For Prof. Gaim Kibreab
With best regards -

4 - 11 - 13 Att

ETHIOPIA:
power & protest

ETHIOPIA:
power & protest
Peasant Revolts in the Twentieth Century

Gebru Tareke

The Red Sea Press, Inc.
Publishers & Distributors of Third World Books

11-D Princess Road   P. O. Box 48
Lawrenceville, NJ 08648   Asmara, ERITREA

The Red Sea Press, Inc.

Publishers & Distributors of Third World Books

11-D Princess Road   **RSP**   P. O. Box 48
Lawrenceville, NJ 08648   Asmara, ERITREA

Copyright © 1996 Gebru Tareke

First Red Sea Press, Inc. Edition, 1996

Cover Design: Linda Nickens

Library of Congress Cataloging-in-Publication Data

Gebru Tareke, 1940-
    Ethiopia : power and protest : peasant revolts in the twentieth century / Gebru Tareke.
       p. cm.
    Originally published : Cambridge : University Press, 1991.
    Includes bibliographical references and index.
    ISBN 1-56902-019-1 (pbk. : alk. paper)
    1. Peasant uprisings--Ethiopia--History. 2. Ethiopia--Politics and government--1889-1974. I. Title.
    DT387.9.G4   1996
    963' .05--dc20   96-5385
                                      CIP

Contents

Contents

Maps

Tables

x

Preface

If understanding the peasantry is important for a truer picture of the Abyssinian past, it is indispensable for a sensible approach to Ethiopia's future.

Donald N. Levine[1]

Until very recently, Ethiopian peasants were consigned to the margins of their own history. Ethiopia's history unfolded in a rural world, but it is one in which warlords have figured much more prominently than cultivators. There is little in rural history in which peasants did not participate directly, and little also in which they have been fully represented, a fate they have shared with peasantries elsewhere in the world.

In sub-Saharan Africa, Ethiopia has prided itself on having a rich literary tradition, one that has been abundantly supplemented by European scholarship on the geography, culture, and ethnohistory of the country. Yet, the peasantry has never been featured prominently in any of these works. Native writers neglected it for two main reasons: first, historical writing generally tended to be ideologically tunneled because it was almost entirely dependent on a patronage system.[2] Those who patronized it were much less interested in the peasants themselves than in their products; at best they ignored them, and at worst, they despised them. Secondly, politics intervened in the production/appropriation of historical knowledge, for the clerics who traditionally chronicled history were members of a literati whose world view was shaped by Christian knowledge acquired within the specific Ethiopian social universe and grounded in variant local traditions. The affinity between the warlords who created dynasties and built kingdoms and the theologians who constructed dynastic legends and ideological precepts to validate kingly authority is quite striking. It is no surprise, then, that what we know about Ethiopia since the thirteenth century, when the manuscripts known as the "royal chronicles" began to be written, is almost exclusively the record of the thoughts and activities of these two privileged groups. In the background there have always been the multitude of toiling peasants of whom we have had only tantalizing glimpses.

Yet, while we fault the chroniclers for their inattention to the common people, we cannot deny the heuristic value of the Ethiopian documents.[3] By the mid eighteenth century, Ethiopians had begun to write on their own initiative, free from direct surveillance by men of power whom they treated with less credulity and ambiguity than their predecessors had done. Their accounts, sometimes interspersed with brief, pertinent analyses, were notable for their assiduousness and accuracy. But even these critical works remained essentially "annalistic," focusing on great men and major events.[4] This dominant historical outlook persisted, with the tendency to biography and hagiography continuing well into the middle of this century.

Foreigners writing about Ethiopia were not free from intellectual and social bias either. With a few outstanding exceptions, scholarly writing showed little deviation from the historical perspective that stressed the role of individual heroes and their perennial idiosyncrasies. It is only in very recent times that the radical shift from political and military history to social history has occurred, and it is a sensible shift. Ethiopia is a society of peasants whose history cannot be fully appreciated without attention to what the cultivators and herders "have passively suffered" as well as what they "have actively lived":[5] attention to the diversity and vitality of their everyday life, their cultural and traditional values, their notions of inequities and injustice, their experiences of solidarity and conflict, and to the various thoughts, images, and symbols through which a great deal of their activities were expressed or channeled. Since Donald Levine made the sage observation quoted above some twenty years ago, a substantial amount of critical and original scholarly work on rural society has been produced, more so by anthropologists than historians. However, a great deal more historical analysis remains to be done before those who have been "hidden from history" become fully visible.

Recent events have disrupted the extended bias in Ethiopian historiography even more thoroughly. The revolution that erupted in 1974 is a great landmark in Ethiopian history for at least two reasons. Undoubtedly the most intense, profound, and protracted upheaval in contemporary Africa, it has eradicated one of the most stable and enduring social orders on the continent. Whatever the capacity of the postrevolutionary society to cope with the daunting tasks of economic development and social reconstruction, for now, Ethiopia has made a sharp break with the past.

Secondly, the revolution has led to a historiographical intervention. The last decade and a half has witnessed a burgeoning of scholarly research on the agrarian society, with the peasantry increasingly occupying center stage in such studies. The emerging historiographical discourse has challenged old assumptions and dispelled old myths (and perhaps created new ones), posed new questions, and advanced new interpretations regarding agrarian class structures, mechanisms of social control, and forms of social identity and struggles. The saga of popular protest has yet to be fully and systematically investigated, however; though their importance has been duly recognized, the significance or legacy of prerevolutionary popular revolts has not been determined seriously. So far, only the resistance in Eritrea has attracted wide (and deserved) attention, in part because it has been larger in scope and intensity and most impressive in its durability. Studies of the Eritrean struggle and the regional insurrections that followed the revolution have raised our understanding of the nuances and complexities of "peripheral nationalism." A fuller account of the story of rural revolts should help not only to challenge prevailing views about Ethiopian peasants but also to enhance our knowledge of the dialectics of popular protest in Africa.

There are few countries in Africa that are as enriched and burdened by the past as Ethiopia. Though it has existed as an independent country for a very long time, it is still riven by deep divisions, largely the result of unequal distribution of power and resources. If its people are distinguished for their long and distinct literary tradition and rich and varied cultural heritage, and admired for their pride, dignity, and valor, so are they known for the incredible exploitation, oppression, and misery they have suffered. If virtually alone in Africa they defied and averted colonial occupation, they are also noted for their relative passivity, deference, and "habitual submission" to authority. They were not, however, entirely docile. People resisted, most of the time individually and in "hidden ways," and sometimes collectively and openly. The intensity of popular defiance steadily increased until it eventually led to what is regarded as the first "social revolution" in Africa, one that destroyed an ancient monarchy, dispossessed an entrenched landed aristocracy, and distributed its lands to the tillers.

For nearly half a century Emperor Haile Selassie I headed a regime that was as impressive for its longevity as for its brutality, though, in comparison both to his predecessors and successors, the emperor appears magnanimous. He was able to rule for such a long time partly because he created a regime of oppression that effectively demobilized the masses. There was no constitutional and little practical limit to the authority of the emperor; no political opposition was allowed and the press was only a mouthpiece of the imperial government. As there was little accountability, public resources were misused, to the painful neglect of the productive sector. The famines that struck the country between the late 1950s and early 1980s are the most poignant and cruel manifestations of the agrarian crisis that imperial policies, in part, produced, but were never able to deal with. There was thus latent discontent which resulted in substantial opposition, sometimes spontaneous and at other times organized, in the towns and countryside. The military coup of 1960 was the most important political event in urban Ethiopia since the restoration of the monarchical regime in 1941. It was significant because it inspired a generation of students who led the most sustained campaign of protest until the fall of Haile Selassie in 1974. They were the catalysts of the revolution.

In rural Ethiopia, popular protest was intermittent but significant enough to dissipate state resources, weakening the government. Peasant unrest was

basically a reaction to two sets of stimuli: state centralization and modernization. Imperial concentration of power through centralism and bureaucratization entailed encroachments upon local and provincial fiscal and administrative privileges. Not surprisingly, segments of the dominant social classes
resisted as best they could and almost always in alliance with the cultivators.
Peasants rebelled not merely because they were instigated by landlords or
overlords to whom they were tied through patron–client dependency networks, but centralization also increasingly impinged upon the subsistence of
the family household. Peasants also rebelled for reasons of social and
cultural or national oppression. Rural revolt was, therefore, an intricate
political affair simultaneously containing elements of class conflict and class
collaboration. Intra-class politics at the top conveniently meshed into interclass politics from below to challenge a monarchical regime reigning over "a
tenuously unified country."

This book is an examination of the ambience of rural protest in twentieth-
century Ethiopia, but mainly focusing on three major insurrections that
occurred between 1941 and 1970. Although theoretically informed, the study
is empirical, and this empirical orientation derives from the fact that the
subject is not well covered in Ethiopian historiography. Of those who have
written about popular protest in Ethiopia, most have chosen to focus on
specific aspects of peasant defiance, while others have drawn broad outlines.
None provides an extended analysis that brings the major revolts together.
Through comprehensive narration, balanced by coherent analysis, this study
seeks to assess the historicity of the insurrections and thereby determine the
extent to which the peasant revolts foreshadowed the revolution.

The book is divided into two parts and consists of seven chapters and an
epilogue. Chapter 1 reviews the scope and mode of peasant resistance,
sketching out the theoretical literature that has informed the methodological
approach to the subject.

Every agrarian movement has a historical context and social content. It
takes place at a specific time and in a particular geographical environment
for specific reasons. Part I reveals the historical and social roots of rural
resistance in Ethiopia. The major events and forces leading to the formation
of a unitary state possessing vastly expanded authority and having a
modernizing orientation are described fully in chapter 2. The following
chapter describes how power and domination were contextualized within
local structures and institutions. The varying and complex ideas and
methods of domination and subversion and visions and possibilities for
liberation can only be understood within the existing structural and cultural
context of social institutions. Hence, by describing the mechanisms by which
individuals occupying similar positions in relation to the forces of production were simultaneously related to one another and to those who
occupied different positions in the social system of production, chapter 3
provides the necessary background to a concrete analysis of the pre-
conditions as well as precipitants of the revolts.

Part II, which comprises chapters 4, 5, and 6, provides extensive accounts of the case studies. I have endeavored to chronicle the events in great detail, describing the geographical distribution of each revolt, the triggers, extent of armed conflict, social composition, organization and leadership, and ideological perspicacity of the rebels, their targets, aims and goals, failures and achievements. A major subject which I do not address is the role of women in the uprisings. At present the lack of sufficient material precludes the serious analysis this subject deserves.

Chapter 7 is a summary of the preceding discussions. It distills the essential characteristics of peasant revolt and it does so in the wider context of social movements. A preliminary analysis of the possible connections between the peasant revolts and the current regionalized movements is given in the epilogue. Recent studies have thoroughly dealt with the causes and motives of these movements, but they say precious little about the exact relationships between the rural population and the guerrilla leaders. Our knowledge of the politics of mobilization and conscientization is limited. The epilogue tries to fill in that lacuna.

The story of the peasant revolts has been reconstructed primarily from archival records and oral testimony. In addition to the material available in the Public Record Office, London, I have had access to the hitherto untapped Ethiopian archives, most of them in the custody of the Ministry of the Interior. The private manuscripts that have supplemented this documentary evidence are meager but valuable. Many of my oral informants were either direct participants in the events or were contemporaneous with them. Others offered either received information or informal opinion on what happened.

It was amidst the revolutionary fervor, well over a decade ago, that I fortuitously hit upon this subject. The Provisional Military Government or *Derg* (Council) that had replaced the emperor was being faced by a galaxy of opponents espousing a cornucopia of clashing ideas and opposing goals. But it was in no hurry to return to its barracks; rather, it turned more violent, assaulting human rights and suppressing newly won civic and political liberties. As their dream of collectively constructing a new society faded, many of the radical intellectuals hurried to the countryside to "save the revolution," albeit without a critical scrutiny of the revolutionary potential of the peasantry. These intriguing events persuaded me to examine the systemic barriers as well as incentives to collective political action by looking at the prerevolutionary revolts. Since then I have become increasingly aware of the centrality of the rural population to an understanding not only of Ethiopia's excruciating current dilemmas but also of its social institutions and political culture. In revising and extending my preliminary investigation of this one aspect of its life, my intention is to contribute toward the general endeavor to restore the peasantry to its legitimate place in history.

Acknowledgements

Scores of people and institutions have been helpful in the preparation of this book, and I wish to acknowledge their assistance. First of all I would like to express my deep gratitude to all those Ethiopian compatriots who willingly shared their experiences with me or provided me with pertinent information. Most of them appear in the notes, and the rest know who they are, for I cannot name them all, but I hope I have presented the material accurately and clearly. My colleagues William Atwell, of whose editorial skills I frequently took advantage, Marvin Bram, James Crouthamel, Richard Dillon, Christopher E. Gunn, Derek Linton, Dunbar Moodie, Daniel O'Connell, and Frank Romer read parts of the manuscript at some stage of its development, and their comments are gratefully acknowledged. I am particularly grateful to two individuals from whose friendship, professional advice, and constant encouragement I have abundantly benefited. My colleague Daniel Singal read an earlier draft and made extensive critical comments. Though not an Ethiopianist, he was right on target on most issues. Donald Crummey, to whom a generation of Ethiopians are heavily indebted, generously shared with me his broad knowledge of my country's history. He read various drafts, including the final one, and his readings were always incisive and insightful. Needless to say, any errors pertaining to fact or interpretation are mine. I am indebted to Amha Wolde Selassie, Alem Seged Hailu, Gabre Selassie G. Mariam, Tsehaye Teferra, Uddin Muin, and Yibza Lakew for the many fruitful discussions; to Dr. Abraham Demoz for his enduring professional support; to Girma Tadesse and Yoseph Tesfaye for their loyal friendship and material assistance whenever I needed it most; and to my late friend Dr. Tesfaye Debessay, who prompted me to undertake the study. Tesfaye, a person known, admired, and respected for his towering intellect, disarming modesty, matchless courage, and an unwavering commitment to an emancipated future was one of the tens of thousands of Ethiopians that the revolution devoured. Thanks to my former and present students for many stimulating and fruitful discussions. I should mention especially Lawrence Copeland, Nicholas Besobrasough, Allison Shutt, Seth Lee, Sarah Crescy, Sarah Merritt, Alan Snel, Karin Munson, Aysha Azfar,

Bettina Malone, Amel el-Amin Mohammed Tatai, Scott Abrams, Dion Thompson, Daniel Weinstein, Brian Sales, Mary Shepherd, Patrick Henry, Mark Darden, Paul Mock, and Jonathan Marston. I fully appreciate the support given me by my colleagues in the History Department and Third World Studies Program of Hobart and William Smith Colleges. My appreciation goes to Ms. Louise Naylor, Ms. Hazel Dayton Gunn, and Ms. Mary Lou Chilbert for typing the manuscript at various stages of its gestation. The cost of typing, copying, editing, and indexing was undertaken by the Mellon/ Hewlett Fund of the Colleges. I am thankful to them and to Cambridge University Press and Praeger Publishers, respectively, for permission to reproduce material published in the *Journal of African History*, 25 (1984) and Marina Ottaway (ed.), *The Political Economy of Ethiopia*.

My deepest gratitude goes to my wife and three children for their forbearance, understanding, and support. With love and respect I dedicate this book to them.

Abbreviations

AA	*African Affairs*
ASR	*African Studies Review*
CJAS	*Canadian Journal of African Studies*
CSSH	*Comparative Studies in Society and History*
IJAHS	*The International Journal of African Historical Studies*
JAH	*Journal of African History*
JCA	*Journal of Contemporary Asia*
JES	*Journal of Ethiopian Studies*
JMAS	*The Journal of Modern African Studies*
JPS	*The Journal of Peasant Studies*
NEAS	*Northeast African Studies*
ROAPE	*Review of African Political Economy*
TAJH	*Trans African Journal of History*

Glossary

abba	father; monk or priest
abegaz	minor district official
Afenegus	literally, "mouth of the king"; chief justice
afersata	officially summoned public gathering
aggafari	superintendent of banquets
aleqa	chief; also religious title
amba	mountain top
ate (atse)	emperor
Ato	Mr.
awraja	district
azaj	commander or superior
balabbat	local notable; gentry
Balambaras	Commander of the fortress
basha/bashai	rifle carrier; lowest title given by Italians to native irregulars
Bejirond	Treasurer
Billatengetta	Chief Administrator of the palace
Bitwoded	literally, "most favored"; Chief Counselor
Blatta	minor official at court
Dejazmatch	Commander of the king's gate
Fitawrari	Commander of the vanguard
Girazmatch	Commander of the left column
Kegnazmatch	Commander of the right column
leul	prince
Leul-Dejazmatch	prince with the title of Dejazmatch
Leul-Ras	prince with the title of Ras
Lij	literally, "child"; title borne by children of the aristocracy
Lique mekwas	king's double; high official
mekwannent	nobility
memhir	teacher; senior clergyman

Glossary

mesafent	princes; aristocracy
mislene	district governor
neftenya	settler; literally, "rifleman"
negadras	head of merchants
negus	king
neguse negest	king of kings
Ras	literally, "head"; commander of the army
shifta/shefta	outlaw, rebel, bandit
shum	chief; official, appointee
Tsehafe-Tizaz	royal scribe; minister of the pen

Explanatory notes

Transcription
To make the transliteration of Ethiopian words and proper names as simple as possible, diacritical marks have been avoided and preference given to well-established usage. No change has been made in the Ethiopian use of praenomens. They are alphabetized exactly as they appear, e.g. Farris Elias.

Calendar
There are differences between the Ethiopian and Gregorian calendars. In the Ethiopian calendar, the year begins on September 11 instead of January 1, and is seven or eight years behind the current year. That is, between September 11 and December 31, the Ethiopian calendar is seven years behind, and from January 1 to September 10, it is eight years behind.

Titles
Ethiopian military and civil titles (e.g. Dejazmatch, Fitawrari) were many – perhaps as many as one hundred or more. Although they were retained until the 1970s, mainly for honorific and status purposes, these traditional titles lost their functional significance following the rise of the centralized imperial state and the concomitant institution of a modern bureaucracy and army. They were abolished completely after the revolution.

Currency
The legal tender in Ethiopia from the late nineteenth century until 1945 was the Austrian Maria Theresa Thaler (*MTT*). Although it was legally abolished in 1945, it remained in circulation for many more years. Its exchange rate varied from two to four dollars with the Ethiopian dollar, which replaced it. The Ethiopian dollar, valued at $0.40 in US currency, was replaced by the *birr* in 1976.

1

Introduction: an historical/theoretical overview

The parameters of revolt

To speak of rebellion is to focus on those extraordinary moments when peasants seek to restore or remake their world by force. It is to forget both how rare these moments are and how historically exceptional it is for them to lead to a successful revolution. It is to forget that the peasant is more often a helpless victim of violence than its initiator.

James C. Scott[1]

This is a study in popular resistance that seeks to rediscover the actions and experiences of masses of people. It is not in search of a heroic past; rather it stresses the historical and continuing damage inflicted upon ordinary people, and their various attempts to redress injustice. To the extent that it illuminates the faces and lives of rural people by focusing on three episodes of resistance, it helps us to understand patterns and structures of dominance, tensions between society and the state (the social formation complex), and the broader question of peasant movements. In so far as it focuses on the common people and their niche in the political economy, it constitutes part of the emerging Ethiopian historiography that gives primacy to social processes over individual actors.

Hierarchies of power, prestige, and occupation, found in the larger social order, generally reflected the varying degree of people's access to material resources. For those people who form the subject of this study, land and livestock were the principal sources of livelihood and the basis of their social relations – not only direct producers but also those who, through various methods, appropriated tribute, taxes, rents, and corvée labor. There are, of course, two or more parties to every conflict, and whatever the precipitants of the conflict may be, in most cases they are connected to existing socio-economic conditions. To study rural resistance in Ethiopia, then, is to understand the institutional arrangements that governed people's relationships at once to each other and to the means of production. These various arrangements have had the contradictory effects of both deterring and fostering overt struggles. It is therefore important to ask not only why

1

Ethiopian peasants rebelled, but also why they did not, for, comparatively speaking, peasant revolt was not common in the country's history.

It is appropriate to define what constitutes peasants before an assessment of their political activities and place in history can be made. It is obvious that theories of social movements differ widely in their definitions of the peasantry as a category for analysis, and the implications of rural differentiation to collective political action. For our purpose peasants are rural cultivators who, by using family labor and simple implements, produce primarily for subsistence but also "for the fulfillment of obligations" to those who dominate them politically, economically, and ideologically.[2] We include in this social category the agro-pastoralists whose household economy similarly relies on family labor and who are subject, more or less, to the same obligations that farmers are.[3] This amendment does not ignore the fact that important differences in modes of livelihood, which are bound to have varying impacts on the political behavior of the rural population, exist, particularly with respect to the dispensation of resources, labor organizations, cultural symbols, and the vitality of social networks linking the producers to one another and to others living outside their immediate world – the village. The fact of the matter is that in Ethiopia farming and pastoralism coexisted within the same social formation.

This differentiated peasant economy has been in existence for many centuries. By comparison, the rise and indeed the continuing decline of the peasantry in sub-Saharan Africa has been associated with the advent of colonialism and the introduction of capitalism in the nineteenth century.[4] Nevertheless, though class divisions and consequent social conflict may have been less articulated than they were in highland Ethiopia, the existence of significant peasantries in precolonial Africa is not to be disputed. Such communities, with varying degrees of differentiation and historical depth, lived in such widely separated areas as northern Nigeria, Ghana, Angola, and Uganda – to mention only a few – surrendering portions of their produce to other actors in the form of tribute, rent, or taxes. The evidence also suggests that there were discernible differences as regards the political dynamics of domination/subordination, distribution of productive resources, organization of labor and quality of equipment. Highland Ethiopia was characterized by a plow culture in which independent producers, using draught animals, raised a variety of crops, part of which was used to support a hierarchy of military aristocracy. In the rest of Africa, where land was relatively more abundant, though not necessarily suitable to cultivation, the agricultural technology mainly consisted of the hoe, and slave, rather than peasant, labor may have predominated in some regions, especially in West Africa. It is also evident that the emerging states in the sub-continent were less capable of directly organizing and appropriating agrarian production than their Ethiopian counterparts; nor were their polities as well equipped with legitimating and sanctioning mechanisms. The Ethiopian polity was armed with written laws and elaborate customs and rituals of

2

social behavior supported by theology that facilitated surplus extraction. In this respect, Ethiopia shares more with Asian and Latin American societies than it does with most African societies. By supporting a social hierarchy that was markedly extractive and exploitative, Ethiopian peasants lived for very many years in a terrible state of ignorance and gruesome conditions of deprivation and poverty. Though it is difficult to gauge their political behavior comparatively, on the surface, it appears that Ethiopian peasants were less prone to challenge those who dominated them than their counterparts in either Asia or Latin America, and when they did, their actions were quite limited in scope and organization.

Peasant defiance in Ethiopia was infrequent and virtually ineffective in its immediate impact, but it did sap the energies of the old regime and inspire a generation of radical students who served as a catalyst in the revolution and are the mobilizing force behind the current insurgencies. The revolts were primarily concerned with specific grievances which the rural population interpreted in terms of ethnic or regional identities and for which solutions were sought at the local level. To some extent, peasants succeeded in redressing their grievances, but they did not end their subordination to other forces. Nor did they provide the "dynamite" that blew up the old regime. The revolution was largely an affair of urban forces. But this epochal event must be seen as the culmination of manifold struggles that were waged in rural and, of course, urban Ethiopia during the preceding thirty years.

Even though peasant revolt is our theme, it is evident that popular protest in Ethiopia, as elsewhere in the world, has occurred in many forms. Reflecting the varied reasons that generated it, protest has expressed itself in a number of ways and guises that, in turn, have produced a variety of outcomes, some of them totally unintended. The forms of protest have ranged from the individualistic, covert, and passive to collective and open acts of defiance; from blind belief in millenarian ideas of justice to willful restriction of output or destruction of property. This book mainly focuses on the open, consciously organized, and often violent forms of defiance: i.e. all attempts by a stratum or strata of the rural population to reduce injustices or simply to renegotiate reciprocal obligations. The terms "revolt," "rebellion," "insurrection," and "uprising" have been used to describe this phenomenon, which with respect to its geographical scope, the broadness of social participation, and the level of violence it entails may not always be easily distinguishable from what are characterized as revolutions or people's wars. Nevertheless, rebellions are invariably provincial and defensive in that they seek to protect a vanishing world or to restore the past, really an idealization of existing cultural values and social conditions. More to the point, rebellions are at once restorationist and reformist in that their makers wish to preserve communal values and to protect existing arrangements of resource distribution even as they struggle to offset injustices or to improve the material conditions of their lives. Viewed in the context of modern history, the crucial difference seems to lie not in the causative conditions but in the organizational capacities and outcomes of these movements.

In either case, collective resistance is rare, though rebellion has occurred much more frequently than revolution. It is not that people do not resist, for protest is an everyday phenomenon, but they do so individually, covertly, and nonconfrontationally, and therefore much less effectively in causing major changes in existing relations of domination and subordination.

Rulers and rebels: domination and peasant consciousness

To speak of collective action is to query the exact link between the unequal social conditions in which people live or are forced to live and popular consciousness. It is to examine the structural and historical constraints ranged against peasants as well as the range of choices and initiatives available to them. What are the factors that deter rebellion in spite of material deprivation, itself largely the product of inequitable access to productive resources? At what point does passive acceptance of wrongs transform into active rejection, or under what conditions do peasants move from passive protest to active resistance? In view of the wide variation in the social bases of revolt, such questions cannot be answered a priori, but only in relation to concrete historical settings.

From a broader view of history, acquiescence to oppressive reality has been more pervasive than organized resistance in peasant societies. Peasants have invariably underwritten the social cost of maintaining superimposed institutional and organizational forces – classes, state bureaucracies, political parties, religious orders – while constantly struggling for economic improvement or even survival. Frighteningly vulnerable to the vicissitudes of nature and the avaricious machinations of those who politically control them, peasants have not always been able to produce enough to meet the basic demands of subsistence and at the same time pay a host of legal and quasi-legal fees – dues and rents to landlords, taxes to the state, tithes to the church or deities, and gifts or bribes to officials. Their response to these exploitative relations has varied from muted apathy to active resistance, giving the imagery of a Janus-faced peasantry. However, apathy is more apparent than activism.

If consciousness is socially produced, how is their relative placidness to be explained, and can they be activated for collective struggle with transformative consequences? Some social scientists have warned against confusing the absence of flashy rebellions with passivity. James Scott, in particular, has argued persuasively that although peasants may appear quiescent or defferential outwardly, they defy obligations imposed on them by using tactics that minimize confrontation and the risk of violent repression. These "weapons of the weak," as he calls them, include such uncoordinated and spontaneous acts as work or output withdrawal, pilfering, sabotage, deceit, banditry, flight or migration, and shift in patron allegiance.[5] Since disobedience and revolt invoke massive reprisals on a scale with which peasants know too well they are unable to cope, it is perfectly understandable why they would prefer to use hidden tactics in order to defy or reject conditions they resent. But peasants do openly challenge established authority, if only too infrequently. Then when and how does individualized rage and noncompliance coalesce into active collective defiance that may modify or alter power relations? Comparative studies on social movements in the modern world have amply demonstrated that the causes and sources of mobilization for collective action are extremely varied and continually changing. An appreciation of the limits and possibilities for popular protest and resistance would require a consideration of the full range of contextual issues: the articulation of classes and institutionalized systems of rights and obligations; peasant relations with each other as well as to other classes, to states, and their opponents; village-based social and cultural networks of cooperation and/or competition; market and transnational relations. Popular and historical traditions of resistance can also be crucial in inspiring collective dissent.[6]

Maldistribution of productive resources and economic inequalities may be the principal factors that stir discontent, but popular outrage is not structurally determined. Peasants generally tend to react collectively and violently when the autonomy of their village is challenged, and especially when customary rights that guaranteed subsistence are violated or when demands of them are suddenly and arbitrarily raised. But economic forces alone do not explain why some peasants are quiescent and others are not, or why some agrarian bureaucracies are more or less vulnerable to rebellion than others, or why revolutionaries in modernizing societies which exhibited basically the same socioeconomic features have had dramatically different political fortunes – some succeeding while others failed. Groups of people occupying subordinate positions in social hierarchies have not only accepted their place, but have, for most of the time, tolerated conditions of deprivation and degradation, more frequently quarreling and fighting among themselves than collectively resisting their common oppressors. Ever since Leon Trotsky said it, one writer after another has repeated it with ample supporting evidence that privation or exploitation – understood as the appropriation of the fruits of labor of one economic category or social stratum by another – in itself is not sufficient to propel people to violent resistance and risk of life. There must be other essential ingredients, one of which is the collective awareness of the fact of exploitation, and that it can be ended through human action. Theda Skocpol has recently restated this point plainly: "What is at issue is not so much the objective potential for revolts on grounds of justifiable grievances. It is rather the degree to which grievances that are always at least implicitly present can be collectively perceived and acted upon."[7] How subordinate groups perceive the dynamics of power, control, and exploitation and then act upon them is very much contingent on historical circumstances as well as state structures and activities. The political choices by which economic grievances might be channeled are linked intimately to the cultural universe in which they are experienced and justified. Varying social structures, historical experiences (though similar historical circumstances do not necessarily elicit the same effects and responses), divergent cultural and political institutions, and environmental factors are bound, inevitably, to have a varying influence on peasant behavior, on forms of protest and resistance and their outcomes. Some peasants have rebelled against exploiting feudal polities and abusive bureaucracies, while others have been ranged against colonial settlers and rulers, capitalist farmers and merchant lenders. The different struggles were contingent upon and in turn led to different forms of consciousness.

Political action emanating from institutionalized inequalities may yet be articulated in nonclass forms of social identity. Many peasant societies including Ethiopia are segmented vertically into numerous groups and horizontally divided by an array of factors such as ethnicity, religion, and primordial kinship affiliations that conceal class exploitation and enfeeble collective solidarity. It may be correct to see animosities or rivalries arising out of ethnic or regional differences as aspects of competing class relationships because nonclass ideologies are articulated within an overall system of power relations. But not every conflict is reducible to class struggle and not every form of consciousness is class consciousness, since "non-class ideologies have a historicity and materiality that are intrinsically not reducible to those of the modes of production."[8] Popular social awareness can be and is mediated by racial, ethnonational, sexual, and religious differences in relative autonomy of class. This does not mean that class and ethnic or national struggles cannot be waged concurrently because there is no natural antipathy between them, but that these differences are not always easily reconcilable on an ideological plane. History is replete with examples of struggles in which these inclusive–exclusive identities have lent themselves far more easily to successful appeals for solidarity than calls for class unity. Hence, if popular consciousness and political action are riddled with ambiguity and adaptability, it is because of the coexistence of multiple identities with overlapping, interpenetrating, or conflicting interests that often give rise to shifting and untidy alliances. Whether these cleavages contradict, clash, or reinforce one another as mobilizing principles of social action must eventually depend on the actual sociocultural and historical conditions.

Not only horizontal divisions but agrarian property relations themselves can have the effect of encasing class consciousness. With specific reference to the French peasantry, Karl Marx enunciated how structural isolation – the atomization and routinization of agricultural work – thwarts unified political activity. Covering a wide range of activities within its own sphere, each peasant household is a fairly autonomous unit of production and cooperation, and approaches self-sufficiency.[9] While broadly concurring with his keen remarks on the constricting effects of the rural economy on popular consciousness and political organization, critics have pointed out that Marx was less sensitive to the strength and vitality of local communal bonds, and to the quite extensive interpersonal relations that exist among peasants even as they strive for self-sufficiency. It is readily apparent, none the less, that the strength (or weakness) of communal ties is, in turn, dependent on resource availability, environmental conditions, rigidity (or flexibility) of political control, and degree of internal stratification. Agrarian relations are actually full of contradictions and ambiguities. In these relations exist conditions that simultaneously promote individualism and communalism, isolation and aggregation, dissension and cohesion. Which aspect becomes predominant at any given time must be dependent on the exact interaction between social situations and historical occurrences.

The ties that bind do not possess the character of universality or continuity. In many instances of nucleated villages that claim common ancestry, hold land in common, and pay taxes collectively, the forces that unify producers have outweighed those that divide them. In other instances, including situations where people are bound by genealogy, history, and property, there is evidence to indicate that cultivators have tended to be competitive for available resources and that this competition tends to intensify as the amount of cultivable land dwindles either because of the expropriation of outside forces,[10] or, as in the case of Ethiopia (see chapter 3), because of the combined effects of partible inheritance and population pressure. The potential for collective action is undermined further by peasant strategies that aim to preserve status, widen the margin of survival, or increase family income and enhance status, for these strategies often impinge upon the interests of other cultivators. Individual aspirations tend to override horizontal links and to strengthen vertical ties. These internal weaknesses in tandem with the political control of the dominant upper classes help to inhibit resistance.[11] And domination can involve more than the control of material resources.

Social control stretches into the realm of ideas because ideas are of consequence both in facilitating subordination and in igniting a process of liberation. Marx and many after him claimed that if rulers govern under stable conditions, it is partly because of their ability to falsify reality by presenting their own interests in universal terms as guarantees of public order.[12] It does appear that in mediating unequal and manipulative relations, rulers have always sought ideological legitimation for their authority, preferring negotiation based on a system of shared values to crude coercion. But a totalizing ideology is, of course, inconceivable in transitional societies like Ethiopia, where cultures are diverse and variable, the class structures and identities complex and plastic, states are insufficiently developed to regulate relations between competing social classes. Even in social formations consisting of two distinct socioeconomic blocks, hegemony can never be complete. Competing classes, which are otherwise routinely engaged in interlocking networks of activities, have ideologies that continually commingle and clash. Ideological domination is precarious, and consent is always negotiated by means of rewards and sanctions.[13] Since it would be impossible to misrepresent oppressive reality, rulers can only try to maintain their domination of civil society by controlling the circulation or transaction of subversive ideas. Peasants (like other subordinated classes) are neither rural idiots who uncritically absorb the world nor supine victims who passively, if not willingly, accept their ordained fate. In their ethos there is quiet admiration for those who openly flaunt normative or codified values. Peasants openly comply, but they also resist, if only in muted or "hidden ways."[14]

Peasants, and the dominated in general, have their language of communication. In preindustrial agrarian societies, counterhegemonic consciousness is expressed usually in the form of metaphors, proverbs, poetry, jokes, songs, and tales which George Rudé conceives as "inherited" values: "the simpler and less structured ideas circulating among the common people, often contradictory and confused and compounded of folklore, myth, and day-to-day popular experience."[15] The popular ideas not only shield the subordinate classes from total ideological hegemony; they also serve as the foundation for radical movements that seek a reversal of the existing social order. Since ideological symbols "are subject to conflicting interpretations," they can help the individual to change the world in as much as they enable him or her to come to terms with it.[16]

How is this revolutionary awareness that the established order can be undone through human action to be attained? Peasants are known for their flexibility in forging alliances with other classes. Whether they become instruments of reaction or forces of change depends on the social character and motivation of their allies. If revolutionary elites have been successful in mobilizing peasants, it is in no small part due to the general convergence (certainly not without tensions) of their radical visions of the future.[17] Rudé offers an explanation of how a radical ideology that might liberate the masses from "ideological servitude" develops. It arises out of the blending of the peasant's "inherent" beliefs and imported ideas that Rudé calls "derived" ideas. The nature of the ideology will depend to a great extent upon the precise mixture of the two categories of ideas, and the historical circumstances under which it is transmitted to the peasants.[18] Exactly how this works in the world of *Realpolitik* is a theoretical as well as an empirical question. Examples, however, are not lacking. We have a most poignant illustration of it in David Lan's magnificent study of the relationship of guerrilla fighters (espousing socialism) and spirit mediums (serving as vehicles of the ancestors) in the struggle against settler colonialism in Zimbabwe (Rhodesia). Lan locates the sources of popular consciousness in a world that was both real and mythical; it arose out of the combination of concrete experiences, authentic community beliefs and practices, and historical myths that were structurally and ritually opposed to the superimposed colonial state and its principles and symbols. In contrast to the chiefs who were coopted by the colonial regime, the spirit mediums remained the stalwart defenders of tradition and community. Embodying undefiled indigenous culture and deeply held popular aspirations for the restoration of stolen ancestral lands, these traditional intellectuals embraced the guerrillas as their legitimate deputies. Thus authentically confirmed, the fighters were able to mobilize a huge portion of the rural population in a successful war of national liberation.[19] The Zimbabwean story is noteworthy perhaps for its uniqueness and not universality, but it is a story that vividly and compellingly demonstrates the interconnection between economy, culture, and insurrectionary politics. We shall have occasion to elaborate (see the epilogue) how a group of radical intellectuals have likewise successfully mobilized a quiescent peasantry in northern Ethiopia by invoking its remembered experience of resistance against oppression, by condemning the prevailing socioeconomic conditions, and by employing images and symbols of communal and regional identity.

Ideas are crucial, but material conditions and organizational possibilities may be even more decisive in determining whether peasants revolt or not. State capabilities and resource availability affect the repertoire of collective action. If rebels have to overcome the moral censorship of superiors, it is even more important that they be able to minimize the damages that the latter can inflict on them. That "tactical leverage" is correlated to their position in the economic scene. As cultivators are segmented internally, not all of them are equally prone to rebellion. Which of them are, and why? The question has been the subject of great controversy ever since Marx contemptuously castigated the French peasantry as a "sack of potatoes" lacking in common political identity and epitomizing backwardness for their support of a revolution that eventually consumed them. A synopsis of two contradictory views would suffice for our purpose. Eric Wolf has posited that "ultimately, the decisive factor in making a peasant rebellion possible lies in the relation of the peasantry to the field of power which surrounds it. A rebellion cannot start from a situation of complete impotence; the powerless are easy victims."[20] The poor and the landless are too closely tied to landlords and, unless mobilized and sheltered by outside forces, they are unlikely candidates for insurrection. What restricts their insurrectionary capacity is their economic dependence and lack of security. Those possessing greater "internal leverage," according to the author, consist of landowning ("middle") peasants, smallholders, and tenants who live in communal villages beyond the immediate control of landlords, and cultivators who live in peripheral zones that are relatively inaccessible to state forces. That "tactical mobility" is reinforced when ethnic particularity merges with geographical marginality.[21]

Jeffrey Paige holds the opposite view: landless cultivators or sharecroppers and not landowning farmers are most prone to collective action. The landless are potentially more rebellious or revolutionary because, it seems, they have little to lose and more to gain. On the other hand,

smallholding peasants tend to be economically competitive, mutually isolated, and averse to risk taking, all of which "in turn lead to political
conservatism, weak organization, and weak class solidarity."[22] This conservative behavior "derives from the peasant's slender survival margin, the
stark alternatives facing the landless, and the risk of landlessness associated
with any social or technological innovation."[23] For Paige, the insurrectionary potential of peasants is not solely dependent on their economic
interests and organizational capacities, but also on those of their class
enemies, a view that Wolf would share. When states and/or dominant classes
are internally divided and weak, they not only encourage defiance but also
undercut their capacity to defuse and quell rebellion. Intergovernmental
relations and the transactions of military hardware and information can be
decisive in determining whether rebels fail or succeed, or whether protest
ushers in change or leads to more repression. Obviously, the validity of the
contradictory theories can only be tested against concrete empirical evidence, and as the results of this study (see part II) will show, the Ethiopian
experience does not fully corroborate either one of them. It bears out some
elements in both of them, which is partly because the sociohistorical processes leading to the emergence of the new state-society in Ethiopia have
their own distinctive features. The conditions that produced peasant rebellions in the rest of the contemporary world did not fully obtain in Ethiopia.

Analysts of contemporary popular movements, including most notably
Wolf, have conceptualized that the key to understanding "peasant wars" of
the twentieth century lies in state building, and in the incorporation of
precapitalist societies into a world capitalist system and the subsequent
commoditization of land, labor, and wealth. The mechanisms of market
forces introduced fluctuating prices for surplus marketable products, altered
patterns of land ownership, and so profoundly modified agrarian class
relations that semiautonomous, or what Wolf calls "closed corporate"
communities, and traditional institutions and strategies proved incapable of
providing sufficient outlets for new social stress and tensions. Unable to
meet the demands of capitalists and state agents, and unwilling to absorb or
accept the hegemonic cultures imposed on them, they began to "fall apart."
The agrarian crisis that colonial capitalism engendered was at the root of
contemporary peasant movements.[24]

Ethiopia's historical experience diverges markedly from that of most
Third World countries which, under colonial or semicolonial domination,
witnessed profound economic and social transformation. Although its
trading contacts with the world economy were old and strong, they involved
no alteration of the productive base and thus no reorganization of the social
relations of production. The colonial encounter (1935–41) was too brief to
cause serious dislocations. Tied to the agrarian social and political structures, nascent industrialism was unable to generate its own expansion.
Transport and communication remained at a rudimentary stage, and there

was no regional specialization in agriculture. In their recent and controversial book, Fred Halliday and Maxine Molyneaux have argued that, with regard to its main politicoeconomic features, the Ethiopia of the mid 1970s was comparable to the absolutist states of France in 1789 and Russia in 1917.[25] Indeed, unlike in the rest of sub-Saharan Africa, neither the state nor the class structures were products of colonial rule. In point of fact, the Ethiopian state arose partly in response to European imperialism. Hence, it is accurate to assign primacy to endogenous factors as the determinants of social conflict in Ethiopia. The explanation for rural revolts appearing since the 1930s lies specifically in the complex interaction between an increasingly intrusive monarchical state, a landed aristocracy, and a subject peasantry. These revolts and the ethnoregional movements that erupted following the revolution are part of a continuing historical struggle to determine the "physiognomy" of the modern Ethiopian state. Even though peasant furies were set off by specific acts of bad government, rural conflict was the outcome of the primary contradiction between the state and the agricultural population.

The Ethiopian peasant: acquiescence and resistance

There have been two conventional images of the Ethiopian peasantry, neither of which is wholly accurate. First, there is the static view of a basically docile and passive agrarian population that silently and fatalistically bore its hardships.[26] These peasants may even have been a contented lot! In rejecting the imagery of a quiescent rural population, a radical perspective portrays the peasants as more combative, prone to rebelliousness.[27] The first underestimates the peasants' disposition to collective action, whereas the second exaggerates it. The dynamics of rural protest are better appreciated in a time perspective. Protest was historically variable. In the main, Ethiopian peasants were neither helpless victims of exploitation nor the resolute resisters of oppression. Although it is difficult to imagine a period in Ethiopian history that did not witness rural unrest, peasants were notably placid until about the first quarter of this century. There were no "spectacular uprisings," only localized outbursts of anger that were contained or resolved within the existing social framework. Peasant political behavior begins to change noticeably after the 1930s, and this was the outcome of innovations taking place at the national level. Important though they were, it was not the roads, railways, or market pressures that breached peasant tranquillity, but state centralism. Needless to say, state centralism was enhanced by infrastructural development.

The increased politicization of the peasantry must be attributed primarily to state interventionism. Between 1930 and 1974 major political innovations were embarked on that, in varying ways, increased pressures on the peasantry, traditional power-wielders, and the state itself. By extending its hold over productive activities, the emerging national state created conditions for multiple grievances. The fiscal and administrative reforms set peasants against the state and dominant classes, class cleavages coinciding with national oppression in some regions. As in other structurally similar situations, the landed upper class was ranged against the state because, while the two were traditional partners in the "exploitation of the peasantry," they were also powerful competitors for control of the cultivators and their products.[28] The unscrupulous behavior of state agents and the brutality of its armed forces further inflamed local conditions. The peasant-based revolts that took place during these years were thus outcomes of old and new sources of conflict. Although they were not immediately evident, the ways in which the rural population responded to the changing social and environmental conditions were interfaced with the undercurrents of class conflict and class struggle. People's social awareness was also mediated by factors other than class. The material, cultural, and regional differences gave rise to multiple forms of consciousness in which class and ethnic awareness either merged or competed with each other in complex ways, thereby affecting rural resistance. Reflecting the intricate tenurial arrangements and the varied historical experience of the agricultural population, political dissent divulged regional variation, mainly between the northern (Abyssinia)[29] and southern parts of the country. This section will lay out the broad pattern of rural politics and state policies that helped to generate peasant unrest.

Life in rural Ethiopia since about the eighteenth century has been generally harsh. The conditions that depressed life arose from the physical and social environments. The Ethiopian farmer, like peasants elsewhere, constantly struggled against the vagaries of nature and the excessive social demands of his fellow man. Floods, locusts, epidemics, drought, and crop failures were frequent occurrences. Famine was cyclical. Time and again he witnessed his crops being wiped out by a hailstorm or eaten by a swarm of locusts or marauding local militia, and frequently by both. He saw his livestock perish from epidemics, the causes of which he rarely understood, and his children die from diseases over which he had little or no control. Whenever he sought restitution and help from a church he so devoutly supported, the priests and monks advised patience, obedience, and piety – advice he accepted in half-belief while enduring the pain.

The other source for the plight of the rural areas was a hierarchy of predatory social forces to which the peasant was linked institutionally. The Ethiopian farmer toiled under backbreaking conditions from dawn to sunset for most of the year, but he was never able to collect the full fruits of his labor. Superior men of the secular and ecclesiastical orders (physically and legally armed) siphoned off a substantial portion of his production, leaving him with barely enough for subsistence. The regional militias constantly interfered with the agricultural season, disrupting cultivation, spoiling farms, and destroying crops and livestock.[30] Such depradations by the truculent troops were so frequent and so severe that the Emperor Yohannes

IV (1869–89) candidly admitted: "We destroy the country instead of occupying ourselves with progress, and so to speak, we feast on human flesh."[31] The emperor was speaking about Abyssinia proper.

Considering the hardships Abyssinian cultivators had to face, one is impressed by their relative calmness. A sixteenth-century governor in Gonder arrogantly told a Jesuit priest: "Father, these villains are like camels; they always cry, weep and groan when they are loaded, but in the end, they rise with the burden that is put on them and carry it."[32] Cleavages and tensions there were, but no conspicuous uprisings occurred between the seventeenth and early twentieth centuries. It is a moot point whether peasant rebellion was overshadowed by the prevalence of warlordism, the perennial warfare between local and regional lords competing for territories, peasants to exploit, and for power and status. The historical conditions that gave rise to millennial movements in other parts of the world also frequently visited Ethiopian rural society, but rarely did millennial beliefs serve as mobilizing myths.[33] Hence the temptation to depict successive generations of mute peasants.

To depict a totally dormant people would be to mislead. Abyssinian peasants were sensitive to class domination, and there are enough indications to challenge the image of a people carrying the yoke of oppression with sheepish timidity. Incumbents who transgressed appropriate norms of behavior within the moral universe or violated customary agreements were deposed or chased from office. The civil strife that consumed the northern regions during the seventeenth and eighteenth centuries was caused in part by peasant unrest. There were heretical movements with strong political overtones which were supported by peasants.[34] Nothing so vividly expresses the outraged grievances of the peasants and the *realization of their potential* to set matters right as this petition written in 1780 and addressed to Ras Ali the Elder, then regent of King Tekle Giorgis I:

> The people of Begemedir's tribute to our sovereign has consisted of giving our breast to the blades of the spears, and our feet to the sands of the earth. We cannot tolerate any more the type of extortion which the Emperor has been conniving to impose on us. If you wish, you can remain and enjoy your office as our representative, subject to our counsel. If you, on the other hand, prefer to remain loyal to the Emperor, we are determined to settle the matter by force.[35]

There were even occasional flashpoints of defiance.[36] Abyssinian peasants generally appeared unruffled, but only within the wider comparative framework of peasant experience.

What accounted for the relatively feeble tendency toward self-initiated revolt in pre-twentieth-century Ethiopia were peasants' direct access to land and the strong links arising out of the institutionalized relationships between the farming community and its overlords. Not only exploitative patron–client ties but also shared cultural values bound the dominant and subordinated sections of the agrarian society. Both fief-holding lord and cultivator

13

were members of an extended kinship group, sharing the same tradition and cohabiting the same parish that was ministered by a priest, himself a kin member and a farmer in most cases. The social order that embraced all of them was not rigidly stratified. The Abyssinian nobility, though hereditary, was not a juridically closed corporate body; any person, including a slave, could ascend the social ladder through acts of military valor or royal patronage. There was practically no social distance between the farming masses and the lower ranks of the nobility. Local authorities and the literati were closely involved in communal activities. Social intimacy blurred class divisions, dissipating social tensions, and mobility reinforced the illusion of social justice.[37] Physical proximity facilitated routine supervision and control through sanctioning mechanisms supported by religious institutions and buttressed by local militias. Village autonomy was severely restricted.

Social fractionalization and vertical orientation meant that it was rare for peasants to organize autonomously. Peasants frequently entered into reciprocal work arrangements, but the norm was to manage the household farm independently, vertical ties of economic dependence outweighing horizontal solidaristic ties. Customary laws regulating property family relations as well as tribute redistribution account for the predominance of patron–client ties manifested in rugged individualism. Peasants engaged in subsistence production on parceled-out diminutive holdings were locked in intense competition for more land. Family-based conflicts, often expressed in the form of litigation, were serious enough to undercut possibilities for class-based revolts. Both Levine and Gedamu Abraha have shown that the dominant traits of the Abyssinian peasant were secrecy, envy, distrust, jealousy, evasion, suspicion, ambiguity, and mendacity[38] – attributes that are actually characteristic of all cultivators living under similar exploitative systems of social production. Peasants, persistently faced with connivance of their neighbors, the insatiable greed of their superiors, and unpredictable natural dangers, are forced to employ various defense and manipulative mechanisms to protect themselves from economic ruin and social indignity, or even to profit at the expense of their neighbors. So, the peasant tries to outwit by telling half-truths or by giving inaccurate information about his output or material possessions.[39] His marked cautiousness or self-centeredness is an outcome of long experience of a world that he viewed as inhospitable. Insecurity created caution about human frailty that bordered on fatalism. Proverbs that express this attitude are legion in the tradition of the northern peasantry: "He who does not suspect will be uprooted," runs one, and "Love, but do not trust man," advises another; "One can trust only a dead person," epitomizes that generalized caution and deeply ingrained suspicion. Such fatalistic views were a product of the peasant's existential conditions, and they were oftentimes reinforced by religious authorities.

Religion may not be the exact reflection of society, but religious ideas can be tailored to fit prevailing sociopolitical realities. They have often helped in making the practice and the cost of domination acceptable. But that religion

14

can have a contradictory effect on popular consciousness is very well known. Religious *ideas* have inspired movements of resistance whereas institutionalized religions, with their high stakes in established social orders, have generally tended to inhibit them. As ideas can be used for domination or liberation, so religion can have an opiating or liberating effect; it at once sublimates and expresses misery. In Abyssinia, though, ritual subordination emphasized political quietism.

By extolling the virtues of a social hierarchy, the Orthodox Church helped stabilize the Abyssinian social formation; it was the cutting edge of relations of exploitation. The religiously inspired customary law declared: "Every one of you must be submissive to the authority of your ruler, since a ruler is appointed by God ... One who opposes the ruler and rebels against him, rebels against the ordinance of God, his Creator. Those who rebel against the rulers secure their condemnation ... "[40] Central to the church's code of morality was the belief in divine omnipotence, the sanctity of royal authority, and the justness of overlordship. Supported by a tradition of awesome antiquity, enjoying direct access to land and to the product of the peasants, and exercising a virtual monopoly in education, the church affected nearly every facet of rural life. The Abyssinian priest was a peasant himself, but possessed a written knowledge. That knowledge gave him enormous ritual authority over the peasant. The teachings of the Orthodox Church, to which the majority of the highland farming population belonged, promoted conservatism, exposing them to a fatalistic world view that finds the causes of poverty and misery either in *edel* (luck) or God. By providing a code of ethics that stressed habits of conformity, deference to authority, and reverence for tradition, there can be little doubt that it helped in the maintenance of tranquillity in a world otherwise filled with misery and tension. The fusion between religion, ideology, and order cannot be idealized, however. Like the imperial court, the church was frequently weakened by controversy and schism. Although it censored any act of disobedience to authority, it itself (or the clergy) became a source of subversion wherever it felt its material interests were threatened or jeopardized. In so doing, it lent justification to noncompliance.

If Christianity was a stabilizing force, Islam might have played the opposite role historically. And that it was coextensive with decentralized and less segmented societies meant that its vitality as a bond of solidarity was even greater. In contrast to the structurally differentiated peasantry, nonstratified communities traditionally have shown greater cooperation and solidarity. Such communities also existed within the Abyssinian Kingdom, and many of them bordered the Abyssinian peasants. It is quite likely that Islam was embraced by a very large segment of the population because of its ability to "indigenize" itself by absorbing elements of indigenous religions. Its expansion in more recent years may be seen, however, as a form of protest or passive resistance against the overbearing and exacting Christian Abyssinians. Indeed, in the last thirty to fifty years, Islam has shown its vitality as a bond of solidarity and as a mobilizing force against a Christian-dominated state, albeit rarely across provinces.

There were other modes of resistance, of which banditry was the most prevalent and enduring. Abyssinian farmers expressed their dissatisfaction through less dramatic forms of everyday noncompliance such as deception, evasion, sullenness, avoidance, and flight. Another phenomenon which may, in the most general sense, be seen as a cultural idiom of protest is spirit possession and exorcism.[41] But all of these outlets might have undermined people's potential for collective defiance by helping ventilate individualized frustrations and anger. So did *sheftnet* (banditry), a precapitalist form of social protest that cannot be separated easily from peasant rebellion.

Peasant folklore and social mores make it manifestly evident that social banditry was a pronounced phenomenon in agrarian societies entering the transition to capitalism. It is also clear that peasants showed great ambivalence in their attitude toward banditry because of its contradictory roles: one of predation and the other of protection of the common folk. Some scholars have celebrated its redeeming qualities, while others have picked on its repressive, reactionary aspects.[42] What is specific about banditry is, in fact, its ambiguity.

Brigandage is something about which it is difficult to be precise; it is an activity in which "self-interested criminality is scarcely distinguishable from socially conscious rebellion and where the sanction is no more than a marginal irritant to the system."[43] In the Ethiopian hierarchical society, banditry provided a safety-valve for releasing social tensions. It was a vehicle of protest as well as of mobility for ambitious nobles and destitute peasants alike. But rarely was the political distinguishable from the criminal act. Consequently, peasants' attitudes towards the bandit were mixed: they ranged from respect and vicarious admiration for his bravery and exploits to fear and hatred of his summary justice and parasitism. To convince themselves that the bandit was quintessentially a social parasite who primarily preyed upon the powerless, Tigrai-speaking farmers of Eritrea recited a typical bandit's prayer:

> Oh God, give us the property of old weak
>   men,
> the property of the blind and limping,
> the property of orphans and women,
> the property of him who has no power
>   and who does
> not remember,
> the property of him who curses [but does
>   not act] ...
> give us!
> I am an unkempt orphan, hoping in thee,
>   I have risen.[44]

On the other hand, peasants of Gonder saw the bandit as a rebel who goes away to the forest to stir up trouble against an unjust authority:

> They say they have burned and destroyed
>   the Tekeze forest,
> The refuge of the wronged and the
>   brave.[45]

It is an ambivalence rooted in the ambiguity of banditry itself.

Banditry was quite rampant in the country between the eighteenth and mid twentieth centuries. What is more difficult to establish with some certainty is the degree to which it was a genuine expression of peasant grievance. Donald Crummey has argued forcefully that, although peasants were far from being passive ciphers, and although banditry "may have served as a dramatic release for social tensions of many kinds," banditry and rebellion in nineteenth-century Ethiopia were nearly exclusively activities of the nobility and gentry who used them as vehicles for social mobility; peasants were drawn into these activities only as followers and with little or no regard to class interests.[46]

This is a compellingly attractive thesis, but the line of demarcation between brigandage/rebellion and peasant resistance appears to be too thin and rigid, and the evidence not so overwhelming. Not only do we know little about rebel composition and motivation, but we also do not see clearly where noble rebellion ends and peasant resistance begins in such a society characterized by fluid and interchangeable class positions. Besides, seldom are political objectives in such peasant conflicts overtly expressed in terms of class interests. If we were to characterize rural rebellions solely on the basis of class consciousness, we would be left without a history of peasant revolts.

Although politically destabilizing, banditry never threatened the Ethiopian social system; on the contrary, by providing outlets for society's tensions, it sustained it. Banditry was the quintessential expression of a compartmentalized and highly individualistic society. Its rampancy is one reason for the nonexistence of large-scale peasant uprisings in the eighteenth and nineteenth centuries. A recent study has concluded that individual lawlessness tended to demobilize the rural population for which it "was a burden of tribute and fear."[47] Bandits operated within the social system and more often than not were easily coopted. Their arrogant disregard for the established order was a short-term phenomenon, for bandits held to the values of the dominant classes to which they normally aspired. To effect reforms or to transform authority bandits needed more than mere personal ambition and their own desire to redress wrongs. From the perspective of the peasants banditry may have propped up the ideology of protest, because by contravening laws and norms they themselves had legislated, noble bandits gave legitimacy to insubordination.

During the period covered by this study banditry played a dual role in peasant politics. On the one hand, coopted bandits became useful tools for increased state authority. But once comfortably placed in the structures of power, they usually became repressive and thus helped to ignite the moral outrage of the populace. On the other hand, peasant bandits were readily absorbed into popular revolts which they greatly assisted by facilitating recruitment and providing skill and leadership. Knowledgeable in local mores, terrain, and guerrilla tactics, they served as indispensable allies of rural rebels as well as critical links between the latter and village communities. Such revolts took place in Wello (1928–30, 1958); Tigrai (1943); Hararge (1944, 1947, 1958, 1963); Gojjam (1942–43, 1951, 1968–69); Sidamo (1960); and Bale (1941–42, 1947, 1963–70).

The revolts were reactions to four sets of factors, all related to the shift of the loci of power to the national state. The insurgency that was ignited in 1960 in the Eritrean lowlands as a dramatic reaction to the unilateral dissolution of the federal arrangements by which the territory was amalgamated with Ethiopia is still raging. With the exception of the resistance in Eritrea, the revolts, usually crushed with vastly improved techniques and means of coercion which the state was able to muster with the help of its Western allies, mainly arose from (1) the reorganization of feudal power, (2) attempts to increase national revenues by abolishing rights and privileges to which the aristocracy traditionally had been entitled, (3) reforms to raise agrarian output by removing structural barriers, and (4) ethnonational oppression. As the state sought to control the rural population directly and more effectively in order to increase extraction, the peasants steadfastly worked to subvert those goals, and oftentimes by manipulating differences and feuds within the ranks of the dominant social stratum.

In northern Ethiopia, centralism meant the devaluation of provincial autonomy and a resulting erosion of noble power: thus it was never surrendered without a protracted struggle. For the peasants, the state represented an oppressive external authority which they resisted as best they could. The concentration of power ineluctably modified or altered the conditions under which overlords, churches, and other holders or repositories of power mediated, influenced, or even determined the fates of ordinary people. Historically, what enabled the northern nobles to limit the role of imperial authority was their entrenchment in the local economy and their affiliational, associational, and multiform functional links to the producing community. Although imperial policies that sought to create a functionally differentiated bureaucracy and a unified fiscal system did not directly interfere with production relations, they did alter radically the functioning of local institutions and mechanisms of surplus appropriation; they had the effect of excluding locally rooted authorities from direct participation in the allocation and distribution of local resources. But this was not achieved without some social cost. By intensifying competition for extractable resources between local notables and those state appointees who took over administrative tasks from them, centralism also created much rancor among the farmers. If peasants felt agitated it was also because the state threatened traditional strategies of subsistence production by shifting from proportional to fixed assessment of taxation and its payment in cash instead of kind. Under the new set of circumstances noble dissatisfaction blended with peasant grievances to pose a serious challenge to monarchical authority. That challenge, which varied according to local context and specific circumstances, must be viewed as a continuation of past politics in which old disputes merged with new sources of conflict and solidarity, creating a veritable tangle of contradictions. Nobles and peasants were bound together by structures of interdependence and a system of shared Christian tradition that provided the basis for unified action transcending socioeconomic differences. A common appeal to primordial loyalties and provincialist sentiments mobilized lord and peasant everywhere in the northern territories; but nowhere was resistance as determined and as bloody as it was in Tigrai. The eventual suppression of the 1943 revolt strengthened the position of imperial authority in the north, but did not deter similar events from happening in the future.

Through a protracted struggle that spread over nearly three decades, Haile Selassie I succeeded in smashing the northern oligarchies, eventually destroying the institutional basis of their power, but not completely. Many of them were retained mainly for administrative purposes; they were useful in the maintenance of order and collection of taxes. Once absorbed into the emerging bureaucracy they seemed to support the status quo unequivocally, but their position was ambiguous and their loyalty always suspect. The continuing presence of these men meant that the state was never able to penetrate the countryside extensively. They remained an influential force with which the fragmented peasantry could make deals in order to resist unwanted state programs or reforms. Conversely, the officials could count on the support of the populace in their continuing competition with state appointees whom they derided as "the outsiders." When grievances converged, the government was in trouble, as indeed was the case in Gojjam in 1968–69. In that year local notables briefly sided with the peasants in a revolt that may be characterized as Vendean, an uprising by an agrarian population under conservative leadership trying to preempt reforms introduced by the central government. The factors that gave rise to the rebellion and the makeup of the leadership in the north sharply contrasted with those in the south.

The Abyssinian conquest of what is today southern Ethiopia, accomplished over many years between the nineteenth and early twentieth centuries, is one of the most pivotal events in the country's modern history. Pre-nineteenth-century Abyssinian domination of outlying regions to the south, southwest, and southeast was manifested in trade, war, and religion. During the period stretching from the thirteenth to the fifteenth centuries, the Abyssinians asserted their hegemony over the frontier regions by establishing an extensive trade network, exacting tribute, and raiding for slaves and livestock. Little attempt was made to incorporate these societies into the

Christian kingdom. In the late nineteenth century, new developments occurring both within the Christian kingdom itself and in its periphery led to the annexation of much of the latter by the former, initiating a kaleidoscopic transformation in the state's sociological and political complexion, and even in its geography. There was wide variation in the societies and landscapes incorporated and imperial policies pursued, but Abyssinian conquest was profound in its overall impact. It was dispossessive, extortionist, and very repressive.

Consequently, the peasant question in modern Ethiopia entailed significant regional differences. The crucial difference was that in the south, land had been expropriated largely by outsiders who reduced the autochthonous population to tenancy. Either by outright seizure or, as in more recent years, through the use of courts and legal pretexts, settlers and officials alike usurped lands that belonged to the kin-based corporate groups. They did this to increase their private holdings, generally with protection from the state. Those who actually tilled the land paid services and rents that were a higher proportion of their product than was paid by tillers in the rest of the country. Consequently class lines, which usually converged with ethnic differences, were more distinct than in the north. Affiliative relations and longstanding shared traditions shielded northern peasants from excessive abuse by local authorities. In the south there was great antipathy between native and settler. The latter did manage to create what might be called the Abyssinian mystique based on the possession of a written script, an institutionalized religion, and a sophisticated military organization. Abyssinian codes of dressing, manner of eating, and other habits were feverishly emulated by many, but that was not enough. Lacking an ideological basis for legitimacy, Abyssinians were primarily dependent on force. The power of settlers, who were at once landlords and officials, was so pervasive that there was little room for legal redress.

The paucity of material makes it almost impossible to assess popular reaction in the south in general prior to 1935. Incorporation into the empire in many cases certainly involved violence and, as elsewhere in Africa, initial conquest deterred organized resistance for at least a generation.[48] Between 1900 and 1935, despite instances of sporadic rebellion, it is likely that the most common form of resistance was avoidance through withdrawal, religious conversion, and scattered banditry.

Administrative centralization enlarged the political space of the southern people, but the state's continuing support for settlers made rebellion a very hazardous undertaking. The consolidation and extension of state authority in the post-Italian period appreciably modified servile relations, landlords losing their unmediated, direct, personal control over their tenants. This must surely have enhanced the cultivator's freedom of movement. However, centralism did not weaken but bolstered the position of settlers, because a more powerful state became their chief defender against a latently hostile population. Consequently, popular perception of the protagonist changed.

No longer was the northern landlord the sole enemy, but the state, as the condensation of Abyssinian power, became the focus of popular discontent.

National and class repression were thus the underlying reasons for the rebellion that swept the state's eastern periphery in 1963–70. Occurring twenty years after the uprising in Tigrai, it was the result of additional burdens borne by ethnic and religious "communities" and the fact that the Tigrean revolt had produced no significant reforms. The causes of the rebellion, which were augmented by external factors, stemmed from the near-colonial situation that southern peasants had endured since their incorporation in the Ethiopian state.

One major source of common grievance in all parts of the country was corruption, the illicit accumulation of wealth for self, relatives, and political cronies. It pervaded administrative, fiscal, and judicial institutions from the summit to the base of the social pyramid, cutting through institutionalized links. It can be said that corruption had become a class activity. With the growth of urbanization, the spread of the cash economy, and relative expansion of communication, there was a marked change in the lifestyle of the dominant classes. The geographical and cultural distance between rulers and ruled, between town and country people, steadily expanded. The desire for imported consumer goods such as cars, household furniture, woolen clothing, silk fabrics, and beverages, as well as the rush for urban real estate, led the emerging classes to increase their share of the agricultural surplus. This they achieved not by developing the productive sector of the national economy, but by simply expanding their holdings incrementally and by enlarging the extractable surplus from the cultivators; since they were not directly engaged in production, they saw little need to promote technological innovation. Instead, they chose to drain a near-stagnant agricultural economy, further smothering it.

Manipulation of the judicial and taxation systems was the most brazen form of unlawful accumulation of property. Local authorities and institutions evaded taxation simply by shifting the burden to the cultivators. As the state raised the stakes in the household economy, these officials tried to maintain or increase the level of their income through more rigorous exactions. There was a scramble for the spoils of office in which tax assessors expected "gifts" and tax collectors charged fees for handing out official receipts, while court clerks and judges accepted bribes from plaintiffs and defendants. Cultural and institutional mechanisms that previously cushioned northern peasants against excessive demands were violated systematically. In the south, where such safeguards had never existed, there was little limit to extortion.

Monetary and labor obligations increased at a time when peasants were increasingly faced with ecological adversity and declining productivity. Holdings, owned or rented, were much too small to support families even in normal times. Yet the demands imposed on them were high and continued to rise. In addition to officialdom's pecuniary cravings, the state shifted its social functions to the rural population in order to minimize its financial costs. Corvée labor, as in bygone days, was used extensively in the construction and repair of roads and offices, and in the cultivation of crown or government lands. Peasants were also coerced to make ad hoc cash payments to support military campaigns and government programs of rural development. These developments placed increased strain on an agrisystem increasingly lacking the flexibility to cope with social stress.

Peasants had more than sufficient reason to grumble, even to resist. Seeking amelioration, they frequently petitioned local officials and the central government, and sometimes sent delegations to the emperor. Whenever such appeals were ignored or met with no action, there might be recourse to armed rebellion. The rural revolts of the twentieth century were thus in large part reactions to increased pauperization of the peasantry, massive bureaucratic corruption, landed exactions, official tyranny, and an increasingly demanding but unresponsive state. Agrarian unrest, however, was not merely a reaction to multiple forms of exploitation, immiseration, and repression. It was also a protest against real or perceived threats to a popular or traditional consensus that governed the relationship between the community, authority, and land in the context of a hierarchical social order. Ethiopian peasants not only had obligations, they had rights as well, rights that rulers violated at great political risk. It is within this popular consciousness "of 'just' rights and obligations" that their grievances operated.[49] It is by recognizing the centrality, even primacy, of land in their consciousness, i.e. their belief in "the common justice of being allowed unfettered possession of [their] land,"[50] that one is able to appreciate the full dimensions of peasant resistance in Ethiopia, resistance that has been notably fragmented and localized, seldom transcending provincial boundaries.

The forces that gave rise to localized but multiclass rural movements must be examined in the historical and social context of an emergent modern state. Along with its emergence, important economic and political transformations have occurred. These changes in turn have had profound and varied effects on the agrarian population of peasant families as well as on local elites and state institutions. To appreciate why and how these changes took place is to understand the peasant rebellions and the intractable nature of the country's current problems. The crucial developments in Ethiopia between the late nineteenth and mid twentieth centuries, in particular, were the reconstruction of monarchical authority in the north, the southward expansion of the territorial base of the monarchical state, and the country's gradual incorporation into the global economy, falling mainly within the sphere of influence of the United States. How these changes were effected is the subject of the following discussion.

Part I

SOCIETY AND HISTORY

2

The historical context

State formation

The processes of state-building are multiple and complex. Different areas were integrated into states in markedly different ways and at different times.

E. R. Wolf[1]

There is no doubt that the consolidation of class and the growth of states have been a joint process, in Africa as elsewhere. In Africa, as elsewhere, they have entailed a contradictory increase in power to oppress and the restraint of power. They have not ended the struggles of the oppressed, but they have changed their arenas. They have also failed to change a great deal.

John Lonsdale[2]

An adequate explanation of the causes, processes, and outcomes of popular protest in contemporary Ethiopia must begin with an account of the rise of the modern state. The main contours of that historical process will be charted by selectively constructing the demographic, political, and historical determinants of the state's territorial and administrative reorganization, the varied ways in which subsequent state centralism affected changing relationships between the dominant social forces, on the one hand, and between them and the producing peasantry they sought to control, on the other.

Definitions lack exactitude, but the *state* here is conceived as an organization of domination and control. It embraces the principal juridical, administrative, and coercive institutions within a territory where it coexists and competes with other formally and informally coordinated organizations for predominance and autonomy as it does with external forces that seek to impinge on its sovereignty.[3] Almost universally the creation and consolidation of the state has been achieved, with varying degrees of efficacy, in the face of tremendous internal (that sometimes meshed with external) resistance, spontaneous or organized, sporadic or concerted. In their endeavor to establish direct and unmediated dominance and control of civil society and in their search for an uncontested sovereignty, "state builders" have sought to subordinate, emasculate, or eliminate existing power wielders and rival organizations either through cooptation or coercion – usually both – but more frequently by force. So the historical evolution of the state has invariably been a slow, often protracted, and nearly always a violent process. The Ethiopian experience is no exception.

The dawn of the twentieth century saw the formation of a new state in Ethiopia. It is difficult to speak of ideal types, and history rarely offers exact parallels, but the "physiology" of the state's evolution in Ethiopia, which has its own spatial and temporal peculiarities, shared some basic similarities with state formation elsewhere in the world. Certain historical processes may not be reproducible,[4] and to be sure, the Ethiopian state is no mere duplication of others, but in its broad phases of development it closely resembled those of Europe. It also shared some major similarities with other postcolonial states in Africa, although their contemporary historical experiences have been quite dissimilar. Its commonality with the latter is easier to establish; it derives from their contemporaneousness, the means deployed in their creation and consolidation, in the relative fragmentation of society and fluidity of classes, in their similarly mono-crop economies, in the relative limitation of their autonomy in the context of the international system of states, and in the incongruity between societal and state institutions. If the African state appears overinflated and all-powerful, though, it is because the society it dominates is too segmented and, consequently, weak. The appearance of the state's omnipotence is illusory, however, because it lacks sufficient economic and administrative resources with which to support its political predominance. Despite their structural similarities, the Ethiopian state is differentiated from others in the continent by its greater organic linkage to society. In the rest of sub-Saharan Africa, state apparatuses were bequeathed by colonialism and thus lack indigenous roots.

In comparative perspective, the similarities with European societies in earlier periods of their history lay in three interrelated areas: first, in the character of society out of which the state emerged and over which it eventually established its dominance; second, in the nature and quality of resistance it had to overcome in order to consolidate and extend that dominance; and third, in the social cost that society was made to bear in the process of the state's territorial consolidation, resource concentration, and the expansion of power through monopolization of coercive instruments. Needless to say, the two societies were not the same, much less identical. The social relations and the class structures and struggles to which they gave rise were different in many respects. What most clearly distinguished Ethiopian state-society from those of Europe in the sixteenth and seventeenth centuries was the fact that it arose in a sociocultural environment that was more diverse and complex. Ethiopian society was more fragmented, its political culture more fractured, and its economy less developed and coherent. Central institutions were weaker, and citizens' loyalty to them more diffused.

Particularistic ties like kinship, ethnicity, and region were more salient and intense, their functional importance greater. The fragmented socioeconomic conditions gave rise to multiple forms of consciousness that competed, in rather complex and shifting ways, with emerging class ties.

State formation in Ethiopia took place in a setting of considerable cultural heterogeneity and under conditions far less favorable than in Europe. The Ethiopian state similarly rested firmly on an agrarian population; but one that was less homogeneous culturally and more diverse ethnically and linguistically. Second, state centralization entailed a high degree of coercion as "state builders" had to deal with many oppositional forces. Internally, as in Europe, there were three such groups: (1) the mass of rural inhabitants who resented new levies on their product and labor and were often pressed to give up portions of their land and to abandon old loyalties; (2) the existing territorial princes and their auxiliaries who were forced "to relinquish or share their power; and (3) the rival claimants to sovereignty."[5] Externally, the challenge came from groups or organizations with competing or complementary interests. Although the basic institutions upon which the new state was erected were derived from its pre-nineteenth-century predecessors, the organizational methods, the technological means, and even part of the financial resources were borrowed from abroad – a feature that it shares with the rest of Africa but one that clearly differentiates it from European states.

Shorn of its mythical origins, the Ethiopian state was formed historically through a long, protracted, and conflict-ridden sociopolitical process. The Abyssinian Kingdom, which traced its lineage from ancient Aksum, was a forerunner of the new imperial state, and existed for at least two millennia before any of the European nations established a major foothold on the African continent. It not only survived European colonial occupation but increased its size by more than 65 percent in the wake of the "Scramble for Africa." Although not conquered by any European power (except for the five-year Italian partial occupation), as was the case with nearly all African states, the Ethiopian state attained, more or less, its present spatial organization during precisely this period, taking full advantage of European capital and weaponry. Ethiopian rulers benefited from diplomatic and commercial contacts with Europeans even as they struggled with these powers to safeguard their independence, or even competed with them for new lands and other resources in northeast Africa. It was European capital and technology that laid down the communication and transportation infrastructure, thereby transforming the means of coercion, and enabling Ethiopian rulers to centralize, unify, and consolidate the state, a pattern unevenly duplicated in the rest of Africa.

The Ethiopian state-society that emerged at the turn of this century from the confluence of endogenous and exogenous forces was qualitatively different from its predecessors, in terms both of its territorial size and of its ethnocultural makeup. It contained a myriad of diverse national and religious groups with economies, polities, ideologies, and kinship systems that radically differed from each other. Levine's argument that, despite this "stunning diversity," Ethiopia has to be perceived as a country that is sufficiently unified both ecologically and culturally, is less than convincing.[6] It is barely a century since a substantial percentage of Ethiopian citizens began to share historical experience with the Abyssinian core. Moreover, the nature and quality of their shared experience has often been as divisive as it has been unifying. In addition to the fraternal bonds that Ethiopians developed through centuries of interaction, the architects of modern Ethiopia hoped to build a single society through political centralization reinforced by cultural homogenization. Amharic and orthodox Christianity were imposed as the state language and religion respectively. However, Amharic remained essentially a language of administration, courts, and schools, of trade, and the small, but expanding, literary elite. Christianity has continued to struggle with residual forms of older beliefs and with Islam, and may have lost substantial ground to the latter over the last hundred years. The policy of cultural integration, let alone homogenization, was ineffectual as autonomous ethnic and regional cultural units persisted. The multifarious groups encapsulated in the nineteenth century, or even long before, were not molded into a fully integrated homogeneous whole. Lack of political, economic, and cultural integration meant the survival of multiple loyalties. Social identities remained in a state of great ambiguity and flux, oscillating between assimilation and rejection of the dominant culture. Many factors molded people's attitudes and political behavior: habitat, kinship, confessional rivalries, variant traditions, and social structures.

State formation was a highly complex process that produced vastly different social conditions and relationships which in turn affected the repertoire of collective protest. Those specific conditions of power, work, and ownership of land, which determined the material lives and political alignments of Ethiopians, entailed regional and temporal variation. It has often been asserted that this variability roughly coincided with the north–south geographical axis of the imperial state. While this is generally true, the range of social experiences, especially in the southern half, has in fact been wide. This variation reflected the extant social formations simultaneously coexisting with each other within the same geographical and administrative region, with some penetrating and dominating the others. It was also the result of imperial policies of rule, policies discussed in chapter 3.

This multifarious society was held together by an imperial state, itself heavily dependent on foreign resources. The imperial state was run by hierarchically differentiated but centrally coordinated civil and military personnel functioning under the auspices of the monarch. Emperor Haile Selassie I erected modern structures of power and authority, claiming sovereign jurisdiction over a national territory that was internationally recognized. That monarchical state has been characterized, with some justification, as absolutist, but it was not a monolithic, centrally controlled polity. The new state was only partially bureaucratized, and there was still a dispersal of power. Although its material base was greatly enlarged, its legitimating ideology refined, its bureaucratic apparatus elaborated, and its cooptive and coercive capabilities improved, the new state never completely destroyed the basis of local power, nor did it fully penetrate and control the rural population. Failing to control it directly, the state was never able to reorganize and regulate rural social relations. What was most characteristic of Ethiopian society until the 1950s was its social stability and continuity; its basic structures and the position of the peasantry remained unaltered.

The country did experience economic transformation and educational expansion that, in turn, gave rise to new social classes. But it was in the northern and southern extremities of the country that peasants experienced greater social dislocation. This was due to the combined effects of land alienation, the erection of new transport facilities linking the hinterland with the coast, and the abundant availability of exportable products in the south. It was there that new commercial classes, directly linked to the world economy, developed. The country's insertion into global capitalism rigidified social distinctions. Landlessness and servile relations in the southern regions, where there was a close correlation between national and class oppression, were the most crucial developments.

One of the eventual results of the combined process of state and class formation was an escalation in regional and ethnic conflicts. Both the imperial state and its successor have been faced with challenges arising from the demands of national and social groups. In the old Ethiopia, regionalism – as an expression of particularistic sentiments anchored in feudal relations – was a major source of conflict. If ethnicity was not a significant factor in Ethiopian political affairs prior to the creation of the imperial state, as Donald Crummey has noted,[7] its politicization in the twentieth century – especially in the period following the end of the Italian occupation in 1941 – became more evident. As Donald Donham has pointed out, "The last and in some ways the most intractable source of conflict created in Haile Selassie's Ethiopia was the developing tension between the definition of national and ethnic identities."[8] Ethiopian leaders have been far less successful in nation building than in state creation and consolidation. State penetration and control of society considerably expanded over the last hundred years but without sufficiently enhancing the identification, participation, and loyalty of the citizen to the nation-state. Hence, the proliferation of a host of peripheral movements as reactions to the twin crises in authority and identity that followed the revolution.[9] Based on their different perceptions or interpretations of Ethiopian society and history, members of the new social classes, more specifically the intelligentsia, have attempted to construct their own communities by violent means. Besides the older Eritrean People's Liberation Front (EPLF), which wants independence, the most weighty, both politically and militarily, are the Tigrai People's Liberation Front (TPLF) and the Oromo Liberation Front (OLF). Despite much

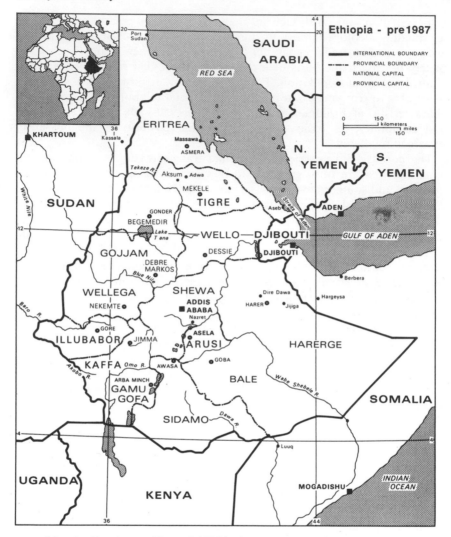

Map 1 Provinces of imperial Ethiopia

ambiguity in their intentions, their main goal is the national state that is strategically placed in the system of production and distribution. Basically reflecting the relative weakness of classes, the state in Ethiopia, much like its African counterparts, preponderantly controls material resources, and those well placed in it use authoritarian methods to defend or expand their corporate interests. The disadvantaged have often sought inclusion in the national body politic by mobilizing ethnicity.[10] Consequently, organizational fractionalization has been their hallmark. From a radical national perspective, they have undermined efforts to mobilize the masses on broad

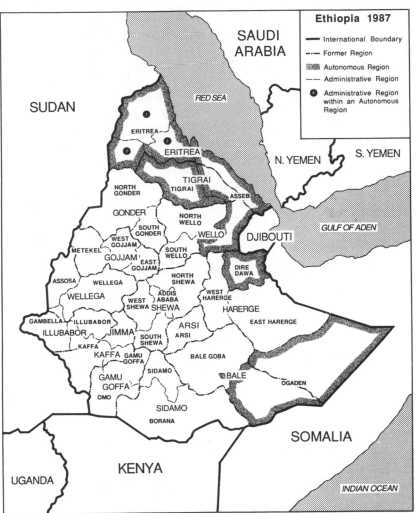

Map 2 Administrative and autonomous regions of the People's Democratic Republic of Ethiopia

democratic concerns and issues that would simultaneously promote national
integration and social transformation.

The existence of these movements is concrete evidence of the continuing
crisis in the relationship between state and society, a crisis linked directly to
the uneven economic development and uneven consolidation of power.
Although rooted in the state structures erected in the preceding century, the
appearance of these groups or organizations is, in part, a direct response to
the extensive centralization that the postrevolutionary government initiated
in order to attain greater coherence and autonomy for the state. The new

31

regime, with an immensely improved coercive apparatus and new legitimating ideas, is engaged in a very costly struggle to determine to whom and how political power and economic resources shall be allocated and distributed in a society that is unevenly integrated and unevenly developed. In order to explain some of the major points raised in the preceding pages, the process of state-society formation in Ethiopia during the last hundred years will be described, focusing mainly on three areas: (1) the dynamic relationship between the human and environmental factors as it affected or shaped the density of social interaction and historical consciousness; (2) the cultural, historical, and social conditions in which the state arose, and how regional polities or ethnic groups tried to maintain economic or cultural autonomy in the face of centralization, commercialization, and power consolidation; and (3) the complexities of the various trajectories of historical change leading to absolutism, and the actors who played prominent roles in the process of change.

Geography and demography: local culture and history

Strategically located in what is known as the Horn of Africa, Ethiopia is a poor but potentially rich country. Over 1,224,480 square kilometers (472,000 square miles) in size and with a population of about 45 million, it is one of the largest countries in Africa; only three are larger, and only two have more people. Although today Ethiopia conjures up images of an impoverished land symbolizing world hunger, the country has ample productive land that can support perhaps as many more people as it has now, providing the material wherewithal for the satisfaction of their basic human needs. Livestock production is both extensive and varied. The country's mineral wealth is as yet not fully known, but gas, zinc, potash, and copper are said to exist in vast quantities. Geothermal and hydroelectric energy can easily be extracted from the volcanic areas and abundant rivers. European colonizers were not unaware of Ethiopia's economic potential and geopolitical importance; indeed, several of them coveted it, but none succeeded in occupying the country except Italy, which seized the extreme north, Eritrea, which was reclaimed in 1952.

Both physically and demographically, Ethiopia is Africa in microcosm; it is a land of great diversity and extreme contrasts. Ethnic heterogeneity is the outcome of migration and conquest, and the great variation in the distribution of population is the result of topography, climate, and history. The contrasting physical environment profoundly affected the evolution of Ethiopian society and its culture, decidedly influencing patterns of settlement, modes of life and production, and social interaction and popular consciousness.

The ethnographic picture reveals the existence of very many linguistic groups, but only a few are numerically significant. Speaking seventy-four languages and twice as many dialects, the Ethiopian population is composed of Cushites, Semites (or Semiticized Cushites), and Nilotes. Occupying the eastern, southern, and southeastern plains that include some of the richest as well as the most arid parts of the country, the Cushitic-speaking majority is mainly comprised of the Agaw, Afar, Oromo, Sidama, Saho, and Somali. Of these, the Oromo are the largest group, accounting for as many as 40 percent of the total population. They are segmented into many branches, the best known of which are the Arsi, Boran, Guji, Karayiu, Mecha, Tulema, and Raya. Dispersed throughout the country, they speak "mutually intelligible dialects" of Oromifa (Afan Oromo), portray diverse cultural traits, and belong to different religions, though the majority are probably Muslim. They have experienced varying degrees of cultural assimilation into Abyssinian society. Close kin of the Oromo are the Afar, Saho, and Somali, who lead a seminomadic existence in an arid region that stretches from eastern Ogaden across Djibouti to Eritrea. Of the many Somali clans segregated from each other by political boundaries, the Isa and subgroups of the Darod, Isaak, Hawiya, and Sab live within Ethiopia, most of them in the regions of Bale, Harer, and Ogaden. The Afar (Dankali), who like the Somali are Muslim, have been scattered in five provinces and in Djibouti, forming a geographic entity that is sometimes called the Afar triangle. With the exception of those residing in Djibouti, they are now unified within the autonomous region of Asseb.

The Nilotes, who may make up about 5 percent of the total, inhabit the warmer hills and valleys of the western parts of the country. They include such groups as the Anuak, Baria, Beni Shangul, Kunama, and Begga, who speak different languages that belong to the Nilo-Saharan family. Though they were politically incorporated in the nineteenth century, they have remained peripheral to the Ethiopian state and society geographically, sociologically, and culturally. Today, Islam predominates in the northern section and native religions in the southern part, with Christian pockets here and there.

The Semitic speakers consist of the Adare, Gurage, Amhara, and Tigrai. The first two are relatively small in size and are largely confined to Harer and Shewa respectively. The second two constitute no more than 50 percent of the total population, but have been the dominant element, culturally and politically, since the foundation of Aksum, with only one major interruption: the Agaw dynasty, which reigned for 135 years. The core Amhara area consists of Gonder, eastern Gojjam, northern Shewa, and western Wello, but the Amhara are found everywhere in the country as settlers, traders, and civil and military personnel. The Tigrai are concentrated in their home areas of Tigrai and Eritrea, out of which they have been emigrating into the rest of the country since the late nineteenth century, mainly for economic reasons. Except for the Adare, who are almost entirely Muslim, the other three are predominantly Christian with significant Muslim minorities.[11]

The historical relationship between these ethnic groups has fluctuated between harmony and conflict. Now feuding and reconciling, now fissuring and fusing, the Ethiopians have cohabited in this vast ecological area for many centuries. They have fought bloody and destructive civil wars at times, but Christians and Muslims have lived there in a state of mutual tolerance. In the southern plateau, a servile peasantry has lived with its northern rulers in a tenuous but markedly less turbulent association. And in the northern plateau, freed farmers have existed along with a landed class in a relationship that runs the gamut from cordiality to hostility. Bound by geography and a tumultuous history, the various peoples of Ethiopia have been in almost continuous association for at least a thousand years, but have not yet fully merged into a single national society. Geography and history have both fostered and frustrated possibilities for intercommunication and solidarity.

Physically, Ethiopia contains a wide range of geographical features and natural phenomena with corresponding climatic conditions. The dominant features are the central highland massif with altitudinal ranges from about 5,500 to 15,000 feet, and the low-lying torrid regions that rise to 5,000 feet above sea level. The highland plateau, which extends for more than 1,600 kilometers (1,000 miles) from the northern to the southern borders of the western half of the country, consisting of vast plains, mountain table-lands, and ranges of hills, looks like a series of islands perched upon a high land mass. Dissected by the rift valley that runs from the Red Sea to Kenya, the plateau is surrounded by a hot, dry, and semidesert plain, very narrow at its northern extremity but widening out as it stretches southward to include the Danakil Depression and the Ogaden, which in turn slowly slopes to the Kenyan frontier and the sea. Despite its proximity to the equator, the plateau enjoys a temperate climate because of its high elevation. But as the temperate highlands slope precipitously down to the tropical lowlands, the climate abruptly changes. In the deep valleys the heat is deadening and the air suffocating. On the plateau, peasants work on small plots with crop rotation typically involving *teff* (the staple cereal), sorghum, wheat, and barley, supplemented by other grains such as millet and maize – crops suitable to the various altitudinal zones. Ethiopian farmers have generally avoided the lowlands, always preferring the cool, better-watered, and healthier highlands.

The distribution of population closely reflects the pattern of topography. The lowlands constitute roughly 53 percent of the total land mass but contain no more than 20 percent of the total population. Density varies regionally from 1.6 persons per square kilometer in the lowlands of Bale to 67.9 in the temperate uplands of Shewa.[12] Not only is the rural population largely concentrated on the highland plateau, but all the major urban centers, with the notable exception of the Red Sea ports of Assab and Mitsiwa (Massawa), are located there.

The country's varied climate, which naturally affects vegetation and the incidence of diseases, thus heavily influenced settlement patterns and human relations. The suitability of the temperate uplands for extensive plow agriculture encouraged the growth of denser settlements (which eventually gave rise to an integrated community marked by Christianity, Amharic, and Tigriniya languages, and a feudal social order). In contrast, in the low-lying drier tropical areas, the material base is limited and societies tend to be small-scale and relatively undifferentiated internally. The lowlands receive less rainfall, and at prevailing levels of technology proved more suitable for pastoral or semipastoral modes of adaptation. The lowland peoples organized themselves into clans or tribes, retained differences of language and ethnicity, and tended to follow Islam. Clearly, the ecological divide also formed a cultural boundary.

Given the pretechnological communications and conditions of life, geography imposed limits on cross-cultural interaction both within and between the two zones. The deserts and mountains hampered social contact, impeded centralized rule, and might have made economic integration a great deal more difficult. D. Donham has analyzed the effect of geography, showing how the escarpments, rivers, and watersheds defined "the boundaries of human interaction." From his penetrating analysis, it appears that Amhara-Tigrean or Abyssinian culture generally did not extend beyond the ecological limits of the highlands.[13]

The geographical and cultural boundary was not uncrossable, however. The highlanders saw the mosquito-infested lowlands as basically unhealthy, inhospitable, and uninhabitable; they dreaded the *nedad* (malarial fever) and feared the Afar, for whom male genitalia were prized as a trophy in war and a license to manhood. (By Afari custom, to castrate the other, non-Afar, man was to affirm one's masculinity, a custom despised by the Christians.) Yet the lowlands were not unknown to them; they frequently traveled there either to fetch edible salt from the Danakil salina or to transport goods to and from the coast. The lowlands served not only as hunting, raiding, and slaving grounds for the "big men," but as hideouts for criminal elements and political malcontents, some of whom built up such wide social bases as to successfully claim supreme authority. Moreover, Abyssinian cultural arrogance coupled with economic imperatives often impelled them to encroach upon the frontier regions. Conversely, lowlanders either traded with or served as conduits between highlanders and merchants at the ports. In times of disorder they led forays into the heart of the weakened kingdom, frequently occupying the marginal lands which would eventually be absorbed by Abyssinian society.[14]

Social interaction within the two ecological zones was also limited through environmental, traditional, and dynamic historical factors. As nomads and pastoralists competed for scarce resources, mainly water and pastures, intercommunal warfare, undeterred by religious or even linguistic commonality, became quite endemic in the lowlands. Such conflicts occurred between as well as within, clans. Raiding for livestock was another source of strife.

In the highlands, the broken and rugged terrain restricted social contact. Mountains were impregnable and rivers, most of which are unnavigable for most of their course, were impassable for much of the rainy season, which lasts several months. No wonder that the Tekeze, Abay, Awash, and their major tributaries formed the historical boundaries between and within provinces in the past. The coincidence of administrative boundaries and geographical definitions reinforced particularistic identities and centrifugal tendencies.

It is not entirely accurate to say that geographical factors were responsible for the fractured political culture of Abyssinia. It was also the outome of a determinate relationship of classes or fractions of them – i.e. activities of hierarchical polities continually competing for productive resources and honorific precedence. Theoretically, power, privilege, and status emanated from the monarchy. But the basis for regional power was not so much the legalization or legitimization of authority by the crown as it was the capacity to muster economic and military resources, which ultimately meant the control of the peasantry, its labor and products.

An inevitable outcome of territorial fragmentation and the existence of multiple sources of power was the fragmentation of popular consciousness. It produced two contradictory tendencies: regionalism/localism and nationalism. The relative insularity of each regional division, combined with the activities of a succession of warrior-rulers, conditioned historical awareness. Regional divisions were fluid and often overlapping, but their impact on popular attitudes was lasting. At certain times, subregional identities were more prominent than regional ones. Thus, historically, it is possible to speak of double or even triple consciousness and loyalty. In relation to one another, Abyssinians tended to identify themselves with their respective locality or region to the exclusion of others, as in Aksum versus Agame or Tigrai versus Gojjam. But in relation to the surrounding people and all foreigners (*faranji*) from far beyond, the Amhara-Tigriniya-speaking Ethiopians regarded themselves as belonging to a supra-region, supra-ethnic community which they called *Habesha*. The Habesha (Abyssinians) saw themselves as a people inhabiting a historically and geographically identifiable region, sharing a common linguistic origin (Geez), a common religion institutionalized in the Tewahdo or Orthodox Christian Church, a mythically derived common cultural frame of reference best articulated in the *Kebre Negest* (Glory of the Kings), and a mode of production that, despite regional and local variations, was essentially the same. That vague consciousness of a national identity frequently expressed itself in a unified patriotic resistance against external invasion during the nineteenth and twentieth centuries.[15]

Abyssinian peasants were less alert to social divisions than they were to foreign threat. Territorial fragmentation had the dual effect of horizontally compartmentalizing the population, helping (a) to discourage interregional alliances against the crown/state, and (b) to weaken class solidarity across regional boundaries; rather, local and vertical ties were strengthened. In their struggle to defend their autonomy and to guarantee the continuity of family rule, warrior-rulers relied heavily on the peasants, whom they otherwise dominated and exploited, and for whose loyalty the monarch also competed. The physical remoteness of the monarch, combined with the nobility's embeddedness in the local economy and its strong cultural ties to the peasantry, allowed local barons to exert greater and direct influence on the latter and to limit the throne's authority and its intrusive tendencies.[16] Local sentiment was particularly intense in Gojjam and Tigrai, two of the northern provinces that tenaciously resisted centralization well into the 1940s and 1950s. As greater administrative consolidation was achieved, however, the regional elites became increasingly more dependent on the state for continued dominance of the peasants, although they allied themselves with the latter from time to time for reasons of expediency. Peasants were likely to be aroused only when they believed that resistance would enhance their own interest, as was the case of Gojjam in 1968. That is to say, the consolidation of the state, a process described below, also witnessed the further crystallization of social classes. The two processes were clearly intertwined.

Foundations of the new imperial state

The new state was formed by the last quarter of the nineteenth century through a dual process of centralization and territorial expansion. This involved the centralization of atomized sovereignty in the core region, on the one hand, and the extension of that sovereignty over autonomous or semiautonomous polities on the southern periphery, on the other. In both instances, there was a good deal of opposition, and the technical means used to break resistance were imported and paid for by the sale of primary products mainly collected from the newly incorporated regions. The territorial limits of the state were finally achieved through collision and collusion with foreign powers. As new territories were acquired to the south, in competition with Europeans, a portion of the northern historical core was alienated by Italy in 1889–90 to form the enclave of Eritrea, a region that experienced greater socioeconomic transformation than the rest of the country. The national and class relationships that developed during the colonial period were to be significant factors in subsequent historical experiences of the region's population. Consisting of numerous and unevenly developed communities, the newly formed empire-state was a mosaic of cultures. The imperial state imposed some degree of uniformity on the sociologically, culturally, and politically diverse features, but without wholly deracinating them.

The imperial state traced its origins to Aksum, a Christian kingdom with an agro-commercial economic base that reached the high point of its civilization by the eighth century A.D., when it began to atrophy.[17] Subsequently, its polity gradually withdrew further inland, setting a new trend of southward movement that was to shape the political geography of Ethiopia for centuries. Aksum's political and cultural institutions were inherited, with little modification, by its successor states, and this enduring legacy was ruptured only in 1974.

In its formation the imperial state passed through four overlapping phases, each of which roughly corresponded with the reign of four powerful personalities, each of whom had his own particular set of goals, problems, and solutions. The forces that began the process of state building emerged out of the crisis of the eighteenth century. Between 1769 and 1855 the Abyssinian Kingdom was engulfed in sterile and destructive factional wars that led to a near eclipse of monarchical sovereignty, albeit without openly challenging the basic principles of social relationships or their broad patterns. The period is appropriately known as the *Zemene Mesafent* (Age of the Princes).[18] Only since the second half of the nineteenth century did the successive Emperors Tewodros II (1855–68), Yohannes IV (1872–89), and Menelik II (1889–1913) reconstruct the Abyssinian Kingdom and considerably expand the material base of a revived monarchical power. By subjecting all citizens to Amhara-Tigrean domination they also initiated a process of "Abyssinianization," an imperial ideal that was only partially realized during the long reign of Haile Selassie I (1916–74). To be sure, urbanization, transregional migration, and transethnic marriages have shaped a society that does not wholly resemble the one existing during the first decade of this century, but the homogenizing effects of the socioeconomic and political changes that Haile Selassie half-heartedly pursued have been variable and very limited.

State construction in Ethiopia was undertaken within the framework of a hazy sense of nationalism and related notions of change and progress. The appearance of the Europeans in the 1830s and then the Egyptians had a perceptible impact on the Abyssinian body politic. What inspired the powerful men to embark on a course of state consolidation was partly the perception that "national" survival was being threatened by a combination of powerful forces unleashed by the expansionist impulses of the European economy and religious fanaticism in the Horn. These historical circumstances gave rise to a state that was uniquely equipped to serve as steward or vehicle of "modernization," a role that was different from the European pattern of the eighteenth century. The Ethiopian experience of state building rather foreshadowed a pattern that would become common in postcolonial Africa: the emergence of a bloated state acting both as agent of and impediment to change. The incongruity between its economic and political structures produced a state that was distinctly autocratic, determining both the direction and pace of its development in relative autonomy from its domestic constituents and its external mentors.

The man who laid the foundations of a unitary state was Kassa, an extraordinarily gifted and ambitious person whose illustrious career began as a bandit in the lowlands of Kwara (Gonder region). His activities as a bandit and his relationship to peasants have been much romanticized. He has been portrayed as a champion of justice who punished the powerful in defense of the weak – a man who looted the rich in order to feed the poor. In 1855, Kassa crowned himself as Tewodros II, King of Kings, after having subdued the warlords one by one. As emperor he tried to ease the burden of the peasantry by creating a salaried bureaucracy and army and by abolishing the church's tax exemptions. He also wanted to initiate technological change, for which he sought European help. His attitude toward Europe was, however, ambivalent, and one that was fully shared by his successors: Europe was at once to be emulated and resisted. With varying degrees of commitment, the Ethiopian leaders wished to benefit from the scientific and industrial revolutions, but they were profoundly suspicious and fearful of Europe's imperialist designs. Indeed, although little technology was borrowed, European activities in the region did consume their energies and resources, including tragically ending the controversial career and life of Tewodros. Some have glorified his rule as an era of reform and change, while others have depicted it as a reign of terror and blood. As is the case with such quixotic characters, there is something mythical about the man. But seen in the context of Abyssinian political culture, Tewodros was an exceptional individual. Endowed with a sharp intellect, a forceful personality, and a visionary outlook, he vigorously challenged the stultifying conformity of a traditional society. As a visionary, he was committed to the creation of a unified and reformed Abyssinia, but one in which Christian dominance was firmly solidified. His vision of a new state-society was rather exclusionary, and in practice he was too harsh in his treatment of non-Christians. His aggressive centralist and reformist programs eventually alienated sections of the privileged strata who successfully undermined them by stirring rebellions that in turn exhausted his energies and resources. Defiant even in defeat, Tewodros killed himself in 1868,[19] but the process he had set in motion was continued after his departure.

Tewodros's successors, by and large, shared his goals, but not necessarily his methods. Though as much intolerant of religious diversity, Yohannes IV was more accommodating to regional autonomy. And whereas Tewodros wanted the church to be institutionally supported, Yohannes increased its endowments in land without even restricting its traditional exactions from the cultivators. He also retained the regional hereditary rulers, bestowing on them titles such as Ras and negus and granting them varying degrees of autonomy. His sovereign relationship with some of them, especially with the rulers of Shewa, was not always smooth, underscoring the existing contradictions among the various factions of the dominant Abyssinian class struggling for political control of the evolving state-society. Menelik's allegiance to Yohannes remained equivocal as he continued to vie for supreme authority, which he must have believed was within his grasp because of the fast-changing geopolitical conditions. Yohannes's preoccupation with the "triple threat" coming from Italian imperialists, Egyptian expansionists, and Sudanese Mahdists prevented him from devoting attention to domestic problems while allowing Menelik to steer an independent course in the south.[20] The "southern marches" brought wealth and power that no rival could match, and Menelik was set to create a more unified and vastly expanded state out of a parvenu of feudal princes and chiefs.

Shewan expansionism was basically an outcome of the internal dynamics of Abyssinian society, but it was the convergence of European commercial interests and those of Abyssinian rulers that made it possible. The frontier has always represented a zone of opportunity for individuals and groups. Rulers encouraged and supported it because it lessened conflicts in the core and provided opportunities for enfeoffment, an advantage which Shewa enjoyed as frontier region. What impelled the Shewans to embark on a much larger scale of colonization in the 1880s was the appearance of European colonialists in the region and the related growth in international commerce. As the Horn was increasingly drawn into the European economy following the opening of the Suez Canal in 1869, the Shewans were lured by the south's lucrative trade and its rich marketable products. By exporting ivory, gold, civet, animal hides, gum, and coffee, the Shewan nobility was able to purchase quantities of firearms with which they were able to expand and centralize the territorial base of the imperial state.[21] Shewa was close enough to the south to take full advantage of the expanding regional trade but far enough from the coast to escape Egyptian and European expansionist thrusts that had engaged the northerners since the early 1870s, depleting their resources. The military and economic balance was consequently tipped in favor of the Shewans, who acquired the new territories lying to the west of the Omo and to the southeast of the Awash rivers in the face of a three-dimensional resistance. The first arose from competing Europeans but rarely involved armed violence. The second came from the rival feudality of Gojjam which was defeated at the battle of Imbabo in June 1882. The third and fiercest resistance came from the indigenous peoples themselves. Yet eventually they lost, largely because their defensive systems and weapons had become obsolete by the nineteenth century and could not match the superior armies from the north which also employed some foreign expertise.[22] In view of the fact that Abyssinian society and state dominated comparable peoples and territory in the fourteenth and fifteenth centuries without marked technological advantages, it might also be argued that the technological disparity explains the rapidity with which conquest took place, not the fact that it did, or even its geographical scope.

The conquerors strove to consolidate their rule by imposing the Abyssinian model of social organization. They did so by conserving and reinforcing compliant local traditional rulers or by creating new ones that eventually became hereditary in some instances. By absorbing the traditional polities Menelik was able to construct a broader social base to the imperial state. The social makeup of the emerging Abyssinian ruling class was thus continually and profoundly being transformed. A new dominant class that was trans-ethnic and transregional was definitely emerging parallel to the evolving state-society. New sources of conflict were also created. By alienating lands of the annexed societies and thereby reducing them to servitude, and by imposing on them Abyssinian culture, the conquerors planted the seeds for national and class antagonism. And as the subordinated ruling groups in the occupied territories accepted Christianity and became fully dependent on the imperial state for the conditions of their reproduction, they lost their organic ties to the indigenous communities. Christianity, which had long provided a unifying ideology for Abyssinians, now became a divisive factor in the multicultural state, since the majority of the conquered peoples belonged to Islam and African religions.

If Imbabo was pivotal in the conquest of the south, so was Metemma in establishing Shewan hegemony over the rest of Abyssinia. In March 1889, following the death of Yohannes in combat at Metemma against a Sudanese army, Menelik decisively seized the hour while the Tigrean notables were still in a state of confusion and disarray, unable to decide between resistance and capitulation. He proclaimed himself King of Kings of Ethiopia on May 2, 1889, accepting the voluntary submission of the other northern suzerains. But even as he consolidated his control over the empire, the emperor still had to deal with Italy, which, in the face of the partition of Africa, had dismembered the northern part of Tigrai soon after the Metemma debacle, naming it Eritrea. Although Menelik had conceded the occupation in the Wichale Treaty of May 1889, Italy wanted to annex the rest of the country. The result was the battle of Adwa on March 1, 1896, in which the aggressor was resoundingly crushed.[23] This was the culminating event in the formation of the Ethiopian imperial state. It assured the country's independence and affirmed the supremacy of the Shewan faction over the rival claimants to sovereignty. Yet the role of the limitrophe powers was treacherous for, while recognizing Ethiopia's autonomy, they did not refrain from undermining its integrity.[24] Their hostile activities would lead to the state's dissolution thirty years later.

Paradoxically, Adwa was both a negation and an affirmation of Wichale.[25] The partition of Tigrai meant not only the loss of the country's major outlet to the sea but also the split of Abyssinian identity, a historical fact that Ethiopian rulers have failed to appreciate fully. When Eritrea was regained some sixty years later, it had already attained its own territorial and historical specificity, which differentiated it from the rest of the country. This major difference finally led to what has become the "longest war" in Africa, the human and social cost of which is staggering. A quarter of a century since the conflict broke out, Menelik's heirs have not been able to find a solution. The Eritrean conflict is a bitter legacy of colonialism and state formation in Africa.

The loss of Eritrea notwithstanding, the Abyssinian dominant social block, led by three prominent individuals, was able to form a multiethnic and multilingual state, drastically changing the demographic and social complexion of "old Abyssinia," in a little over half a century. Centrally located, where all the major trade routes converged, and equipped with a huge armory, which no other precolonial African polity was able to acquire, the Shewan nobility was particularly better placed to quash every resistance in the south, to prevail over its rivals in the north, and, by repulsing Italian colonial onslaught, to assure the external acceptance of the state's sovereignty. The new imperial state was maintained through an intricate web of patrimonial alliances and marriage ties, supported by an expanding military organization. For a quarter of a century, Menelik dominated it by carefully balancing the differing policies of his immediate predecessors. In his cautious drive to transform it into an organization that was more in tune with the changing world, he formed a ministerial system with specialized responsibilities; founded a permanent capital at Addis Ababa; developed a rag-tag army sustained by a fixed levy; and promoted the construction and installation of transport and communication facilities.[26] These changes, in turn, facilitated the growth of a monetized economy that came to be dominated by a small, but growing foreign community. The transformation was, however, limited in scale, a testament to the limited penetration of the world economy.

Haile Selassie I, first as regent (1916–30) and then as emperor (1930–74), expanded, modified, and consolidated Menelik's limited achievements. The inner thrust of his program was to create a unified apparatus of power directly controlled by himself and uncurbed by any law. By decisively undercutting the feudal polity, he sought to extend the state's penetration and control over rural society. The extent of his success in challenging and taming the traditional dominant groups depended on internal and international conditions that broadened the scope of his action. The following pages will pay attention to the changing relationships among local dominant and subordinate groups as well as between the dependent peripheral state and external agencies.

Absolute monarchy, nobility, and peasantry

The imperial state arose from and functioned under dispersed conditions of power. Despite political unification and the introduction of the paraphernalia of a modern governmental system, the monarch's authority remained restricted; provincial overlords still enjoyed administrative and juridical powers, raising armed contingents and collecting revenues with little direct interference from the monarchy. The absence of a permanent standing army, specialized personnel, and a regulated fiscal system belied the existence of a truly centralized nation-state. Haile Selassie instituted these essential instruments of authority, erecting a state whose capacity to control and mobilize public resources and to skim surpluses was infinitely greater than that of its predecessors. Its construction and consolidation entailed heavy reliance on the use of coercive force augmented by foreign support, the cooption or destruction of all intermediary authorities and alternative sources of power and its subsequent personalization, the constriction of political activities despite a democratic façade, and an increased production of cash crops to minimize dependency on the tributary system.[27]

"This government is an absolute monarchy," wrote the Minister Resident and Consul General of the United States in 1928. The minister was quick to qualify his remark by stating that nascent royal absolutism was modified by the relative strength or weakness of the provincial rulers.[28] Absolutism is the expression of a centralized power over a national domain, but it does not mean "untramelled despotism,"[29] nor has it been uniform in its political manifestations. Even at the apogee of his suzerainty, Emperor Haile Selassie never exercised unlimited power over the Ethiopian citizenry, a trait that he shared with other absolute monarchs. In a historical sense then "the monarchy was absolute by opposition to the past feudal scattering of power."[30] That process of power concentration has been historically variable because of the disparity in its social and cultural determinants and monarchical traditions. As Perez Zagorin has expressed it, "Absolutism admits of several degrees and variations and did not present a uniform appearance or conform to a single model. It should be understood as a *relative* absolutism ..."[31] The three decades (1941–74) of Haile Selassie's reign constitute one variant of absolutism.

European absolutism is said to have been achieved through "four major mechanisms: bureaucratization, monopolization of force, creation of legitimacy, and the homogenization of the subject population."[32] How well does the Ethiopian experience correspond to this pattern? Only imperfectly.[33] Despite some marked resemblances, it would indeed be an indulgence in historical simplification to suggest that the postcolonial Ethiopian state was a mirror image of the European absolutist state, either in its pattern of development or in its social and institutional structures. The basic similarities and differences are discernible. Both the Ethiopian and European states controlled agrarian populations, the vast majority of whom were still tied to the land through tributary or feudal relations of production. Second, they both developed uniform juridical, fiscal, and administrative systems, and created permanent armies and functionally differentiated civil bureaucracies. Moreover, they cultivated environments favorable to the growth of an integrated market, thereby creating the apparatuses of modern nation-states. But the differences in class configuration and relation of the dominant classes to the state were equally marked. If Western European absolutism generally meant the consolidation of aristocratic power and the suppression of the masses, and Eastern European absolutism was characterized by the reinfeudation of rural cultivators,[34] then neither variant featured prominently in the Ethiopian case. The Abyssinian nobility suffered the diminution of its political power, its social function increasingly becoming ceremonial. However, the impact of absolutism on the traditionally dominant classes was multifaceted, involving a painful process of alienation, disaffection, and adaptation, in which some benefited enormously and others lost disgracefully, but rarely without a fight – a pattern that parallels the Euro-

pean experience.[35] Except for the Shewan faction, which was safely protected from the effects of centralism because of its closeness to the ruling
dynasty and state power, the northern lords endured indignity and material
loss. That is why resistance to royal power between the 1930s and the 1940s
was largely confined to the northern provinces. On the other hand, although
the peasantry was relieved of the more onerous aspects of feudal relations,
the southern gentry was ennobled under absolutism, and it might be characterized as the "new nobility." The predominance of precapitalist relations
in Ethiopia also meant that the nascent classes were nowhere as significant as
the rising European bourgeoisie and proletariat numerically, ideologically,
and politically. Finally, for its consolidation and sustenance the Ethiopian
state was considerably more dependent on external assistance, assistance
which inevitably impinged upon its autonomy.

The evolution of the Ethiopian absolutist state was never a smooth
process. The state was the product of three major crises, one of which
actually removed the monarch from his throne and had the potential of
modifying or altering the social character of the political system: (1) the
debilitating interclass conflict (1913–28) arising out of the problem of succession to the throne, and policies pertaining to institutional organization; (2)
the dissolution of the emerging monarchical state following the country's
colonial occupation by Italy (1935–41); and (3) its restoration (1941) and
revival in the face of opposition from societal groups and quasi-colonial
restrictions imposed on its sovereignty by Britain. This phase ends with the
gradual replacement of British dominance in Ethiopia by that of the United
States, with whose assistance the emperor was able to establish a patrimonial
absolutist regime that lasted until 1974.

The architect of the state himself was the product of a two-phased political
turmoil facing a rising but still faction-ridden dominant class. The first
involved the rise and demise of the inexperienced Iyassu, grandson and heir
of Menelik.[36] Since he was the son of a former Muslim Oromo chieftain and
then christianized overlord of the Wello, a section of the Shewan nobility
was opposed to Iyassu's enthronement for fear that his rule would herald a
shift of the locus of power from the center toward the periphery. It tirelessly
plotted against the prince, finally deposing him in 1916. The triumvirate that
replaced him was given to Byzantine intrigue and feuding, the Regent, Ras
Teferri (later Haile Selassie I), excelling as the better Machiavellian.[37] The
basis for factionalism was the existence of several rival claimants to supreme
authority and fundamental differences of opinion on a new definition of the
state's character and its place in the international system of states. One
faction was opposed to all forms of innovation because it was suspicious of
European intentions and fearful of losing its privileges. In so far as it had a
program, it sought to insulate the country against foreign ideals and material
influence, to keep a loose union of semiautonomous regions governed by
hereditary ruling families, and to maintain the basic forms of surplus
extraction unmodified or unadulterated.[38] It ridiculed its opponents, called
"progressives" by their foreign admirers, for mindlessly aping the West.

The progressives or modernists, led by Teferri, linked the security of the national state to political, economic, and administrative reforms. Japan was the society to be emulated.[39] A non-European nation, with a monarchical tradition and feudal institutions, Japan had successfully entered the industrial age. It seemed to offer the perfect model for development. Foreign merchants, diplomats, and corporate representatives scurrying for new concessions generally supported the progressives, dismissing the others as the "deadly forces of obscurantism and reaction," in the words of one of them.[40] With their help and commitment and the loyalty of a small but dynamic group of Western educated Ethiopians, Teferri outmaneuvered his rivals so as to capture the throne, closing the second phase of the political squabbles. His rise, which began with the coup of 1916, ended with a pompous coronation on October 30, 1930 at which Teferri adopted a new regal name, assuming the flamboyant title of the Conquering Lion of Judah, Elect of God, King of Kings of Ethiopia and accumulating extensive power and glory for himself. The era of absolutism had begun. Since the struggles that led to his eventual ascendancy were, in part, waged to determine the direction and pace of development of the transitional political economy, Teferri's victory has to be seen as the triumph of a distinct political orientation occurring at a time when the country was coming increasingly into contact with a wider world.

In the first six years of his accession to the throne, the emperor expanded and rationalized the administration by appointing a body of dependent functionaries, established the core of a standing army, and promulgated a written constitution that for the first time introduced a standardized system of taxation. As might have been expected, the main obstacle to reform was the regionalized polities and ecclesiastics. In 1930 Ras Gugsa Wolle, governor of the region lying between the Tekeze and Lake Tana, was the first disaffected noble to rebel against the emperor. The newly constituted army had little trouble in crushing the revolt, killing its leader at the battle of Aychem, to the east of Debre Tabor.[41] Bolstered by the victory, the emperor began to fortify the crown with a series of reforms.

The cornerstone of the prewar reforms was the constitution of 1931. As the juridical expression of the reconstructed state, it provided the legal and ideological framework of absolutism and, as such, it was the ultimate expression of royal supremacy over feudal autonomy. Hitherto, there was no legislative, no judicative, and no written constitution.[42] Although the new document was presented as a social contract between the Ethiopian people and the Solomonic dynasty, the king's supreme authority derived its justification not from popular will but from the religious precept of "divine right." Claiming divine ordination, a claim dutifully supported by the church, the king presented himself as the embodiment of God's authority on earth, to whom submission and obedience were owed, and against whom rebellion was a sin.[43] For its support, royalty generously reciprocated by granting the church huge amounts of landed property, all of it untaxed.

Absolutism was an imperfect amalgam of new and old politics; it was an order in which a new set of central institutions, political relationships, and sources of power were simply grafted onto the preexisting social structure. By fusing aspects of a rational and modern administration with a feudal residuum, the centralizing monarchy both multiplied and complicated the internal inconsistencies and contradictions of the ideological foundation on which it rested so precariously. The conflicting tendencies contained in the operative political system were kept in a delicate balance by the king who, by virtue of his divine aura and inviolable dignity, exercised the power to legislate, to adjudicate, and to distribute a hierarchy of ranks, titles, and attendant privileges and honors. However, to say that the stability of the hierarchical order depended entirely on the religious attributes of monarchical authority is to simplify grossly; after all, Haile Selassie was not the first Ethiopian ruler to claim divine appointment or a "sacred personality." The difference between him and his predecessors was that he had created a military arm of the state with which to support the religious and juridical basis of royal authority.

The constitution, which enormously reduced the crown's dependence on the nobilities, was clearly a historic compromise between monarchy, the feudal polity, and the church. But the concessions were by no means reciprocal, nor was the partnership between crown and nobility equal. Paradoxically, the emperor was both the oppressor and preserver of the aristocracy. As chief of state whose authority was indisputable, the emperor had become the centralizer of resources and power but also the sole distributor of wealth and privilege to the provincial elites, both in theory and in practice. In return for the subordination, although not always willing, to royal authority, the monarch recognized traditional prerogatives and rights of the feudal lords in their respective territories. The violation of these vastly diminished privileges or the desire to reclaim suppressed rights could render the ideology of absolutism inoperative, in which case there would be recourse to military force. This is why such challenges mainly occurred at moments of crisis in the state or when royal authority was perceived to be weak.

The constitutional changes, administrative and military innovations, and the development of new habits in life necessitated fiscal reorganization. To modernize his uniformed army; to support the burgeoning bureaucracy; to remunerate the foreigners whose expertise was sought in the reorganization of the various organs of government; to expand and develop the urban infrastructure of Addis Ababa; and to import luxury goods for which the aristocracy was fast developing an avid taste, the emperor had to create mechanisms with which he could extract surpluses exceeding the costs of state maintenance. Revenue was raised by: (1) increasing taxes on the agricultural population, (2) converting land into a commodity, and payment in kind into payment in cash, (3) raising commodity production to meet the demands of the world economy, and reorganizing the customs administration to provide fiscal centralization.[44] Falling almost entirely on the agricultural population, the new levies in combination with old exactions still collected by feudal lords caused considerable rural strife punctuated by peasant revolts. The rebellion of 1930 had a strong peasant element.

Fiscal reorganization and expansion in international trade during the two decades before the Ethiopian–Italian war had the combined effect of drawing the country into the world economy, a process that had actually begun in the latter half of the nineteenth century. This was due largely to the construction of the Addis–Djibouti railway between 1897 and 1917 and the rise in selected exportable commodities, a development that coincided with postwar consolidation of colonial rule in Africa and consequently full incorporation of the continent into the world economy. As in the rest of Africa, production of cash crops for export became the prime motif of the economy, and the territories south of the Awash attained enhanced importance. By the early 1930s, the size of the exports, of which coffee, hides, and skins constituted the main bulk, increased several fold. Members of the royalty and nobility, in partnership with foreign merchants and traders, had the lion's share of this flourishing trade.[45]

The historical process linking Ethiopia with the global economy had a triple effect on the country's transitional social formation. First, increases in exports led to related economic growth, reinforcing in certain ways the wider material base supporting social formation and providing the means with which to import consumer products and to modernize the state apparatus. Second, by 1920 the Addis–Djibouti railway had become the outlet for the bulk of Ethiopia's external trade, carrying no less than 70 percent of the total. The north's share had diminished to less than 15 percent.[46] The south became the commercial hub of the country, with all trading activities converging in Addis Ababa, itself evidence of a relatively unified economy. Third, the railway and trade in primary products, largely drawn from one sector of the country, had the effect of initiating uneven economic growth in the country, and unevenness had a variegated impact on regions and ethnicities. The disparity was partially due to the enormous variation in the distribution of resources and partly due to the discriminatory policies of the imperial state. The availability of alienable land, an increasing amount of freed labor, the presence of diverse and abundant exportable commodities, and the existence of a transport facility made the southern regions particularly attractive for exploitative investment.[47] It was precisely in this region that an industrial enclave running through a narrow corridor that connects Shewa with Harer came into existence. As there was disparity between and within regions, so was there marked inequality between town and country. Although Harerge received a disproportionate amount of attention, the fulcrum of imperial development was Shewa (home of the reigning dynasty) and its capital, Addis Ababa.

With the steady expansion of commodity production and exchange and the commutation of feudal dues into cash payments, the state's role in navigating the national economy increased. The reorganization of the customs department, the issue of a new currency, and the opening of the Bank of Abyssinia (renamed the National Bank of Ethiopia) – themselves by-products of an expanding market economy – considerably enhanced the state's monopolistic control of the country's financial resources and institutions.[48] A clear pattern was emerging: the state was both to foster and control economic development and class formation. In directing the economy it would appropriate the national surplus, arrogating a large part to itself and redistributing the rest unequally among its various constituents. The absence of oil or minerals meant that that surplus would come almost exclusively from agriculture.

On the eve of the Italian invasion Emperor Haile Selassie had in place the essential ingredients for consolidated and personalized authority. The sudden collapse of the unified state nevertheless demonstrated both the tenuousness of that unity and the precariousness of feudal symbiosis. The sizeable number of noble desertions to the enemy camp or abstentions from the patriotic resistance seem to indicate the great disaffection that regionalized elites harbored toward the crown.[49]

The colonial interlude was noteworthy for another reason: it had the effect of simultaneously weakening the physical and social impediments to centralization and strengthening parochial identities and sentiments. In the first place, by promoting Islam vis-à-vis Christianity, the Italians rekindled sources of religious rivalry. They also promoted Oromifa and Arabic by deemphasizing Amharic.[50] Whereas the occupation might thus have strengthened nationalism, it also heightened ethnic consciousness. Secondly, the prewar social equilibrium was rendered less secure by economic policies that undermined traditional relations between peasants and landlords. Moreover, whereas the colonial state confirmed the collaborationist nobles in their traditional positions, it eroded their power by either limiting or depriving them of their access to peasant labor and products. Finally, by establishing or expanding a broad network of roads, wire, and postal services, the colonialists built a unified communication system that welded together the various regions. It helped the restored emperor to carry out the program of territorial integration and power consolidation that he had begun five years before.

Soon after his return in May 1941, the emperor recommenced his prewar reform policies in the face of mounting opposition. Taking advantage of the weaknesses of a transitional regime, ambitious nobles raised the banner of rebellion, rallying the peasants to their side. This pattern of resistance was particularly noticeable in the heartlands of hereditary noble rule – Gonder, Gojjam, and Tigrai. If the battle of Aychem was the prelude, the 1943 revolt in Tigrai proved to be the last futile act by the nobility to stop centralism. Southern peasants, fearful of the resurrection of northern domination and religious oppression, resisted the reestablishment of Ethiopian administration. Such concerted resistance took place in Bale, Harer, and Sidamo. It was more sporadic in other areas. All over the country, deserters from the retreating army, disbanded native colonial soldiers, laborers who had either lost or been separated from their foreign employers, and various armed fugitives joined brigands to constitute a major destabilizing force. The emperor was able to survive this major crisis because the opposition remained fragmented and the British provided much-needed economic and military support. With their help, he restored tranquillity, firmly reestablishing his authority. In time, he reorganized the administration: boundaries were redrawn demarcating the new fourteen provinces, each with subunits, the taxation system was rewritten, and the church, which had been subserviently linked to the Coptic Church of Egypt, was brought under the monarch's direct supervision, bishops, in effect, becoming royal appointees. By emasculating the two rival sources of authority, the emperor greatly increased the autonomy of the imperial state.

Monarchical authority distanced but did not completely detach itself from the dominant elements because royalty remained rooted in the land and social mores of traditional society. There was no rupture in the organic linkage between economy and polity. Despite the diminution of its power, the aristocracy provided the social basis of the state, and the distribution of wealth was organized in such a manner that it continued to benefit disproportionately from it. The indignity and economic ruin suffered by individual notables, mostly from the north, should not be confused with the eclipse of aristocratic rule. Actually, the nobility continued both to collaborate with and to sustain the centralized monarchical state, while at the same time rejecting full incorporation. Royal supremacy did not and could not supplant the nobility completely. Yohannes's descendants administered Tigrai to the last days of absolutism, and the civil personnel for the north-central provinces were recruited heavily from the localized dominant stratum.[51] Administrative uniformity remained an incomplete process, much as in medieval Europe. According to Zagorin, "royal government never became uniform or monolithic, even in the kingdoms where it suffered least limitation."[52] In concurrence, Perry Anderson remarks that the absolutist state never achieved "any complete administrative centralization or juridical unification; corporative particularisms and regional heterogeneities inherited power." The past order continued to operate down to its "ultimate overthrow."[53] So it was in Ethiopia. Almost to the last days of its life, the monarchical state struggled for domination in the rural areas against powerful hereditary local and regional forces. Inherited patterns of authority and deeply rooted sectional identities and loyalties stubbornly resisted full absorption by the state.

Yet in the face of increasing class crystallization and national antagonism, only the state could sustain the landed class's social preeminence by at once controlling and protecting them. In the south, Abyssinian settlers holding large estates relied heavily on the armed strength of the state to keep a restive peasantry under control; in the north, a semi-impoverished nobility gravitated toward the state for employment or remuneration to supplement its meager income from the land. Abandoning its previous habits and instruments of authority, it slowly adjusted to a settled and more peaceful life, learning "the new avocations of a disciplined officer, a literate functionary," and a court retainer;[54] in essence, it became "a nobility of service."[55]

The other component of the state bureaucracy, against which the nobility of service had to compete continually, comprised men without claims to hereditary office or a regional base of power. They did not have an independent economic base outside the public sector. Commonly of "humble origin," these men owed their position to education they received at home and abroad. As bureaucratization expanded, the state's dependence on the nobility shifted to these "literate commoners." The bureaucrats were mainly the emperor's appointees, and they served him loyally although not always efficiently. Factors such as ethnicity, religion, region, education, and family or personal ties were important in determining entry into the middle and upper levels of the bureaucratic apparatus, but recruitment and retention were determined largely by the chief executive; loyalty and obedience, or the lack of them, were the primary criteria for promotion, transfer, demotion, or dismissal. Shewan Amhara were favored heavily in the *shum–shir* ("appoint–dismiss") imperial system. Few Muslims made it to the inner core of the ministerial hierarchy, and none to provincial governorship.[56]

Under patrimonial rule, social relations were mainly articulated through personal ties, revealing the fundamental weakness and fluidity of classes. Clientalism, which often drew from the affective ties of ethnicity, religion, and region, was the grid of politics, underpinning power relations in the monarchical state.[57] Characteristic of peasant and lord relationships in old Abyssinia, clientalism bound individuals of unequal power and status for mutual benefits. State officials, headed by the emperor, used their privileged access to national resources to reward their political supporters and loyal retainers. As if to stress the material benefits deriving from these extensive networks of personalized relationships, patrons often referred to their clients as *yettut lijoch* (breast-fed children). In the variegated Ethiopian social milieu, patrimonial politics tended to exacerbate regional inequalities in social services and educational and employment opportunities.

If patronage was designed to strengthen class position and mechanisms of social control, it impaired mobilization along horizontal lines. State servants were prone to quarreling and conspiring against each other for advancement and self-preservation, and as such, the state became the arena for class unity as well as class conflict. These factional squabbles and struggles were obviously in direct conflict with one of the group's main objectives – that of strengthening its own social identity and economic position in the emerging state-society. Transregional and transethnic, the dominant class was still far from being unified and coherent, and its activities were not always congruent with its class interests. However, held together by multiple forms of connections, it had become increasingly conscious of its own existence, defending its basic interests against the peasantry and the emerging classes.[58] Its national venue was the parliament. As the emperor was its main patron, the imperial state was its principal weapon in that struggle, notwithstanding its opposition to governmental policies that ran counter to its interest. Clearly, this was a situation in which class and state power were combined, rulers using state power to expand and strengthen their social base. The ruling class had yet to become hegemonic, for it lacked the intellectual and moral aspects of political leadership. Hence its reliance on the coercive tools of the state, which in turn deprived the latter of its relative autonomy.

Authority in the patrimonial state was highly personalized and abusive from top to bottom, provincial officials exercising extensive and generally unsupervised powers. Provincial administration was hierarchically organized with a chain of command that linked the Minister of the Interior at the top to the village headman at the bottom. Offices were institutionally differentiated, but personal ties and nepotism predominated. Men accepted the status and fortune that office holding brought with it, but rarely its duties and obligations. Armed with the power to accuse, arrest, and detain without due process of law, officials used their authority for the extraction of resources. The rapidly proliferating state agents considered their salaries insufficient and they soon became dishonest, accepting bribes and engaging in widespread illicit activities ranging from misappropriation to outright theft. A government-sponsored study in 1969 acknowledged the existence of the problem, but tried to limit it to junior officials, who included the village headmen, judges, and police: "Arbitrary decisions and fictitious charges against poor peasants were mentioned as not uncommon; there seems to be no act of dishonesty and of hidden oppression of which these lower bureaucrats cannot be accused."[59] Actually corruption was ubiquitous and destructive, affecting society at all levels of administration. In the enforcement of the law, which was uneven; in the administration of justice, which was arbitrary and unequal; and in the collection of taxes, which was extortionist, people in power were venal and grasping. The farmers and herders, who suffered most from their activities, made it clear that the burden of corruption had become heavier with the increase in state functionaries. Peasants of Gojjam lamented: "Our country, with its streams and rivers, is kind and bountiful. But this was before the state officials began to multiply like puppies!" And the peasants of Tigrai agonized: "It surely is dangerous to express one's feelings these days, and one is better off when mute and dumb. But thirty administrators for one district! To how many of these can I say master!"[60]

Old methods combined with new mechanisms of predatory accumulation of wealth to victimize civil society as well as the state. The diversion of public funds on a large scale had the effect of reducing governmental revenue as well as productive investment. In the early 1960s the government initiated a program of rural development known as *idget be-hibret* (development through cooperation) in partnership with the people. The rural population was asked to make voluntary contributions in money, in kind, and labor toward self-help development projects like schools, clinics, and roads. In doing so, the state was clearly shifting its social responsibilities and functions to a taxpaying citizenry. Still, the program contained some good elements which might have benefited the rural people eventually had it been honestly and efficiently implemented. As it turned out, it became a useful mechanism for appropriation – a source of graft and fraud. Compulsion was used widely, those unwilling to contribute often treated as tax delinquents. Contributors had little say, if any, in the actual management of the funds. Receipts were rarely given, and no public accounts of expenditures were provided. Government officials exercised broad discretionary powers both in the collection and the disbursement of the funds. What was called *limat* (development) the peasants understood to mean *tifat* (destruction). These extortionist methods contributed toward the agrarian unrest in Bale and Gojjam.

If the authoritarian regime was able to contain or quell popular discontent and dissent, it was partly because it enjoyed foreign economic and military assistance. By uncomfortably marrying advanced imported technology to an essentially precapitalist formation,[61] the regime was able to overwhelm its opponents and detractors. The apparently all-encompassing state was, however, weak because it lacked adequate resources to provide social services, collect taxes, implement its own policies, or even supervise its agents. Yet, those social forces that filled the open political space between state and society were too divided and too weak to pose a grave challenge to the state; its military machinery was enough to intimidate, defeat, and control them.

The bulk of foreign assistance came from the United States, to which Ethiopia became tied in 1953. That alliance, in its politicoeconomic, military, and cultural facets, was mediated solely through the monarchical state itself.[62] In return for its use of a military base at Asmera, the United States promoted the professionalization of the Ethiopian military by organizing, training, and equipping a 40,000-man army. By the end of the 1960s, Ethiopia received about 60 percent of United States military aid for all of sub-Saharan Africa. The military, which consisted of the army, air force, navy, the police, special commando units, and several auxiliary forces, was organized under the Ministry of Defense, recipient of the largest share of the national budget throughout the 1960s and 1970s. The domestic task of the armed forces mainly consisted of maintaining order, suppressing revolts by noble and peasant alike, facilitating the extraction of resources, and protecting the dominant classes, tasks they performed with adequate proficiency and considerable brutality.

Two of the paramilitary forces deserve special mention because of their contradictory role as agents of the state. Whereas they were organized to prevent and/or suppress rural unrest, frequently they were the very cause of it. The Nech Lebash (white-cloth men) were recruited solely from among the peasantry to augment the regular police force in enforcing government orders, hunting down bandits, and raising taxes. With minimal training they were issued with a rifle and ammunition, which they used to harass and intimidate peasants. With no fixed salary, they were prone to looting. The same held true for the Biherawi Tor (Territorial Army), which was reorganized in 1959 and placed under the Ministry of the Interior. Its size probably never exceeded 10,000, but it was better trained and organized than the Nech Lebash. Although the period of service was limited to not more than two months, it was frequently called upon by provincial governors to help in emergency situations, especially in quelling civil unrest. Living at subsistence wages, its members were as notorious as the militia for violating people's rights.

Heavy dependence on coercive methods meant that the absolutist monarch did not have to consult or have the assent of his subjects in making the laws of the land. Representative institutions were primarily designed to serve as a democratic façade for the emperor's patriarchal and patrimonial authority. The constitution of 1931, revised in 1955, "entailed no substantive dilution" of his autocratic rule. On the contrary, it bolstered it. Parliament, to which representatives have been elected by adult suffrage since 1957, was little more than a rubber stamp; drawing its authority from the emperor, it had little independence to initiate and promulgate laws. It could be suspended or even dissolved by royal decree. When it began to exert some influence after the mid 1960s, it was mainly as an obscurantist body defending the interests of the landed and ruling classes. There was no genuine parliamentary system, no independent political activity, no press worthy of the name or in the slightest degree independent of governmental control. Under the autocratic regime there were no means of ventilating popular discontent short of organized violence.

There was opposition, though local and intermittent, throughout the history of absolutism. In the towns and cities, students agitated, workers demonstrated, soldiers mutinied, and aristocrats conspired. In the countryside, the nobility challenged Shewan domination, peasants revolted against taxation and corruption, and the non-Amhara nationalities resisted national oppression. Although in large part conditioned or determined by endogenous factors, the state's very ability to administer repression on its various constituencies was due to the support received from the United States and the West in general. Aids, grants, and loans may have helped absolutism to defuse crisis and to quash dissent, but as the events of 1974 demonstrated, not to eradicate social oppression. On the contrary, by allying itself with absolutism that was so impervious to popular influence, the United States helped to prepare the ground for a violent revolution. In the more than fifty years of his rule, Haile Selassie managed to consolidate a royal autocracy, but one that did not outlast him. The very conditions he instituted to erect that edifice were, in the long term, self-destructive.

This chapter has recounted the political changes and developments that culminated in the formation of a centralized, but partially bureaucratized, unitary state in which old and new sources of power coexisted in varying degrees of coherence and autonomy. This account of how the state overtook and externalized society by either limiting or removing the centrifugal tendencies of regionalized polities in no way suggests that all historical development in contemporary Ethiopia is reducible to the state's history. Its purpose is to establish a direct relationship of popular protest to institutional changes in the political and social structures. Those revolts that occurred in the twentieth century must be analyzed in terms of the relative power of social groups in a changing society. In order to locate the social roots of rebellion, the next chapter will consider the material basis of the Ethiopian state, paying close attention to economic linkages and class relations. Such a discussion has to include the postwar agrarian reforms, their differential impact on the various segments of society, and the attendant reactions. In the short term those reforms strengthened the existing social structure, but in the long run, with the help of the slow penetration of capitalism, they undercut it. The political structure was incapable of providing any adequate basis for a state which became more absolutist after 1974, creating fertile ground for "dissident nationalism," the prime agents of which belong to a fraction of the new social classes.

3

The social context

The agrarian society and state

A moment's reflection on the course of any specific preindustrial rebellion reveals that one cannot understand it without reference to the actions of the upper classes that in large measure provoked it ... Before looking at the peasantry, it is necessary to look at the whole society.

Barrington Moore, Jr.[1]

The Abyssinian state rested firmly on the peasantry and on the produce of the land ... The Abyssinian ruling class was rooted in and drew its support from the peasantry.

Donald Crummey[2]

Although the causes and motives for rebellion are diverse, no politics of agrarian unrest and changing peasant consciousness can be fully understood without a closer look at the institutional framework in which production takes place. This is because in the reproduction of the conditions of their existence people enter into definite social relations, and these relations at once contain elements of cooperation and competition or antagonism. In pre-1974 Ethiopia, land provided the material nexus of social relationships in an agro-ecological system that consisted of cultivation and pastoral zones. The principles regulating production relations varied considerably regionally as did the material conditions of life. Broadly seen, artisan and mercantilist activities were absorbed into an agrarian economy that was based on subsistence production for the satisfaction of culturally determined needs and socially sanctioned obligations, and for local exchange. The purpose of this chapter is to consider the rights and obligations that simultaneously bound and divided categories of people in the social system of production, paying attention to the set of contradictions that underlay these power relations and related forms of consciousness.

The Ethiopian agrarian population was markedly differentiated, functionally and ritually; vertically segmented groups shared the agricultural product unequally. The fundamental schism was between an aristocratic, office-holding stratum, enjoying ideological domination and monopoly of the means of violence, and a mammoth category of agricultural producers. Their relationship was multifaceted and frequently antagonistic; class interests intruded into nearly every conflictual situation (even if the actors themselves were not fully aware of it), cutting across such cleavages as religion and ethnicity, but in many instances coinciding with them. Nevertheless, the social categories were neither tightly compartmentalized nor internally homogeneous. Classes overlapped with a constant mobility in either direction. This plasticity had the general effect of masking flagrant inequalities and of dissipating or preventing group interests from being sharply focused, thereby deflecting or impeding the articulation of social consciousness. Though class antagonism was often acute, social hostility tended to be expressed along ethnic, religious, or regional differences or a combination of them. A spatiotemporal explanation of agrarian conflict in Ethiopia thus raises a whole range of variables: not only tenurial structures, power relations, organization of labor, and technological capacity, but also regional and cultural identities, state policies, market imperatives, and ecological and demographic configurations. These critical issues are considered in the following sections with varying degrees of elaboration and emphasis.

The modern Ethiopian state was created in a socioeconomic environment characterized by low productivity, the absence of accumulation, a resultant failure to promote manufacturing, and a continuing dependence on craft production. To the joint processes of state growth and consolidation of class rule that occurred in the four decades following the First World War, there was no corresponding transformation in the most fundamental aspects of agrarian society. The ruling forces or fractions of them did extensively enlarge the sphere of their economic activities mainly because of the state's dominant role in the development of productive forces and production relations. However, their commercial enterprises fell far too short of destroying feudal agrarian relations and short of upsetting the precapitalist formation. It is obvious that they were primarily engaged in *trade* and not in *production*. They provided the context for capitalist development but ultimately proved incapable of undertaking the historic changes required for the transition.

The symbiosis of monarchy and nobility only led to what might be called "centralized feudalism," in which the semibureaucratized state began to make greater claims on resources previously shared by the mass of farming families and a largely nonproducing but dominant minority. It is this change in the relations between the imperial state and local collectives, combined with ethnic variation and patterns of communal ties, that explains the dynamics of collective action in rural Ethiopia. As in Bourbon France, Romanov Russia, and Manchu China, that conflictual social relationship in Solomonic Ethiopia was two-dimensional: tensions arose from the institutionalized relationship between rural farmers and dominant classes and the state, on the one hand, and from the relationship between the landed aristocracy and the absolutist state, on the other.[3]

On the eve of the revolution, the bulk of the population was still tied to the land, producing most of the domestic surplus for accumulation. The small commercial and industrial sector of the national economy remained inextricably linked to the sociopolitical structures of a precapitalist agrarian society. Agriculture employed more than 92 percent of the active population, accounted for about 65 percent of gross domestic product (GDP), and virtually the whole of the country's export revenue. Industry played a minor role in the national economy, its function limited to the processing of agricultural products. It employed merely 1 percent of the labor force, and while its share of total exports was about 6 percent, its total contribution to GDP was about 3 percent.[4] Urbanization proceeded at a relatively rapid pace after the Italian occupation, but more than 90 percent of the population still lived in the countryside. Using traditional farming techniques and simple tools, peasants continued to work on the land raising a variety of cereals for subsistence and festivities, the local economy, the fulfillment of obligatory payments to the state and the upper classes, and for the replacement of their implements. Over 85 percent of the agrarian population eked out a fragile existence on less than 8 percent of the potentially cultivable land, estimated at 84 million hectares in units averaging 1 hectare. Health and education facilities were scarce and unevenly distributed – both heavily concentrated in the cities and major towns. When available, they were poor and inadequate. With an estimated annual income of less than ETH $120, an infant mortality of 200 per thousand of newly born babies, and a literacy rate of 6 percent, Ethiopian peasants were poor, diseased, malnourished, and illiterate.[5] The general conditions of their life can be described as "nasty, brutish, and short." The landed upper classes lived off the agrarian surplus, investing very little in their holdings and resisting all technological innovations and social reforms. The fact that Ethiopia is one of the least developed and most impoverished countries in the Third World despite plenty of cultivable land, agreeable climate, and a disciplined, hardworking rural labor force is largely due to the pattern of resource and power allocation. Therein lie the social roots of revolt that eventually destroyed an unjust and grossly inefficient system of agricultural production and distribution.

The agrarian system: production relations

The agrarian system that forced the majority of rural producers to submit to the "irreducible demands of outsiders" while preserving their usufruct rights to land was complex and of ancient origin. Although the debate regarding the precapitalist mode(s) of production in Ethiopia is still unsettled,[6] it appears that the relations of production and distribution closely resembled the feudal model. If what preeminently characterizes feudalism is not the existence of a warrior ruling class, hereditary fiefdoms and vassalage, but the exploitative and contradictory relationship between a dominant landed aristocracy and subordinated majority of producers possessing the means of their subsistence in which part or all of the agricultural surplus (whether in labor services or in rent, in kind, or in money) is directly appropriated by the former through political and legal means of compulsion,[7] then such a relationship describes Ethiopian society since at least the fourteenth century. Lords and the crown or the state extracted surplus from the tillers of the soil, the extraeconomic coercion taking the form of corvée labor, tribute, tax, and other customary dues. These obligations expressed the farmers' subordination and "the consequential degree of exploitation" to which they were subject.[8] To be sure, kinship, religion, and residential relations were vital in the allocation and distribution of resources, but the primacy of the exploitative relationship between the peasantry and the nobility is indisputable.

The institutional mechanisms that regulated social relations in Ethiopia had their own distinctive features; they also revealed domestic divergence. To begin with, the attributes of rank, privileges, honors, and duties were in constant flux. The Ethiopian social structure was not rigid, nor was the nobility a hereditary estate like the European aristocracy or a caste like the Indian dominant social groups, although it constituted a hereditary class capable of socially reproducing itself. The territorial and social distances between the two categories were also narrower than they were in other feudal societies. Moreover, the Abyssinian nobility never succeeded in permanently separating the direct producers from the means of production, because the communitarian ethos guaranteed heritable usufruct rights. Not until the nineteenth century was it able to seize and hold vast stretches of arable land as private property by expanding the sphere of its political sovereignty. Even then, the hallmark of the Ethiopian agrarian system was "petty proprietorship," based to a large degree on tenancy and subsistence production. The European seigneurial, or the Latin American *hacienda*, or the Asian estate type where wealthy landlords directly controlled a huge and landless population was an uncommon phenomenon in Ethiopia. Comparatively, and finally, there was little specialization in trade; surplus was low and variable, and the scope of market relations more restricted. The division of labor was scarcely developed, the village collective combining agricultural production and domestic manufacturing. Until the turn of this century there were no cities that served as autonomous centers of commercial and industrial activity. The dividing line between town and country was also extremely narrow, towns serving as administrative outposts in a rural setting dotted with villages. It was in these villages that a hierarchy of lay and ecclesiastical political forces converged and competed for the peasants' products.

Village Ethiopia

The world in which peasants lived, worked, and struggled, then, was composed of a loose aggregate of family homesteads rooted in domestic agriculture and industry. Cultivating a plot of land owned or rented, the household was the fundamental social unit of production, distribution, and reproduction, as well as of taxation. It was a loosely knit extended family that normally consisted of husbands, wives, children, and elderly parents, but also included married sons and collateral kinsmen. Prosperous farmers were often able to add to the family roster retainers and servants and, not in the distant past, slaves, whom they called "children of the house." The formation and organization of a household hinged in part upon economic as well as kinship considerations, so that its size tended to fluctuate along with the size of its holdings. Typically engaged in the production of grains, livestock, and simple handicrafts, the peasant family lived in a single wattle-and-daub or stone hut with a conical thatched roof, one door, and perhaps a window, but not always. This scantily furnished dwelling was used for eating, sleeping, entertainment, and storage purposes. It has been more than thirty years since prosperous farmers began to erect bigger and more capacious stone houses roofed with corrugated zinc; distinctions of wealth have become increasingly more conspicuous.

Agricultural activities took place within a closely interconnected network of farming and animal husbandry. Cultivation was, and still is, a full-time occupation with a marked but overlapping division of labor by sex and age. The primitiveness of farming techniques and tools made the peasants' occupation labor intensive; hence all family members able to work were involved in it. Repetitious and tedious, the drudgery of work was deadening. Using a simple wooden scratch plow with an iron hoe pulled by a pair of oxen, the farmer plowed the land four or five times in order to prepare the seed beds. Sowing, weeding, threshing, and harvesting were all done by hand. Although he raised one of the largest livestock herds in the continent, the Ethiopian peasant used little manure to fertilize his fields, nor did he consume a large amount of dairy products. His main diet consisted of pulses and cereals, and a little fish and some vegetables during fasting periods, while the ruling classes consumed large amounts of meat, milk, butter, eggs, and honey, most of it extracted from the farmers. Enjoying a relatively good diet, these prominent men and their children were likely to have healthier and longer lives. Disease and malnutrition afflicted the peasants, who used their animals mainly for cultivation, payment of dues and exchange, and for ritual and status.

In the hierarchical and patriarchal farming society, cultural division of labor based on gender began at an early age, male and female contributing equally to the household income. But it was the male homestead heads who mobilized and controlled family labor. Children assisted by tending the flocks of sheep and goats, gathering wood, collecting the hay, and running errands. Fathers and sons cleared the land, plowed the fields, sowed the seeds, harvested the cereals, constructed the houses, and made most of the simple agricultural tools and domestic utensils. Mothers and daughters participated directly in some of the agricultural activities such as weeding and winnowing. They were largely responsible for overseeing domestic consumption needs, raising infants, preparing the meals, hauling water, gathering firewood, grinding grain, cleaning the house, brewing beverages, washing and mending clothes, weaving baskets, and spinning cotton threads – all regarded as "light labor" by men. Busy at work from early morning to late in the evening, the peasant woman was treated like a beast of burden. Her work, though exceeding that of men, was never fully appreciated, let alone proportionately compensated.

What purposefully depreciated women's work and injured their dignity was a cultural reality largely constructed by men, who exercised supreme authority both within the homestead and in the larger society. As they enjoyed exclusive control on familial resources, men dominated the household, demanding obedience and loyalty on pain of punishment. According to the dominant patriarchal sentiment proverbially expressed, "Women and donkeys need the stick." Furthermore, not only did few women hold or inherit political office, but the religious discourse supported the objectification of the female, often excluding her from participation in important rites or entry into the place of worship in some cases; sacred space was a male preserve. In pastoral societies, where social distinction was negligible, the conditions of women were considerably better, though they were not entirely free from stereotypical attitudes and treatment.[9] Thus, although all popular cultures glorified masculinity while debasing femininity, the conditions of the Ethiopian peasant woman and her experiences of oppression were quite diverse.

Beyond the family homestead, social organization revolved around a cluster of kin-based small farming hamlets or villages, kinship ordinarily providing the organizing principle for residents. Residential patterns were flexible, though, since people relocated themselves conveniently in order to maximize family resources. There was no particular pattern to the organization of villages, which ranged in size from 5 to 20 or even 1,000 nucleated households in the northcentral highlands, where land was scarcer and each settlement tended to coincide with an ecclesiastical territorial unit, the parish. Villages were widely and thinly dispersed physically, settlement arrangements determined by forms of landholding, land availability, consanguinity, and security needs.[10] Typically, each household was established on or close to its tiny farm, standing apart from the rest; the physical separateness between homesteads and villages was often considerable.

Though vaguely demarcated and socially segmented, the village was the geographical locus of communal solidarity and loyalty. Small or large, every ecological unit bore a name that gave it a corporate identity. It claimed de facto rights to the use of pastures, rivers, ponds, and streams – factors that spatially separated it from neighboring units while serving as material symbols of internal solidarity. However, extensive networks of interpersonal and kinship relations crossed over village boundaries easily, providing vital channels for all sorts of activities.

Although self-sustaining and possessed of a separate organization and identity, neither the homestead nor the village was entirely self-contained or self-sufficient. Households were primarily dependent on family labor and villages were relatively isolated from each other mainly because of difficulty in communication, but there was considerable interdependence between households as well as between villages. Household members frequently worked outside their home units, renting land, oxen, or implements and borrowing seeds from others while they hired out their own means of production. There were occasions in the agricultural cycle when family resources were not sufficient to cultivate the field or collect the crop. Those who could afford it hired wage labor. For others, there were various reciprocal or ad hoc cooperative arrangements in which many members of households worked together.[11] Similarly, no village community was ever able to meet all its immediate subsistence needs from local or internal resources. Whether in the procurement of spouses for unwed sons and daughters, in the pursuit of criminals or outlaws, in the construction of churches or mosques, or in the opposition of governmental acts, villages were ordinarily engaged in a whole series of interactions with one another. Moreover, despite some distinctive features, every village was part of a wider social universe by which it was encompassed and conditioned.

The dominant activity of the peasant family was cultivation mainly for home and local consumption, but villages entered into market relations. Villagers did not consume all that they produced, and a good part of what they consumed was not locally produced. Even though what they exchanged comprised only a fraction of their product, the agricultural population participated in an extensive network of interregional trade. Few of them went beyond the nearest market or town; most would travel weekly or biweekly there in order to exchange or sell part of their products like wheat, barley, and sheep and to purchase domestic necessities such as plowshares, cloth, pans and pots, kerosene, embroidery, guns and ammunition, and in more recent years the much-coveted corrugated zinc. There was a good deal of bartering, for example, trading butter for red pepper or grains for salt, the latter also serving as a currency until very recently. Many of the local products were carried over long distances to the port towns such as Massawa which linked the interior with the international commercial network. If the village economy appeared to be autonomous, it was partly because of the physical distance (often enormous) that separated it from the nearest town, and partly because surplus production was low, the circulation of money limited, and diversification or specialization of production negligible. From one village community to the other, the pattern of economic organization, the technical skills and tools, and the products were markedly similar, if not identical. Crafts, mainly practiced by endogenous outcasts who were dispersed throughout the villages, were intertwined with the predominant activities of livestock raising and cultivation. And a specialized class of native merchants was almost nonexistent because production for export remained essentially part of the agrarian economy. As long as they remained contented with exchanging part of the agricultural surplus for exotic goods, the dominant classes lacked the incentive to diversify production and vitalize the commodity sector.

The other side of the market is its social function. The marketplace has always been the site of social interaction and excitement. Men and women gathered during market days not simply to exchange goods and products, but also to gossip, to disseminate news, to participate in communal and official gatherings, to talk about environmental issues and security needs, and simply to fraternize. For men, the market was an arena of public debate, political discourse, and arbitration, and for women an open social space to which they could temporarily escape from supervised domesticity. Along with the place of worship, the market was the most integrating local institution in rural Ethiopia.

Religion was the other integrative (but also divisive) force. Ethiopia is home to several faiths that either are indigenous or were introduced into the country at different times and under varied historical circumstances. Of the four religious groups that comprise rural society, Muslims and Christians (sub-divided into several denominations) are in the majority. Traditional religions have fewer adherents and are fast disappearing, while Judaism may not have more than a few thousand followers. Neither Muslims nor Christians, however, have completely dissociated themselves from premonistic practices. They still recognize the powers of a wide array of spirits to whom they pay tribute or make sacrificial offerings for appeasement or to enlist their intercession in a cosmic order perceived as mysterious and dangerous. Members of the traditional intellectuals – the clergy or *ulemma* – who interpret social reality, often served as intermediaries. Many adherents wore all sorts of amulets, usually containing words or phrases from the holy scriptures, to ward off evildoers. Such ambiguous beliefs and practices, arising from a mythico-ritual order, in part expressed people's anxieties and their terrible vulnerability to an overwhelming physical world that they were technically ill-equipped to deal with.

Rural life unfolded in an environment where religious and economic activities were intimately intertwined. Both Muslims and Christians adhered to their professed faith, rigorously observing its calendar, rituals, and scriptures even when they did not fully comprehend them. If the agricultural season set the rhythm and pace of social life, religious practices and festivals constituted an essential feature of rural life. Muslims prayed five times a day (which meant, among other things, frequent interruptions of work in the fields), and they fasted from dawn to sunset during their month of Ramadan. Those able to afford it made the *hegira* (pilgrimage) to Mecca, while paying their homage and respects to local saints and their shrines. For Christians as well rural life enmeshed in farming, and ritual tended to be cyclical: "The same cycle of saints' days is repeated every month, the same holidays every year, and every year is the year of the same apostle."[12] Although it was the only institution with direct links to the peasant, permeating most aspects of his life, the church did not have institutional coherence until the 1950s. Rural Ethiopia was dotted with churches that shared common scriptures and rituals but lacked structural unity.

Every village or parish possessed its own church, the hub of community activity. Every church contained a *tabot* (ark) associated with one of the multitude of angels or saints, and which reinforced the parish's parochial identity. The local church (much like the mosque) was a multifunctional institution, serving as a place of worship, learning, and dynamic political interaction. The priesthood (itself part of the cultivating community) performed or supervised elaborate rituals of baptism, communion, marriage, and burial, provided education for some of the young people, and mediated communal disputes and conflicts. Though the mosque served as a school and a place for conciliation, there was no Muslim clergy officiating or performing similar social functions. The parishioners reciprocated through periodic contributions of food and labor. The church was, in short, a place where "normative" values were acquired and social constraints imposed; it was the focal point of the parish where political behavior was ritualized and realized. The clergy were the chief intercessors between the "little tradition" of the parish (many aspects of which were derived from the dominant culture) and the "big tradition" of the Orthodox Church, an institution with strong ideological and material connections to the monarchy. While retaining its relative autonomy, the local church linked the parish community with a larger, overarching politicosocial order.

Village politics, therefore, was articulated within the dominant culture. Household heads and their members were vertically united through diverse kinds of political networks with an overarching regional elite and state representatives in the production process. Political conflicts and alignments within the village, though not always direct extensions or reflections of societal divisions and tensions, were always interconnected with them. The village, then, must be seen as the smallest ecological and social unit at which socioeconomic forces operating over a much wider political landscape converged and intersected for the mobilization and control of peasant labor, the extraction of agricultural produce, and the collection and exaction of fees. It was the primary site of interclass and intraclass conflict, providing the social framework for peasant differentiation and cooperation as well as for relations of extraction.

Relations of extraction entailed temporal and spatial variation, reflecting the complex historical evolution of state-society. The two prominent features of Ethiopian agrarian relations roughly corresponded with regional divisions: *overlordship* in the north and *landlordship* in the south. That is to say, a tribute system operated in the northern regions and sharecropping predominated in the southern part of the country. In both parts land was the epicenter of rural life. It was the basis not only of subsistence, but also of wealth, power, and status. To a very large degree, it determined the distribution and organization of power and the mobilization of labor; it regulated lineage relations and rationalized cultural and social practices, including forms of organized political action. Ligatured to the land through diverse and complex sets of legal and juridical arrangements, the vast bulk of peasants supported several groups, albeit nested in a hierarchy. There were marked differences in their social and legal status, but all peasants lacked freedom, suffering from the worst features of both communal and private tenure which hindered technological change and increased productivity. Inequitable distribution of productive resources, multiple illegal exactions, very high rents, and rampant usury characterized their oppression. The various and elaborate tenurial features made little difference in peasant life. Objectively, all were poor and powerless, and powerlessness greatly constrained their capacity for collective defiance. The concrete institutional arrangements that regulated social relations in rural Ethiopia will now be sketched out by focusing on each region separately.

The north: land, power, and surplus extraction

The Abyssinian polity was founded on the extraction of labor, cereals, and crops produced by landholding farmers. Tribute collection, not landlordism, was its essential quality. Tributary is, therefore, the most appropriate explanatory term for the tenure system that was prevalent in the north, because it was the kin-based village collective that held the right to possession of the land, conditional only on its payment of tribute to the crown, the principal instrument of surplus extraction. In the old provinces of Begemedir, Gojjam, Tigrai, parts of Eritrea, Shewa, and Wello, which together might have contained more than 50 percent of the rural population, kinship was the organizing principle of agrarian relations. Two overlapping basic rights known in Amharic as *rist* and *gult* (or their Tigriniya equivalents *risti* and *gulti*) were superimposed over the same area of land, regulating agrarian production and surplus extraction.[13]

Rist was the expression of property relations defining the intricate connection between agents and means of production. It was a bilaterally inherited, and theoretically irrevocable usufructuary right to land. All "free-born" people who could establish descent from the "pioneer settler" or founding father of a spatially designated cultivating community were entitled to land grants. Since the entitlement was to the right of use and not to any particular piece of land, it was common for individuals to establish claims in more than one hamlet or village. A village corporation included not only those individuals actually residing in it and tilling the soil, but all potential claimants as well. According to custom recognized by crown/state, a person could lease all or parts of his or her share but not sell, bequeath, or mortgage it. Hereditary possession of the land was vested with the village community, which was collectively responsible for the collection of levies.

At the ideal level, *rist* was equitable, but not equalitarian; it was ubiquitous and stable, but not uniform in its social content and applicability or static in its effectiveness. Conditions under which claims could be secured or lost and methods of land allocation, transfer, and retention showed some variation regionally and over time.[14] Not all members of the highland society of northwestern Ethiopia had equal access to land, because the lineage-based ideology was discriminatory on grounds of faith, occupation, sex, and age.[15] Muslims and artisans had the least access, tenancy being their common lot. "The sky has no pillar, the Muslim has no threshing floor" expressed the popular attitude toward that religious community. No land. No threshing floor. The most subordinated group was made up of artisans. Agriculture and crafts were interdependent, the farming village communities largely depending on the weavers, smiths, tanners, and potters for their clothing, domestic utensils, and agricultural tools, and the latter on the former for food. But all artisans were treated as social outcasts, relegated to the lowest status, for "to be landless [was] to be subhuman." Stigmatized for their occupation and feared for their "evil eye," which presumably caused physical harm including death, they were forbidden to intermarry with Christians and deprived access to the only source of wealth, prestige, and self-esteem.

The dominant social groups sprang from and remained immersed in the agrarian society and economy until very recently. Producers and tribute collectors intersected at an estate that was coterminous with a parish. This intersection was articulated in a proprietary right known as *gult* (fief) that was normally granted for life by the crown/state to members of the *mekwannent* (nobility) for service and loyalty in lieu of salary. Grantees kept a good part of the wealth obtained from the direct producers; they were also exempted from tax on their own holdings. *Gult* thus provided the administrative framework within which the imperial domain was organized for surplus extraction. The domain was divided into many units that were governed by a hierarchy of quasi-military feu-holding officers. The lower officials secured their positions from the governors to whom they owed allegiance in a patron–client relationship. "A cow knows its shepherd, but not its shepherd's shepherd" is the Abyssinian depiction of this power relationship. The link between them and the *gebbar* (tribute payer) was the *chika shum* (village headman), the lowest but most vital officer in the structure of power. They were recruited mainly from the *balabbat* (gentry) families, and their offices tended to be hereditary and male dominated. Historically, their main duties included organizing the flow of tribute and taxes, mobilizing corvée labor, maintaining peace, levying armed men for war, adjudicating in civil and criminal cases, and transmitting orders from above and information from below.

Crown and church competed directly with the nobility for surplus appropriation. Not only did it receive the bulk of tribute collected from peasants, but the crown retained substantial amounts of land that were cultivated with corvée.[16] The Orthodox Church was also granted tax-exempt, tribute-bearing lands known as *samon* that were in turn leased to local monasteries, churches, or individual notables, all of whom collected rent and tax from the farmers and part of which they transmitted to the institution.[17]

Peasants of northern Ethiopia supported a social stratum that was linked to them by kin and cultural ties but at the same time was set apart by its predatory claims on their produce and labor. The variety and irregularity of those claims is rather perplexing. Peasants gave considerable portions of their product according to custom, *gibir* (tribute) and *asrat* (tithe) being the most important and burdensome levies. The tribute was collected from the village community, each household contributing its share, which varied from one-fifth to one-third of gross product. The tithe was paid by all producers, the amount not exceeding one-tenth of total output. It was imposed on virtually everything including land, cattle, poultry, honey, looms, and pottery.[18] There were many other dues, also determined by custom but often dependent on circumstances. Corvée was extensively used, the number of work days required from each producer varying from twenty to sixty a year. On festive occasions, which were numerous, officials received some kind of gift for homage. Hence, although more than three dozen of them have been identified,[19] it is difficult to provide a complete list of the specific economic forms through which the unpaid-for part of the product was appropriated; it is doubly difficult to distinguish between what was legally or customarily established and what was de facto social justice.[20] The nonproducing elements frequently infringed upon the limits of equilibrium. Their exploitative capacity was only checked by their own competition for and protection of producers, peasant tactics of concealing or misreporting production, and the absence of transport and communication facilities.

Was this one variant of feudalism? The conflation of political and economic (even religious) powers in property relations makes it appear that there was no ruling class independent of the monarch. From a comparative perspective, the nobility's position was extremely precarious; not only did it lack ownership of the estate over which it had administrative jurisdiction, but its right to tribute was conditional and hence revocable by the crown and then by the state. Clearly, the peasants' inalienable possession of land and the state's ability to control the distribution of fiefs prevented the rise of a typical feudality, but not the emergence of a dominant nobility. Regional fief holders became hereditary ruling families, forming a self-conscious class that defended its interests against the claims of both the crown and the peasantry. Individuals and families rose and fell, but the nobility survived by protecting its economic base in an inequitable social order.

The legitimacy of the social order was supported by customary law and an ancient tradition rooted in religion. The church's intellectual and moral leadership helped the hierarchical polity to establish its material and ideal dominance over the producers using minimum coercion. The operative ideological justification for the rulers derived from the divine right of the Solomonic dynasty. The royal myth directly linked the king to his immortal ancestors, giving legitimacy to his reign and the succession process. The church sanctioned the hierarchical order of society which, it claimed, consisted of the trinity, namely the *negash* (those who ruled: monarchy), *kedash* (those who served the church/prayed: clergy), and *arash* (those who tilled the land: peasantry). Not only were social distinctions affirmed, but those who ruled were endowed with special qualities: not only were they descendants of the kings of Israel, but they were also divinely chosen. As the chosen of God, they were entitled to total submission from their subjects, and in this way power was invested with authority.

The godly minority was armed with moral force to discipline the masses. Of course ideology was supported by armed might. The *Fetha Negast* (Justice of Kings) articulated the link between religion and the feudal organization of power: "Let every soul be subject to the higher powers. For there is no power but God; the powers that be are ordained of God ... For this cause ye pay tribute also: for they are God's ministers ... Render therefore to all their dues: tribute to whom tribute is due ... fear to whom fear; honor to whom honor."[21] Failure to render what was due to Caesar could result in the permanent loss of land. What was the popular attitude or response? The best strategy was to evade power: "The wise man bows low to the great lord and silently farts." Although they rarely challenge it openly, peasants continually contested the rules, means, and cost of the total system of domination in varied and hidden ways. To use subterranean methods of struggle was to avoid the destructive consequences of institutional violence. The lords possessed a permanent nuclei of armed men who could outnumber, outmaneuver, and overwhelm most villages. Cavalry and firearms may have played a critical role also in class relations, working as instruments of terror. But since a state with all its repressive elements is a phenomenon of the twentieth century, ideology was probably the principal weapon of the ruling classes. It is for this reason that the church presented the origin of the Solomonic state as the most important all-inclusive ideology. And that may be why the monarchy never lost its halo of sanctity in spite of the rise and fall of dynasties and the almost total disintegration of the state in the eighteenth and nineteenth centuries.

The south: conquest, class formation, and ethnicity

The annexation of new lands and subsequent establishment of feudal relations added an extra dimension to the Ethiopian social formation. The social relations of production and reproduction engendered in these territories showed geographical and temporal unevenness, the result of the differential impact of Abyssinian rule on preconquest formations. As recent ethnohistorical studies have shown pointedly, imperial strategies of rule and economic organization were affected by ecological and cultural variations as well as by the extant political and economic systems both in the Abyssinian core and in the southern periphery. Much of the political and social history of the incorporated territories was determined not by initiatives taken at the center alone, but also by the varied responses of the indigenous populations and their respective polities to the problems and opportunities arising from Abyssinian occupation. In its decision to establish diverse relations with the subject people, the imperial state had to take into account the geographical location, potential productivity, and demographic density of the occupied regions; the autochthonous elites' resistance or submission to Abyssinian hegemony; and its own administrative capabilities, long-term goals, and security needs.[22] Nevertheless, Abyssinian conquest spawned profound and enduring changes that will reveal the embeddedness of rural rebellion in the total historical and social contexts.

The postconquest social formation was characterized by high extraction. The overriding motif of the conquerors was to harness the labor power of the subject people. Since the whole military enterprise was far beyond the capacity of the tributary system, the subordinated peoples were made to underwrite expansionism itself and to carry the bulk of the fiscal burden toward sustaining the imperial state and dominant classes. Territorial acquisition made it possible to reward loyal servants and troops with grants of land, to provide much-needed agrarian surplus, and to increase the taxable revenue of the imperial state considerably. The new relations of domination and submission that characterized the south were distinctly different from those of old Abyssinia. In contrast to the north, where kinship was the ideological matrix of power relations, imperial authority in the south ultimately derived from its monopoly of force.

The Abyssinian system of territorial control and organization of production can be conveniently classified into two broad categories: (a) *gebbar* or renter regions, and (b) *mengist* or "unsettled" zones. In the highland areas, suitable to large-scale agricultural production and horticulture, northern domination rested on the twin props of the expropriation of vast tracts of land and the subsequent near-enserfment of the indigenous people as tenant laborers for northern settlers and their local allies. The new set-up hastened the process of class formation in those societies that were relatively less stratified while solidifying class domination in others. The social relations that evolved in these regions spawned at least three social groups recognized by their relationships to the means of production. They included the big northern landlords, the indigenous gentry that coalesced with northern settlers and officials, and a large segment of cultivators, itself internally divided.

Highly elaborate forms of land tenure and labor organization were implanted in the renter or production regions. Having claimed ultimate ownership, the crown divided the land among royalty, officialdom, soldiery, and clergy from the north. About one-third was generally reserved for the coopted local ruling families. The settlers were allotted units of *gebbars*, a governor or commander receiving as many as one thousand. However, as there was wide variation in demographic density, so there was disparity in the number of cultivators assigned to men of equivalent title or rank.

There was little land alienation initially, however. Few, if any, of the cultivators were driven from the land; most remained as its occupants, if not possessors. This arrangement suited both the state and settlers. It was suitable for the state because, by granting only proprietary rights to its military and civil servants, it was able at least for the short term to forestall the formation of a landed class capable of challenging its hegemony. It was suitable for the settlers because it provided them with a permanent and cheap labor force. Small portions were none the less sold to northerners in measured units known as *kelad*. This commoditization of land presaged what would become the dominant form of property relations in the southern regions. Though the south was administratively more closely tied to the center than the north, the social system of production instituted there was unmistakably feudal. Pillaging was its essential feature.

As in the north, a network of functionaries mainly recruited from the settlers was charged with the task of raising and channeling resources to the imperial center. Under their supervision, cultivators gave up an augmented amount (or its cash equivalent) of what farmers customarily paid in the north and a host of other imposts. Additionally, they transported the grains, ground cereals, collected firewood and grass, hauled water, built houses and fenced fields, herded animals and portered for troops, tasks traditionally performed by their northern counterparts, albeit in a less onerous manner. Labor services had marked variation in their incidence and severity.

No such dramatic changes occurred in the pastoral or so-called unsettled areas. Very few highlanders ventured into those zones, and when they did it was as imperial appointees whose main objective was the accumulation of wealth beyond the restraining supervision of central authority. The acquisition of those regions had much less to do with their economic potential than with imperial security needs, although places like Ausa and Bena Shangul were considered valuable for commercial and communication purposes. As buffer territories to the Christian kingdom, their acquisition was probably intended to forestall their occupation by European powers. Once it asserted its hegemony there, the imperial state was satisfied with the collection of an irregular annual tax which often took the form of raids for slaves and livestock. This pattern continued well into the immediate prewar years. Not until the late 1940s did the imperial state exert centralized control, and not until the late fifties were portions of that huge expanse of land brought under cultivation. Commercial farms were established along the Awash, Metemma, and Setit–Humera valleys. Capitalism had finally conquered the natural barrier separating the highlands from the lowlands, loosening communal ties and instituting new forms of class relations.

For at least two generations, the imperial state controlled the incorporated territories through the classic system of indirect rule. The vastness of the empire and the absence of transport and communication facilities, the

ethnic, linguistic, and cultural disparity, and fiscal and manpower constraints all thwarted the institution of direct control. Further, indirect rule
was not only a great deal cheaper, but also provided the rationale for
domination and repression. It was legitimating. Hence, existing social hierarchies were absorbed into the imperial administrative structure with
varying degrees of autonomy and coherence. How much autonomy a traditional leadership retained depended largely on its particular response to
occupation and/or spatial location. Those who stubbornly resisted Menelik's invading armies (as happened in Kaffa and Wellaita) lost it almost
completely. Those who timidly submitted (as did the rulers of Jimma and
Nekemte) were allowed to retain considerable power. Similarly, in the
lowlands either ruling families (as in Ausa and Bena Shangul) were ennobled
or community elders (as in Bale) were simply converted into chiefs and
invested with authority to govern with little supervision from the distant
district administrators.

The gentry performed many tasks, for which it was richly rewarded. At the
initial stage, when state representatives from the core areas spoke very little
of any local language and knew nothing of communal customs and religions,
the assistance of the traditional authorities was needed (a) to stabilize or
pacify conditions, and (b) to facilitate the establishment and functioning of
administration. From a long-term perspective, they were valuable auxiliaries
in the maintenance of order, organization of the labor force, collection of
tribute and exactions, transmission of official orders, spying, and supplying
information. That is to say, they were indispensable in the institution and
sustenance of class rule. For their services they were granted *gult* rights and
given land in perpetuity on which they and their children paid nominal tax.
These were the material benefits of derived authority. Office holding led to
the rise of landlordism on a significant and unprecedented scale. The corollary of the rise of a landed gentry was the birth of a landless peasantry; each
was contingent upon the other.

It is not surprising, then, that the position of the gentry was laden with
conflict. This was because its members were simultaneously the representatives of the state and the spokesmen for their people. As class formation
crystallized, the gentry's dual role became increasingly unsustainable. The
peasants' basic interests were in conflict with those of the dominant forces
and were not always congruous with those of the state. While the peasantry
inexorably lost ground, the gentry strengthened its new social position by
Abyssinianizing itself: it learned Amharic, embraced Christianity, and
adopted the social manners and customs of the settlers. The result was that
the assimilated were culturally and ritually divorced from their natal communities. Yet they tried to preserve the illusion of an autonomous base of
authority even as it was being corroded by the imperial state. They vainly
modified local sources of legitimacy to assuage the peasants while meeting
the shifting exigencies of imperial rule. Their hold on the peasantry withered
as the latter turned inevitably to alternative sources of political leadership in

its struggle against the state and class enemies. The gentry competed with, while conveniently using, the traditional and religious leaders who, in many instances, were emerging as cultural and political mediators.[23]

The varied historical relationships between Abyssinians and the societies they helped to form have given rise to two major opposing views. One view emphasizes the exploitative and culturally repressive features of Abyssinian conquest, comparing it to colonial domination.[24] Implicit in this perspective is that every form of resistance waged in the south against the imperial state or its representatives has to be seen as essentially anticolonial in character; culturally framed agrarian protest is thus equated with ethnic or national consciousness. But, perhaps with the outstanding exception of Somali irredentism, there was no such consciousness prior to the 1960s;[25] even then it was an urban and not a rural phenomenon. Although Abyssinians virtually monopolized power, coercively manipulating the indigenous population in order to maximize their economic benefits, the two were held together, in part, by a shared historical experience. It is this fact that led Levine, the chief exponent of the second view, to see imperial expansionism as "*an ingathering of peoples with deep historical affinities*" rather than as "a subjugation of alien peoples."[26] It is true that northerners were not total strangers, but some of the subordinated societies did not have prior experience of Abyssinian rule, and the new state was dominated by a military aristocracy that was ethnically and culturally defined and whose dominance was maintained coercively. The postconquest situation must be seen as a contradictory synthesis in which both dominated and dominant made cultural adjustments for integration. Inasmuch as there were powerful stimuli for hostility and conflicts, so there were instances of cooperation, integration, and symbiosis.

It is evident that formidable cultural and psychological barriers separated conqueror from conquered. Negative stereotyping was mutual, but northerners in general tended to be paternalistic, despising and debasing local traditions and cultures. Exhibiting different manners and habits, the new rulers were not without pretensions to a "civilizing mission." They tried, much like the European colonizers of their times, to justify the exploitability of the conquered peoples by stressing the historical inevitability and moral validity of occupation. It was not without reason that some of the literati depicted the whole process "as struggles between good and evil, light and darkness, attributing victories to the might of God while describing the enemy as being guided by Satan."[27] Paternalistic and arrogant, Abyssinians looked upon and treated the indigenous people as backward, heathen, filthy, deceitful, lazy, and even stupid – stereotypes that European colonialists commonly ascribed to their African subjects. Both literally and symbolically, southerners became the object of scorn and ridicule. The members of the dominant Shewan Amhara elite, while considering themselves dignified and politically astute, had a stereotypical view of nearly all the ethnic groups, including the Amhara of the northern provinces. However, none of their views was as demeaning and degrading as their attitude toward the non-Abyssinians:

The Gurage is thief, the Gojjame
  treacherous,
The Tigrean is flighty, the Gondare
  proud.
The Galla [Oromo] is an animal, the
  Wellamo [Wellaita] slothful and lazy,
Make sure that power always resides in
  us.[28]

The image of an all-powerful, arrogant, and disdainful corporate community juxtaposed against a powerless alien population could be misleading, however. Without doubt, the imperatives of ethnic dominance made it necessary for all members to accept and support the structure unconditionally and without exception, regardless of economic differences within the community. The settlers were none the less neither cohesive internally nor totally isolated from the local people upon whom, after all, they were dependent for their livelihood. They were segmented and factious, individuals constantly competing for resources and status. Nor was there any direct correlation between class and ethnic origin; there were many wealthy and powerful natives in contrast to poor and hapless settlers. Yet, cultural arrogance coupled with anxieties and uncertainties necessitated conformity, and as a minority surrounded by a huge and potentially hostile population, they were remarkably successful in portraying an outward image of solidarity. Their interaction with others, based on imported ideas of deference, was very formal, but it was varied and extensive; it ranged from daily contacts with servants and retainers in the house and with tenants in the field to sexual relations and religious rites. A Manichean view of the setting is therefore too far-fetched, for even in the colonial situation, the colonizer and the colonized were "trapped in a wide range of interactions." There were no culturally defined areas of settlement, and the northerners were far less demarcated from the indigenous population than the European colonialists elsewhere in Africa. Moreover, settler society was open, and anyone could become thoroughly Abyssinianized by adopting Amharic and Orthodox Christianity. The French or Portuguese were far less successful with their policies of assimilation for, in the final analysis, no assimile or assimilado could ever cross the racial barrier. In Ethiopia, the "superior–inferior" complex had a cultural connotation only.

Cultural domination was uneven. The most affected were those nearest to the core and, of course, the coopted polities everywhere; their acceptance of the dominant culture was a precondition for their assimilation. On the other hand, the masses, who chafed under occupation, developed counterhegemonic ideologies either by embracing Islam or by rejuvenating indigenous religions. Force may have had the desired effect of reducing the peasantry to political acquiescence; popular resistance, however, was never completely suppressed. But because of linguistic, cultural, and organizational differences among the various peoples, the antifeudal resistance remained too fragmented and ineffective. It was only in the 1960s that a new generation of leaders, using new forms of organization and struggle, was better able to articulate latent peasant grievances. Those grievances sprang from class and national antagonism.

North–south: rural classes, agrarian crisis

What defines social classes is their specific relationship to the material forces of production and to one another. These relations are fundamentally unequal, most often exploitative, and basically conflictual.[29] In Ethiopia, resource distribution – amount of land, size of animal herds, type and quantity of equipment, and income – largely determined the socioeconomic status of rural families, but political behavior did not always correspond to one's economic position. This is because classes were dynamic social categories the members of which may or may not, fully or partly, have been conscious of their identical interests. What diverted attention from group concerns was people's claims to multiple identities and their involvement in dual or more economic activities. The pervasive ties of kinship, ethnicity, region, and religion, which activated people's passions, cut through class lines, and vice versa. In the peasant economy, many people were at the same time owner/cultivator and part-tenant. The landless and destitute in the northern highlands ritually segregated themselves from the endogenous castes though they shared the same economic status. Among those well placed in the structures of the state, the objective interests of landowning aristocrats and officeholding bureaucrats, while overlapping, did not always coincide.

Rural society comprised several strata, some overlapping but each tending to exploit that immediately underneath it. After the small but wealthy and powerful group of landlords there were intermediate groups whose size cannot be determined exactly. The three-tier ruling class consisted of the aristocracy, the nobility, and the gentry, which also included the upper crust of the clergy. The composition and lines of demarcation between the nobility and gentry were intricate and fluid because they were determined by a combination of factors that included land and office holding, birth, marriage, and religion. Although they owned productive property, neither aristocracy nor nobility directly participated in the process of production. The principal source of their wealth was peasant labor.

The aristocracy, which provided the social base for the monarchical state, owned immense tracts of land throughout the country, concentrated mainly in the southern regions. In the first decade following restoration, they began to move out from the countryside, becoming absentee landlords. They usually lived comfortably in the cities, leasing out their holdings to farmers

73

on a sharecropping contractual basis. Not until the 1960s did the members of this stratum show any interest in capitalist enterprise, converting parts of their estates into large-scale mechanized farms and investing in urban property, transport, construction, and the export–import business. In their entrepreneurial ventures, they were usually connected to foreign residents (Greeks, Armenians, Arabs, and Italians) who dominated the nonagricultural sector of the economy, especially export and wholesale trade.

The aristocracy's closest ally – but regional rival – was the nobility, which was made up of northern hereditary ruling families, military elites, and southern gentry. Compared to their southern counterparts, the northern nobles were land-poor but wielded great political power in the structures of the state because of their special historical relationship to the crown. Unlike the aristocrats, the regional notables remained close to the peasantry both physically and culturally. Many of them were woven into the bureaucratic structure as administrators, judges, treasurers, inspectors, and police officers. This physical proximity and their embeddedness in the rural economy enabled them to mediate between peasants and the state in quite critical ways, often influencing and even directing forms of rural protest and social mobilization.

A caveat concerning the crucial differences between the northern and southern dominant forces is necessary here. As their landholdings dwindled due to the politics of inheritance, and as their political power and autonomy diminished following the abolition of the fief in the 1960s, the northern nobles lost their corporate identity, which was never too strong to begin with. The erosion of their class- and estate-based power meant that they could now survive largely on the basis of their individual relations to the centralizing monarch and upon the degree of his commitment to protecting the old forces and the vanishing world they had created. As individuals, they continued to compete for state gratuities and traditional titles that were merely of symbolic value. The monarchy, while enormously enhancing its autonomy, had thus weakened its class base in the north. No wonder, then, that few noblemen tried to rescue it from the popular onslaught of 1974. On the other hand, the southern gentry had successfully expanded and consolidated its economic base while strengthening its position in the bureaucracy. As an emerging class of landlords, held together by interlocking patron–client networks, and culturally separated from the mass of producers, it had become more unified and coherent. But as it was internally segmented on the basis of ethnicity, area of land and size of herds individual households owned and the amount of labor they controlled, social relations were fraught with conflict. People competed for power and status, quarreled over land, and disagreed over governmental programs. These feuds were, however, largely between individuals or families rather than between class regiments. What held them together as an emerging, and often feuding, social group was their shared interests in the peasant economy, their ethnic particularity, and their continuing dependence on the national state – a relationship that was none the less increasingly being strained on the eve of revolution as a result of the latter's fiscal and agricultural policies.

The peasantry was not a monolithic social category either. Like every other social group, peasants were diverse, ranging from the oxenless and landless to proprietors of sizeable numbers of cattle and extensive farmlands. Peasants saw themselves as consisting of *habtam* (rich) and *deha* (poor) farmers. They were subdivided internally into groups that were distinguishable from each other by their relative access to the means of production as well as by the material conditions of their lives. This differentiation was the result of the whole pattern of land allocation, income distribution, occupational specialization, agricultural techniques and productivity, and environmental and demographic conditions. The three most relevant factors which determined a peasant's social position and material condition were land, labor, and his tools. The Amharic aphorism *yale beriye yalem gebare* ("Without oxen there is no farmer") pointedly demonstrates that not all peasants owning or holding equivalent amounts of land belonged to the same stratum. This was true for at least two reasons: (a) the productive potential of land was variable, and (b) peasants had differential access to instruments of labor. There were four major factors that actually constrained agricultural output, thereby depressing rural life in general while magnifying economic differences among peasants. Forty-two percent of the respondents in a survey conducted in several districts believed that the most important factor limiting their output was the lack of oxen. A shortage of land and scarcity of labor posed the main problem for 32 percent and 17 percent respectively. Another 4.5 percent said it was poverty of the soil that curbed output, while only 0.3 percent thought the market was a decisive element.[30] Another study disclosed that while 29 percent of rural households had a pair of oxen, only 8 percent owned more than one pair. More than 30 percent had no oxen at all.[31] This means that more than 60 percent of the peasants, although not necessarily landless, were unable to meet the requirements for the simple reproduction of labor without entering into voluntary but unequal relations with others. The difference between having an ox-plow or not was survival or utter destitution.

The rise of a huge and immiserated peasantry through a double process of land expropriation and land fragmentation was by far the most significant occurrence in rural Ethiopia during this century. What was basically a middle peasantry – in the sense that rural families independently worked on their plots of land using family labor and producing mainly for domestic consumption – up to about the middle of the nineteenth century had become stratified into four groups by the twentieth. The upper stratum, which might be called rich, and most of whose members were based in the south, was made up of households operating farms in excess of twenty hectares and owning more than a pair of oxen. These farmers hired wage laborers to cultivate their holdings. Under normal or stable climatic and political conditions, they were able to produce surplus far above the needs of simple reproduction on a regular basis. Numerically, this group was insignificantly small in relation to the others below it. What remained of the middle peasantry tended to fall on the poor side of the social divide.

The overwhelming majority of the rural population were poor, unable to meet the demands placed on them by family, community, overlords, and state. Bound to their villages, they formed the reservoir of labor which the nonagricultural sector could not fully absorb. The wage-earning laborers, i.e. peasants whose organic link to the soil was completely broken, were a very small group, but growing rapidly. The line between the poor and the landless was so thin that one Ethiopian scholar felt that more than 81 percent of the rural population lived under conditions of "absolute poverty."[32] Lack or insufficiency of land and implements compelled both categories to lose vast quantities of their labor. The poor peasants sought supplementary income by hiring out family labor, engaging in petty trade or in domestic crafts. For most of them wage income was no longer supplemental but an absolute necessity. The landless worked within the villages simply to earn their daily bread. Many trekked to the towns seeking casual employment for outrageously meager wages or to engage in degrading activities like prostitution and begging. Thousands worked as household servants, street vendors, shoeshine boys, porters, casual messengers, and so on. Forming a vast pool of cheap labor, they were the invisible proletarians.

At the root of rural poverty was the pulverization of household farms. Information on the vital relationships between the size of population, cultivated area, and agricultural production is scarce and, when available, is not always complete or totally reliable. What is an inescapable fact, however, is that whether owned or rented, most holdings were less than one hectare in size and the majority of them were in two or three noncontiguous plots.[33] Consequently, the productivity of labor was extremely low and unstable.[34] Even in the south, concentration of landownership did not mean concentration of production, as landlords seldom rented land in more than four hectare plots.[35]

In the northern provinces it was both the smallness of holdings and the poverty of the soil that diminished agricultural output. By the 1950s population density in some areas had begun "to exceed tolerable limits" and deforestation was already at an advanced stage. The former provinces of Begemedir, Eritrea, Gojjam, Tigrai, and Wello together made up 33.7 percent of the total area but held 37.4 percent of the total rural population. On the other hand, the provinces of Arusi, Bale, Harerge, and Sidamo together occupied 41.9 percent of the total area but contained only 25.7 percent of the total rural population.[36] Not only is demographic pressure greatest in the northwestern highlands, but these areas have been used extensively and intensively by successive generations for several centuries. The difference between the greater fertility and relative prosperity of the southern regions and the near-absolute impoverishment of the northern provinces has a great deal more to do with history than with environment.

There is a close relationship between human settlement, agrarian organization, and ecological crisis in Ethiopia. One of the great merits of the *rist* system was its ability to prevent the rise of a significant landless peasantry, although landlessness was contained in a world of increasing poverty. It acted as a block to outside intervention, serving as a cushion for the existing agrarian system. It maintained a delicate balance between farmers' vested rights in land and the overarching powers of the nobility and state. However, its insistence on the equal partition of land ultimately led to the degradation of the soil and consequent impoverishment for its tillers.

The destruction of the productive base was a long process. Centuries of overcultivation and overgrazing have drastically altered the ecodemographic situation, imposing serious strains on a social system technically ill equipped to deal with the new set of problems that threatened subsistence. Using the same technology and farming methods, people tried vainly to raise production, but the more they worked the land, the lower the yield. Fallow periods steadily became shorter, and common pastures dwindled or completely disappeared as they were claimed by powerful elements in the society. Virtually no land, including hills and mountain tops, was left uncultivated. The earth has lost its plant cover, and as the Haitians, with an apparently similar problem, would say, "the mountains are showing their bones." No root crops are grown in the northern plateau, and the economy is so dependent on rain-fed agriculture that people are extremely vulnerable to the whims of nature, as indeed the recent catastrophic famines have demonstrated.

Outmigration became a safety valve for hard-pressed cultivators, but it had the consequence of dampening possibilities for collective resistance. As many as 100,000 peasants from Tigrai and Wello alone annually migrated to work on plantations, often for several months at a time. In essence, the north had been turned into a type of labor-exporting enclave within the changing national economy. Migration provided an outlet for the social tension that might have arisen from the disequilibrium in the ecosystem. It confined rural misery within the narrow limits of the household while at the same time sustaining the illusion of upward mobility.

Another major source of immiseration was land rent. Tenancy was widely but unevenly distributed throughout the country, showing variation both in the form of rent payment and landlord–client relations. Whereas tenancy in the north did not affect more than 25 percent of the rural population, over half of southern peasants were categorized as tenants.[37] In the areas where private tenure prevailed, its incidence ranged from 32 percent in Wello to 75 percent in Illubabor. Under the sharecropping system, tenants paid rent as a proportion of the crop produced. In theory, the amount relinquished was between one-third and one-half of the total output; in practice, there has never been a legal limit to appropriation other than that imposed by the requirements of subsistence and social reproduction. Even though the tenant bore almost the entire cost of cultivation, he was required to give as much as

77

75 percent of the total product. It has been suggested that landlords may have appropriated as much as 55 percent of the total value of agricultural production; a more reasonable estimate would be about 35 percent.[38] It was not just the intensity but also the irregularity of extraction that was damaging to producers. What was once a sturdy and self-sufficient peasantry was reduced to an immiserated tenantry in barely a century.

Relentless extraction led to indebtedness, the extent of which is another index of rural poverty. During the last fifty to seventy years, more than 80 percent of the rural population experienced a precipitous decline in its share of disposable national income. Usury became rampant as destitute peasants borrowed from merchants and landlords, often at exorbitantly high rates (sometimes as high as 500 percent)[39] mostly for food, clothing, farm implements, medical care, and for the payment of taxes and ceremonies. One regional study revealed that 48 percent of the total number of loans incurred during a three-year period was for the purchase of food, and borrowers included owner-farmers (40 percent) as well as tenants (32 percent).[40] Interest was paid in cash or in kind, and frequently in labor. The need to raise cash to pay taxes and loans placed the farmer in the position of having to sell his crop at the most unfavorable moment, immediately after the harvest. On the other hand, since his food stock normally got low by then, he was forced to borrow when the farming season began. The combined effect of unequal access to land, soil exhaustion and degradation of the environment, and unremitting exploitation has been the pauperization of the rural masses and their increased vulnerability to famine and starvation.

It is evident that the primary antagonism was between direct producers and those who dominated them either through control of the means of production or the institutions of power, or both. Land, rent, and taxation were the basic issues around which battles were fought. Arrayed against the landed upper class were a multitude of dependent, but productively engaged, people whose ability to reproduce themselves was predicated upon their capacity to limit the extent of their exploitability. That parasitic relationship was continually disputed, although consciousness did not always correspond exactly to social reality. Both in terms of their relationship to the means of production and their articulation of that relationship, neither of the primary antagonists was solidary. Social conflict was, in fact, three-dimensional, involving the triple forces of nobility, peasantry, and the state, and in that dynamic process, alliances and loyalties constantly shifted.

The social categories were fluid and historically evolving. And rather than a hegemonic ideology, what held them together was patrimonial imperial authority. Operating within a fractured political culture, the ruling class was unable to impose its ideological hegemony. Though united by their common interest in the extraction of peasant labor and product, the various dominant factions, which were further splintered along ethnic and regional lines, competed for influence at the imperial court. Individual and sectional competition for productive resources, power, and status within an intricate system of patronage and constant disagreements over matters of state and governmental policies weakened their internal coherence. Old and new dominant forces coexisted side by side, sometimes cooperating, sometimes in conflict, and the emperor always calling the tune.

Class and state were not fully independent of each other. Their interests intersected or overlapped, sometimes clashing then reconciling. Old and new institutions were held together precariously under the aegis of an absolutist monarch whose patrimonial power was extensive: individuals gained or lost prominence, families prospered or became destitute, and groups grew or declined in relation to imperial patronage and to the activities, policies, and programs of the absolutist state. The monarchical state both shaped and regulated the formation of classes, conditioning or influencing their political behavior. Yet the state was not capable of fully initiating, legislating for, and implementing reforms seeking to modify relations of power and extraction. For example, between 1942 and 1974 it was frequently forced to concede or surrender to church and aristocratic demands and pressures for exemption from tax liabilities. When it did not suit their interests, the clergy, the monarchy's principal ideologue, never hesitated to subvert central authority. Similarly, despite their integration into the ruling class at the national level, regional polities continued to assert their separate identities to the last days of monarchical reign.

Peasant heterogeneity was not conducive to unified struggle either. The issues that divided the appropriating forces also affected producers at various levels of complexity and with varying degrees of intensity. Peasants' shared interest lay in minimizing or even deflecting their social obligations to those dominating them while retaining control of the basic means of production. This was one aspect of their struggle. The other took place within the divided peasantry itself. In their struggle both to protect their farmlands from rival claimants and to improve conditions for social mobility or sheer survival, family households were locked in stifling competition. Peasant solidarity was transient at the regional level and almost unknown at the national level.

It was the precariousness of material life that demobilized agrarian producers. The tenurial arrangements bred incapacitating fear and insecurity, and social oppression tended to silence rather than activate. As one farmer furiously admitted, peasants were "silent fools" who never dared complain even when spat at.[41] In the north, social insecurity arose more from the rules of inheritance that insisted on the reapportionment of land than from state action. Though it claimed reversionary rights, the state seldom alienated land, for its offensive was stymied by peasant as well as gentry resistance. It was the *rist* system itself that ultimately disaggregated a community that had been agnatically formed. As population growth outstripped available material resources, its elasticity and flexibility became strained. While vigilantly protecting their own diminutive farms for economic, social, and emotional reasons, families constantly maneuvered to acquire more by infringing upon the rights and possessions of others. Under these conditions, peasants knew too well that they could be reduced to total destitution through the unscrupulous machinations of their kin and neighbors. Suspicion and mistrust were pervasive, and solidaristic ties became correspondingly weak. Frictions and litigations were ultimately settled either in the courts of law or through the mediation of the gentry, which used the situation to weaken the peasantry further, to enlarge its own holdings, and to garner more power to itself. Scattered and competitive, peasants undermined their potential to organize and resist collectively, facilitating the appropriation of surplus by lords and state under conditions of relative stability. On the other hand, despite blatant social inequalities, the nobility often succeeded in mobilizing producers whenever its fief and subsidiary rights were attacked by the crown/state.

In the south, insecurity stemmed from unregulated tenancy and the threat of eviction. Possibilities for unified action were further undercut by cultural differences. Asked why they did not act in unison to secure favorable tenurial arrangements, an elderly man from Harer lamented: "Yes, it would be possible if all the people here had the same religion and belonged to the same linguistic group, and had a similar stand against oppression. But there is a medley of people here, and we do not trust each other."[42] The main difference between the regional producers was that, whereas the northern farmer was a tribute payer without legal ties to the soil or lord, his southern counterpart had been divorced largely from the means of subsistence, his condition scarcely better than that of the medieval European serf. State and landlord domination in the south was ensured by their ability to intervene directly in the conditions of production through the control of land and labor. Tenancy arrangements were not regulated by law, and cultivators were at the mercy of capricious landlords. Contractual agreements were casually terminated and without compensation. The implications of all this to peasant solidarity and autonomy become quite obvious: kinship ties, actual or putative, and direct access to subsistence means without legal ties to land or master allowed the northern peasantry greater autonomy than was the case in the south, but weakened its solidary consciousness. The more direct and rigorous control by outsiders, while depriving the southern peasantry of internal autonomy, would have made agrarian relations more prone to hostility.[43] But cultural diversity made unified resistance far more difficult.

Reform and rebellion: prelude to revolution

The fiscal reforms that Haile Selassie enacted between 1941 and 1974 to strengthen central authority were spread over two periods. The first (1941–60) aimed at unifying taxation by eliminating the multiplicity of feudal levies and related scattering of power. The second (1961–74) was designed to generate revenue and to intensify agricultural output by promoting capitalist development, goals that would have entailed a drastic modification of rural production relations, not least of which was the regulation of tenancy. Both objectives were met with collective defiance. The pace and scope of agrarian reform was slow and limited, but sufficient to precipitate the fall of the old regime.

Opposition came from the landed upper classes as well as the subordinated rural masses. Peasant defiance resulted from remorseless extraction and national oppression, fear of dispossession and loss of local autonomy. As has been hinted earlier, the monarchical state and the landed dominant classes simultaneously cooperated and clashed over the redistribution of agricultural surplus. While protecting their access to peasant produce from both cultivators and their main rival, each sought to optimize their income at the expense of the other. This rivalry intensified in the postwar years as the result of the state's attempts to abolish the galaxy of rights, prerogatives, and privileges belonging to the traditionally appropriating forces. Coexisting with the new imperial servants, northern nobles continually clashed among themselves and with a state striving to assert sovereign authority over territory. Nor did the southern gentry readily accept state innovations, despite its symbiotic ties. At the national level these elements had attained enough collective consciousness and organization to be able to compromise, circumvent, or obstruct government measures perceived as harmful to their vested interests.

Soon after its restoration, the monarchical regime passed two major laws that hit the northern nobility the hardest. The decrees disbanded private armies, deprived local notables of the right to appoint their own officials, and prohibited them from sequestering tribute and labor services other than those stipulated by law. But the provisions of the 1942 decree, which aimed at standardizing the tax structure, still lacked uniformity. It provided for distinctions between northern and southern regions and between measured and unmeasured lands. That unmeasured holdings were made to pay the least was undoubtedly due to landlord opposition, and that the new rates applied only to the south-central provinces (exempting Begemedir, Gojjam, and Tigrai) was due to political uncertainty. The basis for distinction was, first, that no measurement had been undertaken in the north, and second, there was a prevailing fear that an abrupt change in taxation might provide the pretext for popular unrest in areas regarded as politically volatile.[44]

However, the decree set off the crisis that it sought to prevent. A year after the enactment of the land tax law, Tigrai rebelled, an event which is discussed in detail in chapter 4. By calling for direct individual taxation, rather than through the intermediary of the village community as had been customary, the state alarmed all peasants in the *rist* regions who feared they would be liable to higher levies, and by eliminating feudal prerogatives it antagonized the regional nobility, or a fraction of it. But it was only in Tigrai that the state was faced with armed insurrection. Why? The imposition of a non-Tigrean governor and the introduction of Amharic in all state institutions seem to have been the focus of popular resentment. In addition to administrative inefficiency and the prevalence of banditry, the emergence of a unitary modern state impinged on the Tigrean nationality with added force.

There is little reason to believe that the government's decision to replace Decree No. 1 of 1942 with Proclamation No. 70 of 1944 was a reaction to events in Tigrai. The amendment, which incorporated the land tax as well as the tithe, was intended rather to increase revenue by unifying the divergent taxes. By requiring all landowners to pay at the flat rates of ETH $35, $30, and $10 on fertile, semifertile, and poor land respectively, the law seemed to apply to all provinces, but the three northern provinces continued to pay at the special rate until the mid 1960s. In the absence of a cadastral survey, systemized land classification and registration, the new law was bound to be abused. The wealthy and powerful were underassessed and undertaxed or not taxed at all. Landlords evaded taxation by simply shifting it to their tenants. Fief grantees were exempted from the land tax on their *rist* holdings but continued to collect it from their estates. The church did not pay any taxes at all, but it collected them from its tenants. Meanwhile, producers paid four different taxes: the land tax, the tithe, and since 1947 and 1958, the education and health taxes respectively. This was a system that penalized and victimized the weakest but most productive sector of society, while rewarding the idle and socially parasitic elements.[45]

The state itself was a major loser. By (a) relieving big landlords from taxation, and (b) allowing them to share in its revenues, the state was not able to raise its earnings from the agricultural sector. The land tax turned out to be regressive, accounting for only 3 percent of the ordinary revenue and capturing only 0.7 percent of total tax revenue.[46] Its overall impact was negative. It failed to achieve a semblance of justice, to generate additional revenue, or to promote economic growth.[47]

The aborted military coup of 1960 demonstrated, among other things, the urgency of agrarian reform. Visibly shaken by the event, prodded by the Kennedy administration of the United States, and counseled by international experts, the regime initiated policies that would promote agricultural development. In a major speech given soon after the coup attempt, the emperor enunciated the principal objectives, one of which was the granting of land to its tillers.[48] However, land redistribution was not the essence of the reform program. The unstated goals were to increase marketable surplus in order to meet the growing demands of a rapidly expanding urban population, and to raise the amount of revenue derived from the sphere of production in order to balance state expenditures. The realization of these objectives, it was believed, would depend on: (a) the protection of tenants by fixing rents and providing security of tenure, (b) the introduction of a system of land registration and taxation of underutilized land, (c) the adoption of graduated tax on agricultural income, and (d) the promotion of tenurial changes that would convert usufructuary to freehold rights in the northern regions. To this end, a series of legislative enactments were introduced in parliament between 1961 and 1971. In the face of considerable opposition from the propertied class, only one major piece of legislation was enacted in a whole decade, and that set off a "tax revolt."

In 1967, after a prolonged and acrimonious fight between government and landlords in parliament, the Agricultural Income Tax Proclamation No. 255 was introduced, replacing the tax in lieu of tithe. The government sought to accomplish two objectives. The short-term goal was to increase revenue from the productive sectors,[49] by abolishing "the classical system of privileged exemptions," as an editorial in a state paper put it.[50] Its long-term objective was to commoditize land by abolishing *rist* and to raise the productivity of privately owned land. It was believed that in order to monetize the economy by capitalizing arable land, productively investing rent, and raising the productivity of labor, the feudal fetters had to be broken through state intervention.

The principal provision of the law was that tax was no longer to be paid on the basis of size and quality of land but on actual income derived from agricultural activities.[51] Except for the church, *gult*-holders could no longer collect tax from their estates. People with taxable income not exceeding ETH $300 were to pay the minimum ETH $1.50. As the total annual income of most peasants was less than the taxable amount, the law would have relieved them of the burden, shifting it instead to those who had avoided it hitherto.[52] For the first time a progressive taxation system had been adopted, and the landed upper class was to be taxed on its actual income. But this was not to be.

The implementation of the law turned out to be even more difficult than its passage. It was systematically obstructed by landlords and former fief holders. Hitherto, the southern landlords had been the principal beneficiaries of the changes instituted since 1941. Whereas these laws undermined the position of the northern gentry, they solidified the base of southern landlords, whose power mainly derived not from office but landholding. The abolition of *gult* rights in the mid 1960s almost wiped out the economic basis of the northern elites. In the south the gentry was able to convert its land grants into private ownership. Moreover, while a more centralized and militarily powerful state diminished the status of northern nobles, it provided southern landlords with a protective shield against a hostile population. For the first time a serious rift occurred between these landlords and the state as a result of the 1967 law. Landlordism had been sufficiently crystallized as a class to challenge the state's hegemony. Having lost the battle in parliament, landlords intimidated, harassed, and even assassinated tax assessors, succeeding in many places in preventing their income from being assessed. They would not dare incite the peasantry, however, because they themselves would have become the principal target. In the north the disenfranchised nobles could have challenged the state only by inciting the peasants.

A major uprising, which forms the subject of chapter 6, broke out in

Gojjam in 1968. There were three closely interrelated reasons for its occurrence. First, the people of Gojjam viewed every tax law as heralding a change and, indeed, the eventual dissolution of "communal" ownership. So, it had to be circumvented. Second, individual notables who had lost *gult* rights in the mid 1960s found it convenient to express their dissatisfaction by fanning political unrest. Third, an arrogant and corrupt governor from Shewa had greatly antagonized the local gentry and peasantry alike. By presenting the tax law as a direct threat to *rist*, their autonomy, and their dignity, disaffected individuals were able to arouse people who were already groaning under an oppressive administration. As a result of a year-long fight, the government was forced to suspend the law in the province. The success of the rebellion in forestalling reforms is the clearest indication of the state's restricted autonomy and of its failure to control the peasantry fully.

The reform era did witness greater land alienation, concentration, and commercialization of agriculture. But these changes fell far short of pulling up feudalism root and branch, though they were sufficient to exacerbate social and political conditions in the southern regions. The privatization of land was actually legalized as early as 1924, but the process did not accelerate until the 1960s. The extensive conversion of fiefs into permanent holdings in a little over a decade resulted in the dispossession of a huge number of cultivators.

The new transactions in land were spurred on by agricultural production on a commercial scale. They caused enormous hardships to the rural population, but without initiating an agricultural revolution. In the mid sixties, international aid agencies began what are known as "small package" programs in a couple of southern provinces, mainly to help small-scale farmers increase their production. The programs had unintended but dire consequences for tenant farmers. The availability of capital, technical means, seeds, and fertilizers attracted an increasing number of landlords to concentrate, mechanize, rent, or sell their holdings, displacing their former tenants. Unencumbered by the exorbitant prices, people from the city – mainly bureaucrats, technocrats, and merchants – purchased or rented land for the production of cash crops, and in a short time these "week-end farmers," as they came to be called, formed the "new rich." The corollary was the rise of an impoverished rural stratum. No similar developments occurred anywhere in the northern regions, because the kinship holding system was resistant to privatization and innovation. Only in the lowland sections were sugar, cotton, tobacco, and tea plantations developed; the inevitable result was the mass displacement of pastoralists from their habitat. Many of them perished in the famine of 1973–74. The urban population was generally protected from the misfortunes which befell the peasantry. Exerting power and influence disproportionate to its size and contribution to the national economy, it had little reason to identify itself with its rural counterpart. It remained oblivious to all the rural insurrections.

The state failed to push its reforms largely because it did not detach itself sufficiently from the landed class. Its autonomous capacity compromised, the state was unable to intervene directly in the countryside and reorganize production. None of the intended goals of the reform policy had been achieved when an aged monarch was counting the last days of his long reign and when the absolutist state he had helped to erect was cracking and creaking at many joints. A Ministry of Land Reform had been put in place, but not even tenancy relations could be amended slightly. A 1965 bill to limit rent payable to a maximum of 33 percent of the crop value and to curtail eviction was quashed six years later by a coalition of liberal deputies who felt it was too conservative and landed senators who viewed it as too progressive.

Failing to expand its fiscal base, the regime became increasingly dependent on foreign sources. Further, the alternative to social reform was the continuing and enhanced use of force to contain or quell agrarian unrest. Rural Ethiopia saw little capital investment and no significant technological innovation. Whereas defense and security might have consumed as much as 40 percent of the combined ordinary and capital expenditure, scarcely more than 4 percent was invested in agriculture.[53] Very little of that trickled to either subsistence farming or livestock production, as much of it was channeled mainly into commercial agriculture and the bureaucratic machinery. As expenditure outstripped revenue, foreign aid and loans were sought avidly to finance the deficit. By 1972 the country's foreign debt had risen to ETH $559 million.[54]

The state was caught in a dilemma, the result of its limited autonomy and contradictory policies. Finally, the regime would collapse under the weight of the agrarian crisis. On the one hand, the state wished to expand the agricultural base of the national economy by removing structural impediments. On the other, instead of taking decisive measures that would have wrested land from big landlords, it soothed and conciliated a landed aristocracy that was not willing to be dispossessed. Even the mildest of reforms was sufficiently serious to evoke resistance – legal and extralegal. While the state compromised and retracted from its own policies and finally capitulated to pressures emanating from the landed upper class, it was bold enough to claim uncollected taxes from the poor, to impose new taxes, and to expropriate land for tax default. In doing so, it only succeeded in fueling class and national tensions that led to an uprising on its eastern periphery, an event that was exploited adroitly by an external meddler. The rebellion in Bale that raged for more than six years – a story fully recounted in chapter 5 – was the prelude to the social upheaval that eventually swept both monarchical absolutism and feudalism into the dustbin of history.

Part II

RESISTANCE AND REPRESSION

4

Tigrai: provincialism versus centralism

Of all the opposition that Emperor Haile Selassie I faced soon after his return from exile, the Tigrean uprising of 1943 was certainly the most formidable. Tigrai became the litmus test of imperial administrative and territorial centralization. The challenge came from a coalition of a significant section of the peasantry, a segment of the dominant nobility, and bandits, many of whom were minor chieftains. The usurpation of provincial autonomy, threats to popular customs and institutions, maladministration, and economic hardship motivated the rebellion. Contrary to official allegations and recent scholarly insinuations, there is no direct evidence of outside conspiracy. The rebellion was triggered mainly by local problems facing a feudal polity. Some of the leaders openly espoused it, but separation was not the goal of the movement. Conservative religious orthodoxy predominated, but Muslims were not excluded. The regime was able to crush the revolt with British help. In offering that assistance, the British hoped to establish a client regime in Addis Ababa.

Popularly known as *Weyane*, the rebellion was a relatively restricted, localized movement with strong provincialist or ethnic overtones. It occurred in 1943 because the interaction of existing social structures with new political events created additional opportunities which reinforced the capacity of the participants for collective action. Specifically, the revolt happened because several disaffected groups in the eastern half of Tigrai believed that they could defeat, or at least extract substantial concessions from, a weak transitional government. The multiplicity of objectives roughly corresponded to the divergent interests of the participants: the semipastoral communities of southern Tigrai, especially the Raya and Azebo, wanted to preempt feudal incorporation because they felt it posed a danger to their communal ideals of egalitarianism and justice; a sectarian nobility wanted a greater share in the regional reallocation of power; and the highland cultivators wished to terminate the predatory activities of petty state officials and the militia. The disorganization of the ruling strata, and the subsequent defection of a segment of the territorial nobility, enormously enhanced the possibilities for popular defiance. But this very heterogeneity compromised

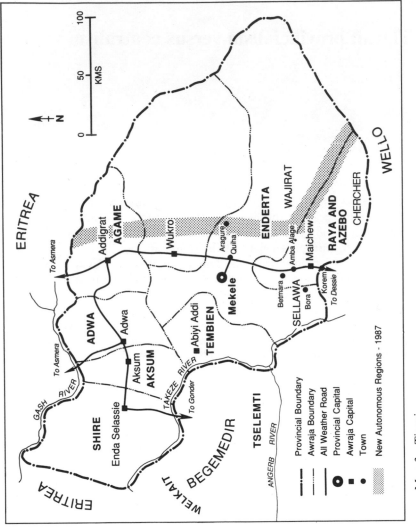

Map 3   Tigrai

the peasants' objectives. What need to be delineated here, therefore, are the complementary and contradictory interests of the various parties who waged the rebellion. That these groups did not share the same ideological outlook and goals produced mixed results. The main beneficiary was the nobility, which got its privileges and prerogatives recognized to the same extent as the gentry in the other northern provinces. The government undercut the nobility's political autonomy, but paid the price of reinforcing its social position. On the other hand, in reaction to the revolt, the state destroyed the social basis of clan authority and autonomy, and reduced the Raya and Azebo to landless peasants.

The precipitants

The administrative region of Tigrai was about 67,000 square kilometers in size before its eastern section was severed in 1987 to become part of the Asseb autonomous region. Of the estimated 4 million people that inhabit it, more than 80 percent are Tigriniya speakers and members of the Orthodox Christian Church. More than 90 percent of them live in the cool central plateau as cultivators and herders. The region has been under continuous cultivation for two thousand years, or perhaps even more. It began to feel the strain of population pressure at the end of the last century, with more people living on smaller and smaller plots. The central highlands are the most densely populated and most intensively cultivated. Demography alone is not to blame for the ecological degradation and attendant recurrence of drought and famine. Decades of interspersed fighting, plundering, and raiding ravaged much of the countryside, reducing some parts of it to mere wasteland.

Whatever the effect of social relations of production and the cumulative impact of decades of warfare and ecological stress in the short run, *Weyane* was an outcome of local events that transpired soon after the departure of the Italians. Of the intricate web of developments that ignited the rebellion in autumn 1943, we can identify the pivotal ones. While at the root of the revolt lay the perennial conflict between state and communal authority and the unresolved problem of centralization versus regional autonomy, the immediate precipitants were taxation, official venality, and the related repressive activities of the militia and bandits.

Taxation and official venality

Haile Selassie moved quickly to reassert and expand his authority in Tigrai, where it was challenged by traditional local leadership and the British, who did not wish to see the province separated from Eritrea, to which it had been amalgamated by the Italians in 1935–41. The emperor did this by (a) appointing his own officials in the face of opposition from British officials, and (b) enforcing the fiscal reforms decreed in 1942. The Italians had canceled all

91

levies except the tithe, and of that they collected little. The reimposition of tax, which was publicized as a guarantee of tenure, turned out to be an unpopular act, and taxation, which was inefficiently and indiscriminately administered, was resisted by the greater part of the peasantry. Abolition of the feudal levies was a tremendous relief, and peasant appreciation was expressed as : "[My big brother], the Italian, with a golden belt, [is] shepherd of the poor, and eats only what is his." The Italian interregnum was an important period in their political experience. The government's claim that the Italians had "abolished the payment of taxes because they wanted to disown your land"[1] was intended precisely to lessen that colonial impact.

The state could have won the reluctant peasantry only by an efficient and rational bureaucracy. The officials it appointed were, however, invariably corrupt and rapacious, further fueling peasant displeasure and anger. As in former times, administration of the tax policy was left mainly to the discretion of the provincial functionaries, who often abused it through fraud, intimidation, and misrepresentation of the tax laws to an illiterate populace. Peasants commonly complained that the officials the emperor "had sent to govern them had taken their money and stock for their own benefit and imposed up to ten times the value of any taxes ever raised before."[2] Even the much-hated militia corroborated this accusation by saying that the rebellion "was entirely due to the maladministration of the Ethiopian government whose representatives had been stealing and oppressing the people for their own gain."[3] Hating his representatives, the farmers were none the less much less defiant in their attitude toward the emperor, as expressed in this poem:

Woe, woe, woe – death unto the officials
of today
Who abuse their authority for a kilo of
grain
And who destroy documents for the gift
of a goat.
The emperor is not aware of these
scandals,
But surely he has sent us hyenas to all
places.[4]

The method of tax collection was as unendurable as the taxes. As in the old days, peasants were obliged to provide lodging to tax assessors, petty officials, and their retinues whenever they were on the move. In addition, the government sometimes stationed detachments of the militia in a district until all taxes due were collected. The producers had to support the militia for the duration of their stay. The militia stationed between Korem and Quiha were particularly notorious; poorly paid and undisciplined irregulars, they often indulged in plundering, looting, and rape.[5] Although initially they encountered little active resistance from the peasantry, they undoubtedly filled it with rancor toward the administration. Even the crown prince is reported to have conceded "that unrest on the main road – Dessie–Addigrat – [was] largely due to lack of discipline amongst the territorial troops, who [were] responsible for the theft, rape and other general misbehavior."[6]

The behavior and actions of unscrupulous state functionaries and irregulars imposed a serious drain on the productive capacity of the population, thereby precluding a return to normalcy and a productive agrarian life. This created a situation in which peasants felt a collective distress that finally exploded.

State versus village community

Fear of loss of autonomy on the part of the much less socially differentiated peripheral communities has always been a source of friction between them and an expanding Abyssinian/Ethiopian state. This overriding fear of being fused with other dependent peoples into a single exploited peasantry often led them even to forge alliances with foreign invaders. We must take a closer look at the social systems of the Raya, Azebo, and Wajirat peoples in order to appreciate the depth of that conflict.

The Raya and Azebo, originally a branch of the Oromo, settled on the eastern edge of the Ethiopian plateau in the sixteenth century and retained some of their ethnic and cultural identity for a long time in spite of their mixing with the Tigrai and Amhara. They basically practiced a mixture of pastoral nomadism and sedentary agriculture and the center of their livelihood was cattle and camels. Wherever cultivation was practiced, mostly at the edge of the highland areas, the *rist* system had been adopted, but social stratification remained at its rudimentary stage. Moreover, since they were predominantly Muslim, they were a religious minority in the heart of Christian Tigrai. Politically, they lived on the fringe of highland society, exercising a large measure of internal autonomy.[7]

The Wajirat were Christians, but in their resistance to the intrusion of the state they had much in common with the Raya and Azebo. Perched on the edge of the Tigrean plateau and clustered around twenty villages, which they called *ambas*, and numbering perhaps no more than 40,000, the Wajirat occupied a variegated and denuded area to the north of the fertile plains of Maichew. It is an extremely rugged and hilly area, much intersected by valleys and ravines. While the villages are located on the lowest hilltops, the tiny agricultural plots are scattered all along the narrow strip of territory stretching from the bottom of the valleys to the hillsides. With other pursuits on the sidelines, especially trade in salt and honey, to supplement their meager income, the Wajirat lived on subsistence agriculture.

Like the Raya and Azebo, the Wajirat enjoyed a great deal of autonomy. Their politicosocial system, known as *kinche*, was based on egalitarian principles, and, despite its exclusion of women from direct participation in the deliberations of communal affairs, it can be described as democratic. All adult males participated in politics, and all elders were councillors. The

Wajirat knew of no chiefs who exercised authority without their consent. Authority was vested in the council of elders representing the twenty villages. Compliance with customary practice was regarded as essential for internal harmony, stability, and continuity of the community. As long as the Wajirat were willing to pay tribute, their system had been allowed to retain its internal integrity.

One major feature of lowland society which became anachronistic in the modernizing state was its proclivity to intercommunal warfare or raids, variously known as *gaz* or *karim*. Whenever raids took place, each affected village was virtually in a state of war. Raids usually took the form of large bands of young, mounted riflemen, led by elders, armed mostly with daggers, short swords, and Italian rifles, generally of the Alpini and Mannlicher type. The raiding party normally split into several groups and attacked the enemy from different corners, then met with the booty to divide it equally among the participants.[8]

The main motive for the intercommunal raids was economic as much as it was ritualistic. They were undertaken primarily for the spoils of war, especially cattle and camels, but were also important social events in which the young men demonstrated their qualities as warriors and potential ceremonial leaders, thus enhancing their prospects "for marriage and political office."[9] The measures of success in these "manly" arts were courage, physical strength, and endurance. Nonparticipants in the raids were not officially censured, but were destined to remain "back-seaters" in their respective communities. Social ostracism could be avoided only through active participation in the campaigns. Thus, since participation was a social obligation by which the young men were expected to prove their manhood and become entitled to wives, this was actually an initiation rite institutionalized to legitimate and safeguard the authority of elders.[10]

The Raya and Azebo, together with the Wajirat, were crucial in instigating the rebellion of 1943. Central to their antagonistic relationship with the state was the fear of losing political autonomy, which meant an increased vulnerability to assimilation into highland society. They perceived the intrusion of the state as a direct threat to their way of life: they believed that the state would severely curtail, if not abolish, the customary raids, thereby undermining the legitimization of traditional authority, their communal way of life, and its attendant heritage. The Raya and Azebo had previously resisted every attempt to incorporate them into the Ethiopian state and into the highland social system. Their location in a fertile, strategic area that straddled the main north–south trade route was attractive to the feudal warlords, and they paid for their success with their blood. Also, cattle were very important to the Raya and Azebo and to their harassers from the highlands. Cattle were particularly scarce in Tigrai, and yet played such a central part in feudal social life; they were the centerpieces of banquets. The Emperors Yohannes IV and Menelik II had carried out occasional punitive expeditions and imposed tributary obligations on them. The campaign of

1942 was simply the last of a long series of military offensives carried out against the Raya and Azebo, whose remarkable persistence and resilience now met their final test.

Personal rivalries and the scramble for governmental positions complicated the relationship between state and communities. In the areas abutting the highlands, where a mixed economy operated, local authorities directly linked to the state had long been in existence. During occupation, the Italians had either confirmed these men in office or created their own village headmen. Haile Selassie Gugsa, the principal colonial collaborator in the region, became their chief patron. The end of colonial rule and the concomitant removal of the collaborator were soon followed by factional rivalries and struggles. The rivalry was between those who were willing to accept and serve the new administration provided they were allowed to retain the titles and positions given to them by the colonial state, and those who wanted to see a transference of chieftainship from one person or family to another. These wranglings frustrated administration efforts to propitiate and control the peasants.

The Raya and Azebo were not unique in their resistance to the Ethiopian state. Other peoples who lived on the periphery of the expanding state in the mid nineteenth century paralleled this story. Such neighbors of the Tigriniya speakers as the Afar, Saho, Maria, and Beja, not to mention the Oromo and many other groups south of the Abay gorge, belonged to different social molds, and fiercely opposed expansion of the feudal state and its tributary extractions. Zewde Gabre Sellassie elaborates the point:

> Although the Saho began to adopt Tigre ways and to pay tribute, the Beja remained fiercely aloof. Even within the core of the Empire, some parts, such as the Azebo Gallas, were rarely effectively assimilated. Thus Arnault d'Abbadie could observe that "Ethiopians regarded the introduction of uniform administration, grafted on to local liberties too severely pruned, as the root of tyranny."[11]

The clash between the Ethiopian state and the Raya and Azebo was one of contradictory political and economic systems. The segmented lowland communities had long had a more democratic and egalitarian social system than the highly differentiated highland society. By contrast with the hierarchical and authoritarian political system of the Tigreans, the lowland communities did not have any specialized institutions divorced "from the communal whole," as political relations were largely coterminous with kinship relations.[12] The state's insistence on subduing the Raya and Azebo arose from the latter's refusal to transmit tribute and accept its representatives. The imposition of village headmen would have undercut the authority of the elders, while direct access to land by the state might lead to social change. Thus, the contradiction manifested itself on two levels: on one level as a conflict between lineage elders and the territorial sovereign of the Ethiopian state, and on the other as a conflict between the communal and tributary modes. Relevant to this situation is Samir Amin's splendid observation that whenever the social structure is based on a tributary mode of production, "the contradiction [is] between the continued existence of the community and the negation of the community by the state."[13] In 1943 the Raya and Azebo conspired with a disgruntled nobility to obstruct their fusion with other peoples into a single exploited peasantry.

Intraclass conflicts within the aristocracy

No less significant a factor in the rebellion was the sharp split within the Ethiopian aristocracy itself. The political disenchantment of the declining Tigrean nobility was as crucial as peasant frustration in triggering the revolt and galvanizing mass support. A dissident gentry allied itself with an aggrieved peasantry and played a central role throughout the conflict. This centrifugalist action was a culmination of many such attempts by the provincial nobility to protect its independence or territorial sovereignty.

By a process of elimination the rival claimants to supreme authority in Tigrai were reduced to two principal families, families that were "equally influential and mutually hostile."[14] By the 1920s, after the long and ruinous civil wars that followed the death of Yohannes IV in 1889, there emerged two strong men, both grandsons of the deceased emperor, each linked to the Shewan dynasty through marriage, and each deeply distrustful of the other. Ras Gugsa was born to Yohannes's son, Araya Selassie, in 1882; five years later his arch-rival, Ras Seyum, was born, the son of Mengesha, Yohannes's adopted son and proclaimed successor. Following the administrative reorganization of the late 1920s, Tigrai was divided between them. Gugsa's domain included Agame, Enderta, Kilte Awlaalo, Maichew, and Aksum. His son, Dejazmatch Haile Selassie, was married to a granddaughter of the emperor. Ras Seyum, whose daughter was married to the crown prince, ruled over the districts of Adwa, Tembien, and Shire. Vying for the provincial governorship and related accumulation of productive resources, they sought to win the support of most of the influential families in the region as well as the emperor's favor. The latter inveterately used their mutual hostility to keep them at bay while undercutting their traditional legitimacy with his centralist policies. In this he was very successful, partly because neither of the men had his political adroitness, or the strength of his personality. The relationship between the rival families, on the one hand, and between them and the monarchy, on the other, rapidly deteriorated after Gugsa's death in 1933. Italian imperialists exacerbated it. Haile Selassie, who succeeded his father, became envious of Seyum and mistrustful of the emperor for three reasons: three areas (Aksum, Bora, and Sellawa) belonging to his family were given to Seyum soon after Gugsa's death; Haile Selassie was not allowed to inherit his father's title; and his rival was elevated above him following Seyum's appointment as military commander of the whole province. Italian colonialism gave him an opportunity to express the bitterness he harbored against his father-in-law and also to challenge centralism.

Believing that he would be able to regain the diminished traditional rights and prerogatives of his family, Haile Selassie Gugsa became the first prominent Ethiopian to defect to the Italians in 1935. In the context of the prevailing political dynamics, his collaboration could be seen as an act of defiance against an aggrandizing dynasty and in defense of material and honorific interests. His rival took part in the initial anticolonial resistance, and only after the defeat of Ethiopian forces at Maichew, the subsequent flight of the emperor to Europe, and the capture of his wife and children did Seyum join the ranks of the defectors.

The different treatment the two men received at the hands of the colonial regime reflected their respective dispositions toward it. For his collaboration and loyalty Haile Selassie was promoted to Ras and confirmed as nominal head of eastern Tigrai, a position he held until 1941. Because of his ambivalent attitude, the colonial administration never fully trusted Seyum; suspected of anti-Italian activities, he was deported twice to Italy between 1936 and 1939. He half-heartedly cooperated with the colonialists for only a year and a half before he switched sides in 1941. He even fought against them at the battle of Alage, after which the British military officials in the country appointed him governor of Tigrai, which included Eritrea. The appointment was neither refused nor formally accepted. Haile Selassie Gugsa was suspended and sent to Asmera, from where he was later exiled to the Seychelles. Annoyed by the appointment and suspicious of British motives, the emperor placed Seyum under virtual house arrest for more than four months in Addis Ababa when the latter went there in July 1941 to pledge allegiance to the throne. The emperor declared Haile Selassie a national traitor and a fugitive, demanding his extradition to Ethiopia. That demand was met in 1946, and upon his return the fugitive was sentenced to death by an ad hoc judicial panel appointed by the emperor, who changed the sentence to life imprisonment.[15] Haile Selassie was to remain in solitary confinement for more than a quarter of a century.

The return of the emperor to power might have marked the political twilight of the Tigrean nobility. The repercussions of the changes introduced in the first few years of the postrestoration decade were far greater than the detentions and banishments of the Tigrean princes. The success of rebel leaders lay partly in their manipulation of the "general fear among the priesthood and local Tigrean authorities and the loss of their feudal privileges under a modern central government ..."[16] These reforms further eroded the nobility's traditional base of legitimacy and power. In the not too distant past, they had reaped economic rewards through their monopoly of political power, a monopoly which gave them access to peasant production through the customary appropriation of land taxes, which best expressed their political autonomy. The legal abolition of customary tributes and services was a severe blow to them. Many felt that the new salaries awarded to them were neither commensurate with the services they rendered to the postcolonial state nor a fair substitute for the old privileges. They could no longer, at least temporarily, appoint or dismiss local officials at will. Asked why he had detained the Tigrean lord, the emperor succinctly answered: "Ras Seyoum had wanted to return as an autocrat to his country, to appoint his own officials, to collect money in his own way, to live on his country and not on a government salary, and generally, to go back to the old form of administration."[17]

While it may have temporarily calmed or reassured his supporters, the return of Seyum in November 1941 as governor general of the province did not alter the fact that the hereditary rulers had lost much ground. Many of the subprovincial governors that the emperor appointed, including most notably Dejazmatch Gabre Hiwet Meshesha (Adwa) and Dejazmatch Abbay Kahsai (Enderta), were believed to be Seyum's rivals and hostile to the traditional ruling families. In their own districts they supplanted his authority, reducing it to nominality. They compounded his problems of governance in the eastern districts; unable to pacify the province fully, the governor was recalled to Addis Ababa in September 1942 and did not return until 1947. His removal further weakened the basis of hereditary authority. Although his teenage son was appointed deputy governor, real power was vested in the director-general, a person from Shewa. A sizeable number of the nobility in eastern Tigrai also found themselves excluded from power by the emperor's new appointees – Shewan Amhara or strangers from other parts of the province. The losers were related to Seyum or Haile Selassie either through primordial or patrimonial ties. Since the political future of their patrons was uncertain, it is possible that they saw their removal from power as permanent. In this sense, the detention of Seyum in Addis Ababa (and the exile of Haile Selassie Gugsa) epitomized an irreversible centralization under the hegemony of the Shewan Amhara nobility. For them the choice was clear: either accept the new status quo with all its perils or reverse it by any means available. They chose the latter. Together with other disgruntled elements, they resorted to manipulating dynastic and provincial identities. They used the pretext of the exile of their hereditary chiefs from the province to instigate subversive activities. Seyum's clients were especially successful in presenting his detention and political crisis as cause and effect. British military officials genuinely believed (a belief shared by governmental representatives in Mekele) that Seyum's detention was in part the cause of unrest, and they strongly urged the emperor to return him "to his province with full powers to establish law and order in Eastern and Western Tigre." In a tersely written message the deputy-chief military officer, Lieutenant Colonel T. R. Blackley, warned the emperor:

> I am directed to state that the Commander-in-Chief will regard any further delay to despatch Ras Seyyum as a deliberate refusal on your Majesty's part to cooperate in matters affecting military operations and that such refusal will be reported to His Majesty's Government with the recommendation that the whole of the territory north of Wollo be placed under complete and direct

British military administration now and remain a reserved area after the signing of the agreement.[18]

Neither the ultimatum nor the many letters that followed it impressed the emperor, who politely ignored them. In the meantime, the situation in the province deteriorated. An overbearing and impudent man, the provincial director, Alemayehou Tenna, helped to provoke his subordinates by calling them mercenaries and traitors, an allusion to the collaboration of the Tigrean princes with the Italians. He also tried to weed out government employees who had presumably collaborated with the Italians. In addition to the emperor's irksome refusal to recognize Italian-bestowed titles, many had been financially ruined, because their fortunes, accumulated in Italian lire, were now worthless.[19] Informants claim that plans to disarm all Tigreans under the pretext of ensuring public order were also deeply resented, and an attempt was made on Alemayehou's life.[20]

The dissident segment of the Tigrean nobility was composed of two factions whose motivation and objectives, though outwardly different, were identical. Their main goal was to recapture lost authority and to arrest the erosion of their local power base. Both groups were centered mainly in southeastern Tigrai, particularly Enderta, Tembien, Kilte Awlaalo, Raya, and Azebo. Dejazmatch Lemlem Gabre Selassie, Seyum's protégé and personal deputy, led the first faction, which organized aspects of the rebellion but took no part in the fighting, maintaining an outward stance of neutrality. Its members were opportunists who looked more towards the rewards of the conflict than to its sacrifices.

Equally alienated but more assertive and combative was the second and smaller group, which identified itself with Haile Selassie Gugsa. Unrest provided a means by which those men who had benefited from the Italian occupation sought to challenge the post-1941 reversal of power. Unlike the other faction, this group openly toyed with the idea of secession and actively took part in the fighting. Led by Fitawrari Yikuno Amlak Tesfai (a relative of Haile Selassie Gugsa), Dejazmatch Fassil Teferri, and Dejazmatch Araya Degela, its principal base of support was in the Bora–Sellawa and Mehoni–Chercher regions. Haile Selassie seems to have actively disseminated propaganda from Asmera saying that upon his return he would lead an independent Tigrai whose eastern boundary would be the river Allawaha.[21] He continued this in exile in the Seychelles; his old associates aided him. They called for independence under a "legitimate" Tigrean dynasty, presumably headed by the Gugsa family, to stir provincial sensibilities.[22] And the disturbed political situation was quite favorable to agitation and subversion.

Banditry

The Italian invasion of 1935 created conditions that gave legitimacy to rebellion. Besides the patriots who continued to resist throughout the five years of colonial occupation, there were renegade elements freely roaming the countryside, often themselves posing as rebels, but primarily advancing personal interests. Indeed, the distinction between patriot and bandit was a very fine one, since more often than not, cultivators suffered equally from the activities of the two. Brigandage continued unabated after the departure of the Italians and became an additional destabilizing factor politically. Reflecting its mixed social composition, it had reactionary and popular components.

Banditry was important for at least two reasons: first, by intensifying the hardships of the peasants, it increased the potential for revolt; and second, when pent-up feelings erupted in 1943, many of the bandits joined the rebellious peasants. Some of the principal leaders of the rebellion, including the chief rebel leader, Haile Mariam Redda, came from the ranks of the bandits.

The correlation between the prevalence of banditry in the early 1940s and the existence of a relatively weak transitional government was unmistakably clear. Brigandage has always been a predominant feature of Ethiopian feudal society, but its rampancy at this time is attributable to the inability of the new government to fill the power vacuum created by the exit of the Italians. One estimate claims that by mid 1943 there were close to five thousand armed bandits in northeastern Tigrai alone, and their activities extended as far as Welkait in Begemedir.[23]

Banditry was not monolithic in composition, motivation, or objectives. An examination of the social origins of the bandits reveals that they included political and social malcontents as well as agitators and criminals. In addition to the large number of peasants displaced by war, the ranks of bandits included dissident nobles,[24] disbanded colonial troops and mercenaries, and large bands of feudal retainers abandoned by their patrons, who could no longer afford to support them. Most of the bandits of nonpeasant origin lived on defenseless farmers over whom they had a repressive control. By their renegade activities, they reinforced the oppressive social order and, in return, benefited from it.

A profile of Haile Mariam may throw light not only on the social background of the bandits but also on the nature of leadership in the rebellion. Haile Mariam was born at Dandiera, Agame, and claimed descent from Sibagadis, chief of the Agame warlords in the nineteenth century. Although he belonged to the gentry of Tigrai, he held no public position of significance until after the arrival of the Italian colonists. On the eve of Tigrai's fall to the Italians, Haile Mariam became a bandit for reasons that are not clear. For a while he proved elusive and troublesome to the Italians, who eventually bribed him into submission by offering him the position of headman of his village in early 1938. He held the position until 1941, when Ras Seyum denied him confirmation. Haile Mariam's family and especially his uncle and mentor, Fitawrari Belai Woldiye, appear to have had a long-standing conflict regarding official appointment in Agame with Ras Seyum. Having to regain his position through personal appeals to authorities both in

Mekele and Addis Ababa, in frustration Haile Mariam once again became an outlaw, a sort of Ethiopian Robin Hood. In slightly less than a year he successfully built up an armed band of about 500 men and became extremely popular among the peasants, mainly for the protection he provided them from oppressive petty officials.[25] By the middle of 1943 he was certainly the *primus inter pares* of the bandits of eastern Tigrai. His fame spread widely soon after many victorious engagements against the militia.[26]

Social banditry fed upon official venality. Provincial officials compounded the hardships of the peasants by their symbiotic ties to coercive and extractive outlaws. On the one hand, they connived with criminals to fleece the populace. On the other hand, they sometimes imposed collective punishment on villages for purportedly harboring bandits, or required peasants by fiat to pay indemnities for crimes committed by bandits.[27] Many people apparently could not endure this existence, and in increasing numbers they simply abandoned their productive lives and resorted to banditry themselves. It is appropriate to call them rebel-bandits since, depressed by violence and economic difficulties, they seem to have believed that they could right wrongs by punishing the avaricious officials. A deep sense of deprivation motivated this form of defiance. These rebels, by and large, lived in relative harmony with the peasants and never lost their links with their home villages. Rebel-bandits always had popular support, and in 1941–43, the peasants were pushed to support them even more. Peasant bandits were among the principal agitators preceding the revolt, and many joined it on its outbreak in 1943. These are indeed the precursors of today's much glamorized guerrillas.

External conspiracy?

What about external meddling? There was widespread belief both in Tigrai and Addis Ababa that remnants of Italian colonialists as well as the British had helped incite the revolt in order to destabilize the regime, or even dismember the empire along ethnic lines. Recent scholarship has tried to give substance to this belief, but without offering fresh and credible evidence.[28] Although external elements may have tried to influence it, *Weyane* was quintessentially an indigenous social phenomenon. The conspiracy theory is highly speculative, and it must be examined with care.

First, the Italian connection. Since Haile Mariam was a collaborator during the colonial years, he was suspected of harboring pro-Italian sentiments.[29] He denied firmly that he had any Italian connection inside or outside the country, a denial confirmed by Fitawrari Tessema Tesfai, then the most celebrated bandit in northern Agame and believed to be in friendly contact with some Italians in Eritrea.[30] There is no indication that Tessema was a conduit for external interest, nor did he himself take part in the revolt. Intelligence reports indicated that many (as many as fifty or more) Italians based in the border towns of Adi Quala and Adi Keyh were engaged in arms contraband and political agitation. That arms transactions might have been taking place secretly across the frontier is not inconceivable, although the British military administration denied the Ethiopian intelligence claims.[31] It is also possible that the military administrators, whose anti-Ethiopian sentiment and annexationist ambition were well known, may have used the Italians as their surrogates to advance their own hidden agenda. However, since in their desire to establish a dominant position in Ethiopia the British were trying to eradicate Italian influence from the country, they would not knowingly have permitted any independent political activities from Eritrea, especially in wartime conditions. Even less credible is the notion that three former Italian officers might have agitated the Raya and Azebo,[32] for it is significant that a government so concerned with Italian fugitives along its frontier should have been so ignorant of their presence in the troubled province itself. There is no mention of them in official records. Allegations of Italian involvement are based on the flimsiest evidence. Indeed, on the eve of their departure, they distributed large quantities of weapons to friendly peasants; and if there was any Italian contribution to the uprising, it lies in their arming and inciting the Raya and Azebo "to attack the British and Ethiopian lines of communication."[33]

For the emperor and his government, the British position was the most intriguing and worrisome. The immediate postcolonial government in Ethiopia could be best described as "dual control." Having helped the emperor to regain the throne in May, the British did not publicly recognize the country's sovereign rights until February 1942. Even then, they continued to exercise a great deal of influence in all spheres of domestic affairs, with many towns and localities remaining under their direct control as provided in the Military Convention of 1942. The political activities of British personnel in the country and of Eritreans spreading anti-Ethiopian propaganda in the north aroused suspicion and gave grounds for offense to the Ethiopians. Ethiopian officials implicated the British in ethnic disturbances that occurred in the southeastern provinces as well as in the Tigrean uprising.[34] The fact that the rebellion was crushed largely with British support sufficiently dispels the notion of their direct complicity, but it is worth while to explore the grounds that gave rise to the belief.

There were two major reasons. First, during the first six months after the restoration, the British military officers adopted the Italian policy of unified administration for Eritrea and Tigrai. They directly administered Tigrai from Asmera, appointing Ras Seyum as governor of the whole region without the emperor's knowledge. It did not help to allay Ethiopian fears of British intentions to secede the north from the rest of the country. The British had to revoke that act, but the activities of the military political officers and advisers in the various provinces continued to cause great pain to the Ethiopians. The emperor, more than once, complained that the officers were meddling in his provincial administration, and that they tried to undermine the authority of his appointees by taking into their confidence other people who supported their own policy, thus sowing the seeds of discord and dissension among the people.[35]

Second, anti-Ethiopian political activities in Eritrea that seemed to have the tacit support of the colonial administration strained relations between the two governments. At that time there was an outburst of nationalist sentiment in Eritrea manifesting two tendencies: the "Unionists" wanted to merge with Ethiopia; countervailing that sentiment, the "Separatists" wished to see a Greater Tigrai (comprising the territory of the same name and Eritrea), possibly under the unsolicited leadership of Ras Seyum, a sentiment shared by some British military officials. By way of undermining the Unionists, the colonial administration enhanced the position of the latter group (a) by elevating the status of the titular leader, Tessema Asberom, and his son, Abraha; and (b) by providing them privileged access to the Tigriniya edition of the *Eritrean Weekly Gazette* (edited by the ardent nationalist and polemicist Wolde-Ab Wolde Mariam), in which they praised "the Tigrean struggle to overthrow Shewan Amhara domination," while belittling the Unionists – accusing them of political naïveté and capitulation. This strengthened the sincere but mistaken Ethiopian belief in the existence of a British conspiracy. Tigrean rebels contributed to this belief by claiming that the British had promised to lend support to their cause.[36] In denying widespread allegations that he himself had propagated this idea, Haile Mariam claimed that the British had offered him material assistance, which in the face of public opposition, he declined.[37]

Had the British government had a single and consistent policy that sought to establish a protectorate in Ethiopia, and had it deliberately provoked the unrest in the north in order to undermine the emperor's position, it might be tempting to say that the Tigrean rebels were being used as a bargaining chip. But the fact of the matter is that British policy in Ethiopia during the first year after restoration was far from clear, often appearing contradictory. Until the Anglo-Ethiopian Agreement which provided for the reestablishment of a sovereign, albeit dependent, Ethiopian state under the emperor was signed in 1942, the British carefully weighed the options available to them. There were two divergent views. Among the proponents of what may be called the colonialist perspective was Sir Philip Mitchell, Chief Political Officer for the Administration of Occupied Territories. Drawing support from military officers beholden to the war and colonial offices, this group argued for "a period of tutelage" that actually amounted to a virtual protectorate, on the alleged ground that the non-Amhara peoples were not treated as they ought to be; and that the emperor was neither sufficiently strong to establish law and order in a "turbulent country," nor sufficiently committed to the abolition of slavery – familiar imperialist tactics. In addition, on the assumption that the Orthodox Christian Tigriniya-speaking population falling on both sides of the border was a historically constituted community deserving autonomous status within a decentralized Ethiopia, the group developed a separate plan that envisioned the creation of Greater

Tigrai (comprising Tigrai proper and highland Eritrea) under "British protection" but affiliated to Ethiopia. It was much less interested in Tigrean autonomy than it was in enlarging its own political space. Its maneuvers were bound to have an impact on the dual struggle emerging in the region, the struggle between a centralizing monarch and a centrifugal nobility, itself divided among rival competitors for power and status. The British unilateral appointment of Seyum and the inability or unwillingness of the British to terminate Haile Selassie's contacts with his followers must surely have sent mixed signals to the Tigrean dissidents. In this sense, the British officers with a colonial project may have helped to foster rural unrest that they did not initiate. Although the "Tigrean question" was resolved by the end of 1941, these men did not abandon their project for an "autonomous" Tigrai until 1943, when the issue was finally settled following the suppression of the rebellion.[38]

The neocolonialist strategy that sought to defend vital British interests in the region by creating a pliant regime was in conflict with the colonialist agenda. This strategy was supported by the Foreign Office, headed by Anthony Eden, the British Legation in Addis Ababa, and senior British advisers to the Ethiopian government. Committed to the reestablishment of Ethiopian sovereignty under the emperor, it was opposed to an imperialist policy seeking to establish a protectorate; nor did it wish to annex Tigrai to the colony of Eritrea. Such an undertaking was believed to be an "extensive responsibility" for an empire on which the sun was fast setting. Second, it was felt strongly that any attempt to violate Ethiopia's sovereignty or territorial integrity would set off a civil war, putting "excessive demands on our military resources" and jeopardizing long-term interests in the country. Furthermore, since the Ethiopian government had influential supporters and lobbyists (such as Mrs. Sylvia Pankhurst) in London, there was concern that a colonialist venture would "provide ground for dangerous criticism at home and abroad," especially in the United States.[39] Fully endorsed by Prime Minister Winston Churchill, this was the dominant perspective all along, and it prevailed. British support for Haile Selassie's government made the idea of a protectorate unpalatable – the creation of a semicolonized Greater Tigrai untenable – but helped to put down *Weyane*, a movement that had no outside inspiration, either material or ideological. That the "pro-Tigrean" colonialists may have encouraged dissent in the north in order to strengthen their claims of (a) the existence of a Tigrean nationalism, and (b) an unstable empire requiring Britain's paternalist intervention is a distinct possibility; but there is no incontrovertible evidence to support their creation of the crisis. In spite of the admittedly subversive activities of its representatives in the field, allegations of a British conspiracy are a bit too far-fetched, deserving no serious consideration. They only help to mystify popular history. It does, after all, seem unlikely that the British government would have supported revolt against the monarchical regime so soon after extending formal diplomatic recognition in 1942. The military measures it undertook in autumn 1943 in Tigrai were consistent with its overall strategy of establishing a client state in Ethiopia. Even the Secretary of War, whose ministry harbored some of the most ardent advocates of a protectorate over a decentralized empire, left no doubt that Britain's primary interest was in the stabilization of the restored regime:

> The War Cabinet ought to face the fact squarely that the War Office has a fundamental military interest in what happens in Ethiopia, owing to the key position of the country in our Middle East Strategy ... the country straddles our land communications between the Red Sea ports and the Indian Ocean. The War Office must therefore try to ensure that Ethiopia is controlled by a well disposed government which will be prepared to concede us the rights and safeguards necessary to protect those vital military interests I have just mentioned.[40]

The British chief representative in Ethiopia was even more explicit: "We desire that the Emperor shall be firmly established to keep his vast country quiet, and we do not want his detractors to be able to point to him as a British puppet being kept there by British bayonets."[41] It was precisely to save "a well disposed government" from drowning that the British helped to crush a rebellion rooted in the social system of Ethiopia and enjoying a substantial popular base. Their willful and direct involvement cemented the neocolonial link to which Ethiopia had been encapsulated before the Italian invasion.

The course of the rebellion

Prelude

Ever since the eviction of the Italian colonialists in 1941, political discontent was evident throughout Tigrai. The transitional state was too weak to maintain "law and order," and the province became a haven for brigands who robbed and molested farmers and merchants alike. The traditional intercommunal raids in the eastern part of the province became an additional destabilizing factor because they frequently interfered with the flow of traffic along the Addigrat–Dessie and Aseb–Dessie roads. Convoys were ambushed and looted, communication was disrupted, and travel along the main route became too hazardous. Large parts of the province were in a state of virtual anarchy, and the "rapidly growing atmosphere of unrest, discontent and lawlessness" created some alarm in the imperial quarters;[42] but although the general pattern of events was recognizable, an armed outbreak was not predictable at this stage.

Of immediate concern to the government as well as to the British was how to safeguard and guarantee the free flow of war supplies, goods, and services along the main highway. The highway, 1,080 kilometers long, was built by the Italians; it connected Addis Ababa and Asmera, passing through the provinces of Shewa, Wello, Tigrai, and Eritrea. It was one of the two routes (the other being the Asmera–Gonder road) along which agricultural products and other exportable products from the north-central provinces were transported to their destination at the port of Massawa. Eritrea, which received a sizeable proportion of its food supplies from the interior, had become a valuable support base for British war efforts in the Middle East. The complete control of the highway was essential for economic and military reasons.

In Addis Ababa's view, the Raya, Azebo, and Wajirat peoples were largely to blame for the "lawlessness"; it sought first to end the intercommunal raids and attendant civil strife in their areas. Every peaceful effort proved fruitless, and the government felt that since its initiatives were not sufficiently reciprocated, the use of force to tame the belligerent would be fully justified. In its first armed clash with the Raya and Azebo on January 11, 1942 the government lost nine of its soldiers and three British officers, and the aerial bombardment of Kobbo was inconclusive. It took two months of preparation to conduct another punitive operation on a much larger scale between April and July. It was organized and led by the crown prince, Asfa-Wossen, and Ras Seyum. To add some drama to the campaign the government raised no fewer than 30,000 men from all parts of Tigrai and dispatched another 5,000 regular troops from Shewa and Wello. The operation, which cost the Treasury some 431,490 Maria Theresa thalers, was relatively long and extremely harsh.[43] Not only had the peasants to sustain the troops for the duration of the campaign, but they were required to deliver 50,000 head of cattle, 50,000 guns, and 50,000 Maria Theresa thalers in penalties. Of these it got some 10,000 head of cattle and 10,000 rifles;[44] the severity of the operation was enough to embitter the people and may have added to the volatility of the situation.

Severe as the campaign was, it failed to diffuse the undercurrents of rebellion. Brigandage increased in scale, and the customary intercommunal raids decreased but did not stop. The districts of Enderta, Kilte Awlaalo, Tembien, Raya, and Azebo, and to a lesser degree adjoining Agame, grew restive. Little success attended the government's attempts to regain public confidence by reshuffling its senior representatives in the province. The new director, Fitawrari Kifle Dadi, who replaced the unpopular Alemayehou Tenna in November 1942, was a very able administrator; he tirelessly but vainly tried to reestablish imperial authority, and in exasperation decided to punish the Wajirat, whom his administration regarded as no less troublesome and bellicose than the Raya and Azebo. The outcome was a harbinger of *Weyane*.

Outbreak and armed conflict: the chronology

The making of the rebellion can be conveniently divided into three stages:

Stage one: May 1943 – the crisis escalates following the defeat of a governmental expeditionary force in Wajirat.

Stage two: June–September 1943 – the government suffers several military setbacks against a coalition of bandits and dissidents. This sets the stage for the battle at Amba Alage.

Stage three: September–October 1943 – the defeat of the dissidents at Alage marks the collapse of the rebellion and the end of provincial autonomy.

The expedition which initiated the first stage was intended not only to raise arrears in penalties but also to punish the Wajirat, who had allegedly taken cattle and other booty from the Afar, refused to accept a governmental appointee, continually harassed travelers and attacked convoys using the main road, and killed one and wounded two British officers. But it misfired. On May 22, the expeditionary force was routed at Anda Abuna near Enda Mehoni, about 15 kilometers southeast of Amba Alage; about four hundred people were killed or wounded in the skirmish and the head of the expedition, Abbay Kahsai, along with several high ranking men, was captured. In accordance with Wajirat tradition, they were dressed like women and kept in detention. This was intended to humiliate and demoralize them in the cultural context of a masculine-oriented society. The booty was never retrieved or the penalties collected. The prisoners were released unharmed at the end of July through the personal mediation of the Acting Governor, Dejazmatch Mengesha Seyum; but the episode proved fatal to the government.[45] Its credibility plummeted so rapidly that even the uncommitted became uncertain of its survival. A local poem expressed the prevailing mood:

> Do not pasture your cattle far from
>   home,
> Bury your money deep in the ground.
> Do not store your grains, but keep the
>   flour safe,
> People of Enderta and Tigrai are locked
>   in a struggle,
> And our ruler is not known yet.[46]

On the other hand, the triumph of the Wajirat badly undermined the image of the Tigrean notables cooperating with the government while giving heart to dissident people and groups who then began to disseminate propaganda aimed at inciting a general uprising in the province. "There is no government; let's organize and govern ourselves" was their slogan. It worked, for in the words of one informant, "After Wajirat dissent spread like wild fire."[47] The areas that were particularly restless were Enderta, Samre, Sellawa, Hintalo, Geraalta, Abergele, Dergaagen, Mehoni, Haramat, Chercher, Wajirat, Menchare, Ebbo, Dayiu, Raya, and Azebo. A major uprising appeared imminent, and concerned officials warned that, unless nipped in the bud, the growing unrest might eventually preoccupy the entire Ethiopian army. The director believed that an additional seven thousand troops were necessary to deal with the crisis.[48] However, few people in Addis Ababa anticipated an armed outbreak, and they were too slow to act. In the mean time, by the end of June, discontented peasants, aggrieved elements of the provincial nobility, and self-seeking bandits formed a coalition under the leadership of Blatta Haile Mariam Redda, and soon began their concerted offensive against the regime. During the rainy season, while peasants plowed their fields and sowed seeds, the dissidents consolidated their organization and established themselves at strategic points between Maichew and Wukro on the main north–south highway. The military garrison at Quiha, not far from the administrative capital, Mekele, was besieged for nearly three months, and traffic between Addigrat and Woldia was frequently interrupted.[49]

Not even the most skeptical officials in Addis Ababa could have failed to realize that these events had turned the prospects of a regional uprising from a possibility to a probability. Hence, on August 26, the emperor appointed the War Minister, Ras Abebe Aregai, to head a full-scale military operation against the dissidents. Accompanied by thirty-four British officers, the undaunted guerrilla leader and widely acclaimed patriot of the five years of resistance against Italian Fascists arrived at Korem on September 17, but was unable to proceed farther to join the commander of the northern troops at Maichew. About six thousand armed peasants from Bora, Sellawa, Menchare, Mehoni, Wajirat, Raya, and Azebo had effectively blocked any troop movements between Korem and Maichew while encircling the main army camp itself.[50] Meanwhile, rebels had opened their attacks on the isolated posts farther to the north.

Armed hostilities began on September 16 all along the highway between Wukro and Maichew, but the rebels mainly concentrated their efforts on overtaking the heavily fortified but beleaguered military garrison at Quiha, a key junction on the main highway south of Wukro. In the early morning of September 17, the rebels tried to overwhelm the garrison, but since it was fenced with trenches and electrified barbed wire, it proved impenetrable. It took nearly six hours of heavy fighting to subdue the defenders who, though numbering no more than four hundred, possessed superior weapons, including twenty-three pieces of cannon and artillery.[51] On the following day a small unit of the Ethiopian army and a large militia, mainly drawn from Adwa, fought as bravely but vainly to defend Enda Yesus, a small fort overlooking Mekele from the northwest. The fort was captured and Mekele fell without resistance, for its panicked defenders had deserted it under the cover of darkness.

Clearly the pendulum had swung in favor of the rebels. In admiration, if not anticipation, Haile Mariam's enthusiastic supporters had been singing cheerfully for months: "You, the youthful Haile Mariam, today you are a bandit but next year, a king." It is unlikely that Haile Mariam had nourished any hopes of becoming a king, but the sweeping events appeared to confirm the wishes of his followers in a rather melodramatic manner. And to their jubilation, he astounded the still sleepy town of Mekele with his flamboyant pronouncement on behalf of the people's assembly known as *gerreb*:

Hear ye, Hear ye,
This is Haile Mariam, voice of the
   people.
Our governor is Jesus Christ,
Our shepherd, Haile Mariam.
The assembly is our government
And our flag that of Ethiopia.
Our religion is that of Yohannes IV,
Catholics and Protestants leave our
   country.
People of Tigrai, follow the motto of
   Weyane
And accept the people's government.[52]

Once the citadel of imperial authority was secured, the rebels moved immediately southwards to seize the strategic mountain fortress of Amba Alage, scene of two major battles during the previous eight years: in 1935, when poorly armed and poorly organized Ethiopian troops were routed by the invading Italians; and in 1941, when the invaders were in turn crushed by a combined force of Ethiopian patriots and British troops. There, more than 20,000 peasants fought a battle of attrition against a smaller but better equipped force of 2,000 soldiers and more than 8,000 territorials. But the design to win a short and decisive victory turned out to be a costly gambit.

The battle for Alage began on September 18. The day Enda Yesus fell to the rebels the Fifth Battalion broke out of the encirclement, and with the support of a battalion of territorials and three armored vehicles, had reached Alage when its advance column was ambushed at Betmara. The British commanding officer, Lieutenant Colonel F. H. Black, was one of the many fatalities. Had it not been for the timely arrival of six more battalions under Lieutenant Colonel Garring Johnston on September 20, the government forces might even have been wiped out. Fierce fighting continued with little interruption until the 23rd, when the troops, having repelled their attackers with mortar and artillery, managed to capture the Alage heights. But their position was still defensive. On the same day, the rebels cut the only telephone line, which was not restored until October 5, and renewed their assault on fortified government positions, especially on the heights and Alba pass. The government suffered its heaviest losses thus far: 84 dead and 62 wounded, including Johnston. There was a deceptive lull for the following two days; but while the rebels regrouped themselves, the irregulars "pillaged the country for some fifteen miles around the area leaving no village unburnt."[53] Taking advantage of the brief intermission, General Abebe Damtew, the Chief Commander, threatened to withdraw unless more troops

109

were sent in. He also asked for air support. There were others who felt that "any show of force which might involve the emperor's troops in a defeat must be avoided at all costs and that settlement should be obtained by peaceful means if possible."[54] Leaflets containing messages from the emperor and echege (prelate of the Ethiopian Orthodox Church) were hence dropped at this time. It is interesting, though, that while pleading, the rulers also threatened, and judging from the content and tone of the messages, the intention was not so much to seek a peaceful settlement as it was to cause friction and discord within rebel ranks. The emperor declared:

> From now onward we are compelled to punish them by the army and air force. You who are our faithful ones and are not involved with the deceivers, gather your arms and punish them. Bring the malefactors to us. Take their property for yourselves.[55]

And the prelate threatened excommunication, perhaps the most dreaded form of punishment to the faithful:

> It is needless to tell the Tigre people, who are learned men, that this is the work of the devil who is a deceiver and who deceived them in the very beginning.
> And now blood is being shed on account of the deceivers and you will be responsible before God for this blood, and therefore oh elders, priests, you should advise your people and flock that they may return from their evil ways and catch the ringleaders and deliver them into the hands of the Government.
> Anyone who transgresses my spiritual advice and fights against his Government and his flag shall be counted like Judas who sold his Master.
> From now onwards anyone who continues in his wickedness and who has not returned from his evil ways the curse of the devil Arios and Hisbros be upon him.
> ... By the authority given to me from God I excommunicate those (who do not give up their evil ways) and they cannot be buried in the churchyard.[56]

The leaflets were apparently ineffective, for the rebels resumed their assault on the 25th, intermittent sharp fighting continuing until the 30th. In multitudes they descended on government forces from three directions, and in some instances advanced as close as three hundred yards. Though heavily outnumbered, the troops "fought with determination and gallantry," and once again unable to withstand the artillery barrage, the rebels retreated and did not return until after five days. As rebel numbers were being depleted, the government was slowly gaining the upper hand; yet the men in the field thought the situation still remained critical, and defeat was not ruled out. The emperor consequently requested air support from his British allies which was granted, but after some hesitation and circumspection: "The Minister of War who is in charge of the operations has justifiable doubts of success in quelling the rebellion, and the Emperor has appealed to us to assist him to pull his chestnuts out of the fire."[57] And so they did, offsetting rebel advantage in numbers with artillery and air power.

The last and decisive battle took place on October 6. An estimated eight to ten thousand peasants commanded by Haile Mariam in person took part in the operation. Through well-coordinated multipronged attacks, the rebels made a relentless effort to exhaust their adversary. Daringly, but vainly, they tried to overwhelm the government forces by flinging themselves in successive waves upon enemy positions, only to be mowed down by mortars and artillery that were deployed with deadly effectiveness. The bombing sorties were terrifying and devastating too. After eight hours of fighting, more than four hundred were dead, and the heavy losses could not be sustained. Rebel morale began to crack, and the chain of command nearly disintegrated. As the officer who was second in command of the British troops reported: "The complete defeat of Haile Mariam's forces broke up all resistance and morale and alienated the various tribes participating with him, the majority of whom were later reported to be retiring to their own country."[58] What ultimately finished the rebels' capacity to continue organized resistance were the three Blenheim aircraft that the British used to drop some 116 bombs, each weighing 40 pounds, on rebel positions, thus controlling places as far north as Mekele. Mekele itself was bombed on a market day. As Peirson wrote, the aerial bombardments had taken their toll:

> The bombing was accurate and inflicted considerable casualties which had their effect in undermining rebel determination. Quite apart from the actual casualties inflicted, however, after one or two attacks the appearance of the aircraft alone was sufficient to cause concentrations of tribesmen to disperse. Ground troops were thus enabled to move forward and occupy key places without opposition.[59]

A local poem also attributed rebel defeat not to lack of courage and faith, but to the effectiveness of air raids:

> An assembly was called in the fatherland
> So that the Orthodox faith may be
>   strengthened.
> Even when the harvest is plentiful
> The farmer never relishes a decent meal,
> Let alone drinks brewed honey,
> And that is what drives him crazy.
> Now your wives have become captive to
>   invaders
> Your cattle have fallen prey to
>   slaughterers
> And your houses have turned into
>   rubble.
> Have you really strengthened the
>   Orthodox faith?
> Ah! a single *gedigedi* [bird] was enough to
>   disperse you.[60]

The government forces were handicapped by lack of adequate training and leadership, but they fought with admirable bravery. The territorials, notable for their "complete lack of training and discipline," were more of a burden as they frequently caused civil disorder, thereby exacerbating local conditions. The supreme military leaders of the operation also lacked some leadership qualities. "The whole force," wrote a foreign participant, "was under command of a General, good, no doubt in shifta warfare, but completely lacking in knowledge of organized fighting tactics ... He himself was under command of a General lacking in any knowledge of supply or administration and incapable of reasoned thought or coordinated action." These inadequacies were, however, fully compensated by the regular troops, whose discipline and indomitable fighting spirit greatly impressed their foreign trainers and combat leaders, including the reporting officer himself.[61]

It is clear that though government troops fought well under difficult conditions, the external factor was decisive in swinging the balance towards the government. A British participant was not claiming undue credit when he remarked:

> I am convinced (and I am certain that the *Ras* and Major General agree) that if the B.M.M.E. [British Military Mission to Ethiopia] had not been participating in these operations with regular troops trained and administered by British personnel, the Emperor's troops would have been destroyed before September 28th, and the consequences of defeat might have been far reaching ... The period September 18th to September 28th was one of extreme anxiety.[62]

Haile Mariam contended that if it were not for the mortars, artillery, and aircraft, his men would have won by exhausting the adversary. Wajirat elders concurred.[63] The plan envisaged was to wear down and eventually liquidate the government troops through encirclement and uninterrupted attacks with superior manpower. Warfare in the open country would have entailed even greater casualties. But their tactics did not work, and in retrospect it was probably tactically suicidal to engage in a positional battle against a better-equipped and well-placed enemy. The alternative would have been guerrilla warfare. The country is broken and mountainous, and was then "covered with dense bush and patches of rain-forest." The Raya and Azebo were described by a professional soldier as "warriors by instinct, particularly adept at surprise action ..."[64] Moreover, given rebel mobility and knowledge of local topography, they would have constituted a formidable and durable force. But they were ill-prepared for a long-drawn-out war, and this error conveys some impression of the quality of rebel leadership, which was handicapped by recurring petty quarrels between Haile Mariam and his allies, the notables, on the one hand, and between peasant leaders and dissident nobles on the other. Thus, once it had lost the tactical initiative, *Weyane* petered out as a coherent resistance.

The events of October 6–7 sealed the fate of the revolt. Their morale broken, the rebels retreated and dispersed to their villages in a disorderly manner. All organized resistance was in effect dissipated, and the War Minister, who was appointed governor of the province soon after the end of hostilities, entered Mekele on October 14. Although a few of the prominent leaders became fugitives in the countryside and managed to elude the militia for a while, none of the participants was willing to wage a protracted resistance, nor would it have been feasible under near-famine conditions. After Araya Degela was killed in 1945 while resisting in the Danakil plains, Fassil Teferri delivered himself up; and not too long after him, Haile Mariam submitted and was subsequently deported to Illubabor, south-western Ethiopia.[65]

Organization and leadership

The extent of popular participation and the rate of escalation of military activities and indeed the level and intensity of organized resistance suggest the existence of a fairly well-worked-out military plan of action. The framework around which such a plan of operation was developed and by which the various component parts of *Weyane* were kneaded into a coherent whole drew heavily on traditional modes of organization of the Raya, Azebo, and Wajirat as well as from the highly structured form of military organization of highland society. Thus, there were two discernible tendencies in the leadership: populism versus commandism or militarism. As these inherently incompatible tendencies vied with each other, the inevitability of conflict in leadership was quite predictable.

At the root of conflict was the aggressive determination of the nobility and bandit leaders to monopolize power, whereas peasant leadership was bent on maintaining a democratic process that guaranteed popular participation. The former saw the peasants as merely a physical force in action; they operated on the arrogant assumption that they were better versed in the art of leadership and warfare, and that they had a command of superior organizational knowledge. In view of the militaristic nature of Ethiopian history, these claims were not altogether unfounded. The nobility's position was also bolstered not only by its primordial ties with the peasants but perhaps also by the trust conferred upon it by the aggrandizing bandit leaders who, by their apparent commitment to the revolt, had won the confidence and trust of the peasant leadership. However, although most peasants might have accepted the claims of the nobility, peasant leaders did not see themselves as simple followers, but as partners in a struggle. The pastoralists in particular were obdurate in their demand that power be deconcentrated, and this demand was consistent with the organizational principle in their social system which then, as in the past, they were unwilling to surrender to those whom they regarded as temporary allies. It is correct to say that the Raya and Azebo knew and hated their neighboring Tigrean rulers as much as they hated the distant Amhara, whom they scarcely knew. The difference in outlook between the major participants was significant because it provided a vehicle for peasant consciousness. On the other hand, although the nobility and bandits were ideological allies vis-à-vis the peasants, their relationship was by no means harmonious, as it was frequently strained by personal ambition and rivalry. Yet it is remarkable that the rebels were able to overcome these differences and pose a serious challenge to the government. Haile Mariam played a key role in both fashioning and sustaining rebel solidarity until their military defeat, from which they were never able to recover.

Haile Mariam was a political maverick. Talented and fiercely independent-minded, he was ambitious and a very skillful mobilizer. Unlike most of the bandits, he was not satisfied with eluding the state from secure sanctuary in the countryside, and among his equals, few demonstrated his stamina and organizational ability to challenge the imperial authorities. His social origin and military experience bolstered his position, but his success in creating a relatively unified leadership lay in his shrewd manipulation of traditional mechanisms of organization and in his extraordinary ability to articulate the respective grievances and aspirations of the participants within the existing class structure.

Rebel leaders, including most notably Haile Mariam, have claimed that the revolt's organizational structure was democratically formulated. A closer examination reveals that this was not entirely true. According to Haile Mariam the nucleus of organized resistance was the *shengo* (general assembly) of 84 elected men representing 12 local assemblies known as *gerreb* (rivers). The assembly, which supposedly selected the abbo gerreb (father or head of assembly), the wanna azmati (chief of warriors), and the haleqa gobez (chief of the brave), was also vested with the power to formulate overall military strategy, promulgate rules and regulations, and administer justice. Eligibility for office was determined on the basis of military prowess and ability to lead in battle, a strong-willed and incorruptible character, and a lack of interest in material acquisition.[66] It is clear that structurally the uprising's organizational composition closely resembled that ordinarily used by the pastoral communities in their periodic intercommunal warfare. In highland Tigrai, the *shengo* was traditionally an informal gathering of adult males in a village or parish to discuss common problems and issues pertaining to taxation, grazing lands, crime and security, elections of village headmen, church affairs, and public relation to local administration. It seems certain that the rebels used this traditional forum primarily to disseminate propaganda, galvanize support, and organize production. However democratic the village assemblies might have been, the nobility exerted enormous influence. It is thus doubtful that all leaders were elected, and that merit was not the sole criterion for leadership is indicated by the number of leaders drawn from the dominant section of the society. It is not conceivable that men who had either been catapulted into their positions by the barrel of a gun or who strongly believed in their birthright to rule would have voluntarily succumbed to the general will. If the nobility had succeeded in forging an alliance and assumed a prominent role in leading the rebellion, it was in part due to their primordial ties with the peasants. And if the dissident nobles and bandits had been more willing than usual to accept aspects of the democratic institutions of village communities, it was mainly because of the demands placed on them by peasant leadership and especially by the Raya, Azebo, and Wajirat. This, then, was more of a concession than an ideological commitment to the general good. Inasmuch as participation in *Weyane* did not suggest similarity of aims, it also did not confirm equal control of the movement by the disparate parties.

Haile Mariam's unwarranted claims must therefore be placed in perspective. In 1974 Haile Mariam was in search of a new role for himself in a society that was engulfed in revolutionary upheaval.[67] Seeking historical legitimacy for the movement, he was prone to exaggerate its popular dimension; he underrated the role of the nobility and minimized the problems that afflicted rebel leadership. Although the militant communities maintained their relative autonomy, authoritarianism was a dominant feature in rebel leadership. The people's assembly was reduced to a titular status; it is interesting that Haile Mariam in his proclamation placed himself immediately below Christ, and at no time did he hold himself accountable to the popular mandate. His megalomaniacal inclinations were a source of friction: as the fighting eventually centered at Alage, the rivalry between Haile Mariam and Yikuno Amlak grew intense. The crisis in leadership was dramatized by the Wajirat's withdrawal from the conflict between September 23 and 27; they then claimed that they had been duped into the crisis by ill-intentioned individuals.[68] In actuality, they had become increasingly suspicious of the motives of the leader and his chief associates and of the quality of their leadership. As a gifted military leader, Haile Mariam first succeeded in inspiring cooperation by accepting the principle of power sharing and delegation of authority; as an ambitious person, he undermined the organization by violating that principle.

The name adopted by the rebels sheds some light on the ideological dimension of the revolt. *Weyane* is sometimes taken to mean statelessness or republicanism.[69] This confuses the term with the social systems of the pastoral communities. It was rather a traditional form of fighting between two groups of youngsters from different hamlets or villages, often separated by a river or rivers. As a ritualized game it was practiced over a wide geographical area extending from Enderta to Yejju, Wello, and was especially popular among the Raya, Azebo, Wajirat, and Yejju. It connotes organized resistance and a spirit of oneness. In practice, the popular sport provided the youngsters with the opportunity to demonstrate to their peers their potential as fighters and leaders. It also taught them the notion of group solidarity, hence the adoption of the word as an ideological expression of the rebellion. In 1943 this sense of solidarity was expressed in the traditional slogan *arriena gerreb* ("We have united around our rivers"). As noted in chapter 2, rivers have had symbolic significance in Ethiopian folklore: "the river is at once a factor of unity and separation, those that are united by it being also separated from others by it."[70] The slogan thus expressed the ephemeral unity of the rebels as well as their inability to transcend their parochial or provincialist sentiments.

Haile Mariam's presentation of the motives for rebellion exemplifies the ideological contradiction that characterized *Weyane*'s marriage of convenience. In trying to construct an ideology of protest, he drew upon a combination of ideas and symbols: ethnic pride and particularism, memories of a "golden past," the symbols of Tigrean royalty and the greatness of Yohannes IV, xenophobia, and religious conservatism. Eclecticism is an appropriate term that describes his approach. Without espousing a single ideology, Haile Mariam dramatized the grievances and aspirations of the various participants. Despite his sworn enmity towards Ras Seyum, the rebel leader called for the restoration of the Tigrean dynasty, thus objectively advocating the cause of some of the dissident nobles; ostensibly intending to placate the conservative clergy, he declared war on the Catholics, Protestants, and on all those town dwellers who smoked and wore long pants, viewing them as importers of alien culture and an outrage to tradition and national honor. To arouse the pent-up feelings of the farmers, he accused the central government of impoverishing them through excessive taxation. In his appeal to provincial sensibilities he accused the Shewan Amhara rulers of ranging Tigrean factional families against each other in order to destroy provincial institutions and thereby establish themselves as the dominant faction in the emerging state-society. He also attacked them for having viciously disparaged the Tigreans as unpatriotic, while it was they who conspired against northerners and bargained Tigrean lands to foreigners – presumably a reference to Eritrea, parts of which had been integral parts of Tigrai. While glorifying the reign of Emperor Yohannes IV, he belittled the Shewan rulers as inept and corrupt but who thrived on feudal intrigue and Tigrean disunity. He cajoled and dismissed the emperor as a coward who had betrayed his people by fleeing the country in the midst of war and who was thus unfit to rule.[71] He even accused him of being an agent of the Catholic Church.[72] These accusations were couched in ethnic sentimentalities; the ideological function of ethnicity was to mobilize people under the false pretext of pursuing common political and economic interests. In this way, what was fundamentally a politicosocial conflict was reduced to a simple ethnic relationship.

Embodying disparate segments, *Weyane* was a typical agrarian protest. Three factors may have accounted for its relative cohesion and effectiveness by mitigating the coalition's organizational problems: oath taking, military experience, and access to firearms. Combatants and their leaders took an oath of fidelity to the movement; it was administered by a priest, a *bona fide* member of the Ethiopian Orthodox Church, at each local gathering. By taking the oath, whose substance was simple enough to be grasped by everybody, the combatants entered into holy communion with one another and with God:

116

May we become lame
May we become blind
May we become dumb
May we become sterile
If we fail to conduct our duties faithfully
And if we fail to work diligently for the
    success of
Weyane and the good of our country.[73]

With regard to the Raya and Azebo, many of whom were Muslim anyway, it was their social system more than the oath that united them. That system provided for organized collective activity such as cooperative labor, ritual, and warfare.

To strengthen the rebel commitment, lofty promises were made and disciplinary rules enacted.[74]

1. The law of the assembly shall be the law of the land.
2. Justice shall be administered by the people's assembly. Citizens ought to disregard all governmental institutions and officials.
3. No man shall rape or dishonor a woman.
4. Looting, robbing, or plundering are absolutely forbidden and punishable by summary execution.
5. Anyone who does not accept and abide by the assembly's rules shall not have the people's protection against robbery, rape, and even murder.
6. Any able-bodied man who fails to support or cooperate with the people's rebel force and to participate in the struggle shall be paraded at market places in a woman's garment.
7. No distinction shall be made between rich and poor and no injustice shall be done to the weak by the powerful.
8. There shall be no conflict and litigation, but harmony and peace.

It is apparent that ridicule and threat were used in recruitment and that many who might have preferred abstention took part in the uprising for fear of intimidation, isolation, humiliation, and social ostracism. Regardless of the method of recruitment, the disciplinary rules were fairly effective. As long as each peasant family was prepared to give one *injera* (pancake-like bread) or its equivalent in *hambasha* (bread) or *tihinni* (flour) a week, no punitive measures were taken against it. Several eyewitnesses have corroborated the exemplary discipline of the rebel forces in the aftermath of their capture of Mekele. Speedy and decisive action was taken against those who looted a few shops.[75] The commanding officer at Quiha, who was himself held in captivity for about a month, claims that rebels were careful not to harm or kill their prisoners for fear of being regarded as effeminate. In contrast to the normal behavior of the feudal armies, who ruthlessly plundered in victory or defeat, the behavior of the rebels was most laudable.

Without the considerable quantities of arms in their possession and without experience in warfare, the rebels would not have been so effective militarily. Itself a participant in many of them, the Tigrean rural population had been exposed frequently to feudal and colonial wars fought in its territory. As a consequence it acquired large quantities of guns and ammunition and became familiar with the art of warfare. In 1935–36 the Raya and Azebo alone received about 3,000 guns from the Italians, and again in 1941 they acquired no fewer than 30,000 guns from the same departing colonialists.[76] Repeated battles in the region had taught the peasants how to operate relatively modern weapons, how to fight, and perhaps, too, how to organize.

Ideologically, *Weyane* was a movement harnessed by the past. It merely wanted to defend existing conditions or to resurrect the past, and not to make the future. It attacked the emperor, but it did not plan to destroy the monarchy; the leadership merely wished to "Tigreanize" it. Apparently prone to the powers and social prerogatives of sacral kingship, Haile Mariam pointed out that his forces were reluctant to attack the royal palace of Yohannes IV at Mekele because they did not want to desecrate this dead emperor's abode. Not only his troops, but Haile Mariam himself proved captive to the ideology of sacred kingship. The revolt defended village autonomy but did not wish to destroy feudalism. Numbers 7 and 8 of the rules enacted have a touch of millenarianism, but *Weyane* was neither millenarian nor revolutionary. The leadership was mainly interested in regaining the locus of power from which it had been excluded by the emperor or his agents. Still, whatever the nobility wanted to make of it and whatever control the nobility exercised over it, the revolt surely had a strong popular dimension.

Repression and aftermath

In the aftermath of defeat, predictable reactions from the imperial center were not long in coming. Defeat was followed by exile, imprisonment, and mopping-up operations. In the process the peasantry suffered enormous depredations which, paradoxically, made the causes of the rebellion appear trivial. Lurid and harrowing stories of whipping, hanging, mutilating, and disemboweling have been heard. All the atrocities were committed in spite of a general amnesty proclaimed for all participants as part of a pacification program. Today, the reminiscences of these atrocities overshadow the movement's lofty ideals and sweeping initial victories.

Weyane was a conflict that involved a great deal of violence. Total human and material losses will perhaps never be known, for specific data on fatalities and damage to property are scarce. Informants could speak only vaguely and in suspiciously exaggerated terms, using words like "large" and "huge"; official sources are more specific but hardly more reliable. One of the participating British officers gave the figures for government losses at Alage as 200 killed, 375 wounded, and 33 unaccounted for.[77] According to the commander of the Ethiopian troops at Quiha, 89 soldiers and an unknown number of civilians were killed and 123 soldiers wounded. The figures for the rebels remain unknown, although in one encounter at Alage alone they lost more than 400 men.[78] In all likelihood, overall casualties on both sides, and especially on the rebel side, were much higher than sources tend to suggest.

Suffering did not end with the cessation of fighting, and of all the participants in the rebellion, it was the nobility that paid the lowest price. Ten of the leaders who had either surrendered or been captured, and several suspected Tigreans of prominence, were exiled to Shewa and imprisoned at Debre Berhan, about sixty miles north of Addis Ababa.[79] Among the deportees was Mengesha Seyum, who was tried and sentenced to death but later pardoned by the emperor. Although he might have sympathized with the rebels at the initial stage of the revolt, there is no evidence of his complicity.[80] Nearly all the detained nobles were released after two and a half years; some were even restored to their traditional positions. Only Haile Mariam was condemned to a long and solitary confinement in southern Ethiopia.

Much less leniency was shown toward the peasants, who endured great hardship during and after the conflict. At Alage resentful and hostile rebels are said to have savagely castrated and at times mutilated some of those whom they captured in fighting. The adversary was no more magnanimous. In retaliation, the War Minister himself executed prisoners of war, while his victorious troops machine-gunned many more defenseless peasants. But these dreadful atrocities still required justification.

> Ras Ababe Aregai was reported to have executed some batches of prisoners, Tigrai and Galla, that were captured and brought in during the battles on Amba Alage. This was war and not by any means a kid glove affair and summary punishment is the only deterrent known to savage warriors of the Galla type who were mutilating their own prisoners. Such executions are not unknown in war between so-called civilized nations according to the news.[81]

The mopping-up operations carried out in the aftermath of the conflict to disarm the peasants were so barbaric that they have left a residue of bitterness and hostility. The militia was ordered to collect arms and hunt down fugitive rebels, especially Haile Mariam and his close associates, in Enderta, Kilte Awlaalo, Tembien, Raya, and Azebo. It was in this process that many acts of vandalism and brutality that sear the conscience of decent people were perpetrated upon the people of east-central Tigrai. The state had neither the machinery nor the will to control the behavior of its troops, who freely roamed the land, destroying crops, confiscating grains and animals, looting property, and burning and pillaging villages. Since it was assumed that there were few peasants without guns, failure to produce one on demand was subject to a penalty of one hundred Maria Theresa thalers, an exceptionally high amount for people whose productive lives had been seriously disrupted for many years. Such acts were despicable and horrifying to some officials. In February 1944, a British adviser to the Minister of the Interior, claiming that his report was based on three "reliable and independent intelligence reports," submitted a memorandum aptly entitled "Primitive Measures in the Tigrai."[82] It enumerated that:

i.   Heavy toll was inflicted on the civilians and farmers, villages were burnt, crops destroyed, cattle and goods taken. There is not much doubt that the Irregulars pillaged the countryside, but it is doubtful whether they ever came to grips with the fighting men, who in time will return and have their revenge, if they can.

ii. General Ababa Damtew with a strong force has been in the Allomata–Cobbo–Cerci [Chercher] district for the last three weeks and has completed the burning and pillaging of those villages East of the Dessie–Asmera road which were suspected of having anti-government sympathies.

iii. The whole of the area of the Cerci [Chercher] has been burned, all crops destroyed and all captured inhabitants known or suspected of sympathy with the Dejazmatch Arriah [Araya] have been killed. Some thousands of head of cattle have been driven off to neighboring districts.

Ethiopian sources corroborated these claims. In one of his formal protests the governor of Raya and Azebo, Fitawrari Yemane Hassen, accused the troops of unlawfully taking away the produce of the cultivators – their grains, butter, and honey – and of expropriating their horses, mules, cattle, sheep, goats, and agricultural implements. He deplored the behavior of troops who ravished married women, abused the elderly, and randomly beat and clubbed citizens, causing deafness or paralysis in some instances.[83] However comprehensive these reports may have been, they failed to mention that each peasant household was compelled to pay ten Maria Theresa thalers to provide for the irregulars.[84] The punishment for failing to comply was even more outrageous. Sadistic acts such as burning faces with boiling water, tying hands with salted ropes, and forcing women to shave off their hair – a practice customarily reserved for mourning the dead – were frequently committed.[85]

In response to the revolt, the state confiscated the lands of the Raya and Azebo, creating a hapless tenantry.[86] The disowned were given the option of purchasing a maximum of 10 hectares per person. Others had the privilege of buying up to 80 hectares. Nearly twenty years later less than 1 percent of the population had bought about 30 percent of the marketable land. The records of the 1960s show that whereas 2,233 persons had purchased a total of 600 *gashas* (1 *gasha* = 40 hectares), another 617, mostly from outside, had freely obtained some 731 *gashas*, which they had then rented to the 8,495 people living on them. The government collected rent in cash and in kind from 3,495 tenants working on 605 *gashas* of its holdings.[87] As pastoralists, many of them had simply resigned themselves to renting sufficient land for grazing their animals. In any case, after *Weyane*, their economic life was greatly depressed. For instance "the number of indebted households and the average debt per household were much higher compared to other areas of Tigre where the *rist* system remained unchanged."[88] Further, as commercial agriculture entered the area, eviction became a common occurrence, giving rise to litigation and social conflict. In the subdistrict of Mehoni alone, land disputes made up 70 percent of total civil cases, while claims to share accounted for 50 percent of land disputes, exceeding the 46 percent incidence of civil cases involving land disputes in the province.[89]

Why were such severe measures imposed on the Raya and Azebo alone? According to the government, the justification for the expropriation of land lay in their repeated defiance of the state (1928–30 and 1942–43) and "notorious" collaboration with the Italians in 1935–36. Total or part confiscation of land by the state for crimes committed against it was an established practice, and the dispossession of the Raya and Azebo appears to have been in conformity with this custom. What made expropriation much easier was the assumption that ultimate ownership of all pastoral lands resided in the state itself. Nevertheless, no punishment of such magnitude had ever been imposed previously in Tigrai. Confiscation marked the beginning of the eventual decomposition of communalism in the eastern lowlands of the province. On the eve of the revolution the dispossessed could thus say with much justification: "Like the colonized [peoples] of Rhodesia, we rented small plots of our own lands from those who disowned us in the first place. We labored hard only to give away what we produced, the amount always determined on the basis of their personal whims; and we delivered at no cost."[90]

Conclusion

Weyane was an uprising with a comparatively low level of class consciousness in spite of a fairly high level of spontaneity and peasant initiative. The revolt was primarily a challenge to a weak monarchical state; it contained aspects of class struggle, but it was not a conflict between landlord and peasant. Exhausted by war, embittered by greedy officials and an ill-disciplined militia, and threatened by feudal incorporation, the rebellious groups mainly directed their disenchantment against the central government. In this regard, *Weyane* has much in common with the peasant uprisings of the seventeenth century in France, Russia, and China, which, according to Roland Mousnier, were essentially, "reactions against the state."[91] Hopeful of a military victory over a weak but increasingly meddling central government, the aggrieved parties united, if only temporarily, around a sense of "provincialism."

Yet the notion of provincialism cannot be stretched too far, for only the eastern part of Tigrai rebelled in 1943; and it is not difficult to explain the rebellion's geographical distribution. Of the four leaflets dropped between September 23 and 27, the last one included Adwa, Aksum, Agame, and Shire, suggesting escalation of the conflict to include those districts. Only Enderta, Kilte Awlaalo, Tembien, and Maichew were fully involved. The local chiefs of Agame, Aksum, and Shire remained on the fence until the outcome of the conflict was known. Gabre Hiwet Meshesha of Adwa went further than most in his active opposition to rebellion by bringing his peasant militia to Enderta to fight the dissidents. It would be tempting but wrong to conclude that the peasants of the western districts abstained from the conflict because of the influence exerted upon them by local nobles who either actively opposed the revolt or abjured it. Underlying the stance of the western gentry, and their relative success in preventing the spread of the revolt there, is the fact that western Tigrai had not been as badly hit as the eastern section by militia and bandit activities. According to British military reports from Asmera, one of the main reasons for its quietism was the "lively commerce with Eritrea."[92] Nothing in the area compared with the behavior of the more than ten thousand militia stationed between Maichew and Quiha, while the east was the base of operations of many of the formidable bandit leaders. Almost all the principal agitators among the disgruntled nobility were centered in the Enderta–Mehoni region. More importantly, the Raya, Azebo, and Wajirat communities, traditionally opposed to feudal encroachment, were also situated there. All this explains why conditions in the east had made the situation ripe for rebellion.

A heterogeneous coalition, embodying divergent motives and interests, engaged in the uprising. Factional alignments cut across class boundaries, but the nobility sought the peasants' support principally to arrest the erosion of its own local power base and to reinforce its position of privilege without changing the social order. The rebellious peasants also gained little from their association with bandits. We must not assume that many of the bandits, even leaders like Haile Mariam, were committed to the peasant cause. It is even difficult to endorse the limited claim that while "Yekuno Amlak's ideas were more often concerned with his own advancement, *Blatta* Haile Mariam was most interested in the province of Tigre."[93] For Haile Mariam, banditry was a means of expressing personal grievances and advancing his interests; he was primarily interested not in destroying or even in reforming the status quo but in finding a comfortable place for himself within it. The aspirations of the leadership, therefore, diverged from those of the peasants. Many of the leaders were aggrieved not so much by the suffering they shared with the peasants as by the contrast between their own positions and that of the new provincial officials. Cooperation with the peasantry was a short-term political necessity.

Although they lacked a coherent set of goals, the rebels showed remarkable unity in action; Haile Mariam skillfully balanced the contradictory objectives of the rebellion's various components. By manipulating traditional symbols of identity and ethnic homogeneity, he managed to maintain a unity which otherwise hung precariously in the balance. In his leadership role we may presume that Haile Mariam was instinctively responding to the competing class interests embodied in his movement rather than consciously manipulating them, since the latter view would require him to possess a degree of political consciousness beyond that for which we have evidence. In any case, whether instinctively synthesized or cunningly constructed, the movement's eclectic goals and ideology were well suited to its various participants.

Paradoxically, the uprising's strength was also its weakness, for the diversity of interests compromised ideological clarity. While from the military side the skill and organizational experience of the dissident nobles, disbanded colonial soldiery, and bandits were great assets, they also posed a serious problem to the peasants because of conflicting political and ideological interests.

At the end, only the dissident nobility benefited from the conflict. It must be noted here, however, that it returned to a diminished territory because Raya, one of the richest districts in the south, was given away to the neighboring province of Wello. Seyum was returned as governor-general in 1947, and most of his associates, including those implicated in the rebellion, were reinstated in the provincial administration. Of all those who engaged in the rebellion, this was the only group which came close to realizing its objectives. But even then, its power had been severely eroded and its political influence greatly restricted. Centralization had effectively expropriated regional autonomy, and as the state became better organized and more powerful, the room for independent political action in the province proportionately diminished. We have already seen that the rise of Haile Selassie heralded the withering of the political power of the Tigrean nobility; that was just one part of the story. For while the imperial state subjugated the nobility, it also retained it, mainly for purposes of administration, as an instrument by which it could control the provincial population.

From the short-term perspective of the peasants, the revolt was not a total defeat. In 1944 the government reverted land tax to 1935 in terms both of the tax rate and the method of levy. Unlike 1935, however, taxes were made payable in cash. The peasants did benefit after the events in Tigrai, and the beneficial effect was not restricted to the province but included all *rist* areas. On the other hand, concomitant with the preservation and safeguarding of the basic interest of the nobility was the repression of those of the peasantry. Incorporation, of which the Raya and Azebo, like all other communities in similar conditions, had always been profoundly fearful, meant an end to village autonomy. Worse, with their lands expropriated, the relatively independent, semipastoralist communities were turned into landless peasants. And from the long-term perspective, the role of the British government may have cemented Ethiopia's link with the Western states whose continued economic and military assistance became critical in the consolidation and sustenance of the restored regime.

Finally, *Weyane* sealed the history of traditional conflict between centralizing authority and provincial sectarianism. The year 1943 was the last time that the Tigrean nobility took up arms against the unitary monarchical state. But it did not eliminate the social roots of popular protest in the region, for the dialogue between the Ethiopian state and the people of Tigrai has continued, albeit in a different fashion and under a different political leadership. Opposition to central authority has shifted from the gentry to the intelligentsia. Whereas the former sought to protect its economic interest

123

and social position by preserving regional autonomy within the existing social structure, the latter wants greater inclusion in a transformed national state.

5

Bale: the nationalities armed

Between 1963 and 1970 the peasants of Bale, heavily supported by an external force but largely unnoticed by the outside world, took up arms against the Ethiopian state. Occurring two decades after the Tigrean revolt, the Bale uprising was set off by a potent combination of grievances stemming from maldistribution of political and administrative powers, land alienation, taxation, ethnic hostility, religious discrimination, and ecological imbalance. Its primary goals were the retention or repossession of land and the reassertion of ethnocultural identities. Diffused consciousness arose out of the community's historical experience and Islamic beliefs and practices standing in structural opposition to the state's Christian symbols. Unlike *Weyane*, it was a conflict that directly pitted peasants against landlords, though its class aspect was not fully manifested at all times. Class contradictions were mostly enacted as ethnic and religious conflicts, as family or personal feuds, and as narrow localism. Despite its geographical restriction, the revolt was the most dramatic expression of the latent contradictions and tensions in the entire southern region of the country.

Though the roots of conflict lay in empire formation, it was the administrative and fiscal changes instituted after the Second World War that sharpened social cleavages at all levels of society. The native gentry, already aggrieved because of its failure to receive land grants, now wanted more administrative power. Its demands and actions intensified interclass competition, which took the form of Amhara versus Oromo–Somali rivalry. The consequent crisis in the state malignantly fused with external meddling. Decreasing access to land and growing insecurity of tenure alienated the peasantry. The state expropriated a hugh portion of the cultivable land under the guise of tax default, slowly turning farmers into landless tenants. Politically insecure, it imposed greater restrictions on people's movements across provincial and international boundaries, severely disrupting trade and the rhythm and cycle of pastoral life. Almost entirely Muslim, the Oromo and Somali also resented the special privileges accorded the northern Christian settlers and the bureaucratic abuses that accompanied the extension of state authority. Conditions became favorable for popular defiance because they were conducive to class alliances and susceptible to outside manipulation. Islam provided the cultural idiom for the mobilization of mass discontent.

Both the timing and scale of the revolt were to a large measure determined by external forces. Events leading to and following the independence of Somalia in 1960 contributed greatly to the growth of a new form of consciousness: pan-Somalism, which drew its inspiration from an earlier Dervish resistance in the Ogaden, quickly gripped a people who had had only the vaguest notion of a larger Somali community, until then divided among four states. The Somali of Ethiopia became attracted to the homonymous postcolonial state of which many of them wanted to become part. These changes had a perceptible impact on the Oromo, who, in the hope of ameliorating their depressed conditions, chose to ally themselves with a foreign power that otherwise coveted their lands. That tactical alliance was not always harmonious, however. There was mutual mistrust among the Oromo and Somali supporters of the revolt. Northern Christian domination stirred them and Islam unified them, but modes of economic activity and ethnic particularity divided them. Somali irredentism was not compatible with Oromo ethnic pride.

A loosely unified leadership without a definite program for political action was able to wage an armed resistance for many years because it operated in a vast frontier region, enjoyed the support of a disaffected peasantry, and received foreign aid that augmented its military capability. It took six years of extensive fighting to quash the rebels, who were armed with sophisticated weapons and utilized new forms of military techniques and organization, an improvement over traditional spontaneity and fragmentation. Despite their impressive military accomplishments, the rebels never initiated any social change. Obstructionism by the Somali state is not to be discounted, but the underlying reason was the lack of leadership with a coherent vision. This was a typical rural protest that sought vainly to redress a multiplicity of grievances.

Pre-conquest social formation

The territory which roughly constitutes the present administrative region of Bale and the autonomous region of Ogaden formed what was the second largest but most sparsely populated province in the empire. Nearly completely embraced by the Genale river to the south and west and the Wabe Shebele to the north and east, the province covered an area of 124,000 square kilometers (before partition in 1987), but contained only half a million people, with density, like the vegetation, tapering off towards the southern edges that reach the Somali border. Very many small rivers drain from the mountains in a southerly direction into the two drainage systems, resulting in a very broken but extraordinarily scenic topography. In the north and northwest the land rises to as high as 4,300 meters at Mount Battu and

126

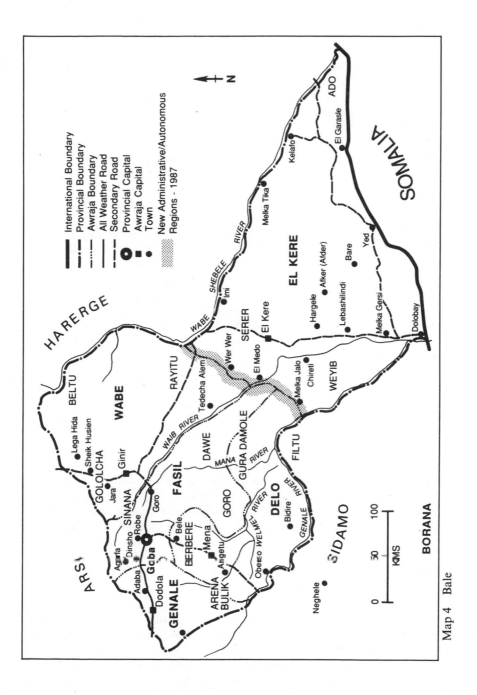

Map 4   Bale

steadily drops away southwards. The plateau is well watered and rich in vegetation, in striking contrast to the dry and semibarren lowlands.

Bale was incorporated within the Ethiopian state in the late 1880s after a brutal campaign mainly directed against the Aweytu and Raiytu of the Arsi clan. The aboriginal population comprised clusters of segmentary patrilineal Oromo and Somali communities; the first were scattered across the lowlying, thorny wilderness, while the latter were confined mostly to the river plains and foothills of the high mountains.

Both communities were classless and stateless. Groups of extended families formed corporate units of production, possessing some cattle, goats, sheep, and camels, and a few rudimentary tools, but none had privileged access to land. There was no centralized authority with specialized agents of coercion to which all inhabitants paid tax or any other kind of levy. Continuous segmentation and mobility combined with shifting alliances among production units to preclude the rise of territorially based stable societies having formal political and administrative institutions. Society was markedly equalitarian and culturally homogeneous. Kinship was the principal idiom of social interaction, mediating economic, political, and cultural activities. Production and distribution, communal solidarity and conflict, ritual and ceremonial activities, jural and political obligations, and people's relationship to the environment were all closely tied to kinship organization.

Egalitarianism did not mean that there was no status distinction. Social rank presupposes privilege, and indeed there was inequality between families that did not have the same number of herds, between elders and juniors, and between men and women. Although adult family members participated in production (hunting, cultivating, and stock raising), not all of them were likely to have equal control of the fruits of their labor. However, surplus above family consumption was too little to allow more than the beginnings of social differentiation and conflict.

A closer observation of each community reveals that the acephalous Somali were fissiparous, clans frequently feuding and fighting over control of water and pastures in a habitat that is extremely inhospitable. As association within each production unit was closely tied to material and security needs, alliances and loyalties constantly shifted. The smallest but most stable social unit was the *diya*-paying group. This was a contractual association that, by paying and receiving blood compensation, provided protection for its member families in an otherwise fractious and conflict-ridden culture. Lineage ties were the most enduring, and the highest form of political cooperation was expressed within the clan, itself an aggregate of lineages. Each clan had its elected head whose main function was arbitration over internal matters. As an authority he enjoyed no special privileges and wielded little political power, for he lacked formal sanctioning mechanisms and renewable resources. Compliance was voluntary but a matter of ritual. The clans were loosely confederated under the umbrella of the *shir* (council of elders) to which, theoretically, all adult males had unqualified access.[1]

The social organization of the Oromo was not markedly different; characteristically egalitarian and democratic, it too was segmented and decentralized. The Oromo were predominantly pastoralist, practicing transhumance with complex and shifting patterns. The land on which they lived and subsisted they treated as *ottuba* (communal property) whose supreme custodians were two senior elders who bore the honorific or symbolic titles of abba biya (father of the land) and abba burka (father of the spring). It appears, though, that in the highland sections sedenterization had already begun when the northerners introduced plow farming. Small and widely dispersed settlements of patriarchal homesteads were engaged in small-scale agriculture and animal husbandry, mainly relying on family labor and rudimentary technology. The basic social unit of production was the *warra* (nuclear family), many families forming a lineage. Like the Somali, the Oromo were organized around clans, a loose confederation of which constituted a tribal cluster known as *gossa*. The two prominent political and cultural mediators were the *burka* and *kallu*; the first was chosen from among the lineage heads, while the latter was a senior clan member whose position tended to be hereditary. The *kallu* was also regarded as the spiritual leader with the power to heal and to mediate between the community and the deities beyond.[2] Islam did not displace these deities; on the contrary, it absorbed them, facilitating its own spread throughout the plateau.

Abyssinian occupation suddenly turned the Oromo into a "subject peasantry" whose social obligations were the same, more or less, as elsewhere in the renter or production regions. By shredding communal relationships, the more legalistic and bureaucratic state increased social stratification and rural misery. It initiated a process of expropriation that half a century later would culminate in massive land alienation. The state claimed for itself most of the fertile, well-watered highland areas, which it then devoted to the production of barley, millet, *teff*, and other cereals, such cultivation being performed by unpaid peasant labor. The highland population was adscripted to northern settlers and officials and their auxiliaries, the *burkas* and *koros*, for whom peasants performed a wide range of services and surrendered a substantial part of their produce through a sharecropping system.[3] Noncompliance or delinquency had its price: according to one observer, the overlord, and more frequently his representative, the *neftenya* (rifleman), "ignores any excuse which the peasant may make, no matter how valid, and imposes a fine, which is collected by the simple method of seizing the man's livestock and household."[4] The settler was often at liberty to whip or flog, chain or detain his subjects even for relatively minor infractions.[5]

Lowlanders were spared these outlandish forms of exploitation and degradation, largely because of geographical and cultural imperatives. The uncongeniality of the climate, the meagerness of exploitable resources, and the difficulty of controlling a fiercely independent and mobile population discouraged settlement in the "fringe peripheries." The imperial state made little attempt to reorganize the nomadic pastoral society other than by

129

imposing tribute on it. Whenever it was possible and suitable, the state confirmed the existing clan elders or, failing this, simply imposed its own appointees on a reluctant population. The new officials were to share in the fixed but irregularly collected tax on livestock. Situated on the fringes of the empire, and adept at manipulating the international border, the nomads were able to retain substantial autonomy until the 1950s, experiencing only periodic military forays from the uplands.

The new and changing relations of domination and subordination were marked by a deeply imbricated history of conflict. Though political, economic, and cultural domination was the basis for communal hostility, underlying that hackneyed encounter was mutual ignorance; the result was mutual exclusion and avoidance. Rigidly parochial and paternalistic, settlers maintained a recognizable social distance from the native population, with whom they shared few or no values. With little cross-cultural interaction, dominant and dominated developed negative images of each other. The conquerors treated the aboriginals as culturally inferior peoples to be uplifted under their benevolent guidance. And the latter viewed the northerners as arrogant, greedy, shifty, immoral, and brutish. To underline the exploitative relationship that bound them together, the Somali dubbed the settler *dubi* (hyena or scavenger), and the Oromo called him *nama gnata* (man-eater), an image they used to frighten children.[6] In Somali popular consciousness the Abyssinian was as vicious and as poisonous as a snake against whom people ought to be on guard at all times.

Popular protest was a recurring phenomenon, collaboration with outsiders a noticeable feature. The best example of armed opposition is the Somali or better-known Dervish movement that began in 1899 under the charismatic leadership of Sayyid Mohammed Abdille Hassan. Using Islam to unify the discordant clans and oral poetry to inspire his followers, the Sayyid led an armed resistance in the Ogaden until 1920, when under the combined weight of British and Ethiopian military might, his pan-Somali movement collapsed.

Imperial rule was again challenged between 1935 and 1947. In the mid 1930s many southerners seized the colonialist aggression against the country to relieve themselves of northern domination by collaborating with the Italians. And upon the return of national sovereignty peasants from Bale and neighboring Sidamo allied themselves with ex-colonial soldiers under the leadership of a certain Nur Gurwein to prevent the restoration of the *gebbar* system which the Italians had suspended. In Bale itself the focus of conflict was Delo, a district in the southwestern part of the province. An uprising, known as *jeghir* and which dragged on for nearly a year, was set off by a power struggle between the hereditary *kallu*, Mohammed Gedda, whom the government had deposed, and its own appointee, Chaka Entele. Their rivalry was a contest in legitimacy. Its localization helped the transitional government to crush it, arresting its politicospiritual leader, who languished in prison until his death in 1961. The imperial state had restored order but not peace, for defiance continued silently and at times openly. The third phase of popular protest marked a transition from localized to mass-based regional resistance that had manifestations of ethnonationalism and which was mediated by new social elements. The rebellion of 1963 belongs to that phase.

Components of revolt

Land, state, and peasantry

The Ethiopian government strongly maintained that the rebellion was insti-gated and sustained by an expansionist Somalian state. Its claim was sup-ported with convincing evidence. However, a realistic assessment of this important episode does not start with outside agitators but with the material and cultural conditions obtaining in southern Ethiopia. The following state-ment by the leader of the rebellion provides an appropriate starting point:

> Notice that when the Amhara occupied our country with the help of European imperialists in 1885–1891, many of our people were massacred. Then the survivors were allotted like slaves to the settlers who also partitioned our lands amongst themselves ... Remember that they have plundered and distorted our historical legacy that is widely known; that they have violated our dignity, calling us the filthy Galla. Do you realize how many times you have been denied justice in their courts of law? You, Muslims, your religion has been denigrated, and you do not share equality with Christians.
>
> Innumerable crimes that have not been committed by the European colonialists on the African peoples have been perpetrated upon you. You have been crushed for eighty years now.[7]

Hardly composed by a typical peasant, but the message underscores the crucial issues in the conflict – land, ethnicity, and culture – and dramatizes the structural relationships of dominance and exploitation within a multieth-nic, socially segmented society. Peasants thought of justice primarily as access to the means of subsistence (land and livestock), and as was generally true of southerners, no experience was as painful as the loss of land.

The agrarian relationship that linked the landowning gentry to state and peasantry had been at the core of rural conflict since the formation of the empire. It assumed greater saliency as the contractual rent system was firmly established. This began with the institution of an enlarged and rationalized bureaucracy and a change in the taxation system, both of which accelerated land alienation. Although the imperial state theoretically claimed much of the provincial land, most producers enjoyed use rights to cultivable and grazing land until the late 1950s when, under the pretext of tax default, venal bureaucrats began to disinherit them.

Methods of land alienation varied from outright confiscation to fraud and deception. The ability of officials and settlers alike to violate existing occu-pancy rights, to confiscate farmlands of alleged tax defaulters without due process of law, and to silence aggrieved protesters depended to a great extent on their ability to draw upon the coercive resources of the state. Governors conveniently confiscated lands, claiming that owners had either failed to pay legal levies or had committed criminal acts against the state. In other instances extensive amounts of land were taken as gifts from quasi-religious figures despite the fact that none of them had authority to give away clan or tribal lands.[8]

The policy of imperial land grants also disinherited many farmers. Between 1942 and 1970 the government granted more than 4,828,560 hectarcs, most of it to dignitaries from the civil and military services.[9] Perhaps as much as 30 percent of this was located in Bale. When the campaign to dissolve *gult* rights began in the early 1960s immediately following the coup, there was a rush to convert them into freeholdings. Proclamation 230 of 1966 accelerated the process of conversion. Men of high political profile in the northern regions were also richly compensated with land grants in the south, mainly in Bale and Sidamo.

The rise of towns and the appearance of large-scale commercial farming increased the farmers' vulnerability. The new towns were built mainly along the Gore–Shashamane highway in the districts of Fasil and Genale, where the best lands for mixed farming were located and where the settlers and principal officials were congregated. There, hundreds of acres of prime land were seized for capitalist development, but largely for speculative reasons, confiscation occurring in relatively populated areas.[10]

More disruptive in its impact was the chaotic taxation system, which provided greedy bureaucrats with the excuse to dispossess hardworking and law-abiding citizens. Until the Italian invasion, tax was paid in the province according to quality of land and number of *gebbar* families, the amount varying widely seasonally. Changes were twice made in the 1940s and 1950s such that taxable land was measured visually and its quality assessed periodically. Visual measurement is hardly a reliable method, and surely discrepancies were commonplace.[11] In 1963, in an attempt to raise its revenue if not to make taxation more equitable, the government remeasured the taxable land with a premeasured wire or rope. Results showed that many holdings had been woefully underestimated, a fact that must have been of particular benefit to landlords with substantial property. Along with the increase in taxable land, tax rates were also raised from ETH $58, $52, and $19.50 to $72, $64, and $24 for a *gasha* of fertile, semifertile, and poor land, respectively. That meant that landlords were to pay on more acreage at a higher rate per acre. As was to be expected, the bulk of the burden fell on the mass of cultivators because landlords simply passed on their shares to tenants.

Many farmers were unable or perhaps unwilling to pay, and they began to forfeit their holdings. According to government representatives, farmers who were undertaxed in the past defaulted mainly because they were unwilling to accept and comply with the new tax laws. Indeed records show that

Table 5.1. *Distribution of land confiscated*

Awraja	Uncollected tax (ETH $)	Land confiscated in *gashas*
Delo	1,799,558.04	8,254
Fasil	2,540,783.14	4,851
Genale	1,165,064.43	2,022
Wabe	2,311,346.15	7,911
Total	7,816,751.76	23,038

Source: MLRA, *Report on Land Tenure Survey of Bale Province* (December 1969), p. 9.

landholders had paid tax on only 25,666 registered *gashas*, which when remeasured amounted to 54,793 *gashas*.[12] But if there was disparity between the amount of land which peasants held and that on which they paid taxes, the disparity would appear to be far greater in the case of individuals with political power and influence with vast landholdings which were either unregistered or underestimated and conveniently misclassified.[13] In the four districts where such holdings were concentrated, nearly 80 percent of the land was classified as poor. Landlords paid significantly low rates, and there is no evidence that they paid more than small landholders. At any rate, failure to pay tax for three consecutive years resulted in loss of land, and very many people defaulted. Arrears rose from ETH $3,381,568.32 in 1953–59 to $8,012,226.20 in 1960–64,[14] and the land confiscated amounted to 27 percent of all holdings excluding the district of El Kere, where land was still held communally.[15] The approximate breakdown by district is given in table 5.1.

To appreciate the depth of the popular resentment that finally drove peasants to armed revolt, it is important to understand the reasons for it. If cultivators failed to pay tax, it was not only for lack of sufficient resources but also because of sheer bureaucratic inertia and red tape. Without roads or communication facilities until the late 1960s, Bale was regarded as a hardship post where tax collectors, customs officers, judges, and inspectors could live on their perquisites, using methods closely approaching those of highway robbers. Official transactions such as land measurement, registration, and classification were rarely performed without the payment of enforced bribes, and many cases of financial mismanagement were reliably reported. A host of illegal fees were collected for routine clerical work, and not infrequently receipts relating to land tax were forged or falsified. Spoils were shared amongst the hierarchy of officials. From time to time additional "gifts" such as honey, butter, coffee, and mutton – most of it grabbed from the hapless producers – were sent to the higher bureaucrats in Goba and Addis Ababa, and in this manner their exploitative relationship was ritualized. Courts were generally pliant instruments in the hands of the powerful. One minor bureaucrat from Sidamo, parts of which were embroiled in the

133

revolt, could thus write: "These officials are blind to truth and justice ... They are only governed and guided by sheer self-interest ... If and when the government takes action against them, the severest possible punishment is transfer to other places ... "[16] He was not the only indignant person. Having uncharacteristically admitted with a sense of equanimity that lands had been confiscated without due regard to the Civil Code of the Ethiopian government, the governor of Bale subsequently ordered that legal receipts be given upon payment of tax, that no land be seized unless proven that delinquents lacked sufficient resources to cover the arrears, and that government representatives be barred from taking part in any land transactions.[17] By then the damage had already been done, and the aggrieved had become restive. The sheikh Ibrahim Lemmu of Goba tried to capture the essence of their indignation: "Ours has been [a history] of deprivation and misery, a story of endless tragedy. In our own country we have lived as aliens and slaves, deprived of our lands and discriminated against on grounds of our tribal and religious identities."[18] Such feelings, which strongly reinforced Wako's claims, may not have been universal, but they were widespread. Even among the loyal gentry a few acknowledged the discriminatory nature of the political system and protested against the harsh and indecent treatment of peasants by officials and settlers alike.[19] Government fiscal policies and the behavior of the government's agents generated such indignation not because some of the levies were illegal but because they were perceived as particularly harmful to the farming Oromo population.

Discontent was rife amongst the pastoralists too. Central to state–pastoralist conflict was autonomy, but lying behind it was a social system to the defense of which autonomy was the key. Elsewhere in the country pastoralism had been eroded through capitalist encroachment. Pastoral land along the Awash Valley and western parts of Begemedir and Eritrea had been converted into large-scale commercial farms producing cash crops of sugar, tobacco, tea, cotton, and sesame. The original owners were pushed into marginal areas that were less suitable for livestock. Many of them became laborers on plantations, working for incredibly low wages in appalling conditions. There was no such land alienation in Bale for the lack of state or private investment. The salt mining in El Kere was too small and inconsequential. There the problem arose from multiple exactions and state policies that tried to restrict the seasonal mobility of nomad-pastoralists. Although the international border imposed restrictions on the physical mobility of the people, squelching access to pastures and water, it failed miserably in preventing nomads from evading taxation. They evaded it by ignoring and crisscrossing the frontier only to return as soon as the collectors had disappeared from the scene. Political offenders and common criminals sought sanctuary on either side of the border using the same tactics. The intensification of Somali nationalist activities on its eastern frontier in the early 1960s presented the imperial state with a new challenge, and mainly for security and tax reasons it began to tighten its control over its borders, regulating nomadic movements. Additionally, in a futile attempt to control what they termed bandit activities, zealous but ignorant officials tried to restrict the seasonal movement of pastoralists in Delo and Wabe, seriously disrupting the cycle of transhumance and exposing livestock to hazardous pests. These unacceptable measures were taken against people whose access to communal grazing lands was already constrained. In addition to taxes paid on their livestock, pastoralists were required to pay for pasturing their animals on what were regarded as state lands, and the greater the concentration of users, the higher the fees. Of state lands in the province, at least 37 percent were leased for grazing. Rent, which was payable in cash only, ranged from ETH $64 in Delo to ETH $24 in Fasil per *gasha*.[20] The police and militia that were sometimes sent to collect these levies ended up committing depredations, thereby provoking the anger of the population. Jamo Ga Ma'Awye of El Kere remembers: "They robbed us. They raped our women in front of us. There was no justice, no courts, no discipline among their soldiers."[21]

The above measures also directly interfered with trading activities. As their economy was by no means self-sufficient, pastoralists were engaged in extensive bartering with their neighbors to the west and east. Agriculture and pastoralism were intertwined activities; grains produced in the highlands were exchanged for such items as salt, honey, butter, coffee, and livestock from the lowlands. The bulk of these products was, however, exported to the Somali coast by itinerant merchants who brought in return clothing, sugar, kerosene, and utensils. These people also acted as the principal agents of the irredentists in the spread of secular political ideas, helping to forge a strong sense of pan-Somalism. As an agent investigating the causes of the revolt saw it, the problem facing the Ethiopian state was rooted in the interplay of environmental, economic, and political forces:

> What has made it possible for our enemies to enter into the sovereign territory of Ethiopia and then to proselytize religion and to spread political propaganda is the market. It is the market that has enabled the bandits to maintain uninterrupted contacts with these people. For example, it is known that Ethiopian nomads cross into Somalia to sell livestock and to buy other essentials for themselves. Somali currency is used in those transactions. Since this kind of relationship might become the basis for a continuing political and economic problem, it will be prudent to establish under government initiative, marketing centers along the border and other strategic locations.[22]

Such marketplaces were never established, but by intervening in their mode of activities, the state created conditions for political unrest. By trying to reduce the flow of people from Somalia in search of water and pastures in its territory, the state increased pressure on scarce resources in their homeland; by trying to discourage its own citizens from moving to the other side, it interfered with the politics of kinship and the logic of the market. The state had become too intrusive and burdensome by trampling upon traditional autonomy. For those aspiring to join the new Somali republic, the boundary was no longer one that could be conveniently disregarded; it had to be removed.

What made the situation in the province more ominous was not only the conjuncture of class and ethnic cleavages; it was also that the state was perceived as religiously discriminatory, a fact that had greater poignancy in Bale. The province prides itself as not only the seat of the medieval sultanate of Bali, but also the sanctuary of the shrine of Sheikh Hussien, the most celebrated Islamic saint in the region, which annually attracts thousands of pilgrims from as far as southern Somalia and northern Kenya. While this institution received no support from the national state, the Orthodox Church, as elsewhere in the country, enjoyed a privileged place, its religious and cultural activities receiving political and financial aid. It drew its sustenance from land grants that were tax exempt and normally rented to Muslim tenants.[23] The *abun*'s (bishop's) authority and influence were surpassed only by those of the provincial governor. Together they symbolized the unity of state and church authority in a region that was overwhelmingly Muslim. In these circumstances, belief in the value to be derived from a connection with the national center was almost nonexistent. If many peasants were ever ready to form alliances with enemies of the Ethiopian state, be it Italian Fascists or Somali irredentists, it is most likely that they were motivated by memories of denial and oppression; implicit in their actions was an element of vengeance. It was this latent popular hostility, now rekindled by additional demands on producers, that combined with the frustrated ambitions of the local gentry to produce the revolt of 1963.

State bureaucracy and gentry

It was argued above that the Ethiopian ruling class was still evolving through a dynamic process of fusions and fissures. The story of Bale is a dramatic illustration of that class fragmentation and ideological incoherence. The provincial dominant group comprised the Christian Amhara minority supported by the native gentry. The latter by no means enjoyed equal access to the state, the principal custodian of material and information resources, and unequal entry benefited or harmed unequally. Perhaps emboldened by political changes in the Horn, it began to demand greater access to one-third of the land that had been theoretically designated to it, as elsewhere in the conquered territories, and a redistribution of administrative power, both of which were adamantly opposed by the settlers. Culturally cohesive, the settlers represented the state, wielding more political power (often translated into economic power) than their numbers would suggest. They jealously defended their corporate identity and interests. Splintered along ethnic and religious lines, these fractions of the dominant class competed among themselves for popular support and influence with the government. Constrained by the settlers' continued domination of the economic system and frustrated by the state's unwillingness to allow substantial devolution of power, the native gentry began to look for outside assistance, which Somalia was too willing to supply. As the dividing lines grew increasingly sharper, Fitawrari Abebe Gabre, the Amhara governor of the province, took the bold initiative of introducing mild reforms with the intention of nullifying Somali propaganda by soothing the native gentry. His efforts were, however, foiled by the settlers, who had the full support of state officials in Addis Ababa.

The policy that the governor devised was simple but quite ingenious, and its purpose was to establish at least a semblance of parity in the distribution of administrative power. The hierarchy of administrative posts in the province were to be distributed among the various ethnic components of the provincial population in such a way that for each Amhara officer there would be an Oromo or Somali deputy, or vice versa. It is improbable that this of itself would have broken the northerners' monopoly of power, yet it received enthusiastic support from the Oromo and Somali, much to the chagrin of the settlers.[24]

No sooner had the governor begun implementing his policy than he was faced with mounting opposition from settlers and petty functionaries which eventually led to his transfer and subsequent termination of the plan. The central aspect of Abebe's reform program was administrative, not political, although it suggested that theoretically the problem in Bale was as much political as economic. Yet the nonindigenous privileged group viewed it as posing an imminent threat to the status quo and began an organized and highly orchestrated campaign to preempt it. The sins of the governor were catalogued: he was accused of having irresponsibly replaced Christian officials with illiterate Muslims who could only "sign with their thumbs." And by appointing untrustworthy Muslims who, it claimed, were sympathetic to Islamic Somalia, the governor had imperiled the security of the country. The settlers cried that the Muslims had grown so aggressive and abusive that they had begun to take away lands belonging to Christians; they also expressed deep resentment at the "equal treatment" afforded to those who they thought were destined to remain "hewers of wood and drawers of water." Ironically they reported that Abebe's "misguided policy" had triggered a political crisis which threatened to "dismantle the fabric of a harmonious community," and unless resolved through the revocation of the plan, would ultimately cause a total breakdown in public order. Reports of increased tension and even of open armed conflict were relentlessly transmitted to Addis Ababa.[25] These unverified stories stirred enough concern to cause the removal of the governor.

Fitawrari Worku Enque Selassie, a Shewan Amhara who replaced Abebe, reversed his predecessor's policy and became a staunch supporter of the settlers. Prejudicial and arrogant toward the indigenous population, which he often contemptuously called "thoughtless nomads," he immediately restored settler confidence. But in reassuring a nervous community he alienated the local people, especially the gentry; the Somali and Oromo loathed him, whereas settlers liked and trusted him. The Worku years were characterized by administrative disorganization and increasing social polarization.

These inconsistent administrative policies illustrate the highly complex and often contradictory pressures placed on the state as a result both of settler interests and the demands of the indigenous population. Viewed in the context of imperial structures of power, Abebe's reformist measures were no more than window dressing, but were serious enough not only to infuriate the dominant groups in the province but also to create some anxiety at the center. The settlers and their allies in Addis Ababa, rightly or wrongly, regarded Abebe's measures not merely as technical or administrative but political, for the implementation of such a policy at the provincial level would have violated the existing pattern of social relations in southern Ethiopia. The evolution and pattern of social relations in the south reflected the relative power, interests, alliances, and conflicts of all those social forces embedded in the structures of the state.

It was, then, the convergence of settler, landlord, and state interests that actually aborted Abebe's plan. The real problem was that general state policy was inseparable from the interests of the local ruling groups. Since the province's incorporation into the empire-state, production under stable conditions had been ensured via the settlers; they were the administrators, security agents, and custodians of state interests. That has always been the unwritten state policy in conquered territories. Hence, whereas the state was fearful that Abebe's scheme might set a dangerous precedent in the southern regions, the settlers saw in it an even more sinister challenge of "them or us," and by calling upon their traditional protector, the state, they succeeded in aborting it. This was all the easier because absentee landlords, who comprised 15 percent of landowners, and many holders of strategic positions in Addis Ababa buttressed the settlers' position. Abebe's removal was meant to safeguard these overlapping and mutually reinforcing interests.

By revoking Abebe's measures the state only undermined its own position. It failed to coopt or appease the restless elements of the gentry that Somalia was aggressively coaxing. They began to desert it in increasing numbers, some turning to banditry and others moving to Mogadishu to work for the Somali government. In the growing crisis, petty officials recommenced their nefarious activities, which the governor had tried, with some success, to curtail. They gave more ammunition to agitators and dissidents. The situation was ripe for external exploitation.

Somali irredentism

Peasant fury might have exploded spontaneously, but the revolt could scarcely have sustained itself with such intensity and for such an extended period of time without Somalia's assistance. The Somali Democratic Republic helped incite the revolt, and it armed, trained, and financed the rebels to achieve its expansionist goals.

By rejecting the inherited colonial boundaries then legitimized by the Charter of the Organization of African Unity (OAU), Somalia wrapped itself in a tangled web of regional conflicts, especially with Ethiopia. Since the foundation in 1943 of the Somali Youth Club, an organization that changed its name to the Somali Youth League (SYL) in 1947, a cardinal aim of the nationalists has been the creation of a state incorporating all Somali-populated territories in the Horn. When the Prime Minister of newly independent Somalia, himself a founding member of the league, made the following declaration, his government was only translating a party slogan into a state policy: "The government of a free Somali state has a special duty towards its countrymen across the border who have a common cultural heritage and origin, and who live, against their will, under a system of government which is not of their choosing."[26] A unified Somali state would then have included not only the former British and Italian Somalilands which constitute the present republic, but also the three territories of Djibouti, the northeastern district of Kenya, and the Ogaden, including a section of southeastern Ethiopia – an extensive area that is not entirely inhabited by Somali but which the nationalists referred to as Western Somalia. Abutting the republic and with a population estimated to be close to one million, the Ogaden became the focal point of Somali irredentism. Deriving its name from the largest clan that inhabits it, the Ogaden plateau (an autonomous region since 1987) is an arid, almost desolate country; covering about 200,000 square kilometers (125,000 square miles) of land that is believed to contain copious natural resources including gas, its sheer size was sufficient to give it prominence in Somali consciousness. Ethiopia gained control of it in 1948 from the British, who in 1954 also relinquished the Haud, an open plateau of about 40,000 square kilometers (25,000 square miles) stretching from Hargeysa to the Ogaden plains in the south and Harer in the west. These territorial acquisitions took place in the face of much protest from the local population. In the first decade of Somalia's independence that protest turned into armed challenge drawing the new state into a war that it was ill equipped to win.

The Ogaden question is of a dual nature: while, on the one hand, it involved the right to self-determination of an oppressed national minority in an empire-state, on the other it was simply a territorial dispute between two sovereign states. To justify their territorial claims, the state nationalists frequently invoked the right to self-determination, yet they arrogated to themselves both the right and the responsibility of not only setting their kinsmen free from "colonial bondage," but also of reconstituting a nation that, they argued, had been fractured by imperialists. On more than one occasion, they went far beyond political agitation to dislodge the Ethiopian state from its southeastern periphery. One such military attempt took place in 1964 following a rebellion the Somali government incited but which the Ethiopians easily quashed since it remained "sporadic and localized, lacking coordination and direction."[27] The invasion was likewise beaten off, and the

Ogadeni were placed under martial rule with the Third Division of the Ethiopian army permanently stationed in their midst. It would take another thirteen years before the expansionists made another disastrous attempt at acquiring "Western Somalia."

Meanwhile the Somali state concentrated on fueling peasants' suppressed grievances by daily broadcasting inflammatory propaganda in Oromifa and Somali. The principal focus was Bale, where the Ethiopian government's ill-timed and ill-implemented fiscal policies and the corrupt practices of its agents served the Somali purpose too well. Up to that point resistance had been passive as peasants vainly petitioned the state for legal redress. But as it became clear that landlords would close ranks with peasants, and that the Somali state would support armed defiance, bandits, disgruntled petty officials, ambitious men of titles and property, and heavily indebted and much abused ordinary people readily responded to such agitation and call to arms. Popular defiance was still far from being spontaneous; it actually unfolded through three stages.

The geography of revolt

From banditry to organized resistance

The revolt was spatially quite limited in its origin and only with added impetus from Somalia did it slowly spread across the whole province, spilling over into another. Taking advantage of government inefficiency, some inconvenienced individuals helped in mobilizing latent discontent first at the village and then at the district levels. These pockets of uncoordinated resistance eventually coalesced into a provincial uprising that reached its peak in the years 1966–68.

The rebellion started near Afker in the district of El Kere under the leadership of a bandit named Kahin Abdi of the Rer Afghab. Kahin was well known for harboring Somali nationalist sentiment and was frequently placed under surveillance. Finally in June 1963, tired of harassment and wounded by his son's detention for alleged tax default, he openly defied the state by becoming an outlaw of the Robin Hood type. He was able to attract a large following that soon began to hit at government installations and sites. In September his armed band burned the small salt mine at Afker and two months later held Hargele under siege for two days. An unsuccessful government attempt to conciliate the populace by replacing the unpopular Amhara administrator of the subdistrict with a long-time Somali loyalist was accompanied by a week-long military operation to clear the area of "bandits." But no sooner had the troops returned to their barracks at Neghele than the rebels seized Lebashilindi and Chireti while threatening others. Buoyed by these easy victories, they began to press on for the total withdrawal of state organs from the entire district.

The resistance could no longer be characterized as banditry, for the intentions of the rebels had become manifestly clear. It was to become part of *Somaalinnimo* or Somali community, an aspiration that the promise of Somalia's independence had helped strengthen. Kindred people live on both sides of the frontier, thus facilitating interaction and comparison of living conditions, and in the buoyant atmosphere of independence, life across the border seemed better. A national state also appeared to guarantee ethnocultural sovereignty. Thus, the rebels wished to sever their links with the Ethiopian state by refusing to pay tax and other levies, refusing to sell cattle, sheep, goats, and other products to government representatives, and by referring interclan disputes to Somali institutions on the other side of the border.[28]

By the middle of 1964 they had successfully mobilized the pastoralists in the district when Kahin Abdi was replaced by Sheikh Mohammed Abdi Nur Takani, another prominent defector.[29] Only three groups remained loyal to the state, many of their members serving in the militia throughout the crisis.[30] These were the Dube, Gherrimero and Gherri, riverine farmers along the Waib–Genale rivers. The reason for their behavior may thus lie in the well-known antipathy between nomads and agriculturalists, but there was a cultural dimension to it. Of Bantu origin and darker in pigmentation, they are believed to be descendants of slaves[31] or *adona*, a Somali term that other clansmen used to identify them. Though linguistically and religiously assimilated, they have been objects of ridicule and social discrimination. Therefore, the resistance they saw not as emancipatory but rather as perpetuating the historical and cultural conditions of their oppression, and they chose to oppose it. The Ethiopian government armed them for that purpose. But neither their loyal service nor the death of Abdi Nur in a skirmish at Yed had any significant impact on the fate of the movement, for popular defiance had already spread to Wabe and Delo.

As in El Kere, it was bandits and disloyal officials who initiated the resistance in those two districts. In Wabe, the most distinguished deserter was Haji Isahaaq Mohammed Daddi of the Raiytu, a senior intelligence officer in Bale and Neghele–Borana. In 1961 he was implicated in the murder of a rival, an Amhara settler, and fled to Mogadishu to avoid arrest.[32] From there, Isahaaq established lines of communication with three bandits in Wabe – Hussien Bunni, Aliye Daddi, and Ismi Hissu aba Washah.[33] With arms generously flowing from Somalia under the auspices of the Western Somalia Liberation Front (WSLF), an organization of Ethiopian exiles from the Ogaden and with which the defector became associated, the bandits banded together under Hussien Bunni and began to incite the peasants. They were not disappointed. Unrest in Delo also grew perceptibly in scale following the desertion of several men, especially the village judge, Balambaras Wako Lugo, between September and October 1964. Wako's defection was occasioned by the longstanding rivalry between himself and Fitawrari Gelchu Togie, a subdistrict administrator. The two men accused each other of abetting the Somali cause, and Wako seems to have enjoyed more popular support, but he was the loser, for his archrival was the more trusted agent. Subsequently, his home was ransacked and most of his livestock confiscated; he made his way to Mogadishu, from where he would emerge as the second most important leader in the expanding insurgency. Such personal rivalries caused administrative paralysis while encouraging defiance.

The government tried to stem the insurgency by offering "liberalized arrangements" under which expropriated property might be reclaimed and tax arrears settled. Moreover, in a desperate attempt to drive a wedge between peasants and landlords allying with them, the emperor declared that the gentry of Bale would be "allotted one-third of the land like the *balabbats* in other regions." He further promised that the tax arrears for the years 1953–62 when paid in full would be used for the construction of roads under the supervision of a special board.[34] The governor's uncompromising will to collect arrears in combination with the extractive activities of subordinates steeped in corruption foiled those gestures, however. Even those peasants of the highlands who had thus far remained relatively tranquil became increasingly defiant at the inducement of rebel agitation. Under Worku Enque Selassie's heavy-handed administration conditions rapidly deteriorated, the state dismally failing to steal the initiative from its opponents. The eruption of intercommunal warfare in neighboring Sidamo and its inept mishandling only multiplied its woes. The civil strife had a catalytic effect on popular unrest in the two provinces.

Intercommunal strife: the widening base

Intercommunal strife that arose from demographic factors, ritualized customs, and conflicting social values was endemic in the lower Omo and particularly in Sidamo. The imposition of political boundaries and new administrations in the nineteenth century further complicated traditional interraiding for livestock among nomads and pastoralists by restricting access to water and pastures. Spatial confinement ineluctably led to overgrazing, seriously dislocating the fragile balance between the environment and its inhabitants, and it tended to intensify frictions and feuds that local officials habitually revived and influenced through levies and bribes.[35] Governmental intervention to end one aspect of the recurring conflict helped to fuel the unrest in Bale.

The most pressing problem for the government was the antagonism between the Boran and Somali. During the Italian invasion of 1935 the latter had moved across the Genale Doriya into Oddo, from where they penetrated farther west into Liban and Dirre. As these nomads did not recognize geographical frontiers but simply responded to the seasonal rhythm of grazing limits for their livestock, the Boran of Ethiopia, numbering about 300,000, found themselves constantly pushed farther west from their original habitat. This normally provoked violent clashes between the two and was frequently the source of a wider civil strife in the region, directly affecting intergovernmental relations. In the early 1940s, British colonial officials in Kenya, where other segments of Boran and Somali lived, believed that the best way to resolve the problem was to drive the Somali back across the Genale river.[36] But the transitional Ethiopian government was hesitant because it did not want to disappoint the Ogadeni, whose territory it wanted to obtain from the British. Actually, that lingering policy was shattered only in the 1960s.

The coincidence of banditry with communal violence in an area where civil administration was fast deteriorating finally persuaded a reluctant government to implement a policy that was inspired by a neighborly colonial regime. A bandit by the name of el Kebir Hussien who may have had a link with the rebels in El Kere raised the alarm, convincing long suspicious officials that the Somali were not only the major cause of the periodic turmoil in Sidamo but politically also the most troublesome group in southern Ethiopia. They saw the removal of the Somali from Borana as the essential precondition for the restoration of law and order. But before plans for resettlement could even be envisioned, the Boran and Gudji – perhaps with the tacit encouragement of some local officers – unexpectedly and treacherously attacked their traditional enemy in October 1964. Perhaps a good half of the Somali fled in panic, losing many lives and hundreds of livestock while they crossed the Genale. Also expelled were the Rayitu, who identified themselves more closely with their Somali coreligionists than with their kinsmen, the Boran and Gudji, whom they despised as nonbelievers.

Subsequent events showed that the government had erred, for its actions coupled with official misconduct helped to stimulate the very revolt they were designed to avert. In Filtu, a border area in Delo, the "refugees" were confined to a kind of "protected hamlet" for constant supervision. Their appeals for a return to their homes were ignored. As their plight worsened under harassing officials, they slowly abandoned passive protest and drifted toward Mogadishu for arms and training. One such group of forty men, which included Girazmatch Cherri Gutu and his brother, Wako Gutu, left for Somalia three months after its arrival in Filtu.[37] Following their return in early 1965 and under the leadership of Wako Gutu, these men played a critical role in organizing what came to be known as the Bale Rebellion.

Escalation of armed conflict and repression

A nucleus of aggrieved but militant persons initiated the armed conflict in El Kere. Similar groups did the same in Wabe and Delo; both by persuasion and intimidation, they built support in their respective localities, transforming individual and communal grievances into generalized discontent. There was no coordination among them, and only after the arrival of Wako Gutu did they create a loose organizational structure of which Wako himself became the supreme commander, with Wako Lugo as his immediate lieutenant. From there on skirmishes and pitched battles – too numerous to be recounted in detail – were fought at frequent intervals.

For strategic and propaganda reasons towns became the initial targets of attack. These were fairly small – no more than a few hundred people – but their symbolic importance far surpassed their size; the administrative officials, police, and settlers were all congregated there. The first rebel action took place on February 8, 1965 when a small force under Aliye Chirri overran Oberso, looting the only church and burning state documents. The Christian residents fled to Mena and Neghele–Borana.[38] Three days later, Wako Gutu himself descended on Bidire with some 250 men. Resistance was stiffer than expected because the police and militia were reinforced with troops from Neghele; the town fell on February 18. These easy victories struck terror among the settlers and officialdom while stimulating popular defiance. From there on, it spread like the proverbial bush fire. The police, who rarely exceeded ten men in each post, and 1,400 territorials lacked sufficient motivation, efficiency, and firepower to halt it.

A belligerent but alarmed governor challenged the state to act decisively, for temporary measures were neither effective nor desirable. Having admonished his superiors for inaction and vacillation, he wrote with typical arrogance that "an ignorant and shortsighted people bent upon fostering outlawry will refrain from such crimes ... " only when it is made to bear the full weight of the state's coercive machinery. He politely reminded the emperor that failure to act in time would allow internal security to disintegrate and "the umbilical cord connecting the rulers and the ruled to break down." To restore order by suppressing the "ill-conceived rebellion" and to ensure tranquillity in the future, he claimed, the state had to station a large military consignment permanently in the province.[39] His overall view was, of course, very much influenced by the settlers, with whom he worked closely; like them, he refused to see the problem as fundamentally political, and was insensitive to the economic grievances of the peasants. His perception (or misperception) of the movement strongly dictated his chauvinistic approach to the problem and the solutions he proposed to the state.

If the state was too hesitant to deploy its armed forces, it may have been because of ignorance and fear. It was too fearful that any precipitous military action might lead to a guerrilla war the like of which had already tied up one division of its army. Yet, it did not make a genuine effort to resolve the problem peacefully; whereas it attempted to mollify the peasants of Gojjam by sending many delegations (chapter 6), not one such mission was dispatched to Bale. This is probably because the state did not fully grasp the depth of popular antipathy. The leaders appear to have fallen under the illusion that they were dealing with bandits who, though sponsored by the Somali state, had neither substantial popular support nor cohesion among themselves. Field accounts that singled out the Somali as the principal troublemakers may have reinforced this false perception. Though Governor Worku repeatedly warned of the serious implications of the unrest to

144

national security, there was an alarming gap between what he reported and the realities of the situation. In his view, only a few traitorous and self-seeking individuals like Isahaaq had conspired with the Somali state to mislead a section of an otherwise loyal and obedient, but ignorant, populace.[40] Whatever its reasons might have been, by being too cautious, the state let conditions deteriorate. While half-hearted measures were inadequate to suppress the insurgents, they were sufficient to exacerbate the conflict.

Two events finally convinced the authorities to change their approach. In November 1965 and March 1966 respectively, two district administrators, along with many police and territorials, were killed. The government was stunned by its successive setbacks and by the steady march of the rebels, who had brought more than three-fifths of the province under their partial control. Even the provincial capital, Goba, was no longer safe, for it was attacked twice in the intervening months. The rebellion had become a mass movement, posing "a threat to national stability and security." Consequently, in December 1966 the government put Borana and all the districts of Bale (except Fasil) under martial rule.[41] Two army brigades consisting of 4,500 men and augmented by police, territorials, militia, and volunteers were placed under the command of the new chief administrator for the prosecution of the war. The military administration was empowered with the authority to detain suspects without trial, restrict people's movements, impose collective fines, disarm the peasantry, and even to confiscate the property of defiant citizens. The army, operating out of Neghele in the south and Robe in the north, had as its primary tasks to cut off main rebel supply routes, to close their infiltration points from Somalia, and to infiltrate their rear bases.[42]

Partial success was achieved early in 1967. In less than three months the resistance in Borana was extinguished, but the one in Bale continued for another three years. The army was able to seal off the Genale Doriya that separated Bale from Sidamo, confining the Degodia and Gherri, the two principal Somali clans in the latter province, to a narrow strip of territory. It was assisted by the Boran and Gudji. Encircled and running out of provision and ammunition, el Kebir Hussien, head of the Degodia and principal leader of the resistance, surrendered in March 1967 and was immediately commissioned to organize a counterguerrilla force that would infiltrate the insurgents' network for information and sabotage. The new title and sizeable number of cattle offered to him for inducement were too alluring to refuse. Among the many factors that prevented a similar sweeping victory in Bale were administrative ineptness and venality, which reached its apogee in the midst of crisis; conflicts between the regular troops and the territorials, who failed to match the high motivation of the rebels; and geography that combined with primitive infrastructure to hamper troop mobility and efficiency.

The actions of petty functionaries whose main interest was to dip into the pockets of others and the public coffers nullified government efforts to restore order expeditiously. They exploited emergency laws to confiscate property and to amass wealth. Rifles and ammunition which the central government sent for distribution among loyal citizens were usually sold or exchanged for handsome gifts.[43] Whether the transaction was purely commercial or political, it undoubtedly benefited the insurgents, who were able to augment their arms' supply with purchased and captured weapons. These functionaries also turned out on market days, using them ostensibly for spying and interrogation but really for harassment and exaction. Former rebels who were drafted as administrative auxiliaries often disguised themselves as guerrillas and pillaged homesteads in order to discredit the insurgents, whom the government characterized as bandits. But the looters failed utterly to deny their former comrade in arms popular support.

Similarly, punitive police measures helped to terrorize even the quiescent peasants. In other words, "the coercion intended to quell dissidence had a contrary effect of enhancing discontent."[44] Some of the more common methods of punishment were beatings, burning the body with red-hot metals, suspending upsidedown from poles or trees, disemboweling, extracting finger and toe nails, and inserting needles into finger nails. Villages were burned and animals slaughtered or appropriated. Mosques were frequently raided or desecrated, and religious leaders intimidated, detained, or tortured. This brutal campaign, waged in some cases without even the knowledge of the authorities in Addis Ababa, was intended both to punish those who allegedly threw in their lot with the rebels and to intimidate potential recruits. The terror benefited the rebels as peasants flocked to them for protection.[45]

Topography was another major handicap. Much of Bale is a guerrilla fighter's dream, but a nightmare to a conventional army. A peripheral province, Bale is a vast region sparsely inhabited by a semimobile population that shared a long border with a hostile state. The vastness and remoteness of the region, the scattered population, and the extreme dearth of communication and transportation facilities were favorable to guerrillas but severely hampered the army's efforts. Three of the five district administrative centers were only accessible by air, and the all-weather road connecting Goba with Addis Ababa via Shashamane, the only one in the province, was not completed until 1969, the year in which the telephone service was introduced. The army was not familiar with the terrain and local cultural mores. Yet, rarely did the leadership respond imaginatively to these challenges. There was no attempt to win the hearts and minds of the people through administrative and economic reforms, and while no permanent garrisons had been established in either Delo or Genale, the army carried out no sustained attacks on rebel strongholds.

Organizational and logistical inadequacies further undermined the proficiency of state forces. Differential treatment affected morale and loyalty. Not only were the troops better paid, but they received such benefits as rations, uniforms, and medical services. The territorials, militia, and volunteers, who were poorly equipped with obsolete rifles, received none of these and were irregularly paid between ten and fifteen dollars – less than a third of what the regulars received. They were left to fend for themselves, and the burden of pilferage was borne by the population. There was a festering discontent, and desertions among the volunteers were quite frequent.[46] Moreover, there was a noticeable lack of cooperation, even sabotage, among the leaders of the various branches of the unified command. Even though the army drew up the plans for combat, the territorials often acted on their own initiative. The commanding generals were constantly at odds with each other and with the governor. There was competition for power between the governor and the army commander in particular, and between military and civilian personnel in general.[47] The governor, himself a military man, frequently interfered in the work of the commander, and the latter's normal reaction was insubordination.

The weaknesses of the state were thus largely responsible for the virtual stalemate that was only broken with the arrival of an innovative and indefatigable governor at the end of 1968. General Wolde Selassie Bereka soon realized that his predecessors' policy of "meting out punishment commensurate with the faults of a people blindly set upon disturbing law and order"[48] was both alluring and illusory. Instead he concentrated on resuscitating the morale of his forces by minimizing differential privileges, weeding out corrupt officials, rewarding the loyal while wooing the not so loyal elements of the native gentry, and more importantly, establishing a new rapport with the peasantry, one based on reciprocity and mutual support.[49] The measures were courageous and the results equally dramatic.

Through terror and reconciliation the governor succeeded in killing the revolt within a year. Ground operations, augmented by aerial strikes, began in Wabe, which formed the weaker flank and where the rebels had already lost substantial ground. The few hundred remnants were easily eliminated. The task in Delo proved much more difficult, and fighting for the balance of the year was limited to this area. Shielded by the mountains, ravines, and thick forests, and supported by the villagers, about two to three thousand fighters under Wako Gutu had secured a solid sanctuary at the confluence of the Mena and Waib rivers. The governor introduced a series of measures to break their backbone. First, a state of emergency was declared in Delo, El Kere, and Genale in August 1969. And since Robe and Goro were far away from the zone of operations, the army opened additional bases on the forest fringes as in Mena (Meslo), cleared roads, and with British aid, constructed a bridge over the Genale Doriya to facilitate troop mobility. Though the governor was extraordinarily careful not to antagonize peasants, villagers who persisted in their support of the insurgency were made to bear heavy bombardment and collective monetary fines. One such fine of ETH $50,000 was imposed on the Rer Afghab and Biddisilin, although there is no evidence that they obeyed.[50] Additionally, Wolde Selassie raised the number of the militia to nearly four thousand men, a large segment of which he put under el

147

Kebir Hussien, charging it with patrolling the border. Despite their unhappy relationship with the army, these men played a key role in siege operations because they knew the terrain very well. Though heavily recruited from the settler community, many of them were indistinguishable from the rest of the population in terms of the material conditions of their life; but ideologically and psychologically, they belonged to a different species – the dominant stratum of Ethiopian society – and so they served the state with dedication and distinction.[51] Overall, the forces of coercion had improved their record enormously. It does not seem likely that the governor was trying to claim undue credit for himself when he wrote that "had the forces stationed in Bale and Borana fought in concord as they do now, the bandits would have been destroyed and peace restored in a much shorter time."[52]

The revolt fizzled out because of internal and external factors. At a time when the Ethiopian government intensified the military offensive, Somalia terminated its support for the rebels. Hence, as the year drew to a close, it became abundantly clear that the war had become one of attrition that the state could afford to fight but the guerrillas could not. Having cornered the hard-core fighters to Arena Bulik, the armed forces carried out coordinated and sustained assaults from the air and ground. Aerial bombardment was not limited to guerrilla sanctuaries, but blanketed whole villages. We have no knowledge of the quantity and quality of bombs dropped, but we do know that the villages of Melka Jimma, Melka Gersi, ElMedo, Bey, and Hawo were strafed time and again, and the livestock were decimated. The human toll steadily mounted, and food became scarce.[53] At this critical stage the new military leaders of Somalia, preoccupied with problems at home and anxious to establish a rapprochement with Ethiopia and the OAU, actualized the spirit of détente that the government of Prime Minister Ibrahim Egal had initiated. As a quid pro quo for Ethiopia's recognition of the new government, they disassociated themselves from the insurgents. Isolated from both their internal and external sources of support, many of Wako's deputies unilaterally accepted the offer for a ceasefire and general amnesty. By January 1970 the rebel force had dwindled so drastically that Wako Gutu had no more than two hundred men under his command, now confined to Welabu, to the south of Arena Bulik. In mid February, Wako Gutu's family, which included four wives and twelve children, and the families of other prominent rebels surrendered.[54] On their heels, on February 23, 1970, Wako Lugo gave himself up, and with great relief the commander announced: "The high point of this week's achievement is the surrender of Girazmatch Wako Lugo, who is no less important in stature than Wako Gutu, and the capture of the latter's depot."[55] Then through Wako's mediation, the rebel chief submitted on March 28, 1970. Again the army commander, who had personally conducted the negotiation, reported exuberantly: "The most significant event of this week is the surrender of the bandit leader, a self-styled general, Wako Gutu. His submission has brought to an end the five years of fighting that has cost a colossal waste of lives and resources."[56] On his arrival at the Goba airstrip in April, Wako was personally welcomed by the governor, an honor rarely given to ex-"bandits." Three months later he saw the emperor who, after a patronizing lecture on Ethiopianity and loyalty, granted him a new title and some land. The movement had been effectively shattered; without a base, supplies, and leaders, the remaining fighters simply dispersed, hundreds fleeing to Mogadishu, where they formed part of a community of Ethiopian refugees that called itself the Western Somalia Harekat. Why such a localized uprising survived for over six years cannot be comprehended without a scrutiny of the quality of its leadership, a subject to which we shall now turn.

The organization of revolt

Both in its origin and the social composition of its leadership the Bale rebellion was primarily a reaction to local needs and pressures. It was organized primarily, but not exclusively, by the local people. Successive Somali governments referred to it as the United Liberation Front of Western Somalia (ULFWS) or Western Somalia Liberation Front (WSLF), implying that it was part of a pan-Somali movement. The Ethiopian government dismissed its leaders as a gang of mercenaries. Both characterizations overlook the essentially indigenous roots of the revolt, diminishing its legitimacy and authenticity. If the insurgents were amenable to external dictates, it was because of the practical needs for weapons and rear bases. The problem facing them, and especially the Oromo elements, was how to make their position palatable to the Somali expansionist state and acceptable to their own people. Not surprisingly the alliance was shaky; it was frequently challenged by the competing interests of the parties, which, in turn, had deleterious effects on the movement.

With the exception of the "Eritrean war of liberation" and the current resistance in Tigrai, the Bale rebellion is the longest peasant struggle in contemporary Ethiopian history, and its longevity was as much due to the resolve and competence of the insurgents as to the ineptness of the state. The latter erred by escalating the conflict clumsily and unimaginatively. A poor command structure and woefully inadequate logistical system, a lack of motivation in the troops, and a cumbersome bureaucracy all combined to undermine its efforts further and were instrumental in prolonging the conflict. On the other hand, convinced of the justness of their cause and operating among a sympathetic and supportive peasantry, the insurgents skillfully capitalized upon the weaknesses of the state, thereby amply compensating for their technical and material inferiority. For more than four years the rebels withstood the state offensive because they had popular support, strong will, sufficient skill in warfare, and the generous assistance of another national state.

It was the insurgent force that began as a curious mixture of bandits and reluctant rebels in El Kere that gradually transformed itself into a formidable guerrilla army functioning under the shadow of an external mentor. The command structure of the insurgents resembled any conventional military organization in which ranking officers were hierarchically tied to one another. Sitting at the top of the pyramid were General Wako Gutu, who headed the western zone in Delo and Colonel/General (?) Hussien Bunni, leader of the eastern zone in Wabe. The other unit chiefs were Colonel Abdullahi Megen of El Kere and Colonel Mohammed Ali Rube in Genale.[57] A complete list of officers is unavailable, but Ethiopian government records show that 2 generals, 16 colonels, 44 majors, 32 captains, and 48 lieutenants had surrendered and/or been killed.[58] Nor is it known how many men each leader commandeered, but it may not have exceeded 2,000 at any time. With the core guerrilla force holding steady at 4,000–5,000 men, the total may have fluctuated between 4,000 and 10,000 in the years 1964–70.[59]

The selection of leaders was an intricate process involving traditional authority, local cultural codes, and a foreign power. The most important qualifications were social background and the ability to command influence and a following in one's community and locality. On that basis and their performance in the training camps, the Somali government elevated either former bandits of reputation or men of traditional status by awarding them military ranks. These men then exercised discretion in the selection of their assistants, theoretically in consultation with clan elders and tribal and religious leaders. If there were any mechanisms of a selection process, they must have been fairly informal, with the opinions of men of status and authority carrying greater weight. This is why most of the high-ranking officers were *burkas* and clan heads.

It is now easier to explain Wako's eventual rise to supreme leadership. Of *balabbat* origin, Wako could appeal to gentry and peasantry alike; bilingual, he could claim to represent both the Oromo and Somali. As a young man in his early thirties, he had received three months' military training in Somalia.[60] Thus, enjoying a traditional base of authority, he possessed new skills in the art of warfare and military leadership, both crucial to peasant insurgents. It needs to be stressed, however, that although Wako was the most widely acknowledged leader by rebels as well as by the two hostile states, it is difficult to measure accurately the extent and effectiveness of his authority. This is because the highly decentralized set up of rebel organization does not reflect a chain of command within the framework of a unified strategy.

Rebel leadership not only lacked full autonomy from the Somali state or its surrogate, the WSLF, but was territorially segmented, and this segmentation reflected the complex interplay of demographic, historical, cultural, and political factors. The Oromo and Somali participants, who were engaged in different modes of economic activity, exhibited varying degrees of ethnic and social consciousness and an intricate set of objectives. The interaction between ethnic, local, and external factors was reflected both in the genesis and the organizational structure of the revolt.

That structure bore striking parallels with the Kenyan peasant revolt of

1953–56 commonly known as Mau Mau. Mau Mau had a certain duality: Kikuyu ethnicity versus Kenyan nationalism; the Kikuyu primary goal of land reclamation versus nationalist aspirations for independence and freedom; and magicoreligious beliefs versus secular, rational ideas. Moreover, although the revolt had a translocal and transethnic organization known as the Kenya Defense Council headed by the enigmatic Field Marshal Dedan Kimathi, localism was its predominant feature. Fighters of the Land and Freedom Army were more strongly tied to their local leaders than to the wider organization, and the chief leader could not easily dictate policies unless he received voluntary support of the lower echelon of the leadership.[61]

The Bale rebellion showed the same ideological ambiguity and as such was saddled with similar problems. The fire that set it alight originated in El Kere, but the revolt was by no means spontaneous. Only in time did locally based groups coalesce to form a province-wide movement. These localized groups grew into sizeable and relatively cohesive guerrilla units, each maintaining strong ties to its own leader and locality and cherishing its identity and relative independence. Fragmentation coincided with provincial, but not necessarily ethnic, division. Historical as well as existing realities determined this territorial attachment. First, most peasants were clannish and therefore reluctant to move away from their own villages, and in spite of shared interests vis-à-vis the state and landlordism, they were primarily concerned with their own welfare and the autonomy of their villages. The general tendency on the part of the local elites, then turned guerrillas, to protect their traditional base of power and indeed to compete for higher status and authority only reinforced this parochialism. Second, there was no problem with Somali mobility and readiness for armed struggle, but the segmentary politics of pastoralism was in conflict with the militarized structure of the leadership. Clan members constantly pressed for more discussion, consultation, and delegation of authority, demands that contradicted rebel organizational structure. Clan decentralization was incompatible with military centralization. Third, from the practical, military point of view, it would have been easier to wage a guerrilla war in one's own locale or region, where the terrain was more familiar and the people generally supportive. At home there could be greater affinity between fighters and producers, which made recruitment, supply, and security easier. But the very factors – ties of kinship and locality – that made this possible also obstructed the formation and operation of a wider, extra-local organization. Only the Western Command Zone, which incorporated a large number of recruits from Sidamo, came closest to having a nonterritorial character, for it freely operated in Delo and parts of El Kere and Genale. There, as in Kenya, the size of guerrilla forces as well as the mixed character of the leadership "tended to diminish, though not eliminate, the importance of territorial segmentation" among the insurgents. Like Field Marshal Dedan Kimathi, General Wako Gutu, an Arsi from Sidamo, transcended the "territorial identification," but this, too, may have been a political liability, for some regarded him as "the man from beyond the big river [Genale]," an outsider.[62]

A corollary of territorial segmentation was the decentralization of power and authority. The original pattern of organization in which ties between leader, followers, and locality were prominent was preserved throughout the conflict. Decentralization was reinforced by the varying degree of loyalty to one's own constituency on the one hand, and to the Somali state on the other. There is reason to think that while the Somali lowlanders may have owed greater allegiance to the Somali state than to their own organization, the atti- tude of the Oromo was discernibly ambivalent; Oromo leaders were appre- hensive of, if not antagonistic toward, Somali motives and tried to remain accountable to their constituency. Whereas leaders like Kahin Abdi and Hussien Bunni may have sought legitimacy in either the Somali state or even the WSLF, for the Oromo leaders the legitimacy of their authority arose pri- marily from local recognition, and its effectiveness rested upon the loyalty of local guerrilla fighters. If those fighters recognized Wako's authority, it was only because of their leaders' voluntary affiliation to the central leadership. As was true of Dedan Kimathi, it is doubtful whether Wako Gutu, whose authority was partly legitimized by the Somali state, could have obtained their allegiance without the consent of local leaders.[63] Vertical segmentation of power and authority, then, meant that horizontal ties between the prin- cipal chiefs were far less significant than vertical loyalty binding guerrillas and their territorial leaders. It is not surprising, then, that there was little or no centralized planning and unity of action. There were no joint operations between the two command zones, and territorial units rarely coordinated their activities. Consequently it was far easier for state forces to isolate one district from the other, as, for example, Delo from Wabe. Localism provided a considerable degree of self-sufficiency, and decentralization may have facil- itated greater "flexibility of maneuver and individual initiative," but they prevented the emergence of an ideologically cemented and militarily more effective force; they were two of the major organizational frailties.

The main strength of the insurgents lay in their popular support. They were solidly rooted in the masses. Although the majority of peasants did not take an active part in the fighting, they were prepared to harbor and supply insurgents. The Somali government occasionally provided guerrillas with an undetermined amount of rice, corn, sugar, and cooking oil. It also reportedly paid between 400 and 750 Somali shillings to the senior leaders. But the main- stay of the rebellion was the peasants. They supplied cereals, milk, butter, honey, and pack animals, and furnished information about the movements of state forces, sanctioning Mao Zedong's dictum that the peasantry is for insurgent guerrillas what water is for fish.[64] The relationship between peasants and guerrillas should not be idealized, for neither was support total nor were the rebels entirely virtuous. There is evidence that guerrillas used coercion to recruit adults and that they behaved like brigands, demanding food, taxes, and tribute from villages.[65]

The insurgents used guerrilla tactics, which goes to explain the revolt's endurance. They avoided well-fortified posts and fixed fighting with a superior army. There was only one case in which the rebels engaged an estimated four thousand men in a running battle lasting four days.[66] Making use of concealment in a suitable terrain, their main tactic was hit-and-run raids and their principal targets were police stations and military convoys. Their effectiveness astounded the antagonist: "As a result of this unanticipated [good] performance by the rebels," wrote a perplexed brigade commander in Borana, "enormous damage was done to our troops; many lost their lives and many more were disabled. Thirty-two vehicles were destroyed. It was very difficult to understand."[67] This was repeated in Bale on an even larger scale, and bewildered officials looked for an alien or invisible hand. The Minister of Defense expressed his anxiety about communist influence unequivocally: "The manner the bandits operate in Bale, their aim, cruelty, and their impressive performance, exemplifies the communist credo and practice, which the rebels seem to have embraced like a matter of faith. This possible communist infiltration raises deep concern and deserves serious attention."[68] Good fighters the rebels were, but communist influence is hard to detect and was merely a figment of the official imagination.

Without the military training and sophisticated weapons that Somalia provided, the insurgents would not have been so effective in arousing the envy of the other side. Those peasants who traveled to Somalia during the first two years of the rebellion were introduced to the elements of guerrilla warfare and the use of such weapons as rifles, bombs, grenades, and machine guns. Most of the training was given at Luuq, not far from the Ethiopian border, lasting from three weeks to two months. More specialized training, which lasted over a year and in which as many as five hundred men may have been involved, was given between 1964 and 1965 at Gerewey, near Mogadishu. This training was in the use of heavier and more sophisticated weapons such as antipersonnel and antimechanized explosives, bazookas, mortars, land mines, and artillery, which were given freely to the rebels.[69] Both in its scope and method of warfare this was no ordinary rebellion in contemporary Ethiopian history; but it still has to be characterized as a typical peasant revolt in which the insurgents closely resembled what an eminent authority on popular movements and people's wars has called "roving rebels." Such rebels lack well-enunciated goals and base areas from which they could launch the protracted armed struggle without which a politicomilitary victory is unattainable.[70]

The question of ideology was just as crucial as the political and military question. Ethiopian officials saw the revolt as little more than an aberration of an ethnic movement that drew its inspiration mainly from Somali irredentism and Islamic fanaticism. One Ethiopianist thought it was a militant reaction against national oppression which gradually assumed a socialist orientation.[71] Neither view is wholly accurate: the first because it completely disregards objective conditions that gave rise to the revolt, and the second because it overestimates the qualitative aspects of the revolt – class consciousness and class struggle. That ethnic and religious parochialism, which may have limited popular consciousness, was a fundamental feature of the rebellion is certain, but this merely reflected the character of the Ethiopian state-society. Since the agrarian question in the multiethnic feudal state was intricately linked to the ethnic equation, agrarian grievances in the south highlighted the coincidence of class and ethnic oppression. From this view, the revolutionary aspect of the revolt was its persistent demands for the return of alienated land, lost dignity, and freedom. The revolt was still essentially restorationist, not revolutionary.

It was also a bifurcated movement that used religion to suppress internal fissions. Even though the more specific grievances centered around land and material security, a good number of the Somali insurgents unambiguously expressed their wish to be part of the Somali national state. That was basically a democratic demand, but it was tarnished by the Mogadishu nationalists' dream of obtaining a slice of Ethiopia. To achieve their objective they stirred ethnic sentiment by dramatizing the assumed continuity in Somali historical resistance against alien domination and its heroic symbols, the Imam Ahmed ibn Ibrahim al Ghazi (1506–43) and the Sayyid Mohammed Abdille Hassan.[72] Somali lyric poetry, continually aired over Radio Mogadishu, praised the celebrated leaders, and official propaganda immortalized them. The rallying cry was the liberation of Somalis from "black Abyssinian imperialism" and the eventual reconstitution of a fragmented nation.

One could not have mobilized Oromo peasants, of course, by appealing to Somali ethnic particularity. What is evident is that despite the religious confraternity between the Arsi and Somali clans, there was an underlying tension and incompatibility in goals. Oromo aspirations for cultural affirmation and land reclamation were not harmonious with pan-Somali sentiments and tendencies for secession. By appealing to their ethnic, linguistic, and religious distinctiveness from both the settlers and the dominant nationality in Ethiopia, the Somali state was able to fan the latent discontent of the indigenes; but since the multiethnic composition of the peasantry presented a major problem, it drew upon their religious unity to deemphasize the ethnic rift. Religion was used for reasons of ideological obfuscation, and it helped not only in camouflaging Somali motives but also in diluting the class dimension of the conflict.

Islam served as the ideological matrix of organization and mobilization, but as an ideology of emancipation, it failed explicitly because it was shrouded in hopeful messianism. In Islamic eschatology, as in the Judeo-Christian tradition, there are principles that justify rebellion as much as others legitimize authority and enforce submission to it. The Koran abounds with verses that support the "struggle against corruption and decadence." One such verse exhorts the believers: "O ye who have believed, fight the unbelievers who are near to you, and let them feel a rough temper in you, and know that Allah is with those who show piety" (K. 9:123). When religion sanctions the rejection of established authority, allegiance to it is called on to enlarge the scale of resistance. The mediating elements were local religious leaders. The provincial governor verbalized their vital role:

> They [the *sheikhs*] preach about *izbullahi* [Hizb Allah] and say that *izbullahi* means someone who does not submit to the rule of man. They scold and ridicule those who have remained loyal to the state and call them the people of *jehanem*. Since the preaching derives from their religion, the people have accepted it. Moreover, the *sheikhs* say that the times of the Amhara are over; that the Amhara will not pass this or that river, and if they did, they say, then we will burn our Koran in shame.[73]

The sheikhs and *kallus* validated the revolt by invoking the name of the venerated saint Hussien and by espousing millenarian ideas. They proclaimed the inevitable end of Christian settler domination and reminded the faithful of their obligation to support the uprising for a new order. They even raised the specter of a *jihad* (holy war), obliging their faithful followers to take up arms against "the infidel and debased rulers." Whereas nonparticipants were condemned to *jehanem* (hell), martyrs were guaranteed a place in heaven. Through the combined threat of eternal damnation and promise of salvation, the spiritual heads helped the insurgents to form a regional movement by surmounting clan and ethnic divisions and loyalties.

Religion confirmed the justness of the rebellion and lent substance to the belief that ultimately right would prevail over might. Rebels saw the eventual demise of settler domination and subsequent return of lands as a providential design. They appear to have believed that in their unequal struggle with the oppressor state, justice would prevail and that in the Horn, like in Vietnam, the powerful would be vanquished. In the words of the insurgents:

> We shall not surrender, for we have gone out for a *jihad* in God's cause. You have to remember that the conflict between us and you is just like that between the Vietnamese and the Americans. One of us may be destroyed, but we shall persevere in our struggle to regain our land. We would rather die than submit ourselves to you. Our struggle is gaining force like a gathering storm.[74]

Determination alone could not compensate for major weaknesses that faced the insurgency. Even though religion was useful in inciting and sustaining defiance, it was much less helpful in expanding the base of popular support. This is because Islam, unlike Christianity, has not been able to express itself institutionally at a national level despite its deep historical roots in the country. The consequence of this has been the lack of an enduring Islamic awareness cutting across regional, ethnic, and cultural barriers. Thus, with a restricted territorial base and festering internal tensions and without a secure rear base and dependable external ally, it appears that the destruction of the rebels was almost foreordained.

The price of revolt

At the end of the resistance a few concessions were made, but no fundamental changes in the organization of state and society. The foundations of the imperial state may have been shaken momentarily, but the status quo with its predatory culture remained unaltered.

If there were no rewards, what was the price of revolt? Little is known about the extent of human and material loss, for neither party to the conflict kept complete and reliable records. While former rebels could not offer any believable figures, government sources covering the period 1964–68 are meager and suspect, and those for 1968–70 inconclusive. According to these official sources the state had lost the incredibly low number of 54 men, as opposed to 871 for the rebels, and about five million ETH dollars.[75] In conflicts such as this one, truth is one of the main casualties. However, the important point is that underlying those sterile statistics was untold human suffering, which cannot be computed easily.

It was the peasants who suffered inordinately; they fought while producing, and as in all guerrilla wars, they did most of the fighting and endured much of the dying. The price of sheltering, concealing, and supporting rebels was also very high. State forces, often unable to retaliate directly against the elusive guerrillas, vented their wrath on the farmers by callously destroying their hamlets, animals, and crops. They slaughtered as many cattle, goats, and sheep as they could consume and turned over the rest to the state, which in turn auctioned them at abnormally low prices.[76] In the period 1968–70 alone, by official accounts, over 60,000 cattle (slightly over 4 percent of the livestock in Bale), 18,698 camels, 7,060 pack animals, and 22,215 sheep and goats were confiscated.[77]

The rebels were no more charitable, for they did not spare those who were reluctant or refused to throw in their lot with them. They robbed merchants, burned villages, violated women, and looted the property of peasants who refused to collaborate or were suspected of assisting the state. These acts of brigandage may have violated "the Somali warrior ethic."[78] They also treated the settler communities cruelly and indiscriminately.[79] Eyewitness accounts confirm that at the close of the conflict the countryside lay plundered and in ruins, and peasants were diseased, emaciated, and in rags.[80] Certainly not an unfamiliar sight in Ethiopia even under normal conditions, but the effects of the war were unmistakably apparent.

When it was all over the state treated the peasants with remarkable restraint and leniency, in marked contrast to its brutal actions in Tigrai in 1943. None of the rebel leaders was deported or incarcerated; on the contrary, many of them were allowed to retain their former titles and social positions. Wako Gutu, who was given the title of Girazmatch, became a wealthy man owning many livestock and plenty of land in his new village of Meda Welabu near Mena and enjoying considerable influence and prestige among the local people, who regarded him as their de facto administrator.

On the other hand, whereas a weak state was unable or unwilling to restrain its forces from brutalizing the already famished peasants of Tigrai, there was no similar looting, burning, and pillaging in Bale in the aftermath of revolt. Additionally, the state canceled all arrears in land taxes up to and including the year 1967.

The elevation of some of the indigenous people to administrative positions only bolstered the social position of the gentry and strengthened the state. The appointment of Major General Jagaama Kelo, an Oromo who together with Wolde Selassie Bereka coordinated the repression of the revolt, as provincial governor, and the promotion of a handful of indigenous elements[81] were more of a reward to loyal and faithful servants of "king and crown" than a genuine concession to sectarian sentiments. To be sure, such acts implicitly recognized the saliency of ethnicity, and in light of the earlier settler resistance to such appointments this was definitely a change; but the concessions were too meager, ineffectual, and short-lived. Once it was felt that conditions had returned to normal, the state slid back to the policy of appointing officials from among settlers and outsiders; in 1973 in El Kere, where the crisis had begun and the most significant changes in administrative personnel were made, all senior officials, including the district governor, were of Amhara-Christian origin.[82]

No agrarian reform was undertaken; it was not even contemplated. The state also reneged on its promises to return alienated lands to their original owners. In 1964 an imperial proclamation had made it theoretically possible for peasants to reclaim their confiscated lands, but in 1973, the official deadline for submitting petitions by claimants, there were only 279 applications from peasants reclaiming 417 *gashas*, as opposed to 6,780 people applying for grants amounting to 9,129 *gashas*.[83] The continuation of the patronage system, which was likely to have increased absenteeism or encouraged emigration from the central province of Shewa, left no illusion on the part of the peasants as regards the state's depth of understanding and appreciation of their basic concerns. The negligible number of peasant applicants reflected their lack of confidence in it. Meanwhile, two long-term projects, neither of which took the cultivators into serious account, were being entertained. One was to balance the ethnic composition of the provincial population, mainly for security reasons, by resettling peasants from the Amhara regions. The other envisioned the development of commercial agriculture by leasing portions of the confiscated and government-designated (22.9 percent) lands, which together made up about half of the cultivable land,[84] to foreign concessionaires. Neither was actualized; but mechanized agriculture on individual farms had begun, and by 1971 some twenty-nine tractors were used in the cultivation of at least 4,000 hectares in Fasil alone. Inevitably, an unknown number of tenants were displaced, a worrisome trend that the Security Department was quick to grasp. Fearful that such evictions could be cause for another crisis, it advised that a program of agricultural and industrial development be initiated in the province to absorb the unemployed.[85] Its warning was impudently shrugged off.

The impact of the revolt was therefore quite negligible. Among some of the visible changes were the construction of a semifunctional dry-weather road connecting Goba with Ginir and the installation of telephone lines in Adaba, Dodola, Goba, Goro, and Robe.[86] A hospital that was begun in 1965 was not, however, completed ten years later. Between February 1970, when the revolt ended, and February 1974, when the imperial regime collapsed, precious little had changed in Bale, as indeed in the rest of rural Ethiopia, with regard to the conditions of life of the peasantry. That was the raison d'être of the cataclysmic upheaval of 1974.

Conclusion

In the early 1960s Bale was pregnant with a cogent set of contradictions. Ethnic animosity and religious discrimination had combined with land alienation and bureaucratic corruption to create an explosive situation. The coincidence of rising social tensions and the decolonization of the Horn provided the spark that kindled the rebellion. An Ethiopian state that put the whole blame on outside conspirators and their domestic dupes or puppets was utterly unable to appreciate fully the depth of bitterness of the peasantry and the scope of the insurgency.

If one element distinguished the revolt of 1963–70 from earlier collective acts of resistance, it was the extent of its popular support, organization, and durability, not the reasons for it. Although some of the grievances that led to it were of recent origin, the revolt was an important event in a continuing conflict brought about by the imposition of Abyssinian domination and the consequent alienation of land from its original owners. Because of the dispossession and indignities they had suffered under the Ethiopian state, peasants gravitated toward Somalia. Yet the true local roots of the rebellion were confirmed by its links with earlier events of resistance in the area. Earlier resistance cannot be explained merely by the fundamental incompatibility of a prefeudal democratic social system with an imposed mode of production; it also involved the particular extractive and repressive features of the new system. Memories of anticonquest resistance are very much a part of the Bale oral tradition, and the memories are both bitter and energizing. More important than the story of the resistance itself is the fact that those who nursed this long tradition of opposition to the state were essentially the same people – the peasants.

The activities of newly independent Somalia in the Horn heralded a dramatic shift in peasant attitude. Peasant militancy increased perceptibly as relations between the Ethiopian and Somali states rapidly deteriorated. It must be stressed that it was not the objectively oppressive conditions alone that caused the shift from passive to active resistance, but also the peasants' belief that hostilities in the region may have undercut the repressive capacity of the Ethiopian state.

The role of the Somali state has still to be seen as a catalytic agent. It was important in that it disseminated propaganda highlighting the national oppression of the southern peoples of Ethiopia and in that it provided training, arms, provisions, and organizational skills for the rebels. The Somali aspect only helps to explain the timing and duration of the conflict, and not the reasons that gave rise to it. The Ethiopian government, however, deliberately orchestrated the Somali factor in order to underrate the popular basis of the movement. It is not uncharacteristic of such besieged states to rationalize that popular defiance has to be instigated from the outside because the people are too ignorant to manage it themselves. To assert that there would have been no rebellion without the Somali stimulus is really to beg the fundamental question about the character of Ethiopian society. In its structural origins and symbolic expressions the revolt was authentically indigenous, and so was its leadership.

The religious and ethnic orientation of the revolt does not detract from its essential peasant character. The ethnic or national question in southern Ethiopia was quintessentially a peasant question. Somalia's stress on the more pronounced forms of social oppression – i.e. its simple presentation of the problem as a contest between Christian Amhara and Muslim Oromo/Somali – critically undermined the class aspect and the transformative potential of the revolt. Hence, it was fundamentally reactive, not revolutionary, much less a movement with a socialist orientation. There is no known political program or manifesto that envisioned an alternative social system. The suggestion that repressive measures by the state turned "an essentially peasant revolt into a national revolutionary movement"[87] can be dismissed as wishful thinking. If the rebels sometimes styled themselves *sewra*, perhaps a corrupted derivative of the Arabic *thwar* (revolution), between 1969 and 1970, they were only imitating the revolutionary rhetoric of the Somali military regime. And when they attempted to draw a parallel between the Vietnamese struggle and their own, the insurgents were only seeking wider recognition. Their movement was no more than a typical peasant protest, whereas that of the Vietnamese was a nationalist cum social revolution. In point of fact, when such a revolution exploded, many of the rebels joined counter-revolutionary forces to impede it. That the Somali invasion of 1977–78 which they fully supported as its avant-garde immensely contributed to the entrenchment of an authoritarian military regime is beyond question.

6

Gojjam: a vendée revolt?

In 1968, a quarter of a century after the bloody suppression of *Weyane*, and at a time when the imperial army was tied up in Bale and Eritrea, unrest broke out in the northwestern province of Gojjam. Despite rumors of peasant agitation and scattered instances of civil disorder, the government was apparently caught by surprise, as one of its dramatis personae later revealed:

> Accidents happen to people, don't they? So they can also happen to an Empire, and in 1968 this is what happened to us in Gojjam Province. The peasants jumped on their rulers' throats. All the notables found it inconceivable, because we had a docile, resigned, God-fearing people not at all inclined to rebellion . . . if the peasants in such a country go on a rampage, they must have an extraordinary reason.[1]

Both the causes of and government reaction to the rebellion in Gojjam were markedly different from those in Bale. Except for the non-Christian and non-Amharic-speaking lowlanders, who were subjected to the indignities of cultural domination like most southerners, the people of Gojjam experienced no such domination; and since there were no outside settlers, they suffered no land alienation. But government was as bad and corruption as pervasive as in the rest of the country, and the Gojjame resented the state's increasing intrusion. The other major difference lay in the government's extraordinary reluctance to react with any substantial amount of force against a region in revolt. One is apt to ask whether the restraint in using violence, which might have seemed normal against the Oromo or Somalis, or even the Tigreans, was not due to the fact that Gojjam is an Amhara region. The reason, however, lies in the government's realization of the limitation of its own coercive capacity since the state was already militarily engaged in other provinces. More importantly, the rebels of Gojjam were not nearly as threatening as those of Bale or Tigrai, either militarily or ideologically. Firstly, the rebels of Gojjam had no external connections like those in the eastern region, and unlike the northerners, they were not suspected of having drawn inspiration and support from outside forces hostile to the Ethopian state. Secondly, not only were they weaker organizationally, but the rebels never contemplated secession as did their Somali counterparts or sought the restoration of dynastic rule as did some of the Tigrean insurgents, though they equally resented Shewan domination. There is no reason to think that the monarchical state would have been as merciful had the rebels challenged its legitimacy.

Though there were many reasons for popular discontent, the revolt was sparked off by the new agricultural income tax of 1967, which it wanted to circumvent. Its principal objective was, however, to defend the cultivators' unfettered access to the means of production. Lasting for sixteen months, it was more durable than *Weyane*, but the level of armed conflict was markedly less intense and the outcome less dramatic. It was the third armed outbreak in the province since the restoration of the monarchical regime, thus betraying the image of a docile peasantry. What, in fact, distinguished the provincial population from its northern neighbors, living under more or less similar conditions in the three decades before the revolution, was its propensity for militant resistance.

The occurrence of three revolts within barely two decades leads ineluctably to at least three conclusions. First, the unusual frequency of rural unrest in Gojjam would seem to suggest the relative economic autonomy of the peasantry, inhabiting a region where land was relatively more abundant and the soils more fertile. Second, geography, history, and a kinship-based culture tended to foster class collaboration. Third, because of their deeply seated genuine mistrust of the regime, the farmers consistently and obstinately resisted all taxation reforms including those that might actually have lessened their customary burdens. Their fears were manipulated by the local gentry, which stood to lose from the fiscal reforms. On the other hand, in the face of popular opposition, the state either revoked or merely postponed its new agrarian policies, a clear indication of the limitations of centralization and the concomitant weaknesses of the monarchical state.

Regionalism, local gentry and peasantry

Gojjam (now subdivided into three administrative regions) is located on the Abay bend, to the southwest of Tigrai. Surrounded by the Abay river in the northeast, south, and southwest, and by the Dinder river and Lake Tana in the north, Gojjam looks like a river island. Its population of about three million is ethnically and religiously mixed, but most of them are Christian Amharic-speakers. Some 64,000 square kilometers in size, Gojjam is a surplus-producing area; among its marketable products are *teff*, wheat, barley, *dura*, and oil seeds. Most of the cultivable land is located in the eastern mountainous sector, where the population density is also greater. There the average size of family household was 3.6 people and the average cultivable land per holding 1.15 hectares in the 1960s. This compared favorably with Tigrai, where there were on average five people per hectare, and in some places, nine. Density was even smaller in the tsetse fly- and

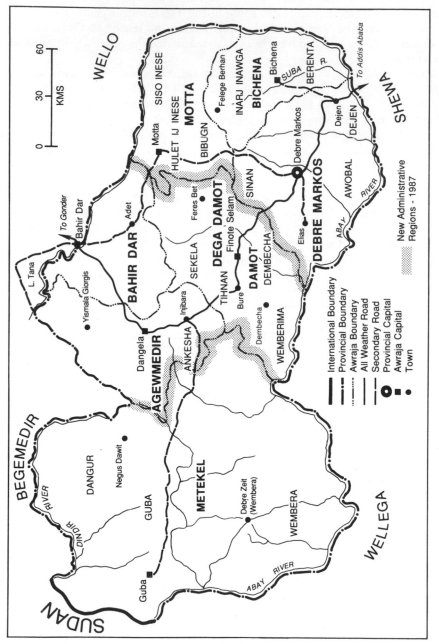

Map 5   Gojjam

malaria-infested region of Metekel, which otherwise constituted nearly half of the province. Further, in contrast to Tigrai, which was the theatre of nearly all the wars of colonial aggression, because of its proximity to the coast, Gojjam was not only spared the ravages of such wars, but remained secluded from foreign influence until the first quarter of the twentieth century. Its only external link was interregional trade.

Historically, the province consisted of three main parts, namely Gojjam proper, Agewmedir, and Damot. In the Era of the Princes it was fragmented into many principalities, each enjoying autonomy from the monarch while being independent of one another.[2] Claiming royal descent and hereditary rights over all the territories within the great bend of the Blue Nile, the lords of Damot reunified the region in 1873 after their chief, Ras Adal Tessema, triumphed over the ruler of Gojjam, to whom the Gonderine emperors had entrusted the nominal governorship of the province. Eight years later, Yohannes IV crowned Adal tributary king with the regal name Tekle Haymanot, affirming the territory's incorporation into a loosely integrated kingdom.

Despite military setbacks and the gradual diminution of power, the provincial dynasty survived until the close of the first half of this century. Tekle Haymanot's ambitious designs to build a prosperous and strong fiefdom through territorial aggrandizement in the southwest brought him into conflict with the Shewans, resulting in the disastrous defeat at Imbabo in 1882 from which the Gojjame rulers never fully recuperated militarily. Thereafter, they were merely content with safeguarding their regional over-lordship, and so long as they transmitted part of the tribute collected from the peasantry, there was little direct interference in their internal affairs by the imperial court;[3] but whenever that feudal fidelity was breached, the province suffered the consequences, as in 1889, when the emperor's punitive campaign against the king brought enormous distress to the peasants.[4]

There were fluctuations in the political fortunes of the provincial gentry following the death of Tekle Haymanot in 1901. Without formally abolishing the dynasty, Menelik II partitioned the province into three administrative units that, more or less, coincided with the historical divisions of Gojjam, Agewmedir, and Damot, assigning them to men directly appointed by and responsible to him. As one of the appointees was from Shewa, centralization through dilution of the local elite had begun in earnest. However, Menelik's physical incapacitation, caused by the multiple strokes he suffered between 1905 and 1909, helped the centrifugal elements to reassert themselves. In 1907 the dynastic rulers regained much of their power, which they enjoyed for another quarter of a century, when Ras Hailu, son and heir apparent of Tekle Haymanot, was appointed governor over the entire Gojjam.

The rise of Haile Selassie saw the eclipse of hereditary rule. In their futile attempt to reverse centralization, the lords of Gojjam, found themselves entangled in post-Menelik Machiavellian court intrigues and conspiracies, thereby precipitating Hailu's disgraceful fall and the eventual demise of provincial dynastic rule. In 1931, a year after he became king, Haile Selassie I unceremoniously deposed Hailu and kept him under detention in Addis Ababa until the Italians freed him and conferred the title of negus on him. His elevation to the provincial kingship might have quenched his boundless ambition for power, but it did little to reverse the diminishing political fortunes of the provincial dynasty, since much of the province remained under the control of guerrilla leaders resisting colonial occupation in defiance of their collaborationist traditional leader. The price of collaboration was loss of legitimacy. Hailu's confinement to Addis Ababa following the restoration of the monarchy, where he languished in well-merited obscurity until his death in 1950, put the final nail in the coffin of the provincial ruling elite, who had been grudgingly yielding ground to the centralists since the closing decade of the nineteenth century. Although it neither eliminated the roots of provincialism nor ended the local gentry's hold on the peasantry, the termination of Hailu's brutal reign did bring some respite to the producers. The implication of that reign to the postrestoration revolts is that exploitation alone was not the reason for collective defiance. What was so remarkable of the Gojjame peasants during this period was their outward passivity despite legitimate grounds for revolt.

Hailu's rule was as ruinous to the peasantry as it was typically tyrannical. Described as "a blustering, ebullient, and ambitious show off" by one author,[5] but with "little claim to any outstanding qualities as a leader or administrator" by another,[6] Hailu surely proved himself capable of devising new mechanisms of exploitation. Virtually autonomous for more than two decades, and with an avaricious taste for power and wealth, Hailu introduced new forms of taxation, auctioned political and church offices, nearly monopolized provincial trade by controlling the export side of it, transacted obligatory labor into monetary rents, and, though little is known about them, enlarged his estates with a manifest arrogant disregard for the customary judicial process of land allocation.

The sale of political office to raise additional revenue from the propertied classes in Ethiopia was perhaps as old a practice as feudalism itself, but Hailu's excessive use of it was without precedent in the history of Gojjam. Offices and titles were offered normally to the highest bidders from amongst the gentry who, in turn, in their "right" to appoint subordinates, charged the same exorbitant prices. In order to recoup itself through "licensed privileges and corruption," the hierarchy of officials simply shifted the economic cost of office to the farmers. This unprecedented growth in the transaction of public offices reflected not merely an individual's insatiable greed; it was the outcome of the increased monetization of the public economy and the correspondingly relative rise in mercantilism. It was a useful device that served both economic and political functions by "making the acquisition of bureaucratic position a market transaction." It undermined the network of feudal clientship, theoretically dependent on the monarch, while enhancing the benefits of office dependent "on the personal connections and prestige of a great lord and his house."[7] But from the perspective of the peasants, this arrangement was not merely an exchange of parasitism dependent on patronage for venality; it was an intensification of official parasitism.

The cultivators' burden increased with the introduction of new levies payable in cash.[8] In 1910 the governor imposed two Maria Theresa thalers on farmers owning a pair of plow oxen, and a decade later decreed what is known as the *tis* (smoke) tax which, incidentally, was comparable to the hut tax in colonial Africa. To avoid this dreaded levy, hard-pressed producers often huddled together into fewer huts. And with some poetic exaggeration, "I ate my cabbage raw," they cried pitifully, "as I cannot cook it for fear of the smoke tax." The generalized plight only helped to inspire an unmerciful tyrant to oppress his groaning subjects. Nearly all the marketable products became subject to taxation, the amount varying with quantity and quality. At the customs gates established in border areas his representatives imposed a toll on every animal and product passing through the gates. Just as burdensome was the method of enforcement known as *mechie*, a method by which a force of irregulars raised in one district was quartered in another until payments were made in full. In the meantime, the militia freely fed itself on whatever was available – chicken, sheep, goats, etc. – while it abused its "hosts" and stole their valuables.[9]

The suppressed, but universal, hatred for Hailu's administration was rarely translated into organized collective resistance. Apart from scattered acts of banditry and minor clashes with the militia here and there, the general reaction was one of resignation bordering on fatalism. "You have looted my property and expropriated my cattle," lamented the hapless farmer, "but there is one thing more, Ras, that you have yet to take, and this is my stomach so that I may sleep [rest] in peace."[10]

Hailu's acumen for business and love of money earned him the appropriate nickname "*birru* Hailu" ("dollars Hailu"). Any attempt to estimate the amount of wealth he accumulated and the manner of its dispensation would be purely conjectural, for we have little knowledge of the baron's bookkeeping. The widespread belief that he was "the richest warlord in Ethiopia"[11] is suggestive only of his wealth's enormousness. What is generally known is that whereas a fraction of the ill-gotten wealth was spent on office buildings, road construction, small scale irrigation schemes, and, of course, periodic public entertainments, the bulk of it was invested in real estate and lucrative business enterprises such as hotels, night clubs, cinemas, and taxis, all operating in the growing city of Addis Ababa.[12] Coffee was grown on his estate at Zaghie on Lake Tana. A foreign admirer can thus write: "Money is power in this country as elsewhere, and the power is of superior quality when the money is in the hands of so intelligent, astute, and resourceful a man as the ruler of Godjam [*sic*]."[13] Clearly, the man was one of the very few feudal lords engaged in the primitive accumulation of capital, and interestingly, quite in tune with the emerging bourgeoisie in the rest of

Africa, he exhibited a proclivity toward an indulgence in luxuries. It was reported that during his short visit to Europe in 1924 he went on "a vast shopping spree which subsequently filled his storehouse at Debra Marcos with cases of champagne and vintage wines, cigars, tinned goods, masses of suits, shirts, and women's dresses, and a motorcar ..."[14] It is significant, however, that a feudal baron located in the geographical periphery of the empire was so extensively involved in mercantilist activities, an indication of the measure to which the country had already been drawn into the world market. Yet, it did not inaugurate any transformation in production relations.

The Italian episode was just as indecisive, but notable in one respect. By constructing a road that bridged the Blue Nile linking the hitherto isolated province with Addis Ababa, the Italians increased the vulnerability of the local elite. The economic significance of the road was not immediately realized, but the political implications were grasped by the gentry, which frequently contemplated dynamiting the bridge. These changes facilitated centralization, but were not sufficient to break the backbone of the lesser gentry. As was evident in the revolts of both 1950 and 1968 it remained influential, and its ability to arouse the peasants against the state lay in the tenure system as well as in its primordial ties with the peasants, notwithstanding glaring social distinctions. By presenting a surface image of social harmony, anchored in the politics of kinship and regionalism, they succeeded in stirring the peasants.

Antecedents: the moral economy of resistance

Though not as spectacular as the Tigrean revolt, there was public unrest in Gojjam between 1942 and 1944. Popular reaction to cadastral surveys, land measurement, registration of individual holdings, and fiscal reform was violently negative there because such measures were universally perceived as dangerous infringements upon the kinship-based landholding system, which guaranteed control over subsistence. Since the collective payment of land tax has traditionally been regarded as the sole evidence of "communal" ownership, it was widely but erroneously believed that taxational changes were inevitably bound up with alterations in land use. To reject land measurement and tax reforms was, therefore, to defend the integrity of *rist*, even though this would mean perpetuation of the tributary system. What the tillers wanted to avoid was the dreadful fate of their southern counterparts. In their view, if southerners had been disinherited, it was because they were colonized peoples. But the Gojjame were free citizens, and the basis of their freedom was the heritage of collective ownership of land. As their elders unequivocally stated before the emperor in 1950, to tamper with the existing production relations was to destroy their liberty and identity:

> When the Italian colonialists invaded our country to seize *rist*, to shed blood, and to denigrate history, your countrymen, the Gojjame, made a valiant

resistance, bearing the burden of sacrifice, for five years ... Yet, we now understand that we are to be deprived of our traditional rights. There is no *rist* without liberty and no honor without *rist* ... The Honorable Dejazmatch Kebede Tessema has interfered with our freedom. We are gravely concerned that his administration is planning to alter a system that has been in practice for at least 200 years and to institute in its place something similar to the system now operative in the frontier lands occupied by force. The *balabbats* of Menz and Tegulet know very well the cruel history of the Galla. Your Majesty, it is not disputable that our fathers helped in the conquest of those territories, and to contemplate governing Gojjam like them is not only to deny the contribution of our fathers but to institute a system of oppression in our land. The fact that it has been stated before your August presence that the Gojjame live by custom and have no *rist* rights confirms our belief that the Governor's intention is to govern Gojjam like an occupied territory. Your Majesty, the real intention of the Governor you have given us is to drive us out of our "country" slowly by raising taxes annually ...[15]

In 1942–44 and again in 1950, when vigorous attempts were made to universalize the tax schedule then fully operational in the south-central provinces, popular anxiety erupted into major rebellions. The state was forced to retreat on both occasions, which were dramatized by personal aspiration. In the first instance, the aspirations were those of Belai Zeleke, a person of soaring ambition whose larger-than-life exploits in the patriotic resistance against the Italians had turned him into a hero of legendary proportions. Disgusted with both the office and the title given to him in the postliberation administrative reorganization, Belai made the ill-fated decision to defy the government by turning to banditry. He did not last long, and before his captors he is said to have enraged the emperor by remarking that "God created every one of us, but did not appoint anyone to rule." By contesting the divine basis of kingship, Belai provided his persecutor with additional reason to sentence him to death by hanging. The national fame and prestige the rebel enjoyed, and his personal courage, were too much for the emperor to stomach.

The revolt of 1950 was even larger in scope and longer in duration than that of 1944. The government's decision to measure land and rationalize taxation in that year was woefully ill timed because a drastic fall in the price of cereals had hit the farmers very hard,[16] precipitating widespread unrest. Some notables, the most prominent of whom was Dejazmatch Aberre Yimam, found it opportune to challenge a government they had reason to resent. Aberre was one of those redoubtable wartime heroes who had been wounded by failed expectations; in his case it was his subordination in the administrative hierarchy to a person with whom he had had a longstanding political feud. Under his able leadership, the rebels waged a guerrilla war for nearly a year, serious enough to force the government to concede to their demands: a general amnesty was declared, the provincial governor was replaced by a local noble, peasants were exempted from a third of the taxes, and the new tax bill was rescinded. Only Aberre suffered the consequences of his action. Like his counterpart in Tigrai a few years earlier, he was tried as a criminal against the state and sentenced to death; the emperor commuted the sentence to life imprisonment. Subsequently, the rebel chieftain spent sixteen years of his life in jail.[17]

In the face of overwhelming popular opposition, no land measurement, and therefore no taxational reforms, had been undertaken in Gojjam, or indeed in any of the northern provinces. Between 1942 and 1966 only 0.1 percent of the total land in Gojjam was measured, as compared with 2 percent in Tigrai, 4 percent in Shewa, 23.8 in Arusi, and 30.4 in Kaffa.[18] The mechanisms by which village elders determined the distribution of the tax levied among parish members remained unaltered. The cultivators had thus successfully prevented the state from establishing a direct link between themselves and the central authority; only the names of the founding father of the descent corporations and that of the village intermediary known as *tetterri* (representative) appeared on the tax register. When the government once again tried to tinker with customary practice in 1967, it set off an uprising that forced it to recoil from its actions.

Much like its antecedents the revolt of 1968 was a spontaneous reaction to a new tax bill which, as before, was regarded simply as an ominous harbinger of a change in property relations through the commoditization of land. This time that assumption was not entirely unfounded given the long-range goals of the regime. Apprehension that the bill would lead to increased obligations was evident in the popular cry, "This year it is only $1.50, but next year it will be $150."[19] However, fear of heavier taxes alone might not have ignited the crisis, for did not Hailu multiply the agrarian levies without stirring up open opposition? According to popular tradition, Hailu, oppressive and exploitative as he was, could not disown tillers of the soil, for he was their kinsman; only outsiders, now represented by the state, could violate cherished custom. Ergo, "the primary and immediate cause of the revolt was the conviction that the government intended to measure land and alter or abolish the rist system of land tenure."[20] Some of the provisions of Proclamation 255, which was not fully explained in advance, reinforced that conviction.

The proclamation provided for the distribution of legal receipts to all taxpayers including tenants. In Gojjam many of the tenants, estimated at 19 percent, were social outcasts with no right to land. The granting of tax receipts to all was interpreted by the landholders to mean that tenants too would be entitled to the right to use of land, until then limited to the ambilineal descent groups. In that case, they argued, the source of the farmers' social status, the traditional identity and particularity of the descent groups, and indeed their security of tenure, would have been irreversibly destroyed. The fact that Muslims were granted the right to purchase land within urban municipal zones since 1960 seemed to support their concern. Although popular justice discriminated against some sectors of the agricultural population, the driving motive behind collective resistance was to defend use rights against the incursion of exclusive rights in private property.

Other factors, which are not sufficiently stressed as the underlying reason by previous analyses, were eloquently recited to arouse the people and to sustain the resistance. If, as has been often and rightly assumed, local nobles and institutions played a central role in agitating the peasantry, it was partly because these secondary factors contributed immensely toward the latter's readiness to revolt. And if popular fury tended to focus upon personalities rather than on public issues or concerns, it was, in part, because authority was highly personalized and social awareness too limited.

The precipitants

The Agricultural Income Tax was decreed at a time when discontent was rife in Gojjam. Contributing to that discontent were bureaucratic abuse, habitual repression by the security forces, state unresponsiveness, and a general feeling that Gojjam received fewer social amenities "than its tax money should pay for."[21] The following testimony voluntarily given on July 4, 1968 in front of a large assembly by an elderly priest touches upon these salient issues:

> I personally have not suffered any inconvenience, but in presenting the people's woes on oath, I know I may have put my own life in jeopardy. Come what may, it is my duty to speak, for here we have with us high-ranking state officials willing to listen. The revolt has not been caused by the levy, which in fact hurts the state more than it does the taxpayer. But the country is being plundered, wives are violated, and men are still forced to work on private estates. People have little time left to work on their own farms as they are frequently called upon to plow the fields and to harvest the crops of those in authority. It has become a common obligation to transport their flour mills from place to place, and fatal accidents have occurred in the performance of such [illegal] services. The officials kill. They never sit in their offices to carry out their duties; instead they travel around the country in pursuit of other benefits, and they deposit their [ill-gotten] money in the bank. Whenever visitors come here we are always reminded to speak of the pleasantness of life under their "good" administration; punishment is the price of disobedience. We have even become pitiful servants of the militia; and the village judges have become like pests, for they have no regular allowances from the state. We cannot appeal, and suits are dragged out for years since delays are profitable to judges. The people have lost hope in the cause for justice.[22]

A disrespectful and abusive governor from Shewa only helped to magnify the repressive and exploitative character of the state. He made it easier for political agitators to incite general support against imperial administration. No one better personified authoritarianism at the provincial level than Dejazmatch Tsehayu Enque Selassie, governor of Gojjam from 1960 to 1968. Born to an influential family in Shewa, Tsehayu, along with his four brothers, grew up and succeeded in politics under imperial patronage. He

169

received little formal education, but later joined the civil service, where his meteoric rise was only interrupted by the Italian invasion. Five years later Tsehayu, who had distinguished himself as a guerrilla fighter in the resistance movement in Shewa, rejoined the emperor's government and rose from one position to another in rapid succession. His appointment to the governorship of Gojjam was the high point of his political career and, as it turned out, the most challenging one.

Flamboyant, overbearing, and supremely arrogant, but enjoying the confidence and trust of the monarch, Tsehayu exercised administrative and judicial powers without constraint, to the great consternation of his nominal supervisors at the Ministry of the Interior and to the envy of most of his counterparts in the rest of the country. His status was no less prominent than that of the two princes then governing Eritrea and Tigrai, both of whom were related to the emperor either by blood or by marriage.[23] Taking advantage of this special relationship to the emperor, Tsehayu single-mindedly set out to accomplish what his predecessors had failed to do: to bring Gojjam under effective centralized administration by enforcing "measures which had been in force for a number of years in most Ethiopian provinces, but had been suspended or ignored" in the province.[24] It was a colossal undertaking.

In his fanatical determination to subdue an administrative region that had been regarded in Shewa as the "most stubborn and independent of the provinces,"[25] to collect overdue taxes and prosecute defaulters, to raise funds ostensibly for developmental purposes, and to humble a generation of illustrious patriots, Tsehayu alienated a cross-section of the population, eventually driving it into armed rebellion. His aristocratic countenance, arrogant disposition, and the court method of "appoint–demote," which he so ruthlessly used to reward "friends" and to punish "enemies," antagonized many of the local nobles. The behavior of the district and subdistrict administrators he appointed, the general conduct of the irregulars he organized, and the periodic cash contributions he collected, on the other hand, earned him "a particularly unsavory reputation" among the peasants, most of whom otherwise had little or no direct contact with him during his term of office. Just as Alemayehou Tenna had arrogantly, but clumsily, inflamed Tigrean sensibilities a generation earlier, and just as the governor's brother, Worku Enque Selassie, had notoriously created conditions that led to the rebellion in Bale, so did Tsehayu's despotism help to initiate the uprising in Gojjam.

The first indications of dissatisfaction were seen as early as 1963, when the governor, having vowed to eliminate all forms of lawlessness – especially brigandage – in the province, began to enforce a law that had up to then been in abeyance. Through sheer ignorance or defiance, few in Gojjam had complied with a law that required citizens to have their guns registered upon payment of two dollars. The governor, who believed that ignorance was no less excusable than defiance, ordered all gun-holders to comply with the law within three months of the issuance of the directive or forfeit their property. The hasty, clumsy, and often brutal manner of its enforcement soon became a source of public outcry. Little explanation of either the purpose or the procedure of registration was given in advance to dispel a lingering suspicion that the real intention was to disarm the population. Former patriots bitterly confessed that they could not understand how a regime they had so gallantly fought to restore would wish to disarm them in peace-time.[26] There were others who complained, perhaps not without foundation, that their failure to obey was only because registrars were charging two dollars in excess of the nominal fee. The administration began to confiscate weapons upon the expiry of the notice. The governor's admirable courage and vigor were, however, matched by an unbending determination on the part of his opponents to frustrate his aims.

Complaints began to reach Addis Ababa by early 1964. In response, the emperor twice formed a commission, mainly consisting of his senior ministers, to investigate the matter, but each time the outcome of their work was not revealed, nor was any action taken. Meanwhile, as the governor, "supremely confident of his own power [continued] to defy everyone and everything,"[27] conditions in the province steadily deteriorated and a mood of frustrated anger arose.

There were many additional factors conducive to unrest, especially the economic sacrifices that the people were periodically asked to make toward ineffectual projects. An umbrella organization known as Gionawit Gojjam was created in the province to direct the program of "development through cooperation." The governor, who was also the self-elected chairman of the organization, appointed the council members and heads of branch offices and supervised its functions.[28] On paper it appeared that this was a semiautonomous project in which the people voluntarily and freely participated; in practice there was no popular participation. The contributors, who were also the intended beneficiaries, were not involved in planning, decision making, implementation, or evaluation of the project. The normal practice was to impose a compulsory contribution in the form of money and labor either on individuals or parishes, and to punish those failing to cooperate.

There is little information on total public contributions and the manner of their dispensation, but allegations of misappropriation and embezzlement abound. As officials left no financial records, the question of how much was raised and how much stolen will probably never be settled. The scanty evidence that throws some light on this comes mainly from the peasants themselves. Here are a few examples: the residents of Bichena and Kola-Dega Damot claimed they raised ETH $140,000 in 1965–66, a portion of which was used to erect the emperor's statue at Finote Selam in commemoration of his "triumphant" return from exile in 1941. Dembecha alone might have raised 20,000 dollars in two years. Dega Damot reported that it was designated to collect 10,000 dollars per annum, but did not say how much was actually raised. Similarly, while the inhabitants of Inabise, Motta, inform us that each family household in the subdistrict was required to pay 44 dollars annually, they are silent on how many of them complied and for how long. According to the same sources not all contributions were intended for development. In 1964, for example, when a military conflict broke out between Ethiopia and Somalia, people were asked to make generous donations to the Ogaden Campaign, as it was known. At least 800 quintals of grain and 30,000 dollars appear to have been collected, and this from only two districts.[29] In the collection of contributions the threat or use of force was quite common; the militia confiscated farm implements and physically abused those who were unwilling or unable to pay.[30]

Statues are the single most important legacy of Tsehayu's administration. Two small statues of the emperor were erected at Debre Markos and Finote Selam at an unknown cost. Many believed that the cost ought to have been quite small since materials as well as labor were supplied largely by the peasants. No schools, clinics, or roads were built. Even the existing health centers remained understaffed, ill equipped, and chronically short of supplies. Where did the money go? Once again we will have to let the contributors speak for themselves. Peasants invariably claimed that the bulk of what they gave under a variety of designations was simply "eaten up" by the officials. They asked: how is it that a district administrator like Demiss Alamirew of Bichena, making a monthly income of ETH $250, was able to acquire fourteen flour mills and many houses in barely seven years of service? Is it conceivable that a subdistrict administrator could own several houses in the administrative capital and a bar at another in less than four years at a monthly salary of ETH $150?[31] It was also widely rumored that the governor owned several trucks, many houses, and real estate in Addis Ababa. He had certainly built several villas and a mansion in the capital where he might have vainly hoped to spend his retirement in splendor and tranquillity,[32] but we do not know how much of the property was acquired illegally. Given the fact that the administrators had no public institutions or facilities to show for all the money they collected, allegations of graft and corruption do not seem to be entirely unfounded, however.

The militia were no less predatory than the officials who recruited them. These men were drafted from amongst the peasants, but most of them had previous criminal records. Their exact number is not known, estimates varying from one to two thousand.[33] In theory they were supposed to help in the fight against brigandage, a common phenomenon in the province, and in the maintenance of public order both as an auxiliary to the police force and a reserve army; in practice, they served as spies, private guardsmen, and hit-men for the governor and his lieutenants, who used them unsparingly to punish their suspected opponents or "enemies." Armed with state authority, they terrorized peaceful peasants. Normally, men recruited in one village were sent to another for a particular task or mission; but under the pretext of hunting down bandits, distributing court orders and notices, or collecting overdue taxes, they frequently traveled around the country, living off the peasants. They even exacted feudal fees long abolished by law.[34] Peasants complained that they carried the militia on their backs and that as a burden they were much heavier than all the taxes combined. They were often accused of having taken liberties with women, including wives of the clergy, blasphemous behavior in that Christian community. Either to solicit bribes or simply to vent personal vendettas, they falsely charged innocent citizens, subjecting them to mental and physical torture.[35] A "highly confidential" report to the Prime Minister, the authors of which included the Minister of the Interior and a crown counselor, found these assertions generally incontestable:

> Although the services that the militia render to the state are by no means negligible, it is equally evident that they are a cause for the current public unrest. We continually heard complaints of grave and extensive damages they have committed, and we have realized that they are almost universally hated. The reasons are obvious: the majority of them are former outlaws who had spent time in prison before set free on clemency. Always claiming that they are under orders by the administration to hunt down bandits, deliver court summons, collect taxes, and other pretexts, they move around freely living off others, often committing degredations, looting property, and abusing wives.
>
> In our opinion, the meager allowances of ETH $50, 25, 23 and 15 assigned to a lieutenant, sergeant, corporal, and private, respectively, are too small to sustain them even for one month, let alone a year. It is the meagerness of the allowance that drives them toward predatory acts, and we trust that what we have heard from the people is credible ... On their part, though they do not admit every complaint brought against them, the militia do not deny that they never carry provisions but that they live on food and drink freely provided by the people ...[36]

The trouble was that there was little difference between the militia and the administrators. On his arrival in the province, Tsehayu discovered to his great chagrin that nearly all the district and subdistrict officers were of local origin. Since their sources of power and status were locally rooted, they were not suitable instruments of centralized rule, a goal that the governor had set out to achieve. Moreover, as former patriots, many of them were rather indignant at subordinating themselves to outsiders whom they looked upon with a mixture of contempt and fear. In order to strengthen his own position as well as to ensure compliance with his administrative policies, Tsehayu began to dismantle the administrative hierarchy. Using insubordination and incompetence as useful pretexts, he removed administrators at all levels and replaced them with his own appointees, men who had no claim either to "noble birth" or to an independent source of power. What the chief administrator wanted to achieve through this unprecedented assault on the gentry was not merely cooperation but subservience, and true to the Ethiopian adage that "a dog knows its master and not the master of its master," they served him loyally and faithfully. But, highly abusive and repressive, the new administrators soon became a great liability to the state. One intelligence report sadly admitted that:

173

Of the seven district governors three are native Gojjame; these and many other subdistrict officers were formerly bandits. They were appointed to their current positions with the hope that they would be instrumental both in the maintenance of law and order and in ensuring public safety by tirelessly combating brigandage and related lawless activities in the province. They may well be able to do that, but for now, by punishing those who despised them while rewarding those who supported them when they themselves were outside the reach of the state, they have become terribly divisive; and although people's attitude toward them is divided, it is apparent that their liability by far outweighs their usefulness.[37]

A profile of one of these men helps to illustrate the character and *modus operandi* of the administration that Tsehayu had set up. It was common belief that the governor's most trusted henchman was Demiss Alamirew, a former bandit leader whose activities had earned him fame and notoriety throughout the province. First designated thief catcher in his home district of Bichena, Demiss completely cleared the area and adjacent villages of bandits in less than a year. On that record he was successively appointed subdistrict and district administrator with the title of Fitawrari. For more than six years he ran Bichena with an iron fist; for minor infractions, often trumped up by his lieutenants and the militia, he meted out the severest punishments. Confiscation of property, whipping, flogging, and even hanging became common. Demiss had turned Bichena into "a land of tears and blood." In his savage use of power and in his greed to amass a fortune, he was Ras Hailu's prototype. Demiss also acted as the chief law enforcer in much of the eastern half of the province, frequently traveling from one district to another, presumably in pursuit of bandits and always spreading terror and misery. No wonder that "the hatred he provoked among the people surpassed even their hatred for the provincial governor."[38] Yet fearful of antagonizing a powerful governor, concerned officials were reluctant to take any measures against him; if anything, they praised him. The chief security officer of the state, clearly contradicting intelligence reports by his own men, staunchly defended him, and it was with hesitation and regret that he finally recommended his removal from the province.

There is no doubt that the reason for the unpopularity of Fitawrari Demiss Alamirew is his hard and indefatigable work. That he has restored peaceful life by eradicating banditry is undeniable; I myself strongly believe it. This he has done by faithfully following the governor's instructions and at great personal cost, for it is true that he has lost close relatives in the various armed clashes against outlaws. However, he is widely hated and the government cannot afford to lose credibility by incurring public hostility. Now is thus the right moment to have him transferred, but this will require tact (I will explain orally).[39]

Although they were not always consistent, what the intelligence reports invariably attested to was the official corruption that had greatly disturbed stability in the province. They presented a picture of a volatile situation in which men in power unethically, but blithely, enriched themselves, while "the truly rural poor and weak, having lost all hope for protection and justice from the state, [were] in a state of great distress and anger."[40] While still wavering between passivity and militant action, the peasants themselves poignantly expressed the prevailing mood of frustration.

> The poor works harder, but has lost
>   hope,
> Greatly diminished is our beneficence.
>
> They looked at the land and then
>   increased our burden,
> The grace of the past is surely gone.
>
> When you see that what used to be five
>   loads has become one,
> You are but greatly saddened.
>
> The cow gives no milk and the bee
>   produces no honey,
> The earth is no longer bountiful.
>
> Do not mislead the people that it was
>   decided by a council,
> The burden you have imposed on us is
>   not simple [light].
>
> Hoping for the better, the poor ploughs
>   ten plots of land
> But when June passes this is not even
>   enough for planting.
>
> This is life, and somehow we will subsist
> But the king does not know our
>   difficulties.
>
> For thirty years we have had light,
> But the king has changed his attitude
>   toward us.
>
> Now that the customary tax has been
>   altered,
> Only seven days are left before the people
>   are dead.

175

Nay, the Council has erred and the
  decision ought to be rescinded,
Whom will they rule when all the people
  are dead.

Let us mourn in the monasteries
For what the Gojjame understands is not
  war but sorrow.

The Gojjame has been used to a feast by
  the king,
Do not change tradition, hold on to
  custom.

Are not God and king the same?
Can the word of a king be altered?

If you say do not eat or drink
Then the king has become cruel, and one
  must die silently.

If, however, we petition the king and he
  turns a deaf ear to us,
War being better than hunger, we shall
  perish in struggle.[41]

Two administrative measures, which were otherwise consonant with overall state policies, helped to crystallize and to turn latent anger into violent defiance. First, by revoking church privileges, and second, by demoting, removing, or expelling local officials of esteem and great influence, the governor created conditions favorable for class collaboration. Ever since the clergy, supported by the peasantry, thwarted state attempts to secularize and unify administration in the years 1942–44, the great churches and monasteries in Gojjam continued to enjoy their traditional privileges of collecting land tax and of exercising administrative and juridical authority over their parishes. In his attempt to mobilize rural resources the governor terminated these prerogatives on the grounds that the churches were no longer capable of maintaining law and order, a drastic move that enraged the clergy. Their reaction was predictable: as in 1944, they refused to accept the new measures, and in 1964 they sent some three hundred priests to Addis Ababa to put their case before the emperor. When they discovered that he was less amenable than he had been twenty years before, they began to agitate, for "when satisfied, they preach[ed] loyalty and obedience, but when dissatisfied they foment[ed] discontent among the populace."[42] The same was characteristically true of the gentry. There were many who had sufficient reason to forment trouble: local nobles who had suffered a loss in status and prestige as a result of the administrative changes undertaken in the 1960s, former patriots who had never been happy with the distribution of offices and feudal honorific titles following restoration, and an array of personalities who had axes to grind against the governor.

There was no overt participation from the urban population, but it was not wholly irrelevant. The towns served as safe havens for agitators whose activities ran the gamut from channeling funds and ammunition to the villages to spreading rumors and false news that, at times, had apocalyptic overtones. From the towns they transmitted coded messages urging peasants not to accept the tax bill, to drive out Tsehayu's appointees and protégés, and to resist or, as one of them simply put it, "to disturb in order to rectify."[43] In addition, there was restlessness there because of two interconnected factors: first, most of the townspeople still had rural ties, many holding *rist* land, and were thus as apprehensive of the tax bill as their relatives in the countryside. Second, the governor's efforts to promote and facilitate the establishment or expansion of town municipalities caused a great deal of anxiety and provoked considerable silent opposition. As the municipalities were chartered to acquire, mortgage, or sell land, and to raise additional revenue by imposing higher taxes on the land within the boundaries of their jurisdiction, people became fearful that the introduction of land transactions would lead to the end of the *rist* and that Muslims would be able to own land in the countryside. It is evident that there was some link between rural strife and urban discontent even though the latter had little impact on the genesis of provincial unrest. More crucial in setting off the rebellion was the desertion of the rural clergy and gentry.

The uprising: outbreak and expansion

Six years after its suppression, a former state dignitary recaptured the drama of the uprising: "reports are coming in from Gojjam Province that the peasants are brawling, rebelling, bashing in the skulls of the tax collectors, hanging policemen, running dignitaries out of town, burning down estates, uprooting crops. The governor reports that rebels are storming the offices and that whenever they get their hands on the Emperor's people, they vilify them, torture them, and quarter them . . ."[44]

There was great alarm and fright throughout Gojjam when the income tax bill was officially announced there in September 1967. Yet the immediate reaction of the peasantry was not the same everywhere: it varied from passive acceptance to outright rejection of the proclamation. Only Agewmedir and Metekel, the two western and predominately non-Amhara districts, refrained from antigovernmental activities throughout the crisis. On the other hand, Damot and Motta were the most belligerent, refusing to elect or to admit tax assessors and preventing others from obeying the law either by persuasion or coercion, and often by both. But even in these core areas of stubborn resistance there was little use of violence in the first few months as

177

Table 6.1. *Tax assessed and amount collected, 1968 (ETH $)*

District	Population	Percent	Tax assessed	Collected	Uncollected
Agewmedir	157,000	11.7	71,175.00	2,155.00	69,020.00
Bahir Dar	276,800	20.6	54,360.75	4,207.50	50,153.25
Bichena	184,600	13.7	11,078.50	5,409.00	5,669.50
Damot	315,400	23.5	40,812.25	1,650.00	39,162.25
Debre Markos	206,000	15.3	115,085.90	24,762.50	90,323.40
Metekel	—	—	13,420.50	4,696.00	8,724.50
Motta	204,000	15.2	351.00	30.00	321.00
Total	1,343,800	100.0	306,283.90	42,910.00	263,373.90

Source: CSO, *Report on a Survey of Gojjam Province*, p. 7. Ayalew Berhanu to Kifle Ergetu, July 7, 1968, MIA G 29/60/3.

initial protest took the form of petitions, appeals, and personal presentations. Only when these methods proved fruitless did peasants resort to violent tactics.

In October, enforcement of the law began in earnest, but tax assessment was not easy and its collection was even more difficult. Although there was little organized disruption until February 1968, work proceeded at a snail's pace because people were generally uncooperative. It was also severely handicapped by technical difficulties and administrative irregularities. Guesswork is bound to arouse suspicion, and right from the start there were complaints of "unfairness and corruption." Elected village elders did not always know their specific tasks, while some administrators, too eager to finish work on schedule and thereby please their superiors, simply ignored the electoral process by appointing their own men to do the assessment or undermined the job of legally constituted committees by imposing their own estimates.[45] In either case they gave credence to public accusations of corruption and foul play. Few paid their income tax on schedule, and as table 6.1 shows, between January 8 and June 8 not more than one-seventh of the total tax assessed had been collected.

By early 1968 peasants had moved slowly from differential petitioning and noncooperation to insurrection with manifest anarchist tendencies. It all began in Damot and Motta, though there is disagreement about the exact place of origin of the revolt;[46] according to official accounts it started in northern Motta on February 2 and almost instantaneously spread into northeastern Damot.[47] On February 7 rebellious peasants from the two districts met at the Azwari river and took a solemn oath of unity and action, electing their respective district and subdistrict governors. They agreed to expel all state officials, to boycott government courts, to withhold agricultural produce from the markets, and to destroy the property of "all traitors." Tax assessors summoned to the gathering were mercilessly criticized and scolded, while the unrepentant ones were beaten; peasants who had paid the new tax were cursed and ostracized, losing their huts and cattle in some instances.[48] By February 25 nearly all state officials had retreated to the subprovincial capitals, and for nearly two months thereafter rebels were in almost full control of the two districts, governing themselves and urging others to act in a similar way.

Their efforts were not in vain, for resistance expanded into the adjacent districts of Bichena, Debre Markos, and Bahir Dar. The administration had little trouble in regaining control of Bahir Dar and in containing the trouble in Debre Markos; the situation in Bichena, however, rapidly deteriorated as rebels evicted most officials and elected their own leaders, vowing to stand firmly with their kin in Damot and Motta. By the middle of March about 60 percent of the population in eastern Gojjam had openly defied the state and could be said to be outside its immediate control. It is remarkable that little violence was used in all of this – mainly because the state was reluctant to commit its troops – and the police and militia, heavily outnumbered, were less inclined to go into armed combat. Conditions changed following a small incident in Debre Markos.

It began in Awobal in the subdistrict of Yedawaraj in a rather theatrical manner. It was Sunday afternoon, March 9, and the villagers were enjoying a feast in their parish church when they heard the disturbing news. The deputy administrator, escorted by the secretary of the subdistrict, who was also the chairman of the assessment committee, and a few policemen, had begun to measure a plot of land on the holiest day of the week, a double insult to the villagers. There was pandemonium in the gathering: women began to cry while men sang war songs and the priests gave their blessings to those ready to defend the sanctity of the *rist*. As was to be expected, men and women, armed with spears, clubs, and machetes and blowing horns and trumpets to alert others, flocked to the field and pleaded with the officials that measurement be stopped. After firing a few shots to frighten them, the administrator, who was apparently in a state of intoxication, contemptuously told the men: "Let alone on your lands, I have authority on your wives."[49] That set off an angry exchange of words and fists, but no physical harm was done since the policemen agreed to give up their weapons. The chairman of the assessors was, however, beaten up, his gun was taken away, and his house, along with the government documents in his possession, was burned. The following day, people from all over the subdistrict and neighboring villages met near the Bogena river and decided to disarm the militia, expel all officials, and elect their own leader.[50]

The governor responded with unusual alacrity. A contingent of the militia under the command of Demiss Alamirew was dispatched to Awobal to teach the villagers an unforgettable lesson. There the militia were let loose; they burned homes, looted property, and apprehended seventy men. Fifty-six of them were later sentenced to prison on the basis of flimsy evidence, by the government's own admission.[51]

If the reprisals were intended to terrorize the population, they apparently did not have the desired effect. On April 6 more than three thousand rebels from Bichena, Damot, Debre Markos, and Motta headed for Mengisto to set the prisoners free and to punish Demiss. About seven kilometers short of their destination, the rebels were stopped by a combined force of territorials and police. The principal target, Demiss, narrowly escaped and sought refuge in a nearby church. After two days of continuous fighting, government forces ran out of ammunition, and only the timely arrival of regular troops saved them from extinction. This marked the first direct involvement of the army in the conflict. When hostilities stopped through the mediation of the bishop of the province, the government had suffered four fatalities, including one district governor, to six rebel losses.[52] It was at this point that the central government in Addis Ababa became sufficiently concerned and began to send one commission after another to investigate the matter.

State intervention and repression

The preceding account has shown that by the mid 1960s the situation in Gojjam objectively contained ingredients for rebellion which the Agricultural Income Tax sparked. During the first few years of Tsehayu's administration the relationship between the state and the citizenry had been so severely strained that the outcome seemed fairly predictable. Between 1961 and 1964 there was a marked outpouring of frustrated anger upon the symbols of that frustration. After the governor refused to countenance their complaints, frustrated peasants sent a delegation to Addis Ababa to make their grievances known to the emperor and to seek the intercession of influential people in the capital. The emperor chose to ignore them; by failing to take appropriate measures that might have helped to diffuse the growing tension, the state ineptly allowed conditions to get out of its control. When it eventually decided to send an official delegation to try to persuade the rebels to abandon their "misguided actions," it was a bit too late. Other delegations were to come and go, giving little and accomplishing nothing. The state was finally able to regain control of the province by using "the stick and the carrot" at the same time.

In its judicious but futile attempt to restore tranquillity by peaceful means, the government sent three commissions between April and July 1968. Their task was essentially the same: to explain the content and purpose of the proclamation, to advise citizens to respect the law, to find out the motives behind the unrest, and to suggest means of ending it. I will describe briefly the makeup, findings, and recommendations of each commission in order to show how the ineptness of the state in part helped both to incite and sustain the rebellion.

On April 10, two months after the outbreak of hostilities, the first commission left for Gojjam. Consisting of five prominent people, it was headed by a senator, Dejazmatch Dereje Mekonen, who incidentally was instrumental in bringing the revolt of 1951 to an end. Having spent six days in eastern Gojjam talking to officials and peasant representatives, it returned to Addis Ababa accompanied by seventeen elders from Motta (nine) and Bichena (eight). Damot refused to be represented.[53] On April 17, in the presence of commission members, the elders presented their complaints to the emperor both orally and in writing. They informed him of their misery under bad governors and a rapacious militia and reminded him of the state's "benign neglect [that] had kept this province in darkness." They asked for better government, better educational, health, and transport facilities, and demanded the cessation of tax assessment, the withdrawal of assessors, and the abrogation of the tax law.[54] The emperor is reported to have flown into a rage upon hearing their forceful remonstrations. He rejected their demands, warning them in veiled language that if they failed to stop their "misguided and unlawful activities" immediately, the state would use all means at its disposal to protect its law-abiding citizens and to restore law and order. There was, none the less, a vaguely conciliatory tone in his uncompromising response; he capped his emotional peroration with a gentle plea to the elders, urging them to return home without delay and help bring peace to their troubled land.[55] Deeply disappointed and empty-handed but no less determined, the elders returned home. It soon became clear that while no military campaign was to be resumed, neither would the governor and his deputies be removed from their posts. Equally obdurate, the peasants chose to persist in their struggle until their demands were met in full.

The first test of their resolve came in early May when the administration sent the governor of Dega Damot back to Feres Bet to resume his duties. Under heavy police protection he vainly tried to reassert his authority. He even gave a banquet to make reconciliation. Rebuffed and frustrated, the governor abandoned the town on May 9 and for another two and a half months the rebels ran the subdistrict with little interference from the state. Similar attempts in Motta also failed. For all practical purposes, governmental activities had ceased to exist in those two districts, and there was a general paralysis in state institutions in the entire eastern half of the province.

The government was not yet ready to give up its efforts to resolve the crisis peacefully. There was a genuine belief in Addis Ababa that the otherwise innocent people of Gojjam were being "misled by deceitful individuals with harmful designs for their country and people," and that, through patient counseling and guidance, they could be dissuaded from their "injurious activities."[56] So, on June 1 the second commission, made up of representatives from the Ministries of the Interior and Finance and the Departments of Police and Security, was sent to the province.[57] Led by the Vice-Minister of the Interior, Girazmatch Tafesse Tebikie, the committee spent eleven days moving around the districts of Bichena, Debre Markos, Damot, and Motta, talking to people, gathering information, and giving counsel whenever and wherever circumstances permitted. It had a mixed reception; in some places it was welcomed cheerfully and treated respectfully, in others not. For instance, on June 2, it used its influence to dissuade an estimated force of 3,000, mostly armed peasants from Bichena, Damot, and Motta from attacking peasants from Sinan, Debre Markos, after the latter had agreed to lay down their arms. Similarly two days later it intervened to save Dembecha from possible destruction by 4,000 rebels. But when on June 7 it sought the release of the governor of Motta, who was being held by rebels, the committee almost jeopardized the lives of its members. Angry men assaulted and disarmed them, then impetuously threw them into a small hut where they passed "a dreadfully cold night fighting bugs and lice." After they were freed through the intervention of the clergy, they hurriedly returned to Addis Ababa, apparently convinced that the rebels had "renounced their ties to the state."[58]

Obviously fearful of displeasing and antagonizing a powerful governor, the commission submitted a two-part report that was a mishmash of hearsay and subjective impressions. Highly selective and too judgmental, it was an equivocal endorsement of the governor's views. In its opinion, the cause of discontent was not what it had heard all along – i.e. fear of land measurement or *kelad*, increased taxation, and repression – but a conspiracy concocted by unnamed enemies of the state residing within and outside the province. It did admit that accusations directed against the militia were not totally groundless, but found the governor and his deputies entirely blameless. Those rebellious peasants "who could hardly distinguish the good from the evil," it timidly reported, were simply led astray by people who had selfish reasons to disturb the peace. Included in the list of agitators were state employees who had lost their jobs, collaborators with and beneficiaries of Italian colonialism, thieves, murderers, and all sorts of criminals turned highwaymen, men who idly passed their time in courts seeking titles and/or appointments, idle members of the gentry, state employees who had failed to receive salary raises or promotion in rank, losers in parliamentary elections, and senators.[59] Except for one former parliamentarian none of them was identified by name, nor were the allegations supported by concrete evidence.

Similarly, when it suggested military means for ending the challenge to the state, the commission was merely repeating what the governor had recommended all along. Specifically, it advised that lines of communication between the conspirators in Addis Ababa and the population be broken by deporting the conspirators to remote regions, and that the belligerent peasants of Damot and Motta be made to bear the full weight of the state's power. According to the plan, state forces augmented by six hundred fresh troops and supported by fighter planes – the very sight of which, it was believed, would terrify the rebels – were to carry out surgical operations from three strategic locations: Felege Berhan, a border town between Bichena and Motta, Jigga (Damot), about 75 kilometers from Debre Markos, and the town of Motta, 230 kilometers from the capital. If these measures were adopted, it confidently predicted, the state would regain full control in less than three weeks, forcing the population to pay taxes as scheduled. Any further delays, it warned, would only embolden the peasants, who had mistakenly taken state leniency for rebel strength.[60] Ensuing events did make it abundantly clear that there was no alternative to the military option, but the commission's optimism concerning a speedy end of the crisis was not borne out.

Evidently troubled by the sudden increase in the level of violence, the government took what it considered were deterrent military measures. Between June 18 and 20, several skirmishes occurred in which both sides suffered heavy casualties. Horrified by the people's "arrogance, pride, and proclivity to violence," a weary and nervous governor dispatched urgent messages requesting a reinforcement of two battalions.[61] Wasting no time, the government sent nine hundred troops, most of them going to Motta, which along with Bichena was placed under military administrators.[62] At the same time leaflets which carried messages from the emperor were dropped there. Expressing regret and dismay that a few districts had opposed the tax bill through "sheer misunderstanding," the emperor tried to convince his suspicious and defiant subjects that the new revenue was to be used mainly in the eradication of diseases, expansion of education and transport, and promotion of agricultural and industrial growth. These maneuvers made little impression on the rebels.

Additional peaceful overtures followed. The third and last commission, which included two of the most senior and influential ministers, arrived at Debre Markos on July 5 to have a direct dialogue with the rebels. Led by Dejazmatch Kifle Ergetu, Minister of the Interior, and Dejazmatch Kifle Dadi, Crown Counselor, the delegation traveled widely by air and by road, stopping in remote villages and always listening and lecturing.[63] For more than two weeks it heard, with distressing frequency, stories of repression, of hardship, and of fear of alterations in land use. Upon its return to Addis Ababa, the commission submitted a comprehensive report that contained an objective evaluation of existing conditions and bold proposals for remedying the situation. In its view, state officials had lost the trust and confidence of the people, and their retention would only prolong a crisis that had the potential of spreading into other provinces. At least three changes had to be made in order to avert a bigger problem: remove the governor and replace him with a person acceptable to the people, reshuffle his deputies within the province, and integrate the militia into the police force. If these changes did not bring about the desired ends, the commission concluded, then it was incumbent upon the state to protect its law-abiding citizens by armed means, for which two additional battalions were thought to be sufficient.[64]

The report was favorably received and acted upon. On the emperor's official birthday (July 23) Tsehayu was transferred to Kaffa and Dereje Makonen was brought from the senate to replace him. Two of Tsehayu's arch rivals, Haile Yesus Filate and Ayalew Desta, were reinstated in their former posts in Damot and Motta respectively, while two other local nobles were appointed governors of Bichena and Debra Markos respectively. A few subdistrict governors were elevated to higher positions elsewhere, but most of them simply exchanged posts in the province. A few days later, a general amnesty was declared; rebels were ordered to lay down their arms and return to their farms by September 7, and all farmers were exempted from all penalties for tax default provided they submitted arrears by December 1972. The jubilation and rejoicing that followed these announcements gave added hope that the troubles would soon be over. That was illusory. Since withdrawal of the tax bill itself was not among the concessions, peasants were not convinced that land measurement, the main source of their anxiety and unrest, was not to be instituted. The hasty actions of the new appointees only helped to reinforce that lingering fear. Unscrupulous officials inadvertently subverted the government's program of pacification. Before conditions were sufficiently stabilized, overzealous administrators began to collect taxes using coercion in some instances. This was especially true of Haile Yesus Filate and Ayalew Desta, the two men who had been suspected of instigating the rebellion. Wondering "if he had been inciting them to rebel only to prepare the way for his coming home,"[65] elders claiming to represent the district angrily told Haile Yesus to leave along with the chief of police. Many other incidents occurred, the most serious being the fighting that broke out on October 17 following rebel attack of the police at Dembecha. After two days of fighting that involved the air force, the rebels retreated, leaving behind 50 dead and many more wounded, with five killed and six wounded on the other side.[66] Gravely concerned, the emperor sent out another emotional appeal:

> It has deeply distressed us to learn that despite our efforts and appeals, the people of Dega Damot and adjacent areas have continued their lawless activities.
>
> Whereas we desire to create an atmosphere in which every citizen would be able to live in peace and prosperity, exercising his rights fully and enjoying the fruits of progress, it is regrettable that such a problem should have been created in these few districts.
>
> Therefore, since we do not wish to see the destruction of lives and property of our loyal citizens by a few conspirators, you are again instructed to return to your normal pursuits as soon as you have received this order and warning.[67]

The message was ineffectual. Although the governor of Damot was able to return to his post at the end of October, the district remained ungovernable, conditions bordering on anarchy. Rebels moved wildly around burning huts, destroying crops, slaughtering livestock, and killing suspected saboteurs. While the air force raided some targeted villages in northern Damot and western Motta, the governor, in exasperation, informed Addis Ababa that three battalions of the regular army and seven hundred policemen were required additionally to end the crisis.[68] And once again the emperor warned that "Those malcontents who impudently continue to violate the rights of others, to harass the administration, and to disturb security" would be punished.

The military threats designed to compel acquiescence were paralleled by civil action. The state's police commissioner paid a one-day visit to the province in mid December and recommended that a delegation including nobles from Debre Markos be sent to Damot to mollify the peasants, who were "hoodwinked by evil persons with blind ambitions and unattainable goals," and that an armed force with adequate logistics be permanently maintained in the province to guarantee order. Incredibly, he added that "since, as is historically known and as I myself have witnessed, the people of Gojjam are too malleable and fickle, quite susceptible to propaganda, and since their basic attitude will never be reformed by time, it is imperative that appropriate measures are taken to teach them a lesson for their current behavior."[69] None the less, a delegation headed by the prominent Gojjame, Haile Mariam Kebede, arrived at Feres Bet on December 21 and addressed a huge gathering, emotionally appealing to the people to lay down their weapons and spare the land more violence, and pledging that although the income tax was irrevocable, land would never be measured. Some of the rebel leaders, including most notably Bamlaku Ayele, surrendered, and resistance subsided significantly. Only Dega Damot, Kwarit, and Bibugn refused to submit.[70]

It had become apparent that the resistance was fast losing steam, and the military offensive that the government finally opened proved terminal to the insurgency. Supported by the territorial army, the police, and some regular troops, peasants from Agewmedir invaded Kwarit and Bibugn while those of Wemberima, Yeshihudad, Sekela, and Tinhan of Kola Damot were mobilized against Dega Damot. The conflict was turned into interclass warfare which was brutal and decisive. By February all resistance had been broken and the situation fairly stabilized. In May the emperor made his long-awaited visit; he toured the province, paying his respects to the monasteries and great churches whose traditional privileges he restored, giving promotions and banquets, and awarding titles and medals. All this was intended to please the gentry and clergy, but the peasants too had won significant concessions: most of the unpopular bureaucrats had been removed, tax assessors recalled, and the income tax indefinitely postponed. Moreover, farmers were exempted from tax arrears for nineteen years (1950–68), a sum which would have been in the neighborhood of ETH $1,054,478.[71] All received clemency; a few of the rebel leaders even got titles. In terms of overall results, there was a striking resemblance between the revolts of 1951 and 1968. Twice the state gave way to public pressure, and in both cases the regional gentry channeled public grievances in ways that reinforced their own position and the existing social order.

Organization and leadership

The image of a ragged band of Damotian farmers, armed with ancient rifles, a few rounds of ammunition and spears, setting out to defend themselves and

185

their rist against the modern forces of the Imperial Ethiopian Government may seem quixotic. Pathetic would be a more apt term; for the men of Dega Damot did not expect to win. Their attitude toward their land and their chances of successfully defending it were summed up in the slogan: "Die for your rist!"[72]

Allan Hoben's description of the Damotian rebels is remarkably accurate and holds true for the whole provincial movement. Relatively ill equipped and fragmented, the rebels lacked a permanent, province-wide organizational structure. Without doubt their slogan "Die for your *rist!*" was most appropriate for that moment, for land was the central unifying issue, and it was as popular and as powerful as the all-time mobilizing slogan "Fatherland/Motherland or death!" But the peasants' apparent determination to sacrifice themselves in defense of their lands was not matched by organizational resources and commitment. Compared to those of Tigrai and Bale, the rebels of Gojjam lacked unifying leaders, and the various inchoate segments remained militarily ineffectual.

Structurally, rebel organization closely resembled that of *Weyane*; operationally, it was less effective. In organizing themselves, rebels drew from local resources and experience. The traditional process allowed all those who supported the insurgency to participate directly both in public discussions and in the selection of leaders. Normally at the sound of a horn or trumpet, informed villagers would assemble at the parish church, the village market, or a river to elect officers, work out plans, and pass binding resolutions under oath. Reminiscent of *Weyane*, the oath was intended to strengthen bonds of solidarity and loyalty while minimizing the risks of dissension and betrayal. Every gathering had its ritual, the common pattern being one in which a public prayer was followed by festive activities that included dancing and singing to war chants. Then after long hours of deliberation, the *shengo* or assembly chose its leaders, usually by acclamation, from a list of nominees.[73]

Leadership was typically hierarchical; it included, from top to bottom, the yegobez or awra aleqa (chief of the brave), yewenz aleqa (chief of the river), yabat dagna (judge of the fathers), and sebsabi abal (summoner). As far as can be ascertained, the much coveted office of yager azmatch (country war leader) remained vacant, and the incompleteness of the pyramidal structure means that there was no single, unified leadership. Each district was loosely organized under a chief of the brave who acted as supreme military and judicial authority at that level. Immediately under him was the chief of the river, who exercised a great deal of power since the village cell was the nucleus of the structure. The judges provided counsel and arbitrated in matters of local conflict, while the summoners were mainly responsible for calling meetings and transmitting messages.[74]

What was the criterion for office? One author asserted that the chosen officers were "often men of position and title,"[75] while another claimed that "The main qualification for office seems to have been the possession of a gun and the will to oppose the tax."[76] It was more than that. Of the 32 known prominent leaders, all of whom were men, only 4 had titles and only 5 held administrative positions before their defection. Merit, character, and social status were the main criteria for office. "It is believed that those [men] known as chief of the brave," reported observers from the other side, "were elected because their fellow villagers thought they had the moral power and fortitude to counsel and guide people as well as to admonish or punish wrongdoers ..."[77] Leaders were chosen from among those considered "of forceful character," commanding the respect and trust of their fellow villagers. That trust was earned and deserved. Consider, for example, the case of the legendary one-eyed Bamlaku Ayele, who distinguished himself in the uprising of 1951. Outside officialdom, few people were better known than this person, whose demeanor could hardly conceal the reputation and influence he enjoyed in eastern Gojjam. A good number of the officers, like Bamlaku, were rehabilitated bandits. They were men known for their courage, aggressiveness, and decisiveness – men respected for their magnanimity or feared for their cruelty. In addition, there were those from the gentry whose claim to office was justified by their high position in the community and willingness to oppose the government.

Although leadership enjoyed a popular mandate, not all officers operated democratically at all times. As a matter of fact, some were more concerned with making private gains than with correcting public wrongs. Considering the fact that in such rural movements leaders are usually self-appointed, the extent to which peasants in Gojjam were involved in determining the makeup of rebel leadership was impressive; it shows the degree to which kinship relations and the truncated autonomy of the village community intruded into and indeed competed with feudal relations of power. Leadership was democratically elected. However, once elected or confirmed, some officers lost touch with their constituency, engaging in intrigue, pettiness, and grudges. As there was no popular mechanism for power control, including the absence of a single supervising authority, they became notoriously abusive and as demanding as those officials they had replaced. "After they expelled the state officials," noted one report, "they became the main power wielders, collecting fees and imposing penalties at will ..."[78] Surely the principal targets were people unwilling to join the resistance, suspected spies, and "double-dealers," but those who supported it were not spared either For minor infractions, such as making contact with disgraced tax assessors or local officials, individuals were reprimanded, sanctioned, or forced to pay a penalty of up to fifty dollars, often pocketed by the "chiefs."[79]

A lamentable absence of unity was another feature of the revolt. Just as the anticolonial resistance in the province thirty years earlier was encumbered by internal friction, so was the insurgency of 1968. Rebel leaders were unable to form a cohesive organization as they continuously vied for honorific precedence, frequently feuding amongst themselves. These disputes blunted the effectiveness of their resistance. There was no one among them capable of exerting authority that transcended his own locale, and none,

187

with the possible exception of Bamlaku, had the stature that was remotely comparable to that of Haile Mariam Redda of Tigrai or Wako Gutu of Bale, although one of them, Mekonen Mengiste, was ambitious enough to call himself leul (the prince).[80]

It was not only petty rivalry and friction between leaders that plagued the resistance; correspondence between villages or subdistricts leaves no doubt that there was mutual suspicion, mistrust, and even recrimination among peasants supporting the rebellion.

> March 28, 1968 (21 Megabit 1960)
> To our respected fathers and brothers of Inarj Inawga and Yinach:
> We have secretly and solemnly agreed to die together. It grieves us to inform you that the contents of our confidential agreement have been leaked out by one of your members. Though we have abandoned you today, we have not retreated. Regrettably, we will expose the person responsible for revealing our secret at our next meeting. May the Lord of Gojjam help us!
>
> Respectfully,
> Chiefs of Ine Maijara[81]

> To our respected fathers and all the *balabbats* concerned with the welfare of Gojjam:
> There are no people who have not suffered for their *rist*; many have given their lives. We are all mortal beings, and we beseech you to believe us that the reason why we failed to attend the meeting is because most people had gone to market early in the day before our messengers could notify them about it. You should not doubt our motive. We assure you that not only the men but the women too are ready to die!
>
> The people of Wondessa[82]

Even though peasants were determined to protect their unfettered access to land, they lacked a strong sense of solidarity. Collective ownership, augmented by kinship affinity, created "a sense of common identity," but fell short of providing territorial symbols of unity. Only in Motta did the population of the four subdistricts achieve sufficient and sustained internal cohesion to expel all state officials, assuming the reins of local administration for nearly a year. Not even Damot, the other area of stubborn resistance, witnessed such organizational unity, because the southern half was not nearly as involved or committed as the northern half of the district.

Solidarity was most genuinely expressed at the village level. The parish, ranging from about 100 to 2,000 people in size, was the matrix of social cohesion. Usually demarcated by a ravine, stream, or path, and claiming its own *tabot* (holy ark), the parish "joined the population of individual settlements into well-defined territorial groups, the village communities," and was thus "the most important territorial unit of affiliation and identification."[83] Most peasants were undoubtedly committed to the defense of their rights to land, but were more willing to fight near their neighborhood symbols.

Hence, the reason why resistance remained so fractured was precisely that the concept of parish solidarity was too restrictive both organizationally and operationally.

The movement's problem was not merely one of organization but also of mobilization, for neither fear of privatization of land nor kinship affinity was enough to guarantee universal support for the uprising. It is well known that the inhabitants of Agewmedir and Metekel, separated by cultural and linguistic differences as well as mode of livelihood from the dominant Amharic-speaking population, abstained from the rebellion; what is less known is that a sizeable fraction of the Amhara never supported the insurgency. Not only did Bahir Dar, the greater part of southern Damot, and southern Debre Markos refrain from most of the fighting for most of the time, but the latter two areas were instrumental in the suppression of the rebellion. Excluding Metekel, all of them were part of the *rist* system. Then what explains their political behavior?

One view holds that the peasants occupying the open plains of Debre Markos and vicinity avoided the rebellion mainly for economic reasons. Inhabiting an area that enjoys a mild, temperate climate and fertile soil, farmers there were considered more prosperous than those occupying the mountainous districts farther to the north and were thus likely to regard the rebels askance.[84] But Kola Damot, which was only peripherally involved in the rebellion, lies outside this climatic zone. Moreover, since the richer peasants would have been targeted for higher income taxes, there was all the more reason for them to resist. The militancy of the northerners and the relative passivity of the southerners probably lay in geography more than in economy. Mountainous and without roads, northeastern Gojjam has served historically as a haven for rebels and bandits alike. It provided for greater tactical maneuverability than the flat plains, which were not so easily defended.

The inability to stir up peasants solely on the basis of *rist* forced rebel leaders to resort to propaganda and coercive tactics. The ideology of protest drew upon religious bigotry, gossip, rumors, and messianic news, Rudé's "confused" and "contradictory" ideas. Not only was it rumored that the emperor was dead, but that his successor would be a Muslim. Muslims were singled out for abuse and victimization for their alleged support of the tax bill. Rebels were deliberately using hate and scare tactics by drawing upon the community's historical experience and existing religious cleavages. At the same time, men disguised as hermits and prophets spoke of an imminent disaster in apocalyptic terms: the country, they preached, was to be embroiled in political turmoil for at least three years, cataclysmic events leading to the fall of the regime and the subsequent rise to power of a saintly Gojjame who would then rule the province with justice and in peace. So, they urged peasants to fight on for another three years, assuring them that the government would be censured at the United Nations if it ever dared to bombard their villages.[85] Not all of these ideas were attributed to the

189

peasants themselves. Some of them originated either in Addis Ababa or Debre Markos, and were then transmitted to the countryside either by word of mouth or in the form of coded messages. It was rumored that one of the chief contacts between town and countryside was a former member of the Imperial Bodyguard who had fled there after the abortive coup of 1960. He was staying in a monastery at Koga, Motta, disguised as a monk.[86]

In addition, fictitious letters were circulated in some of the districts in order to boost the morale of dissidents or to warn their detractors and enemies. One such letter, purportedly received from neighboring Begemedir, was actually concocted in Motta:

> Greeting to our kin in Damot and Sekela:
> Measurement of land is a plot to change the landholding system. The people of Begemedir and Gonder are ready to sacrifice themselves in defense of their *rist*. You, too, should be firm. We counsel that you rather go to jail than allow measurement.
>
> We are your kin from Begemedir and Gonder.[87]

Propaganda was supplemented with the threat or use of force. The rebels usually communicated their objectives, warned their opponents, and proclaimed the justness of their actions through threatening letters.

> To our dear brother Ato Aderaw Hailu:
> That you, in connivance with Fitawrari Abeyto Tesfaye and Kegnazmatch Kassahun, are engaged in hostile activities is known to us. Unless you submit yourself to us as soon as you have received this letter, your house will be destroyed and your livestock will be confiscated.
>
> Chiefs of the brave, Berkegn and Telim.[88]

Threat was often translated into destruction of property, those cultivators who allowed measurement or paid tax suffering most. Their crops and huts were burned, their animals killed, and their property looted or confiscated. They were treated as social outcasts who could be beaten or flogged at will. Antirebels or passive peasants were ostracized as religious heretics or, as they were often called, "the children of the missionaries"![89] Too often popular justice was arbitrated by personal hatred and vindictiveness.

That such a splintered movement survived for well over a year was due much less to its own resources and organizational sophistication than to the state's inability to take decisive measures. At no time did the state try to exert the full weight of its might, and the major operation against the locus of resistance was not taken until almost a year after the inception of the insurgency. The government used its troops sparingly, primarily for defensive purposes; this was by no means owing to the reluctance or refusal of state forces to "fight against their fellow Christians,"[90] although some native policemen were not unsympathetic to the rebels. Because the army remained on the sidelines, the confrontation between the rebels and the police (supported by militia and "volunteers") was bound to be an unequal match. Whereas the resistance could mobilize as many as 4,000 fighters at a time in one district alone, the number of policemen at each station in the countryside barely exceeded ten – often it was six – and the total size of the auxiliary force was at no time larger than two thousand men. These forces were largely ineffective because they lacked organizational unity and discipline and because their weapons were as outdated as those of the rebels, and in some cases even inferior. Moreover, many of the police were native Gojjame who were thus cautious not to antagonize their fellow countrymen, and also reportedly expressed their sympathy and solidarity by smuggling arms for dissidents.[91]

The state's reluctance to take strong punitive measures, as recommended by the governor and the first ad hoc committee assigned to review the situation, was based upon two factors: a strong belief in the generalized innocence of the rural population and a contagious fear that repressive measures would only inflame conditions both in the province and in neighboring provinces. Since it was commonly believed that the innocent peasants were manipulated by "evil-minded" people, they could be mollified through protracted and calculated negotiations. Although it grossly underestimated the peasants' ability to make independent decisions as rational beings, the state's uncertainty in the military option was not without justification. At a time when it was still engaged on two fronts in Bale and Eritrea, hundreds of miles apart from each other, the opening of a third front would have meant overreaching its military capabilities. This fear was reinforced by the notion that any overt popular discontent had the potential of spreading over a much wider geographical area because of the commonality of land tenure, culture, and rural social structure in the northern regions.[92] However, the state had greatly overestimated the potential for peasant unity on the one hand and rebel organizational skills on the other. In contrast to Bale or Tigrai, leadership was amorphous and extremely reluctant to lead peasants into action.

Lacking strong internal solidarity, rebels showed no commitment to wipe out state forces. An eminent Ethiopianist was absolutely correct when he commented: "Neither the peasants nor the government undertook a coordinated effort to sweep the opposition from the field."[93] This was not the result of lack of arms or inability to fight. They were not, of course, as well armed as their counterparts in Bale. Their weapons, consisting primarily of Italian Alpini, Manlicher or Minaser, Demofter, and other brands such as Wetterly (Wechefo) and Snider, were somewhat outdated, although some of the rebels possessed automatic machine guns smuggled in through Borana-Sayint, Wello.[94] Given the rich legacy of patriotic resistance and revolt in the province, peasants were not lacking in the experience of warfare either. Their problem was mainly organizational.

The hallmark of rebel military activity was spontaneity, lacking effective coordination and harmony. Military operations were erratic and spasmodic, with as much interruption by mediations as actual fighting done. Consequently, initiatives were never sustained, rebels failing to consolidate initial gains. Threats to blow up the main bridge linking Gojjam with Shewa were never followed up, and only rarely did rebels interfere with highway traffic and communication.[95] This lack of planning and organization was nowhere better manifested than in their spontaneous attempts to burn police stations and/or towns, which were often abruptly and rather awkwardly dropped because of the intervention of third parties, usually the bishop, the clergy, or even government officials. This demonstrates the bankruptcy of their leadership and their ambivalence, and, indeed, their lack of a specific program of action. If military and political considerations had not precluded swift and forceful action by the state, it is doubtful that the revolt would have lasted so long without a radical reformation in rebel commitment and organization. That, of course, would have required a fundamental reorientation of the parish mentality.

Conclusion

The revolt was a coalition of discontented groups, participants trying to protect their economic interests both as individuals and as members of a class. The economic and social issues that united them divided them at the same time. Households were separated from each other by distinctions in ownership of land, livestock, and tools, but were united by a community custom that upheld collective possession of land. Since an assault on the *rist* would have threatened all, antagonistic cooperation was deemed absolutely necessary. But cooperation was conditional, and there were abstentions, desertions, and frictions. By supplanting them, but only partially, the state created an alienated segment of the regional gentry – men who always maneuvered as the stalwart guardians of tradition and valiant leaders against outside interference. They abandoned their allies as soon as their limited goals were met. On the other hand, while the often ambiguous political vocabulary of the insurgents contained instances of class animosity, peasants did not act harmoniously. The landed cultivators excluded, and even terrorized, the landless and least harmless, targeting them as strategic enemies. They were minimally class-conscious. This duality was characteristic of a differentiated agricultural society that rested on affective ties of kinship, confessionalism, and feudal rituals of subordination.

In spite of its mixed social composition, the revolt of 1968–69 was fairly specific in its objectives, which were realized by and large. It wanted above all to preempt the Agricultural Income Tax Law, which it did. It also wished to terminate corrupt administrative practices; in this it was only partially successful. Although the revolt was eventually suppressed by force, the government capitulated to nearly all the rebel demands. After much hesitation and inaction, it transferred unpopular officials, relieving them of their duties in some cases. Some of them were even replaced by local nobles who had been suspected of abetting the unrest. Not only was the tax decree postponed, but all tax arrears were canceled. No rebels were punished. Once again the imperial state acquiesced to provincialist forces opposed even to minimal agrarian reforms. Its failure was a measure of the extent to which it had weakened local intermediary authorities.

Previous studies of the revolt have incorrectly portrayed it both as anti-Shewan and as antimodernization. Hostility against Governor Tsehayu has been taken to mean popular hatred for Shewan Amhara.[96] However, peasant fury was directed only against officials believed to be corrupt and unjust. The most unpopular of them all was Demiss Alamirew, himself from Gojjam. The districts under Shewan administrators were, in fact, extraordinarily quiet.[97] This is not to imply that the uprising entailed no parochial senti-ments, for in its unyielding struggle against the state and its agents from Addis Ababa, the local gentry did fall back upon provincialism to mobilize the peasantry.

To present the rebellion merely as a clash between tradition and moderni-zation is to deny its political and social content. An attempt has been made to portray the state as an agency of change whose developmental policies were frustrated by conservative and reactionary forces consisting of the gentry and peasantry.[98] Even more than *Weyane*, this rebellion demonstrates social conflict at the point of production – the parish. The gentry, otherwise an ally of the state in its exploitation of the peasants, was opposed mainly to further state intrusion into its traditional domain and to the burden of taxation. The peasants' fear and mistrust were rooted in their existential experience and social relations of production. Their precarious life hinged upon their ability to control the basis of subsistence – land. What they feared most was its alienation and commoditization which, according to popular belief, only outsiders could have accomplished. And the state controlling from Addis Ababa was an alien intruder. Peasants were not averse to change per se, but to changes which did not involve them directly and which they believed would be harmful to them in the long run. The rebellion in Gojjam was only one more manifestation of the continuing dual struggle in rural Ethiopia, but one in which peasants successfully preserved their partial autonomy by exploiting interclass conflicts at the top.

7

Conclusion

Agrarian rebellion was repetitive. One revolt resembled another, following a similar pattern and aiming at similar goals. Peasant rebels lacked either a political program or an ideological inspiration to direct their eyes beyond immediate grievances toward basic reforms or institutional change.

Perez Zagorin[1]

Every rebellion is historically specific, and as such it contains distinctive qualities of its own. The causes and forms of agrarian protest vary with time and place; wide variations exist in the breadth and depth of popular participation, in the quality of leadership and organization, and in the degree of urban cooperation. Some revolts are manifestly more extensive, durable, and violent, some more egalitarian in their vision, and others fairly concrete in their objectives. Yet, there seems to be an element of timelessness in peasant uprisings. To speak of peasant revolts as spontaneous, localized, particularistic, discontinuous, and limited in objective and impact is to stress the phenomenology of rural resistance. In summing up the discussion on the sociology and contours of insurrection in twentieth-century Ethiopia, it will be emphasized again that not only were the three revolts sufficiently similar in origin and outcome, but their basic limitations are characteristic of nearly all peasant rebellions.

The causes of popular protest in contemporary Ethiopia lay in an iniquitous and coercive social order, itself experiencing increased pressures from extraneous forces. Although there were considerable differences with respect to precipitants, social composition, and goals of protest, at the root of every revolt were many grievances rising from a multitiered social structure that rested on a feudal base. Tensions originating from capitalist penetration were important, but hardly decisive. Novel and expanding relations with the West did produce new problems and possibilities, but the manifold and cumulative reasons for the conflict were domestically rooted. The parameters of resistance were set by the extractive activities of the state with a bent toward modernity, and in so far as they were reactions to the politics of

194

"modernization," some of the revolts can be described as futile attempts to reverse historical trends and processes set in motion by powerful domestic and international forces. In its endeavor to extend its autonomy by pruning lordship, undermining local autonomy, and centralizing fiscal resources, which meant an increasing intrusion into the household economy, the imperial state created a situation generally unfavorable to its goals. In that epic contest between an incorporative and innovative state and centrifugal forces negotiating and fighting for better or favorable terms of incorporation into the emerging state-society, the latter were handicapped by the obvious disadvantages of inferior resources, technology, and organization. They drained the state's energies and resources, but, with the exception of *Weyane*, none of the revolts posed an immediate threat to the monarchist regime. Spatially confined and lacking any long-range goals, they easily dissolved when their demands were met or else fizzled out in the face of sustained repression.

Peasants alone did not initiate, organize, and direct the revolts, but did so in coalition with other social groups; that interclass solidarity was feeble, however. Amid the tangled web of social cleavages and shifting alliances, fractions of the landed upper class were ranged against the state: tenants against landlords; village communities against venal bureaucrats; national minorities against ethnic hegemonism; Muslims against Christians; and periphery against core. Peasants were at the heart of all of them, but the course and outcome of these Jacqueries were, to a very great degree, shaped by continuing struggles among the dominant social strata. Rural protest thus must be seen as part of a broader social conflict stemming from a transitional social formation (in which merchant capital was uncomfortably combined with existing forms of surplus appropriation) and directly involving various segments of society. Guided by a mixture of old and new ideas, discontented as well as ambitious groups constructed alliances by cutting across class, ethnic, and religious boundaries, but without ever merging. They were separated by unbridgeable contradictions, organizationally unable to overcome structural vulnerability. The objectives of struggles waged by such a mélange of class representatives were unavoidably mixed and so were the outcomes, although some of the results were not what the rebels had desired or even anticipated, but were consequences of their actions.

There was direct correlation between the predominance of a peasant-based economy with regional divergencies and the mobilization and organization of social action. As in early modern Europe, the preponderance of an ethnically and culturally segmented agricultural population meant that (a) in the struggle to achieve greater administrative and fiscal uniformity the imperial state had to rely heavily on the dominant forces even as it tried to tame them, or to put it differently, segments of the landed upper class "became indispensable allies and formidable enemies";[2] (b) the issues, strategies, and organizations around which opposition coalesced were preeminently locally rooted and without projects to redesign the state; and (c) the bulk of the social cost of the conflicts was borne by the peasantry.

Monarchy and aristocracy ultimately established a precarious equilibrium that lasted until the 1970s. The monarchical state did attain its goal of destroying rival sources of power, but only partially, for the regional nobility was able to maintain, albeit in diminished form, its access to the rural product and its preeminent social position. In the northern provinces (Eritrea excepted) a high proportion of the middle- and lower-level state functionaries were drawn from local dominant groups until the fall of the regime. Unable to eliminate them completely, the imperial state could not bring the countryside under its immediate control and thus was never able to carry out its reforms fully. The *rist–gult* dialectic simply was not amenable to imperial centralization and innovation, although the ideological basis of the Solomonic dynasty provided the justification for the collection of tribute by the monarch and his representatives. Similarly, the southern gentry, while dependent on the state for its privileged position, frustrated governmental efforts to initiate limited agrarian reforms. Its members' obstructionist activities eventually helped to pave the way to the revolution that destroyed all of them along with the old regime.

Meanwhile, the main losers were the peasants. Their condition grew worse with each revolt, leading some observers to write off the uprisings in the northern provinces as "a mindless struggle on behalf of class privileges."[3] Undoubtedly, by using longstanding patron–client networks, the nobility was able to transmute genuine popular discontent into support of its own cause. However, it would be wrong to assume that peasants were completely subaltern, and subalternity does not necessarily mean utter powerlessness. The revolts in Gojjam and Tigrai were more than elite responses to state policies, since they required popular participation in which peasants were active and creative agents. Their development is a good example of grassroots anger spontaneously jelling into violent action. Peasants did not just provide food, shelter, and information. They made up the majority of the combatants who were united by a consciousness of denial and oppression; that collective awareness was relatively low, but sufficient to sustain bloody struggles that demanded great sacrifice of livelihood and life. Peasants are rational beings who take calculated risks. Their low degree of consciousness was a function of history and of the cultural milieu in which popular discourse took place.

Despite the apparent ambiguity between social position and political action, the revolts must be treated as integral parts of continuing class conflicts and struggles. If class conflict is seen primarily as a struggle over the appropriation of surplus and property, then it certainly was epifocal to popular protest. We may not be able to see class ideology and organization explicitly articulated, yet the only adequate context within which we can comprehend usefully the historic actions of the peasantry is that of social antagonism. That many, perhaps most, of the participants did not make an accurate assessment of their enemies or that they were not fully aware of their fundamental interests should not be surprising, since people are not always fully, or even partly, conscious of their class relationships so as to make them the basis for collective action. Class consciousness entails not only awareness of common and conflicting interests; it also means the capacity to assert collective interests by organizationally instituting radical changes in the existing social order. Consciousness was less evident than hostility, and this in part explains why peasants benefited the least although they made the greatest sacrifices.

Why was peasant consciousness so diffused? At least two interrelated explanations can be suggested. First, the Christian Amhara of Shewa monopolized political power to the near-exclusion of all others. As a result, preferential institutionalized arrangements were made for Amharic and Orthodox Christianity. Under these circumstances, consciousness took the form of cultural and/or ethnic assertiveness. Second and more importantly, the Ethiopian peasantry was not a monolithic social category. Although they comprised a class in relation to the broader society, Ethiopian peasants were internally stratified, objectively and subjectively. Rural differentiation had a cultural dimension that greatly affected social experience and political choice. Perceptions of self and of others were not determined solely by economic factors, nor were these images transfixed. Political preferences were in part determined within a cultural universe. For example, the possession of material resources or wealth had little to do, if at all, with how Christians and Muslims viewed each other and interacted with or against one another. Regardless of their position in the economic niche, Muslims were viewed generally as of lowly status by Christians. Northern peasants, poor and rich alike, had the same perception of their southern counterparts; southerners were seen as heathen and, therefore, undeserving of equal treatment with Christians. Common economic grievances failed to transcend cultural barriers and provincialist identities. One major outcome of social and cultural fractionalization was fragmentation in political action.

Practically no possibilities existed for class-based action by a national peasantry. Because of the atomization of the peasantry and the dissimilarity of interests that were not at all favorable conditions for crystallization of national goals and symbols, the mobilization of discontent was extremely difficult even at the regional level. There *were* feelings of solidarity, as these proverbs illustrate: "When spiders' webs unite, they can tie up a lion," and "If only the country could unite, the king would be in trouble." But, in practice, such sentiments proved illusory because there were few channels for cross-cultural cooperation. Rich, poor, and tenant farmers and landless agricultural laborers saw little reason for unified action. Poverty, insecurity, and cutthroat competition for dwindling resources undercut possibilities for collective action. Patron–client ties and a host of other "vertical coalitions" competed with cooperative, solidaristic ties, often outweighing and overriding them. The country's vastness, difficult terrain, and poor communications hindered social intercourse on a wider scale.

Peasant resistance was defined primarily in terms of local issues. The different modalities of oppression appear to have little differential impact with respect to public mobilization. Northern Ethiopia shared a common mode of production, a common polity, the same Christian tradition, and an "etiological charter composed of a script, art, and literature" derived from Aksum. These were powerful enough factors to unify the population against foreigners. The perennial competition for honorific precedence among the regional overlords, and the rivalry between them and the crown for agricultural surplus, however, helped to develop provincialist identities. In other words, the activities of the ruling classes reinforced peasant parochialism. Internally, members of descent corporations did not have unifying symbols beyond the parish. And the ideology of kinship was more useful in invoking land claims – a source of litigation and conflict – than in organizing scattered households and villages. However, when authority became too abusive, violating law and custom, and when the gentry was willing and cooperative enough, collective defiance was possible. The essentially provincial forms of resistance against the state might have attained a regional dimension had the powerful people conditionally collaborating with the peasants chosen to form an interprovincial common front. Although they shared the same material interests and outlook, they were also locally rooted, however, lacking an institutionalized corporate identity. In the south, on the other hand, national and class antagonism had an almost perfect correlation and, as the Bale rebellion demonstrated, objective conditions for wider collective action existed. Nevertheless, ethnic and linguistic particularisms precluded solidarity across national boundaries. Perhaps the greatest obstacle to class mobilization in both sections of the country was the fact that cultivators were preoccupied routinely with their narrowly defined day-to-day activities and their own realization that their problems were essentially of a local nature.

Localism, then, was the underlying weakness of rural rebellion. Indeed, it is exceptional for peasants to move beyond spontaneity and localism without assistance from organized insurgent forces. Reflecting the low level of national integration, none of the revolts was able to promote solidarity across provincial frontiers. Each remained confined to one or parts of one province, unable to transcend its parochial origin. And when there was temporal coincidence, no attempts were made to coordinate activities. Each revolt operated in relative isolation, with little or no awareness of or even concern about what was happening elsewhere in the empire. Official suspicions that Eritrean rebels might have collaborated with those of Bale were utterly groundless.[4] Variant historical experience, ideological diversity, and divergent interests produced a mixed and highly ambivalent leadership that was incapable of providing a new basis of solidarity above the more restricted and restrictive ties of locality, kinship, and ethnicity. The state's instruments of coercion – the army, air force, police, and militia, largely equipped and trained by the regime's external supporters – were sufficiently strong to deal with the incoherent actions of the rural population.

None of the revolts, therefore, was capable of upsetting the whole system of social organization, nor was that its goal. The rebels attacked neither the legitimacy of the monarchy nor the broader ideological roots on which the political and economic power of the ruling classes rested. With the exception of the rebels in Bale they never directed their fury at the monarch, giving substance to an Abyssinian adage, "God cannot be blamed, the king cannot be accused." The rebels of Bale attacked the emperor and his regime, for they did not have strong historical or symbolic links to the central institutions. The Tigrean rebels, who, as in other similar contexts, were prone to dynasticism as a political movement, did the same, but they were clearly more ambivalent. In Gojjam, the emperor was exonerated from any responsibility for wrongdoing. "May God forgive the people of Gojjam, and may God give our king a longer life. It is the officials here who have hurt us, not his majesty's government," said the aggrieved.[5] As is common with peasant societies, the problem was always believed to be not with the sovereign himself but with the evil people who surrounded him. Insurgent Russian peasants "worshiped the Tsar." For them, "there was no 'system' within which Tsar and nobleman fitted as complementary elements within a common exploitative class."[6] In Europe, too, "the peasant movements operated largely within a world of received conventional assumptions respecting the right relation between the king and his people. It was to the king that they addressed their appeal for justice and redress of grievances."[7] Similarly, the targets of Ethiopian peasants were the most visible symbols of authority at the local level – judges, inspectors, administrators, police, and militia. The emperor was far removed from the peasant world. Frequently he pleaded ignorance in front of his officials, whom he sometimes scolded in public for having betrayed his trust. Hence the tendency of peasants to submit their plight to him over the heads of his representatives.

"With rare exceptions they envisage an adjustment in the social pyramid and not its destruction, though its destruction is easy to conceive," wrote Eric Hobsbawm about peasant revolts.[8] Like the bulk of agrarian movements, the rebellions in modern Ethiopia had only limited goals. Their main objective was not to overthrow or destroy the system of domination, but to redress wrongs, to evoke concessions, or, to use Hobsbawm's apt phrase, to work "the system ... to their minimum disadvantage."[9] They sought the restoration of "violated rights" or the recognition of existing ones. What they demanded were those things which they believed the king or his government was capable of delivering: better administration, fewer or lower taxes, respect for communal autonomy, reduction of corruption and repression, and the return of stolen lands. The peasants' aspirations also directly reflected their own experience as well as the conditions of their existence, which were relatively fixed and the same everywhere. To the extent that they attacked the legitimacy of the regime and the structure of power relations, the rebels of Bale could be regarded as more radical than their counterparts in Gojjam and Tigrai. But they made no attempt to construct a new system of social relations. To say that their movement had a revolutionary orientation is to read into the revolt evidence which it does not contain.[10] It is not correct to say that peasants do not envision the abolition of exploitation, for they actually do; but it has seldom been within the scope of rural movements to seek social transformation. Their goal has invariably been ameliorative, not revolutionary, although few revolutions, if any, have been made without peasants in the modern world. In their limited ability or inability to envision a different reality, Ethiopian rural rebels were quite typical of peasant insurgents.

Despite the narrowness of their goals, however, the rebels fought with great emotive intensity and tenacity. Assuming quite distinct organizational forms, they used different tactics of resistance that ranged from conventional to guerrilla warfare. What motivated the combatants was a strong belief in the legitimacy of their grievances, but leadership used rumors and propaganda to garner more sympathy and support from the populace. Women were conspicuously absent in that leadership, although they sometimes served as intermediaries, messengers, and spies. They were also the key element in the production and distribution of food; without them the male combatants could not have sustained the horrors of warfare. That warfare employed different strategies. Believing that it was possible to win an instant victory against a relatively weak transitional government, the Tigrean rebels fought determined but disastrous positional battles. By choosing positional warfare they made themselves an easy target for the superior technology of destruction supplied by the British. In Gojjam, where the leadership was more amorphous and hesitant, rebels sporadically attacked defenseless towns, driving out petty functionaries and looting and destroying their property. They avoided both positional and guerrilla tactics, and the overall impact of their armed action was limited. It might be mentioned that rebel leadership in both provinces suffered from internal tensions, antagonisms flaring up even as they fought a common adversary.

The rebels of Bale employed a superior method in their struggle, taking advantage of local and international conditions. With large tracts of forest and mountainous terrain, Bale was an ideal location for effective guerrilla warfare. The province is peripherally located and inhabited by distinct ethnic groups, both facilitating factors for insurgency.[11] The tradition of resistance and the vitality of Islam as an ideology of protest were helpful factors, but the fact that there had never been a rebellion of such magnitude in the region underscores the significance of Somali assistance. Despite their determination and dedication, the rebels were unable to form a more cohesive organization or to expand their territorial base, eventually sharing the fate of the others.

Failing to move beyond localism, the revolts were doomed to piecemeal annihilation. And when it was all over, little or nothing had changed; only death and suffering resulted. A landed class that sought protection from the state, while at the same time competing with it, was scarcely interested in innovations, and the existing social order, though not crumbling, was visibly under increasing stress. Growing land scarcity and rising rural impoverishment foretold the collapse of the agricultural system. Subjectively, however, the revolts provide remarkably little evidence of the existence of a "revolutionary situation" in the countryside, including in those parts which were stirred to open rebellion. In spite of sporadic clashes between peasants and landlords in the south, rural Ethiopia remained extraordinarily calm even when the monarchical regime was being incapacitated by combinations of worker strikes, student demonstrations, army mutinies, urban riots, and a generalized civil disobedience in 1974. In contrast to the French and Russian peasants who in 1787–89 and 1917 respectively hastened the collapse of the Old Regimes by directly assaulting landlords everywhere, the contribution of Ethiopian peasants to the national crisis that led to the monarchy's fall was rather limited, much like that of the Chinese cultivators in 1911.[12] What obstructed social action on a national scale were the divergent production relations, community traditions and customs, and historical regional and ethnic divisions. It is precisely by appealing to ethnic or regional particularism that the leaders of the post-1974 insurgencies have tried to activate and mobilize the peasants.

A major feature distinguishing rural revolt in Ethiopia from most others is its weak urban linkage. Leaders as well as followers came from the rural population, and the revolts were conceived, organized, and waged in the countryside. Elsewhere, there has been some connection between urban and rural peoples in times of political crisis. The urban plebeian joined insurgent peasants, or urban riots and strikes overlapped with rural revolts. In France, for example, "town insurgencies frequently accompanied [rural] risings. Conversely, peasants acted as auxiliaries in town revolts."[13] There was such fusion between rural and urban discontent during the Mau Mau uprising in Kenya. Mau Mau was, in fact, distinctly an urban movement in its origin.[14] The impact of the forces of market integration was far less small in Ethiopia, and the role of townspeople in the rebellions far less discernible. When *Weyane* broke out in 1943 Tigrai was predominantly rural. So was Bale. Whatever urban dimension there was to the Bale rebellion came from its link with a modern political organization (WSLF) which was located in Somalia's capital city. In Gojjam, Bahir Dar was a fast-growing town with a sizeable work force engaged in textile manufacture, but there, too, the urban population played no direct part in the rebellion of 1968. To say that no urban riots occurred in conjunction with rural revolts is not to suggest that the urban element was altogether irrelevant. After all, an increasing amount of the agricultural surplus was transferred to the urban sector in the form of taxes and rent. Since the 1950s many of the landlords who skimmed off the peasants' product and were the focus of their rage have lived in the towns and cities. The urban laborers and the mass of unemployed people were barely a generation away from their rural origin, and as their lives were full of misery, it is not difficult to surmise where their sympathies might have lain. In addition, a few of the agitators in Gojjam and Tigrai came from the towns. Ex-colonial soldiers participated in *Weyane*, while some of the native police in Gojjam assisted rebels by smuggling guns and ammunition. Petty traders traveling frequently between town and country served as channels of communication. Thus, although the rebellions took place in an essentially rural setting, they were not totally isolated from urban forces.

Rural resistance had a perceptible and lasting impact on one section of the urban population: the students. In 1965, in reaction to and support of peasant struggles, they adopted the slogan "Land to the tiller" and began to agitate for agrarian reform. In 1969 the militant university student publication *Struggle* hailed the continuing resistance in Bale and Eritrea as a legitimate popular expression for self-determination by oppressed nationalities. Peasant resistance was radicalizing in its effect, but the national question became a thorny and divisive one because the student movement itself began to splinter on the interpretation and application of the principle of self-determination. That Ethiopia was a multinational state in which the nationalities deserved to be treated equally was not in question; what was debatable was the strategy by which the right to equality was to be achieved. One group held that the national and class struggles were dialectically connected and that the end of class exploitation would inescapably lead to the end of national oppression. Another thought that the struggle for self-determination ought not to be contingent upon class struggle; it assigned primacy to national repression. The students were never able to settle this fundamental disagreement. In point of fact, their diverse personalities and intellectual backgrounds, ideological predispositions, and ethnic identities that bedeviled their movement were to play a crucial part in the fratricidal political disputes that followed the removal of the *ancien régime*.

Meanwhile, students continually demonstrated, serving as the crucial catalyst in the events leading to the revolution. As was evident in one of their revolutionary songs, they even propagandized the idea of popular armed struggle:

> Rebel spread out into the country (2)
> Like Ho Chi Minh, like Che Guevara.
> Rebel go into the forest (2)
> To lead the struggle
> In the valleys and mountains.

The movement, however, offered neither Ho nor Che to politicize and organize dissident peasants around national issues. In the mean time, the peasant revolts in Bale and Gojjam were suppressed, and when the revolution erupted in 1974, the radical intelligentsia were caught almost by surprise. Creatively and courageously they tried to play their historic role in the unfolding struggle, but through fatal tactical and strategic errors, they were outmaneuvered, outgunned, and nearly eliminated from the political scene by rival claimants to popular leadership. They did not disappear completely, however. Today armed struggle is being waged against the postrevolutionary regime in many regions, including Bale, Gojjam, and Tigrai. Their leaders (except for Bale) are no longer bandits, local notables, or even rural rebels, but young intellectuals, products of the student movement. In terms of their social composition, motivation, and ideological orientation there are marked differences between the pre- and postrevolutionary rural movements, but are there discernible connections?

Epilogue

From rebellion to revolution?

The crisis consists precisely in the fact that the old is dying and the new cannot be born; in the interregnum a great variety of morbid symptoms appear.

Antonio Gramsci[1]

The Ethiopian revolution, itself the product of profound social contradictions and historical conjunctures, detonated long-repressed (and thus, whimsically regarded, perfunctory) sectarian sentiments and loyalties that have proved a severe test not only for the current regime but also for the existence of the state itself. The dislocations in the structures of power and consequent crisis in authority unleashed a crescendo of dissident organizations and regional movements, ensnaring the postrevolutionary regime in a politicomilitary imbroglio from which it has yet to extricate itself.

Despite superior human and technical resources, the incumbent government is already reeling from major setbacks, and its collapse appears imminent. If it survives for much longer than anticipated, then it will be mainly because of the opposition's failure to unify and pull its resources together. The government commands an army that is ten times bigger than that of its predecessor, and it has a huge arsenal of destructive weaponry at its disposal. The extent to which it has subjected the peasantry to the state's control was unimagined by the imperial regime. Yet the state's mass and territorial base has steadily shrunk as vast areas have been nibbled away by its indomitable opponents. After fifteen years of relentless and destructive warfare the "armed equilibrium" has been shattered, for the insurgents have clearly moved from strategic parity to strategic offensive. The political and military achievements of the various rebel organizations have been uneven, however, because of divergent structural, historical, and cultural features of peasant life. Peasant political behavior has also been directly influenced by the conflicting demands and activities of the adversaries. If some organizations have been more successful in advancing their goals than others, it is precisely because they were able to expand the critical base of peasant support and loyalty by exploiting the state's structural and ideological weaknesses and vulnerabilities, and by using slogans and historical symbols that express the political and cultural rationality of their resistance. This epilogue will assess the cause and scope of popular participation in the inchoate movements, locating points of continuity and discontinuity in peasant consciousness.

The precise causes of the protracted and costly insurrectionary warfare are subject to conflicting interpretations. Some have placed emphasis on its economic and social underpinnings, whereas others have tended to see it as externally inspired and fueled. Although in some instances the regional insurgencies were encouraged, incited, and supported by foreign agencies or governments, they broke out under the disruptive and creative effects of the revolution and were primarily determined by sociohistorical conditions germane to Ethiopian society. Every social formation is a historically constituted complex of material forces, politicocultural institutions, and ideas. The social forces that defend or challenge it are historical products of that constellation, exposing the degree of its internal coherence as well as dissonance. The fact of transnational relations means, however, that external structures and resources can and do impinge upon national institutions and cultural processes, greatly influencing the course and outcome of localized conflicts. The diminution of external aid, from which both parties have benefited to varying degrees, would contribute significantly toward the demilitarization of the Ethiopian conflict just as it has been instrumental in its prolongation.

Underlying the conflict are perceptions of material deprivation and the heritage of cultural repression. John Markakis has aptly argued that the whole array of movements challenging the military regimes in the Horn of Africa are products of economic grievances arising from inherited spatial inequalities – unevenness existing both interregionally and intraregionally.

A corollary of uneven development was incomplete and thus weak national integration. The infrastructural and economic linkages built since the late nineteenth century were not sufficiently extensive to act as a countervailing force to the centrifugal elements of geographic fragmentation, linguistic diversity, and cultural variability. Multiple identities and loyalties have not been transformed into a culturally and politically coherent entity. Rather, as Halliday and Molyneaux have correctly observed, the transitional society was marked by fluid and shifting patterns of class alliances as well as competing and overlapping identities. "If we add to these complex and overlapping rivalries based on ethnic and regional origin," they wrote, "it can be seen that each group in Ethiopian society was subject to multiple pressures for cohesion and dissolution."[2] As was previously mentioned, the absolutist monarchical state was an amalgam of old and new institutions, resting on the precarious balance of centrifugal forces. It was at once exclusivist and accommodationist. Although desirous of national homogenization through the universalization of Abyssinian-Christian culture, the Amhara-dominated state was admirably tolerant of religious pluralism, as it was heedful of provincial privileges and communal customary immunities. The revolution destroyed the basis of that "centrifugal equilibrium." Determined to achieve greater administrative centralism and political integration by undercutting primordial, cultural, and historical forces that had constricted the growth of a modern secular nationalism, but without fully abandoning the exclusivist politics of its predecessor, the postrevolutionary regime inescapably inflamed autonomist aspirations.[3] Hence, as the revolution triumphed, it also fractured into political factions and orientations, some of which crystallized into regional movements largely by mobilizing peasants on the basis of ethnic identification or affiliation.

Regionalism has been a permeative and powerful force in Ethiopian history. The recrudescence of ethnoregionalism as the organizing principle of collective political action is evidence of national malintegration and of the enduring significance of nonclass bonds as foci of identity and solidarity. The durability of the regional movements is, to a large measure, due to the leaderships' ability to manipulate these otherwise malleable and mutable identities. And the tenacity of the dissidents, claiming to represent geographical collectivities, is in no small measure due to their conviction that, despite the revolution, the instrumentalist purpose of the state has not changed. In other words, the privileged access of the Amhara to the material, coercive, and symbolic resources of the state has not diminished. Because of its strategic position in the system of production and distribution, the state apparently does help to promote or hinder subjective identity claims that subliminally embody common objective goals. Inequitable distribution of societal benefits breeds discontent, and the aggrieved invoke cultural identities to justify claimed rights or to rationalize opportunities denied.[4] Put differently, material grievances are translated into political conflicts through the medium of cultural attributes or cleavages.

Economic grievances alone do not account for the mobilization of social identities, however. The connection between ideas and political praxis is too complicated a matter to be satisfactorily explained by material discontent alone. Perceptions of inequality are not sufficient to explain either the regional focus or the scope and intensity of collective action. In the Ethiopian case, it would be difficult to demonstrate that there is a center–periphery cleavage perfectly coinciding with ethnic boundaries, or that the most intense rural movements involve those collectivities which have suffered the greatest marginalization, economically and politically. There is also ample evidence to suggest that in multinational societies like Ethiopia, equitable distribution of resources does not necessarily lead to a corresponding reduction in social tensions. Popular protest must then be seen as a concatenation of historical, economic, political, and psychological factors. Social injustice may be at its root, but political dissent in Ethiopia is also a reaction to perceived cultural marginality and frustrated ambition for social mobility. The prime agents of the regional movements, who are mainly drawn from the nascent classes, seek empowerment by removing socio-cultural prohibitions historically imposed on their natal communities. They particularly resent the limitations imposed on their languages, for language is the most poignant expression of cultural authenticity. Culture, therefore, they see as the terrain of political contest between the hegemonic forces and their own desire for self-expression and affirmation. The quest for cultural autonomy also serves as a veneer for narrow interests such as personal ambition that seek to secure a niche in the bureaucratic landscape of the national state.

As in the past, the present rural movements thus arose from mixed grievances of peasants and other social strata. And as in the past, they are distinctly localist or provincialist. However, they differ considerably in motivation, scope, and intensity both from each other and from the peasant revolts of the past. Except for Bale, where there has been marked continuity in leadership, the men and ideas that initiated and organized the ethnoregional movements (so characterized on the basis of the dissidents' own claims to ethnic particularity which does not always coincide with territoriality) came from the cities. These intellectuals might have been inspired by class ideology, and they are not lacking in visionary projects, but the impetus for resistance has come from ethnoregional aspirations. And as ethnicity circumscribed transregional solidarity, the movements have remained fragmented much like the society that produced them, and their political fortunes have been markedly different. Those organizations that managed to establish a broad and secure enough territorial and popular base amid the political turmoil of the 1970s have been able not only to withstand state repression but also to grow, successfully erecting a rival dual power. The rest have either disintegrated into political oblivion or are militarily inconsequential. The ebb and flow of the movements is inextricably linked to the rugged history of the postrevolutionary state.

The insurgencies: a profile

None has grown as rapidly and as menacingly as the Tigrai People's Liberation Front (TPLF), a movement that traces its origin to the tumultuous years of student activism in Addis Ababa. Inspired by Marxist ideas of class struggle and redistributive justice, university students eloquently popularized the depressed social conditions of the Ethiopian masses in general and the cultural repression of sociological minorities in particular. But as they did so, there emerged two contradictory tendencies in the movement. The dominant orientation was toward unity in that the majority saw the struggle of the oppressed Ethiopian people as indivisible. Drawing upon Lenin's polemic on the principle of the right of nations to self-determination, the other tendency held that a new and democratic republic of Ethiopia could be constructed only through the voluntary and consensual association of its parts. In that sense it was an orientation toward fragmentation. The issues of nationalities became so divisive that tension between the Amhara and Tigrean students became quite sharp, eventually leading to the formation of a Tigrean organization.

At the turn of the 1970s some of the provincial students at the national university formed the Union of Progressive Tigreans (UPT), later called the Tigrai National Union (TNU), whose purported aim was to assert and defend the identity, dignity, and interests of their nationality. The formation of the student association foreshadowed their tangled relationship with other organizations. Their autonomist aspirations, which the revolution helped to crystallize, were at odds with nationalist sentiments. The intervention of a centralizing military regime and the subsequent curtailment of popular participation in the revolutionary process steadily pushed them to embrace new forms of resistance. The students' romantic encounter with Third World revolutionaries and revolutions and their idealization of the Eritrean fighters with whom they shared cultural affinity were additional factors that propelled them into the countryside to wage an armed struggle under "the least unfavorable conditions possible."

The transition from a student to a guerrilla organization took place at a time when the state was gravely weakened following the collapse of the *ancien régime*. Its successor was beset by many difficult political problems. Daily pressed by popular agitation at the center, the government seemed to lose its grip on the periphery. While Somali irredentists were bracing for war on the eastern frontier, Eritrean nationalists were encircling or overrunning major towns and military outposts. In adjacent Tigrai former high-ranking officials, led by the deposed governor of the province, Mengesha Seyum, were trying to mobilize the peasantry in an effort to reverse the gains of the revolution and thereby to restore the status quo ante. These developments, coupled with the Left's failure to agree on the right course of the revolution in the face of increasing repression from the new regime, led a dozen members of the TNU to launch an armed insurrection that they called *kala'ay Weyane* (Second *Weyane*). Calling themselves the Tigrai People's Liberation Front, about twenty young men led by Gessesse Ayele, a former bandit, began operations on February 18, 1975 at Dedebit in the subdistrict of Asgede, Shire, far to the west of Assimba, a hilly place where a multinational organization, the Ethiopian People's Revolutionary Party (EPRP), was establishing a rural base. The initial camaraderie masked the ideological and political differences that were to lead to fratricidal fighting between the two, significantly contributing to the ultimate defeat of the Ethiopian Left.

Governmental detractions, hesitation, and vacillation were undoubtedly helpful, but it was mostly through sheer determination that the TPLF established its supremacy over Tigrai, otherwise a contested area between 1975 and 1978. With no previous military knowledge, hardly any experience in popular mobilization, and without clearly defined objectives, the organization was apparently ill equipped to deal with the adverse conditions that soon confronted it. Its ultimate triumph was, to a large degree, the result of human will and endurance.

The young rebels had to deal with several contentious groups before they could establish themselves as legitimate leaders of the "national resistance." In its quest for legitimacy, the TPLF first quarreled with the Tigrai Liberation Front (TLF), an avowedly anti-Shewan group that, with some assistance from the Eritrean Liberation Front, had begun clandestine political work in the province in the early 1970s. The reasons for the antagonism and the consequent elimination of the TLF are not fully known. TPLF has claimed – a claim that its opponent never got the chance to counter – that these arose from basic disagreements regarding the character, motive, and leadership of the resistance. TLF is said to have defined the resistance in Tigrai as an anticolonial struggle cutting across class and under the unifying leadership of Mengesha. TPLF's alleged position was that, as a struggle for self-determination within a unitary Ethiopian state, the resistance was national in character and its leaders were the progressive intellectuals. Independence was, therefore, an option, not a maximalist objective. It saw the Tigrean nobility as class enemies to be destroyed along with the Ethiopian aristocracy.[5] Whatever the story's veracity, the issue was finally settled violently, setting a pattern of armed confrontation among the contestants in the territory.

Since the resistance was perceived as national, the presence of multinational organizations on Tigrean soil was seen as an impediment to achieving that objective. Having annihilated the TLF, whose internal friction only hastened its own demise,[6] the TPLF then turned against the Ethiopian Democratic Union (EDU), an organization of fallen bureaucrats, dispossessed landlords, and some anti-*Dergist* intellectuals, and the Ethiopian People's Revolutionary Army (EPRA), the armed wing of EPRP, both of which it eliminated from the area between 1976 and 1978. Taking full advantage of governmental disarray and drawing support from the Eritrean movement, the front was able to consolidate its position fairly rapidly, establishing control over most of the countryside. By "restoring" historical boundaries, it redrew the provincial map, vastly enlarging Tigrai's territorial size and the population it contained.[7] Today, with about 20,000 guerrilla fighters and twice as many armed militia under its command, the front is the second most powerful (second only to the EPLF) organization in the Horn of Africa.[8] In July 1985, on the tenth anniversary of its founding, the TPLF created the Marxist-Leninist League of Tigrai (MLLT) to serve as its political and ideological guide. The reorganization was followed by internal purges or dissensions which, however, appear to have had no visible impact on the front's relationship to the peasantry.[9]

Meanwhile, other organizations had suffered major setbacks on the eastern periphery. Under the sway of the Somali government and encouraged by an explosive, highly unstable, spontaneous popular upsurge, veterans of the Bale rebellion and other Ethiopian refugees in the Somali republic hastily regrouped themselves to recommence armed resistance against the beleaguered regime in Addis Ababa. None the less, the complex interplay of ethnic, cultural, geographical, and transnational factors made it quite difficult to enlarge opportunities for political mobilization. The Oromo and Somali insurgents who succeeded in creating a viable alliance in 1963–70 were now split along national lines. The meddling of the Somali state only helped to exacerbate their fundamental differences. The conditions that were nearly ideal for stirring up unrest and unified opposition in the preceding decade had changed perceptibly, and the resistance, comprising several disparate groups, was suppressed as quickly as it was ignited.

There were three major groups with overlapping territorial claims but mutually exclusive 'nationalist' missions. Organizational fragmentation inevitably resulted in the splintering of mass support and loyalty, which in turn weakened the factions. Partly encouraged by the considerable unrest in the Ogaden, the first to appear in January 1976 was the Western Somali Liberation Front (WSLF). It was led by veterans of the Bale rebellion, some of whom had received further military training in North Korea, Syria, and other countries between 1970 and 1975. The majority of its members were from the Ogaden, but its territorial claims extended as far as the Awash river in the north and Moyale in the west.[10] With an arrogant disregard for the non-Somali people inhabiting the region, its Secretary proclaimed, "The Awash, that's where we are going to stop ... And we are not going to stop the war while an inch remains to be liberated."[11] Between 1976 and 1977, the front steadily escalated its operations in Bale and Harerge, attacking police and military posts, sabotaging the railway, and terrorizing the Christian population. Although it enjoyed wide sympathy and support among the Somali population, WSLF was too dependent on the Somali government, the latter choosing the core of its leaders, laying out military plans, and providing arms and provisions. This was damaging to its image as an authentic national organization. And its extravagant territorial claims were contested by other organizations operating, more or less, within the same geographical zone. These claims placed them at odds with each other.

The first challenge came from its own offshoot, the Somali and Abbo Liberation Front (SALF), whose members asserted a dual identity (Oromo and Somali). Although bilingual, most of them were Oromo, and their claim to a sort of split identity set them apart from Somali and Oromo movements. The organization was formed in mid 1976, under Somali patronage; its leaders were Wako Gutu and Mohammed Ali Rube, both prominent leaders of the 1963–70 revolt. Except for its anti-Christian stance, SALF had no clearly defined policies. As an organization with an appeal to Oromo- as well as Somali-speakers, SALF was designed to dilute growing Oromo ethno-nationalist sentiment. As such it displayed a mercenary character that was also manifested in the earlier rebellion when leaders were reportedly paid between 1,500 and 2,000 Somali shillings while ordinary fighters may have received from 200 to 800 shillings.[12] The front began its armed activities in the highland farming areas in close cooperation with members of the Oromo gentry, who were opposed to the land proclamation that had dispossessed them. By claiming Arsi, Bale, and Sidamo, they found themselves in conflict with WSLF, whose claims also included most of Bale and southern Sidamo. They were both unmindful of the fact that virtually no Somali are found in Sidamo and only a minority in Bale. Despite Wako Gutu's fame, prestige, and undiminished charisma, SALF had little success in winning over the Oromo peasantry, whose allegiance was actively being sought by the Oromo Liberation Front (OLF).

Unlike its immediate rivals but like the TPLF, the OLF was organized mainly by university students who began guerrilla warfare in the Chercher mountains of Harerge towards the end of 1976 and successfully attracted a mélange of disaffected Oromo gentry, former civil servants, and some of the peasant rebels of the 1960s. Claiming to be the only authentic and legitimate representative of the Oromo, a vastly dispersed people with no history of political unity since the sixteenth century, the OLF was utterly disdainful of SALF, which it regarded (with justification) as an avant-garde or naïve instrument of Somali irredentist aspirations. Rightly pointing out its nonexistence on the ethnographic map, OLF asserted that "the coinage of the name Somali Abbo served as proof of Somalia's [sic] ambition to annex and Somalicize the neighboring Oromo communities."[13] But the front was equally saddled with ideological ambiguities. Though the nationalities problem is inextricably linked with the crisis of the state, it stubbornly insisted on projecting its cause as one of denied decolonization. In contrast to SALF, whose objectives were never fully expressed, OLF's main goal was to establish an independent state called Oromia over a territory that stretched from Harerge southwards to Moyale on the Kenya border and westwards to Wellega on the border with Sudan. Nearly 600,000 square kilometers in size, the territory would absorb all the lands claimed by WSLF and SALF, save the Ogaden. Since this vast span of territory is inhabited by diverse ethnic groups other than Oromo and Somali, it is most astonishing that the fronts, much like the TPLF, scarcely cared about the rights of others.

In any event, before any one of them could establish a secure base, the Ethio-Somali War consumed them all. Following the Ogaden War of 1977–78, in which the Ethiopians, supported by thousands of Cuban and Soviet troops, smashed an invading Somali army, the organizations lost whatever ground they had gained during 1976–77. WSLF and SALF disintegrated into squabbling factions, constantly intriguing and conspiring against each other. Neither organization is currently operating militarily; they are, therefore, little more than an annoyance to the regime in Addis Ababa, and it does not seem likely that they will ever rise from the doldrums in which they are languishing. In 1982–83 OLF moved its base of operations to the southwestern regions of Wellega and Illubabor, primarily to ensure its own survival. Indeed, it has survived, but its fighting force scarcely exceeds 3,000 armed guerrillas.[14] With such puny numbers, its military and political achievements have been less than spectacular.[15] Nevertheless, unpopular government policies, especially those pertaining to resettlement and villagization, may well reverse these short-term trends by shifting popular support

211

and loyalty toward the guerrillas. And indeed, the OLF has already resumed its activities in Harer.

The mobilization of social action

How does one explain this wide variation in strength and performance by the "liberation" movements? As was pointed out earlier, any satisfactory answer would consider a host of contingent circumstances. But to understand what motivates people to engage in activities that entail the risk of loss of life, it is necessary to appreciate the exact relationship between popular consciousness and political leadership. In his study of guerrilla movements in Africa, Basil Davidson stipulates that "an ideology of liberation cannot develop except in step with the potential of a people's consciousness in any given and specific time and place. That is where the art of leadership has been decisive."[16] And consciousness, as we have argued earlier, is "intrinsically historical" as it is formed or shaped by lived experience as well as objective conditions of life. Most popular movements embody a range of ideas and ideals that motivate and galvanize their supporters. The relative success (or failure) of a leadership in mobilizing masses of ordinary men and women must surely depend on the degree to which the ideas and values it enunciates are shared by these men and women. If it were not so, then every movement that has managed to arouse a multitude of people into armed insurrection must be said to have done so either through compulsion or manipulation of the proverbial gullibility or idiocy of the rural masses. The historical evidence supporting either proposition is too thin. The cases of Bale, Gojjam, and Tigrai help to clarify the point.

The pattern that emerges from the peasant resistance in Bale is one of greater continuity in historical consciousness among the Somali than the Oromo. During the six years they resisted the imperial state in the 1960s, rebel peasants of Bale exhibited varying degrees of social awareness. Although they were bound by common material problems, they were separated by cultural differences. In that precarious alliance, Somali cultural nationalism was more concrete and assertive but not necessarily dominant. As ethnicity competed with class loyalty, popular discontent was provided with a religious context. Hence, common material grievances were expressed through Islamic cultural symbols. Islam was a mobilizing and validating force, religious ideas providing the basis for a critique of the existing social system and the justification for change. In this way, Islam helped to diffuse the internal fissures that persistently threatened the negative unity of the rebels.

As an ideology of mobilization Islam was much less effective during the uprising of 1976–78, for it could no longer submerge Oromo identity and self-expression. The erosion of its saliency was due partly to the sweeping political and economic changes that had been introduced in the preceding two years and partly to the emergence of a secular ethnonationalism among

212

the Oromo, a new phenomenon mainly propagated by the urban intelligentsia. I. M. Lewis has claimed that in their "mutual opposition to Amhara domination," Oromo and Somali were united by the cult of Sheikh Hussien, whom the author describes as "a multifaceted symbol of local Islamic (and anti-Christian Amhara) identity, bringing together Oromo, Somali and Arab elements ... a Cushitic time-bomb in the contemporary Ethiopian powder-keg."[17] Actually, the drastic changes in social relations had rendered Islam less potent. Why was it that bilingual dissidents like Wako Gutu, who reluctantly accepted it in the 1960s, were less willing to "assume the ethnic identity of Somalia" in the 1970s? One answer is that objective and subjective conditions had been significantly transformed in the crucible of revolution. The land reform bill of March 1975 was most effective precisely in those areas where exploitative landlordism had been entrenched and national repression was most intense. By legally entrusting land to its tillers the reform dealt a deadly blow to the opposition forces. Conversely, it shielded the fledging military regime "against the one source of ethnic opposition that could have been fatal to it."[18] Oromo peasants chose to help defend, consolidate, and increase the revolutionary gains because it was no longer in their best interest to ally with Somali insurgents, many of whom aspired to changing state allegiance. The same reason accounted for the inability of other dissidents to inspire the peasants. The Oromo gentry failed because of the incongruity between class and ethnic politics; contradictory economic interests made ethnicity dysfunctional organizationally. And the intellectuals failed because the land question, the basis of national oppression, had been resolved, denying them the mobilizing weapon of the 1960s. What this means is that social action is invariably grounded in material conditions. It was historical and political realities that imposed limitations on the actions of the dissident forces, supporting Marx's dictum that, "Men make their own history, but they do not make it just as they please; they do not make it under circumstances chosen by themselves, but under circumstances directly encountered, given and transmitted from the past."[19] It is the disjuncture between social reality and popular ideology that neither the dissidents nor Lewis could fully appreciate.

Somali intervention had, of course, complicated matters. However, it is idle to speculate what the situation in southeastern Ethiopia might have looked like today had the Somali state refrained from meddling in Ethiopian internal affairs. But had the aggressor state succeeded in achieving its ambitious goals, it is not difficult to imagine that it would be fighting an OLF that is as powerful, if not more so, than the TPLF today. By seizing their lands and replacing Abyssinian with Somali domination, it would have helped in forging and solidifying Oromo group consciousness, which the OLF was unable to achieve on its own for historical and objective conditions.

It is easier to rationalize the defeat of the rebels in Bale than to explain the phenomenal growth of the Tigrean movement. The rate of its growth and the scale of its activities are hard to fathom. What factors or circumstances helped the young dissidents to mobilize the provincial population, one that had remained relatively quiet since 1943, against a state of which it has been a part for many centuries? What may be called the "nationalist perspective" sees the current resistance simply as the culmination or "highest stage" of a struggle in which the people of Tigrai have been engaged against domination and control by the Amhara of Shewa since the nineteenth century. If *Weyane* is the forerunner of the current conflict, then its leaders are the precursors of the present generation of "dissident nationalists."[20] However, unless feudal warfare among Abyssinian lords is confused with ethnoregionalism it is hard to establish such remarkable continuity in peasant consciousness. To suggest that *Weyane* was a nationalist revolt is really to indulge in myth-making. That the TPLF would, as indeed it did, hark back to the past is hardly surprising, for have such movements not tried to thrive on nationalist mythologies? Speaking about the movements in the Horn, Markakis has remarked, "Nationalism ... is always invoked as the primary cause despite the fact that as far as it refers to the forging of group identity, consciousness and solidarity, it has more often than not emerged during the course of the conflict and is, therefore, not a cause but a consequence of it."[21] Although it is argued here that the TPLF's rise and growth are to be explained in part by its ability to tap an existing residue of ethnoregional consciousness, its epiphenomenality in Ethiopian political history cannot be controverted.

The perspective that evinces a conspiratorial vision must be rejected equally, because it historicizes events in the wrong way. Attempts are sometimes made to present the ethnoregional movements as mainly foreign-inspired.[22] Such conventional formulations need to be transcended, for they detract attention from the real issues. It would be naïve not to imagine alien influence, for in these times no respectable dissident organization can or does function effectively without some form of outside assistance. But to suggest that the Tigrean movement lacks authenticity is to deny its endogenous roots and the popular support it commands. The ethnoregional movements cannot be understood apart from the broader sociocultural context in which they are embedded. The cultural patterns that define a group's identity and its struggle for self-determination are not arbitrarily constructed or externally imposed; rather they are products of concrete historical experiences and institutions. So, the question is not whether the TPLF is an endogenously rooted movement, but why it has been so successful in mobilizing the Tigrean peasantry.

What accounted for the relative success of the TPLF was a configuration of many factors, the most crucial of which, perhaps, was its own organizational effectiveness. But if the weapon of organization was effective, it was because a set of circumstances made it possible to create alliances by winning the support and active participation of a desperate peasantry faced with many intractable problems. Wolf has suggested that a generalized crisis could drive peasants toward embracing dissident movements.[23] There is such a crisis in northern Ethiopia, a crisis that has been evident since the 1950s. Ecological distress, drought, famine, and consequent disruptions in normative patterns have had the cumulative effect of undermining the agrarian political economy and social structure. Under conditions of scarcity and increasing insecurity, peasants who rarely acted in unison now sought collective solutions to collective problems. In a situation of rising landlessness and destitution, individual strategies long used to ensure access to land and subsistence were no longer effective or relevant. One of the main reasons the rural population gravitated toward the TPLF was that it provided them with an organization within which they could more effectively grapple with those problems. In other words, the intervention of these elements has helped to harness latent grievances by channeling them into controlled collective action.

There is a direct correlation between a perilous physical environment and the ecology of insurrection. As elaborated in chapter 3, Tigrai (along with Wello) is the most depressed region in the country. There are no industrial establishments to compensate for the agricultural decline. The activities of the Tigrai Agricultural and Industrial Development (TAIDEL) were mainly limited to the collection and processing of wild incense grown in the western lowlands. Employment was variable, not exceeding 300 at peak seasons. Famine and death have visited the land, with greater frequency and magnitude since the 1950s. It is this crisis in subsistence that has facilitated politicization and mobilization of an otherwise socially atomized and politically quiescent agrarian population. The peasants' militant response to the depressed conditions of life in the 1970s was in striking contrast to their passive suffering in the 1950s, when they were hit by crop failures and a devastating famine. It was not merely the further decline in subsistence during the intervening years, but the emergence of an organized human agent capable of politicizing latent discontent that has made the difference. And these political agents need not be Tigreans only. According to former members of the EPRA, their multinational organization was able to win many villages in Agame within a short time. It was only when the balance of armed power shifted toward the TPLF that those peasants deserted the EPRP. Even the *key kesoch* ("red priests"), lamented one of them, "abandoned us in the wilderness."[24] As it demonstrated its military capability, peasant loyalty and trust in the TPLF increased because the probability of success became higher and the anticipated rewards greater.

The revolutionary upheaval has had quite a different impact in the northern and southern regions. Whereas it turned the world upside down in the south, taking the "steam of revolution" out of the dissident nationalists, the land proclamation had little immediate impact on production relations in the north, where the cultivators had always enjoyed direct access to communally owned land, and where continual parceling and soil erosion had a socially equalizing effect, greatly reducing class tensions. And as the abolition of feudal exactions was soon followed by the imposition of new levies such as taxes and fees, the revolutionary benefits quickly disappeared, raising the potential for revolt.

The political turmoil that followed the fall of the monarchical regime clearly had adverse short-term effects on the rural economy. The evidence suggests a correlation between migratory labor and peasant support for guerrillas. Since land parcels are not large enough to absorb the labor potential of family households, a large number of peasants from Tigrai and Wello yearly migrated for temporary employment. Tigrai alone "accounted for 27 percent of all migrants" in the country.[25] These migrant workers, who remained tied to their villages, were inevitably exposed to new ideas and conditions of life which, in turn, affected their consciousness. Working far from home and with people of diverse ethnic and cultural backgrounds, they tended to band together for security. On the plantation where most of them were employed, and in the voluntary associations which they formed for mutual assistance, the migrants were able to acquire the valuable experience of working collectively. In prerevolutionary times migration helped to defuse latent discontent. When the military government severely constrained the free movement of labor in the 1970s by restricting peasant inflow to the towns, forbidding "the private hire of agricultural labour," and by increasingly resorting to coercive practices instead of offering attractive wages on state farms,[26] not only did it put additional strains on the peasant economy, but it inadvertently enabled the guerrillas to tap this reservoir of a relatively conscietized rural manpower.

The regime's war policies also had the effect of alienating more people. As troops on transit to and from Eritrea interfered with rural production, further squeezing the peasantry, and as the air force bombed villages for sheltering or supporting "outlaws," they made rebel recruitment that much easier. To avoid forceful conscription into the government militia, many peasants joined the insurrection; pressganged, ill trained, and poorly paid, a good number of the recruits also chose to desert, many of them embracing the rebellion.[27]

Two interconnected factors, both stemming from weaknesses of a transitional government, were critical to the ultimate success of the TPLF in institutionalizing a peasant-based movement. Inasmuch as the inability of the restored imperial regime to establish administrative and military control in the province allowed a dissident gentry to instigate a discontented populace in 1942–43, so did the inability of the postrevolutionary regime to reestablish state authority quickly help the radical insurgents to mobilize an impoverished peasantry. The disintegration of the locally rooted hierarchical polity, following the removal of a hereditary governor, loosened political and social control in the villages, enabling the peasants to interact with the insurgents more freely and with enhanced self-confidence. The rebels were able to strengthen this alliance before the new regime could establish its legitimacy and moral authority. The regime's failure to establish centralized control over the province was partly the result of its preoccupation with enemies elsewhere in the country.

It is quite sensible to suppose that had the government waged a sustained campaign against the TPLF during its formative and thus critical stage, the organization's strategy of peasant mobilization may not have been as effective. The success of the TPLF was neither predictable nor inevitable. Time was of the essence. Believing that the Somalis and Eritreans posed the greatest and most immediate threat both to its own survival and the existence of the Ethiopian state, the government concentrated its forces on the two fronts, to the utter neglect of all other dissidents. No doubt its forces were overstretched, but it is also clear that the government grossly underestimated the TPLF's potential; it saw little or no reason for such a movement to succeed in the Abyssinian heartland.[28] In retrospect, this was a major miscalculation, for government inaction gave the TPLF ample time to organize the peasants by displacing the much-weakened administrative hierarchy and local gentry. When the regime finally turned its full attention to the simmering crisis, it was a bit too late, for the insurgents had already established a solid mass base from which it has become impossible to dislodge them.

Yet the growth and continuity of the insurgency in Tigrai ultimately hinged on the TPLF's stupefying determination and organizational talent to erect rural Soviet bases and create mass organizations in the face of an escalating war. Using effective mobilization techniques that combined cultural symbols, propaganda, and coercion, it was able to overcome the negative features of an atomized society and to rally vast numbers of the rural poor, with whom it has established a stable and creative relationship. Success was, in turn, dependent on the front's ability to maintain its corporate identity and internal cohesion, and not always by democratic means.

Persuasion may have been the preferred method, but mass mobilization and organizational discipline often involved coercion. There is strong evidence that the TPLF has used force to organize the rural population, especially in the initial critical stage when many peasants who appeared unsympathetic or tended to tilt toward one of the other organizations were harassed, intimidated, and often penalized.[29] Even harsher methods were used to quash internal dissent. In 1977–78, precisely at a time when it had to meet the dual challenge from the EPRP and EDU, the TPLF was faced with an internal crisis known as *hinfishfish* (chaos). This was a factional struggle within a bifurcated movement, one that was characterized from the beginning by a fundamental duality. Behind the façade of professed ideological unanimity and organizational coherence, there were two opposing currents: secession and regional autonomy. In addition, there were strong disagreements with regard to representation in the leadership. The source of the problem was *awrajawinet*, or localism. These competing tendencies and the resultant factionalism were kept in check by force. Four men charged with spearheading the protest to the alleged domination of the front by persons from Adwa, Shire, and Aksum (run together as *asha'a*) were executed.[30] Imposed unity ensured survivability, and indeed expansion, but had a stultifying effect on democracy as dissent became a hazardous political enterprise. If the TPLF has held together well, never splintering decisively like the organizations in the eastern front, it is partly because of its small, highly centralized, and secretive leadership. Despite the leaders' often-repeated claims to the contrary, the exigencies of guerrilla warfare, combined with the inherited feudal culture, seem to reinforce tendencies toward militarism. However, since successful mass mobilization is inconceivable without reciprocal collaboration and mutual support between elites and peasants, the front cannot afford to suffocate all democratic channels of political work. The secret of a people's war then probably lies in the leadership's ability to generate sufficient and active support for its cause and actions through constant dialogue with the rural population. The glue that holds the elite–mass alliance together is the delicate synthesis of democracy and centralism, although greater emphasis is likely to be given to the latter, as experience elsewhere in the world has amply demonstrated.

The front's organizational structure is pyramidal; there is a hierarchy of people's councils known as *baytos* from the village to the province. At the top sits the front's central leadership. This organizational framework, which includes functional mass associations such as the Farmers' Association, Women's Association, and Youth Association, was established before the government had the chance to create its own peasant associations. In 1975–76 there were just over one thousand of them, with more than 311,000 registered households. Six years later the number of associations and household membership had plummeted to 157 and 55,988 respectively.[31] They were simply lost to the rebels, who by then had also established extensive extraterritorial links. The front is believed to draw substantial support from organizations of Tigreans in the Middle East, Europe, and North America.

In contrast, the EPRP had had little success in inspiring the peasants of Gojjam, and not for lack of grievances to exploit. Like cultivators in the rest of the country, farmers in Gojjam deeply resent the state-imposed production quotas; the fixed market prices for their produce; the conscription of their young men; the payment of agricultural income tax and a variety of ad hoc fees for such things as military and literacy campaigns, resettlement, and public works; and the pervasive corruption and nepotism of state bureaucrats and party functionaries, most of whom are one and the same. True, Gojjam is relatively rich and its people have never experienced the kind of deprivation that the Tigreans have. It is also true that the peasants there do not regard EPRP fighters as *ye-wonzachin lijoch* (children of our rivers), since few of them are originally from that region. They are sceptical and profoundly suspicious of the motives of these outside agitators. But the party's failure to mobilize them is perhaps due to its inability to penetrate the tightly state-controlled peasant associations that link villages with districts and districts with the administrative regions. Moreover, the government has an additional reason to tighten security measures in an area that is not particularly difficult to guard against guerrilla infiltration because of its near encirclement by the Abay gorge. Gojjam is a surplus-producing region that, along with Arsi and Shewa, accounts for between 75 and 90 percent of the marketed grain.[32] As in the rest of Africa, the government's success in keeping the burgeoning cities relatively passive is, in part, dependent on its ability to feed them. That the regime in Addis Ababa has managed to meet those subsistence needs by relying mainly on three provinces is itself an indicator of the relative smallness and poverty of the urban population.

The outward calm of the Gojjame nevertheless raises a more fundamental question: why did those peasants, who were often provoked by mere rumors of change in the landholding system in the two decades before the revolution, accept the actual land reform of 1975 fairly peacefully? One of the reasons for this obvious discrepancy lies in the fact that unlike in Tigrai, where an active and popular hereditary ruler was able to arouse sections of the population by appealing to provincialist sentiments, there were no such figures in Gojjam, since the regional dynasty and the authority that derived from it have long been destroyed. The fact that the regional nobility, which remained physically close to the peasantry, was less affected by centralization meant that traditional patron–client ties as the matrix of sociopolitical cohesion were stronger in Tigrai than in Gojjam. Even though the nobility failed to sustain the resistance it itself initiated, its behavior helped to give legitimacy to the insurgency that a new generation has successfully organized. No such generation could have so readily established a "liberation front" in a region that never experienced cultural domination (since it is Amharic-speaking). Secondly, it was simply a matter of force majeure to which the peasantry had to submit. Following the imposition of the land reform there were signs of unrest in Bichena and Motta that two former parliamentarians, along with two other disenchanted members of the *Derg*, vainly tried to transform into a popular revolt.[33] In contrast to its reluctant predecessor, the government nipped the unrest in the bud with harsh measures that may have cost as many as three hundred lives in Bichena alone.[34] There were other factors that contributed to the quietening of an already intimidated peasantry: the land reform did not radically upset the traditional tenurial system, and the villagization program, which is reportedly 80 percent complete, has been carried out with remarkably less coercion and social disruption than in other parts of the country, Arsi excepted. And by using many of the churches as focal points of the reorganized villages as well as by helping restore some of the well-known but decaying monasteries, the government has been able to placate the clergy, notwithstanding their ideological hostility.

Where the EPRP has achieved greater success is among the previously dormant inhabitants of Metekel, the vast but sparsely populated lowland region. The Nilo-Saharan communities there sublimely abjured all the provincial rebellions against the imperial state. The EPRP's relative success in activating them today is mainly due to their resentment of the government's resettlement policy, which threatens their habitat. Even though shifting cultivation is the principal mode of livelihood of the native population and even though the ecology is not best suited to heavy and intensive tillage, plow and mechanized farming is being developed along the Beles river, a major tributary of the Blue Nile, on a large scale. Mechanization, besides supporting the more than 80,000 peasants who have been resettled at Pawe, is intended to produce exportable crops. These changes have, of course, upset the precarious balance that existed between a delicate ecology and the hitherto marginalized commune of the Gumuz. There is evidence also that the local people have been used as forced labor on state projects, a practice that must have rekindled memories of the slave trade. Is it any surprise that they have reacted with armed revolt?[35]

To complete our abbreviated story of the Tigrean resistance we need to look briefly at its military strategy and mass mobilizing symbols and slogans. Its method is guerrilla warfare, one that allows surprise and maximum flexibility and mobility. In contrast to the *Weyane* rebels, who fought pitched battles only to be destroyed by superior firepower, the TPLF never engages its unequal adversary at a time and place of his choosing. But as very recent events, in which the front overran many military posts and towns, demonstrate, it has moved from guerrilla forays to highly mobile operations using heavy weaponry such as artillery and rocket launchers, some of it, no doubt, captured from government forces. Having completely secured Tigrai, it has extended its operations as far as Gonder and Shewa. This military strength derives from peasant support and the leadership's resourcefulness, but Tigrai's peripheral location has been very helpful. The insurgents not only received vital assistance at the initial stage of their struggle, but from time to time have coordinated their operations with the EPLF, the most formidable guerrilla force in the region. Geographical contiguity or a base of support in neutral or friendly neighbors across the border has always proven invaluable to rebels everywhere. In like fashion, the TPLF has used Sudanese territory to import much-needed weaponry, ammunition, provisions, and clinical and educational materials with minimal interference from the government, a privilege that their counterparts on the eastern side were denied, which undoubtedly contributed to their decline and weakness.

How did the front motivate the peasants on whose active support its military strength rests? What issues were invoked, what promises made, and what benefits delivered? Basically, what animated the rural population to resist on such a scale and with such tenacity were the poor and ever-declining conditions of material life; collective action was a response to the unprecedented challenges facing an agrarian community. But this collective social action must be attributed to the combined organizing genius of a few inspired intellectuals and the generalized repressive violence of the state. The leaders have stressed Tigrean identity of the cultural and historical heritage of the region whose impoverishment they attributed to a conspiratorial act of the Shewa Amhara ruling oligarchy. In their literature and propaganda as well, they have consistently presented the poverty and hardships of the region as the outcome of unduly extractive centralization. To arouse collective passion and identification, they have relied heavily on historical memory. And the unremitted and indiscriminate violence unleashed by the state to subdue the rebellious populace has only helped to crystallize solidarity sentiments. So, the success of the TPLF's mobilizing efforts must have depended on the extent to which its slogans and objectives converged with concrete historical experiences or realities and perceived identities of the popular masses.

In a country marked by weak societal integration, it has not proven difficult to politicize ethnicity as a medium of social action. Reference has been made to the fact that Ethiopia is a society in which a growing sense of national identity has competed with particularistic loyalties; affiliation to region or even locale has not been eroded by national attachment. In the northern regions in particular, physical fragmentation, patron–client dependency relations, and the rivalries among hereditary ruling families tended to entrench provincialism while constricting supra-regional consciousness. Ethiopians have, therefore, a long history of cultural awareness and linguistic self-assertion. This has been particularly true of Tigrai, where there is significant overlap between region, language, and religion, the three salient unifying/divisive factors. However, these cultural attributes were rarely translated into political demands. Contrary to the TPLF's claims, the current "nationalist" sentiment has been thrust upon the peasantry by the intelligentsia.[36] This has been done by reactivating ethno-regionalism. Although the issues (economic neglect, cultural oppression, and discriminatory state policies and programs) that spurred the current movement are quite contemporary, there has been some tendency to locate the origins of popular grievances in the misty past. In particular, the historical memory of *Weyane* has been used as a means by which a sense of an oppressive past and the popular resistance to it is revived and codified. When nationalist historiography interprets the rebellion as "one of the spectacular examples of Tigrean resistance against the dominance of the Amhara nation,"[37] it is to construct a culture of resurgence that would inspire, energize, and unify the masses. Now that the TPLF has moved from the regional to the national terrain, criticizing its initial actions as manifestations of "narrow nationalist deviations,"[38] these parochial mobilizing issues have become virtually defunct. The front will have to repoliticize ethnicity for purposes of national unity.

It is instructive that where the TPLF operated in a relatively compact region, compact both culturally and historically, the OLF tried to arouse the Oromo peasantry in a historical void. This is not to deny that Oromo grievances are spawned by widespread historical consciousness. Speaking mutually intelligible dialects and having commonly shared Abyssinian domination and a related sense of collective humiliation, there is no doubt that the Oromo intelligentsia have cultivated an ethnonationalist consciousness that has grown incrementally since the Bale rebellion and the foundation of the Metcha and Tulema cultural association in Addis Ababa in the mid

1960s. That consciousness has crystallized in the rise of the OLF, whose legitimacy is none the less being contested by the Oromo People's Democratic Organization (OPDO). Yet Oromia suggests a misleading cultural homogeneity and historical particularity. The *Gada* institution which could have provided a common frame of reference is nowadays practiced only in Borana. Ethnographic distribution does not perfectly coincide with geographical delimitation (though ethnonational identity can find expression without reference to any territorial definition), and peasant life and attitude have been shaped by varying structural and historical elements. The Oromo are found throughout the country (save Eritrea), but it is in the region that roughly encompasses Arsi, Bale–Goba, Sidamo–Awasa, and western Borana that one can speak of an exclusively Oromo population that is also predominantly Muslim. Geographic dispersal has been accompanied by varying degrees of cultural assimilation, the inhabitants of Gonder, Tigrai and Wello having experienced by far the widest intermingling with the Amhara and Tigreans. On the other hand, Wellega, which now serves as the OLF's principal base of operation, was never subjected to the same degree of economic exploitation and cultural domination as the southern Oromo have been. These historical-cultural disconnections and regional differences, as Christopher Clapham has rightly remarked, were bound to generate varied peasant response to the intelligentsia's strive for a common identity and the construction of a "national" community. If the OLF has been less successful in mobilizing the Oromo peasants on a large scale and sustained basis, it is no less due to the latter's physical and cultural fragmentation than to the conjuncture of unfavorable domestic and international political conditions. As land reform and Somali interventionism prevented it from establishing a secure base in the area that mattered most – the Arsi–Bale–Borana region, which is the cradle of Orofima and the repository of the *Gada*, a region where ethnocultural homogeneity and memories of exploitation and consequent resistance are very strong – the convergence of ethnonationalist ideologies has precluded its penetration into regions of mixed ethnological composition (such as Harerge, Tigrai, and Wello). Whether the peasants finally embrace Oromo nationalism by crisscrossing regional and cultural barriers will very much depend on their material conditions, political calculations, and imponderable historical circumstances, not the least of which is the fate of the Ethiopian national state.

Their counterparts to the north faced no such objective limitations. In point of fact, state repression had the opposite effect of increasing or heightening the ardor of ethnoregionalism. In addition to the economic misery and natural disasters, the forced resettlements, the extractive demands, and the destruction and mayhem have all given peasants objective reasons to take an active part in one of the most tenacious and durable movements in contemporary Ethiopian history. Social engineering in the midst of war would have only enhanced the front's stature. Winning the trust of the peasants in considerable part depended on its demonstrated ability to provide such scarce commodities as salt, cooking oil, sugar, and kerosene; to cater for the most basic health and educational needs; to construct feeder roads; and to introduce a system of afforestation so that the despoiled land could be reclaimed. It directly participates in the distribution of food donated by international organizations. The Tigrean movement is, in fact, one in which the classic guerrilla–peasant relationship appears to have been reversed; instead of being dependents, guerrillas have become providers.

This peasant–elite partnership cannot, however, be interpreted to mean the existence of total harmony or even agreement on either how social reality is objectified or how social justice is envisioned. In such movements that comprise diverse social groups, "divergent visions of order and justice" inescapably arise to become a constant source of tension among participants. As James Scott has succinctly stated it, "Although radical elites and an insurgent peasantry may have a common enemy, their divergent motives, aspirations and styles make their partnership an uneasy one at best."[39] The radical people leading the insurgencies are not wholly alien to the sociocultural milieu of the village, as many of them are of peasant origin. But, by virtue of their modern education, they have acquired new habits and styles of life that are sufficiently different to set them apart from the rural population. They belong to a different class altogether. Although some of them have rebelled, primarily because of thwarted ambition or failed expectations, there is no doubt that they are engaged in a struggle that demands discipline, dedication, selflessness, and denial of personal aspirations. Yet, no matter how well they may integrate themselves into the peasant world by "committing suicide as a class,"[40] it is inconceivable that these people can "peasanticize" themselves culturally. And it will be a very long time before the peasants can develop a new consciousness correlating to a transformed mode of production. Hence, although the armed struggle may bridge the cultural gap, it is practically impossible to close it. Tension between the futuristic orientation of the revolutionary intellectuals and the backward-looking tendency of rebel peasants will persist. The official adoption of Marxism-Leninism by the insurgent movement in a world that is almost entirely rural and still deeply religious is likely to heighten, not lessen, that underlying tension. As political guidance without domination and conscietization without indoctrination are nearly impossible, the peasant elite alliance will remain tenuous, notwithstanding the mergence of the "inherited" and "derived" ideas that gave rise to it in the first place.

This analysis of peasant experience in three regions has shown that people's political behavior and action are interwoven with their material interests and activities. But, although predicated primarily on social experience, popular consciousness in the multiethnic Ethiopian state has been expressed in cultural terms, locally variable conditions giving rise to different levels of awareness of solidarity. Consciousness, as intimated before, is a subjective phenomenon that evokes a range of identities, and the circumstances under which these identities are submersed, activated, or heightened

223

are historical and dynamic. As the density of social interaction across regions was thin because of a dispersed economy and a poor communication system, ethnicity tended to serve as the mobilizing weapon of collective action both before and after the revolution. It is important to add, though, that ethnic boundaries are porous and malleable, as they are cross cut by religious and class cleavages. The analysis has also revealed that people make history within circumscribed limits and under material and symbolic constraints. The political activities of the dissidents on the eastern frontier were circumvented by the combined effect of the land reform bill of 1975 and the Somali invasion of 1978. If the regime's preoccupation had not given the TPLF the breathing space to organize the peasants when the latter were relatively free from the control of the traditionally dominant social forces and from state repression, its fate might have been entirely different. Finally, the Ethiopian case leads to the conclusion that many others have reached: peasants can become revolutionary agents, but only in alliance with other forces. The relevant question that needs to be asked, therefore, is not which segment of the peasantry is more prone to rebel, but under what circumstances and with what kind of ideas an external agency can enlist the active participation of the rural population in order to wage a sustained resistance against the modern state or those who dominate and control it.

The question of the Ethiopian peasant's revolutionary potential has become even more pertinent today. Will the Ethiopian People's Revolutionary Democratic Front (EPRDF) be able to unify the diverse peasantry for a collective reconstruction of state-society? The EPRDF is a united front of three forces the strength and staying power of which are extremely difficult to discern, though the TPLF is by far the dominant numerically and most effective organizationally. Its junior partner, the Belessa Democratic Movement (BDM), then renamed the Ethiopian People's Democratic Movement (EPDM), was established in November 1979 in Wello by defectors from the EPRP. Though professedly multiethnic, its exact composition and size are unknown. Critics are prone to dismiss it disparagingly as a tail or more precisely as the "Amharic department" of the TPLF. On the other hand, its leaders have vociferously defended its independence, claiming that the organization's fighting force has attained parity with its ally.[41] The EPDM is still relatively small, but its prominence will undoubtedly increase as the United Front consolidates its hold on the Amharic-speaking regions. The third parner is the OPDO, a group formed quite recently by Ethiopian troops who were prisoners of the TPLF and EPLF. Its armed strength is estimated at between seven and ten thousand, but whether it shares the Marxism of the other two is uncertain. There is absolutely no question that this force has been created under the tutelage of the EPRDF in order to counteract the OLF, an organization that wishes to expunge past humiliations and to affirm its identity by founding a new state on the ruins of Ethiopia. In this sense the United Front is a negative unity of unequal partners whose immediate common objective is to remove one of the most ruthless tyrannies in the Third World. Militarily they are succeeding at an astounding speed, no doubt because a repressive regime has alienated the masses, and a huge but terribly demoralized army has lost the stamina to fight ever since its disastrous defeats at Afabet (Eritrea) and Enda Selassie (Tigrai) in July 1989 and February 1990 respectively. Peasant fighters from Tigrai and Wello, two provinces that the regime has virtually lost to the rebels, have subsequently overrun Gonder and Shewa, apparently with local cooperation and assistance. Whether that cooperation holds or not will very much depend on the conjunction of peasant grievances and insurgent goals and activities. Nevertheless, as the EPRDF closes on Addis Ababa, it faces daunting strategic and political problems: How readily will the multiethnic peasants reconcile the parochialist activities (history) of the TPLF and its pan-Ethiopianist aspirations? Will the conspiratorial action taken against the OLF misfire as the United Front enters deep into Oromo territory? What measures have been taken to assuage and accommodate the interests of the EPRP, which controls substantial areas in Gojjam and Gonder? What provisions have been made for Afari and Somali irredentist aspirations? What formula has been devised to settle the Eritrean question that has eluded two successive regimes for almost three decades? These are some of the basic questions with which the coalition has to grapple if it hopes to mobilize the peasantry nationally and begin a peaceful reconstruction of the country.

Ethiopia is at a critical transitional period, its people facing an uncertain future. Feeding on factitious history while denying historical causes for present political predicaments, the incumbent rulers have squandered multiple opportunities for a democratic construction of a state-society. Their predecessors, who none the less were never confronted with political problems on such a scale and intensity, were far more willing to allow a measurable degree of regional autonomy. They were keenly aware of the limitations of the state's coercive capacity. In contrast, the military men, supported by the might of the Soviet Union, have sought militaristic solutions for fundamentally political problems. Their actions alienated large sections of formerly excluded groups that have readily embraced ethnonationalism. The ensuing conflicts have devastated the country, wreaking death and destruction, the sheer scale of which cannot be determined with any degree of certitude, but the bulk of which has been borne by the peasantry. The state crisis that the military rulers so ineptly mismanaged has thus led to further national and social fractionalization that, in turn, has prolonged the passing of the old and delayed the dawning of the new order that the revolution had promised fifteen years ago.

Constructing the future

As the military dictatorship nears its terminal stage only a strategy that is at once democratic and unitary (one that does not exclude federal or

225

confederal arrangements) would save the country from more civil strife and economic distress. When the last embers of revolt are extinguished, the cacophony of forces tugging the country in different directions will have to devise a political formula that takes into account the need for national sovereignty and ethnoregional self-determination while ensuring the primacy of the general interest of the producers. If, in the words of Gramsci, the "multiplicity of dispersed wills, with heterogeneous aims, are welded together with a single aim on the basis of an equal and common perception of the world,"[42] they are more likely to cement the revolution in a united pan-Ethiopian state, a state in which diverse cultures are accepted and celebrated and civil liberties and human rights are respected and protected. By failing to free themselves from the morbid confinement of sectarianism and ideological absolutism, the insurgent intellectuals stand to waste the liberatory potential of their divided struggles. The result is pervasive conflict, more fragmentation, and greater misery.

Ethiopian peasants were stirred to revolt by economic inequities, political injustices, and cultural denials. Localized and reactive, those revolts seldom posed a threat to the existing social order. Unless they can break out of their ethnic and regional enclaves, the current movements risk the fate of their precursors. Ethnoregional aspirations for self-determination and peasant struggles for greater autonomy and self-sufficiency should not be seen as opposing but rather as mutually reinforcing goals. These goals are more likely to be realized when genuine representative institutions are erected. Wartime collaboration between peasants and elites has increased popular participation in politics, enhancing possibilities for the institution of popular sovereignty. The great test is whether that alliance can be translated into a sustainable partnership that transcends ethnicity and regionality. No doubt there will be strains and rifts, not least because, firstly, the collective visionary agenda of the intellectuals dramatically conflicts with the individualistic and parochial tendencies of the peasants; and secondly, the dominant elites will be continually challenged by two contradictory tendencies that have afflicted historical revolutions: the striving or quest for justice and the temptation of power, or in other words, the search for liberty and the hunger for state power. When peasants are no longer benevolently guided by others but enjoy greater political space for self-initiated and self-directed action, then it can be said that another major phase in the stymied revolutionary process has begun, and the oldest peasantry in sub-Saharan Africa will have opened a new and exciting chapter in its long and rather depressing history.

Ethiopian peasants may have ended their political peripheralization; there is, however, a major dilemma that will continue to face them. Whereas they wish to free themselves from the burdens of its authority, the rural producers will remain dependent on the state for a long while. It is a historical dilemma from which they cannot easily escape. Hence to stress peasant autonomy is not to be oblivious to the state's paradoxical but inescapable and continuing

226

intervention in civic life. Abjectly poor and illiterate, the Ethiopian peasantry is too fragmented to act for itself. During the long transition to an undifferentiated free citizenry (for the peasantry is a passing social category) it will need constitutional and institutional support in its struggle to improve the conditions of its life through self-motivated and self-reliant activities. It is not state intervention, then, that is in question but rather the nature and extent of that intervention. In the past, the country was ravaged by a hierarchy of warring rulers whose descendants a centralizing authority was able to tame at the turn of the century but without ever deracinating their hold on the agrarian population. Hindering all forms of innovation, they continued to impoverish the most productive sector of society until their demise only a decade and a half ago, sometimes in collaboration and at other times in competition with an extractive state. Today, "socialist" parasites who control the state have led it closer to an abyss by instituting wasteful methods and policies that thwart and frustrate initiative and creativity, frequently disrupt productive activities, and generally favor the city at the expense of the village. Unless that symbiotic relationship is finally broken, Ethiopian peasants cannot hope to free themselves from the grinding and degrading poverty and misery in a country otherwise endowed with ample and fertile land, water, and an almost idyllic climate. And a sure way to tame the state and limit exploitation is by strengthening popular organs of power and production.

The peasants' most pressing problem is one of material *scarcity* and not simply the lack of political freedom (although it is possible to show the close correlation between the two). If despotism and bureaucratism have tended to thrive on scarcity and backwardness, then it may be that one way of deflecting them is to satisfy the material wants of people, a goal that may be difficult to attain without the democratization of state–society relations. Without state policies and programs that give top priority to the agricultural crisis, the peasantry cannot increase food production and domestic consumption. And it is reasonable to assume, an assumption supported by historical evidence from elsewhere, that that existential problem might be better addressed if those radical intellectuals who have constructed a creative relationship with the peasantry are strategically located to help direct the activities of the state. They have proven to be the most conscientious and consequential actors in the struggle for power in rural Ethiopia. The costly civil wars must then serve as the defining experience of the Ethiopian nation to be – one in which political democracy and social justice are instituted and protected constitutionally. For this to be realized the various political organizations, now fighting against the incumbent regime and against each other as well, must be willing and able to form an interim coalition government that will lay the foundation for a pluralist electoral process. No organization, whatever its ideological coloring, ought to be allowed to have a monopoly over politics. Rather, political society must accommodate all democratic forces and be tolerant of informed dissent as well as respectful of legal opposition. Only a regime that has a popular mandate will be better positioned to channel collective energies, individual talents and skills toward rebuilding and restoring the dignity of a land that has been ravaged and wounded by the twin misfortunes of war and natural calamities, to resuscitate an economy that is in tatters and gradually to close the national, regional, and income inequalities that are at the heart of the political crisis. One hopes that the conflicts of the last fifteen years will lead to greater national unity, social cohesion and stability founded on genuine peace, freedom, justice, equity, and prosperity.

The history of Ethiopia is largely about oppression and exploitation of peasants who carried it with habitual obedience and servility. They challenged their subordination too infrequently and always unsuccessfully. That cycle has been broken and peasants are engaged in a struggle to rid themselves of the shackles of feudal culture and the tyranny of material poverty. Liberation would entail a fundamental change in the patterns of authority, labor organization, and habits of work. And as such the struggle for economic and political empowerment will be long and protracted, one that the peasants are more likely to win in alliance with other sets of groups that compose subordinate society. The evolution from a long oppressed and abused people to a free and active citizenry that is in control of its own affairs will thus be neither smooth nor simple. And Ethiopian peasants, along with the other sectors of civil society, may never subordinate the state completely; but they have acquired new experiences, tools, and organizational means with which to impose limitations on its extractive and repressive capacities. By paying an incredibly enormous cost they have been mobilized to a degree never imagined before, and in constructing a culture of opposition or resistance, Ethiopian peasants have entered a new phase in their own history.

Notes

Preface

1 D. N. Levine, *Wax and Gold* (Chicago and London, 1965), p. 55.
2 Gabre Hiwet Baykedagn, "Ate Menelik ena Itiopia," in *Berhan Yihun* (Asmera, 1912), pp. 336–37.
3 Though they were extremely laconic in recording events pertaining to the lives of ordinary people, the chronicles did cover a range of subjects. In addition to court life, royal succession, imperial appointments, dynastic conflicts, and theological controversies, they yielded some interesting pieces of information on such issues as ecology, epidemiology, famine, and taxation systems, shedding light on broader social themes.
4 Sven Rubenson, *The Survival of Ethiopian Independence* (London, 1978), pp. 20–27; Sergew Hable Sellassie, *Ancient and Medieval Ethiopian History to 1270* (Addis Ababa, 1972), pp. 2–6.
5 Expression borrowed from Jean Chesneaux, *Pasts and Futures, or What is History For?* (London, 1978), p. 11.

1 Introduction

1 James C. Scott, *The Moral Economy of the Peasant* (New Haven and London, 1976), p. 203.
2 Teodor Shanin, "Peasantry as a Political Factor," in T. Shanin (ed.), *Peasants and Peasant Societies* (London, 1971), p. 240.
3 John S. Saul and Roger Woods, "African Peasantries," in Shanin, *Peasants and Peasant Societies*, p. 105, n. 2.
4 *Ibid.*, p. 106.
5 James C. Scott, *Weapons of the Weak* (New Haven and London, 1985), pp. xvi, 28–37.
6 Among the important works are Scott, *The Moral Economy*; Theda Skocpol, *States and Social Revolutions* (Cambridge, 1979); Jeffrey M. Paige, *Agrarian Revolution* (New York, 1975); Eric R. Wolf, *Peasant Wars of the Twentieth Century* (New York and London, 1969), and Barrington Moore, Jr., *Social Origins of Dictatorship and Democracy* (Boston, 1969).
7 Skocpol, *States and Social Revolutions*, p. 115.
8 Goran Therborn, *The Ideology of Power and the Power of Ideology* (London, 1980), p. 39.
9 Karl Marx, *The Eighteenth Brumaire of Louis Bonaparte* (New York, 1975), pp. 123–24.
10 Paige, *Agrarian Revolution*, pp. 337–39; 342–45.
11 *Ibid.*, p. 339.
12 Karl Marx and Frederick Engels, *The German Ideology* (New York, 1970), pp. 64–65.
13 For a fuller discussion of the mechanisms of ideological domination see Therborn, *The Ideology of Power*, pp. 93–100. See also Scott, *Weapons of the Weak*, ch. 8.

14 Scott, *The Moral Economy*, p. 239; *Weapons of the Weak*, pp. 28–32.
15 George Rudé, *Ideology and Popular Protest* (New York, 1980), p. 9. See also Scott, *The Moral Economy*, p. 233.
16 John Lonsdale, "States and Social Processes in Africa: A Historiographical Survey," *African Studies Review*, 24, 2/3 (June/September 1981), 160–61; Therborn, *The Ideology of Power*, pp. vii, 102.
17 James C. Scott, "Revolution in the Revolution: Peasants and Commissars," *Theory and Society*, 7, 1 (1979), 124–25.
18 Rudé, *Ideology and Popular Protest*, pp. 23, 28, 35.
19 David Lan, *Guns and Rain* (London and Los Angeles, 1985).
20 Wolf, *Peasant Wars*, p. 290.
21 *Ibid.*, pp. 290–93.
22 Paige, *Agrarian Revolution*, p. 342.
23 *Ibid.*, p. 27.
24 Wolf, *Peasant Wars*, pp. 280–95; Scott, *The Moral Economy*, pp. 167–82.
25 Fred Halliday and Maxine Molyneaux, *The Ethiopian Revolution* (London, 1981), pp. 15–16.
26 Robert L. Hess, *Ethiopia* (Ithaca and London, 1970), p. 148.
27 John Markakis and Nega Ayele, *Class and Revolution in Ethiopia* (Nottingham, 1978), p. 26.
28 Skocpol, *States and Social Revolutions*, p. 49.
29 Abyssinia used interchangeably with northern Ethiopia refers to the geographical area that roughly included Begemedir, Gojjam, Wag, Lasta, Tigrai, and highland Eritrea, and which also generally shared a commonality of polity, land tenure, culture, and religion. The regions which were conquered in the nineteenth century and which henceforth will be referred to as the south approximately include the former provinces of Arusi, Bale, Gamu Gofa, Harerge, Illubabor, Kaffa, and Sidamo, as well as southern Shewa.
30 For vivid descriptions see Afework Gabre Yesus, *Dagmawi Ate Menelik* (Rome, 1901), pp. 2–5; Gabre Hiwet, "Ate Menelik," p. 349; Richard A. Caulk, "Armies as Predators," *IJAHS*, 11, 3 (1978), 465–71 and Addis Hiwet, *Ethiopia* (London, 1975), p. 20.
31 Cited in Richard Pankhurst, *Economic History of Ethiopia 1800–1935* (Addis Ababa, 1968), p. 569.
32 Cited in Richard Pankhurst, "Some Factors Depressing the Standard of Living of Peasants in Traditional Ethiopia," *JES*, 4, 2 (July 1966), 91.
33 Merid W. Aregay, "Millenarian Traditions and Peasant Movements in Ethiopia 1500–1855," in Sven Rubenson (ed.), *Proceedings of the Seventh International Conference of Ethiopian Studies* (Berlings, Arlov, Sweden, 1984), pp. 260–61.
34 Girma Beshah and Merid Wolde Aregay, *The Question of the Union of Churches in Luso-Ethiopian Relations* (Lisbon, 1964), pp. 84–87, 97–104; Andrzei Bartnicki and Joanna Mantel-Niecko, "The Role and Significance of the Religious Conflicts and People's Movements in the Political Life of Ethiopia in the Seventeenth and Eighteenth Centuries," *Rassengna di Studi etiopici*, 24 (1969–70), 5–39.
35 Cited in Zewde Gabre Sellassie, *Yohannes IV of Ethiopia* (Oxford, 1975), p. 4.
36 See Pankhurst, *Economic History*, p. 563.
37 Donald Crummey, "Abyssinian Feudalism," *Past and Present*, 89 (November 1980), 137–38; F. C. Gamst, "Peasantries and Elites without Urbanism: The Civilization of Ethiopia," *CSSH*, 12, 4 (1970), 373–92.
38 Levine, *Wax and Gold*, pp. 242–56; Gedamu Abraha, "Wax and Gold," *Ethiopia Observer*, 11, 3 (1968), 230.
39 Paige, *Agrarian Revolution*, pp. 31–32; Levine, *Wax and Gold*, p. 93.
40 Richard Pankhurst, "'Fear God, Honour the King': The Use of Biblical Allusion in Ethiopian Historical Literature, Part II," *NEAS*, 2, 1 (1987), 46.

41 Herbert S. Lewis, "Spirit Possession in Ethiopia: An Essay in Interpretation," in Rubenson, *Proceedings*, pp. 419–27.
42 For contrasting views see Eric J. Hobsbawm, *Bandits* (New York, 1972; 2nd edn, 1981); Anton Block, "The Peasant and the Brigand: Social Banditry Reconsidered," *CSSH*, 15 (September 1972), 494–503.
43 Nigel Harris, "The Revolutionary Role of Peasants (1)," *International Socialism*, 41 (December 1969–January 1970), 20.
44 Enno Littmann (ed. and trans.), *Publications of the Princeton Expedition to Abyssinia*, Vol. II, *Tales, Customs, Names and Dirges of the Tigre Tribes: English Translation* (Leyden, 1910), p. 203.
45 Gratefully obtained from Dr. Alem Seged Hailu.
46 Donald Crummey, "Banditry and Resistance: Noble and Peasant in Nineteenth-Century Ethiopia," in D. Crummey (ed.), *Banditry, Rebellion and Social Protest in Africa* (London, 1986), pp. 137, 140–43; and Rubenson, *Proceedings*, pp. 263, 265–66.
47 Timothy Fernyhough, "Social Mobility and Dissident Elites in Northern Ethiopia: The Role of Banditry, 1900–69," in Crummey, *Banditry*, pp. 152–53; see also Block, "The Peasant," 498–502.
48 Basil Davidson, *Let Freedom Come* (Boston, 1978), p. 89.
49 Therborn, *The Ideology of Power*, p. 62.
50 Rudé, *Ideology and Popular Protest*, p. 30.

2 The historical context

1 Eric R. Wolf, *Peasants* (Englewood Cliffs, N.J., 1966), p. 11.
2 Lonsdale, "States and Social Processes in Africa," 205.
3 Charles Tilly, "Western State-Making and Theories of Political Transformation," in C. Tilly (ed.), *The Formation of National States in Western Europe* (Princeton, N.J., 1975), p. 638; Skocpol, *States and Social Revolutions*, p. 29.
4 C. Tilly, "Reflections on the History of European State-Making," in *The Formation of National States*, p. 81.
5 *Ibid.*, p. 22.
6 Donald N. Levine, *Greater Ethiopia* (Chicago and London, 1974), pp. 21, 69.
7 Donald Crummey, "Society and Ethnicity in the Politics of Ethiopia during the Zamana Masafent," *IJAHS*, 8, 2 (1975), 271–78.
8 Donald Donham, "Old Abyssinia and the New Ethiopian Empire: Themes in Social History," in D. Donham and Wendy James (eds.), *The Southern Marches of Imperial Ethiopia* (Cambridge, 1986), p. 34.
9 Christopher Clapham, *Transformation and Continuity in Revolutionary Ethiopia* (Cambridge, 1988), p. 195.
10 John Markakis, *National and Class Conflict in the Horn of Africa* (Cambridge, 1987), pp. xvi–xvii.
11 This account is based on Levine, *Greater Ethiopia*, pp. 33–39 and Edward Ullendorff, *The Ethiopians: An Introduction to Country and People*, 3rd edn (London and Oxford, 1973), chs. 3, 6.
12 Mesfin Wolde Mariam, *An Introductory Geography of Ethiopia* (Addis Ababa, 1972), pp. 171–73.
13 Donham, "Old Abyssinia," pp. 19–21.
14 *Ibid.*
15 I have benefited from the insights of Levine, *Greater Ethiopia*, p. 118; Donham, "Old Abyssinia," pp. 22–23 and J. Markakis, *Ethiopia: Anatomy of a Traditional Polity* (Oxford, 1974), pp. 42–47.
16 Markakis, *Ethiopia*, p. 48.

17 The most comprehensive accounts about Aksumite society and culture are provided in Yuri M. Kobischchanov, *Axum*, trans. Lorraine T. Kopitanoff, (University Park, Pa. and London, 1979); and Sergew Hable Sellassie, *Ancient and Medieval Ethiopian History* (Addis Ababa, 1972).

18 M. Abir has discussed these events fully in his *Ethiopia* (London, 1968), especially chs. 2 and 6.

19 Rubenson, *The Survival of Ethiopian Independence*, ch. 4 and *King of Kings, Tewodros of Ethiopia* (Addis Ababa, 1966); D. Crummey, "Tewodros as Reformer and Modernizer," *JAH*, 10, 3 (1969), 457–69.

20 For a detailed and sympathetic study of Yohannes's reign see Zewde, *Yohannes IV of Ethiopia*.

21 R. H. K. Darkwah, *Shewa, Menilek and the Ethiopian Empire 1813–1889* (London, 1975), pp. 155–79.

22 *Ibid.*, pp. 190–99; Mohammed Hassen, "The Oromo of Ethiopia, 1500–1850: With Special Emphasis on the Gibe Region," unpublished Ph.D. thesis, University of London, 1983.

23 S. Rubenson, *Wichale XVII* (Addis Ababa, 1964) and "Adwa 1896: The Resounding Protest," in R. I. Rotberg and Ali A. Mazrui (eds.), *Protest and Power in Black Africa* (London, 1970), pp. 113–42.

24 The Tripartite Treaty of 1906, in which Britain, France, and Italy impudently declared that they would partition the country should it disintegrate following Menelik's death, expressed not only harmful intentions but also the fragility of the new state.

25 Why the Ethiopian leadership failed to turn its military victory to a complete Italian evacuation of Eritrea has remained a perplexing question. The Eritrean question has also left Menelik portrayed in the conflicting images of a great nationalist and colonial collaborationist. The Ethiopian author Tekle Tsadik Mekuria has speculated that Menelik abandoned the idea of regaining the lost territory (a) for fear that his prolonged absence from the capital would encourage rebellion in the conquered territories, and (b) because the prospects of success were uncertain since Italy had reportedly dispatched about 15,000 troops to reinforce Asmera, the colony's capital. A conspiratorial vision would suggest a third and perhaps overriding reason: that Menelik's intention might have been to weaken the northern rivals by permanently dismembering their territory and denying them direct access to the sea, access that had enabled them to enjoy a virtual monopoly over arms imports up to the nineteenth century. If indeed that was Menelik's plan, then he seems to have succeeded, for Adwa witnessed the virtual eclipse of the Tigrean dynasty. Tekle Tsadik Mekuria, *Ye Itiopia Tarik* (Addis Ababa, 1968), pp. 83–84. See also H. Marcus, *The Life and Times of Menelik II* (Oxford, 1975), p. 176.

26 Marcus, *Menelik II*, pp. 198–204.

27 This section has benefited from T. M. Callaghy, "External Actors and the Relative Autonomy of the Political Aristocracy in Zaire," and N. Kasfir, "Relating Class to State in Africa," both in Kasfir (ed.), *State and Class in Africa* (London, 1984).

28 Addison E. Southard to Secretary of State, Addis Ababa, June 19, 1928, in Borg G. Steffanson and Ronald K. Starrett (eds.), *Documents on Ethiopian Politics*, Vol. XI (Salisbury, N.C., 1977), p. 74.

29 Perry Anderson, *Lineages of the Absolutist State* (London, 1979), pp. 49–50; Perez Zagorin, *Rebels and Rulers, 1500–1660*, Vol. I (Cambridge, 1982), p. 74.

30 Immanuel Wallerstein, *The Modern World System* (New York and London, 1976), p. 101.

31 Zagorin, *Rebels and Rulers*, Vol. I, p. 91.

32 Wallerstein, *The Modern World System*, p. 95.

33 Bahru Zewde is the first to draw attention to this issue in his "Economic Origins of the Absolutist State in Ethiopia (1916–1935)," *JES*, 17 (November 1984), 6–11.

34 Anderson, *Lineages*, pp. 47–48.

35 *Ibid.*, pp. 18–19.

36 The unwritten story of Iyassu is complicated and controversial. At any rate, in opposing him, the Shewan nobility accused him of disloyalty to the throne, of apostasy, and sexual impropriety, accusations orchestrated by the British and French legations in the capital.
37 The other members were the Empress Zewditu and the War Minister, Fitawrari Habte Giorgis.
38 Southard to Secretary of State, June 19, 1928. Also Haile Selassie I, *My Life and Ethiopia's Progress 1892–1937*, translated and annotated by E. Ullendorff (Oxford, 1976), p. 180.
39 Addis, *Ethiopia*, pp. 77–78.
40 Reverend Ashly Brown, *Australian Church Standard*, enclosure in James Loder Park to Secretary of State, Addis Ababa, September 7, 1927, in Steffanson and Starrett, p. 68.
41 The emperor claimed that the revolt was instigated by Italian propaganda: *My Life*, pp. 156–63. James McCann in his informed essay has argued that it was a reaction to multiple domestic events and developments. See his fascinating study *From Poverty to Famine in Northeast Ethiopia* (Philadelphia, 1987), ch. 7.
42 The *Fetha Negest*, which served as the main source for secular and ecclesiastical legislation since about the sixteenth century, was not such a constitution.
43 M. Perham, *The Government of Ethiopia* (Evanston, Ill., 1969), pp. 70–71.
44 Bahru, "Economic Origins," 11–23.
45 Addis, *Ethiopia*, pp. 38–44; H. G. Marcus, *Ethiopia, Great Britain, and the United States, 1941–1974* (Berkeley/London, 1983), pp. 3–4, 44.
46 Bahru Zewde, "An Overview and Assessment of Gambella Trade (1904–1935)," *IJAHS*, 20, 1 (1987), 77; Addison E. Southard to Secretary of State, Addis Ababa, April 22, 1919, in Steffanson and Starrett, p. 30.
47 Markakis, *National and Class Conflict*, p. 97.
48 Bahru, "Economic Origins," 20–23.
49 Alberto Sbacchi, *Ethiopia under Mussolini* (London, 1985), chs. 14 and 18.
50 *Ibid.*, pp. 160–65.
51 According to Patrick Gilkes, between 1944 and 1966, 72 percent of the district governors in Tigrai came from the province itself. The distribution for Gojjam, Shewa, and Wello was 52, 83, and 68 percent respectively. In contrast, a substantial majority of the officials in the southern provinces were not of local origin. See his *The Dying Lion* (London, 1975), pp. 39, 49.
52 Zagorin, *Rebels and Rulers*, Vol. I, p. 93.
53 Anderson, *Lineages*, p. 51.
54 *Ibid.*, p. 48.
55 Zagorin, *Rebels and Rulers*, Vol. I, p. 96; Skocpol, *States and Social Revolutions*, pp. 86–88. Again, the similarities with Europe are quite striking.
56 For the most comprehensive account of governmental organization and patrimonial ties see Markakis, *Ethiopia*, chs. 9 and 10; C. Clapham, *Haile Selassie's Government* (London, 1969), and J. H. Spencer, *Ethiopia at Bay* (Algonac, Mich., 1984), especially ch. 7.
57 This is a major feature that Ethiopia shared with other postcolonial states in Africa. See Kasfir, "Relating Class to State," pp. 13–14; Callaghy, "External Actors," pp. 64–71.
58 For analytic inspiration, I am indebted to Callaghy, *ibid.*, especially pp. 70–71.
59 Quoted in Gilkes, *The Dying Lion*, p. 47.
60 My source is Dr. Tsehaye Teferra, to whom I am thankful.
61 For similarities with East European absolutism see Anderson, *Lineages*, pp. 197–98; Addis, *Ethiopia*, pp. 78–79.
62 The evolution of that relationship has been fully recounted by Marcus, *Ethiopia*, chs. 1–4 and Spencer, *Ethiopia at Bay*, pp. 102–279.

3 The social context

1 Moore, *Social Origins*, p. 457.
2 Crummey, "Abyssinian Feudalism," 122, 126.
3 In formulating these views I have drawn especially from Skocpol, *States and Social Revolutions*, p. 48.
4 Siegfried Pausewang, "Peasant Society and Development in Ethiopia," *Sociologica Ruralis*, 13, 2 (1973), 174–75.
5 *Ibid.*
6 Crummey, "Abyssinian Feudalism," 115–38; Addis, *Ethiopia*, pp. 24–28; Michael Stahl, *Ethiopia* (Stockholm, 1974), p. 22; Allan Hoben, *Land Tenure among the Amhara of Ethiopia* (Chicago and London, 1973), pp. 1–2; Gene Ellis, "The Feudal Paradigm as a Hinderance to Understanding Ethiopia," *JMAS*, 14, 2 (June 1976), 275–95; Donham, "Old Abyssinia," pp. 8–17.
7 Maurice Dobb, *Studies in the Development of Capitalism* (New York, 1970), pp. 35–37; R. H. Hilton (ed.), *The Transition from Feudalism to Capitalism* (London, 1976), pp. 34–35; Marc Bloch, *Feudal Society*, vol. XI (London, 1971), p. 446.
8 Dobb, *The Development of Capitalism*, p. 66.
9 For various stereotypical views of women, see Levine, *Greater Ethiopia*, pp. 54–55.
10 Mesfin, *An Introductory Geography*, p. 178.
11 These reciprocated activities (harvesting, house-raising, etc.), known as *dobbo* (Amharic) or *woferra* (Tigriniya), could involve a good amount of expenditure, since sponsoring families had to prepare food and beer for the festive occasion.
12 George A. Lipsky, *Ethiopia* (New Haven, 1962), p. 142.
13 The most comprehensive analyses are provided in Hoben, *Land Tenure*; Joanna Mantel-Niecko, *The Role of Land Tenure in the System of Ethiopian Imperial Government in Modern Times*, trans. Krzystog Adam Bobinski (Warsaw, 1980); Markakis, *Ethiopia*, chs. 4 and 5; Gilkes, *The Dying Lion*, ch. 4; John M. Cohen and Dov Weintraub, *Land and Peasants in Imperial Ethiopia* (Assen, The Netherlands, 1975).
14 The criterion for eligibility and allotment of land was modified in parts of Eritrea and Tigrai, perhaps in response to demographic changes. By making coresidence or domicile the sole requirement, a land-share system put a time limit to collateral eligibility. Equal distribution of cultivable land among resident households and newcomers was made periodically by lot, the time for repartitioning ranging from four to seven years. Sale or transfer was prohibited, and absenteeism was not allowed, departees automatically forfeiting their shares. Under increasing ecological strains, this tenurial arrangement may have provided better security to producers, but it affected only a small percentage of the total population in the two provinces. For the most informed study see John W. Bruce, "Land Reform Planning and Indigenous Communal Tenures: A Case Study of the Tenure Chiguraf-gwoses in Tigray, Ethiopia" (unpublished SJD Law dissertation, University of Wisconsin, Madison, May 1976).
15 The violation of the principle of bilateral descent often worked against women. Power was also translated into land. Hoben, *Land Tenure*, pp. 55, 182.
16 According to Cohen and Weintraub the state may have controlled about 12 percent of the cultivable and 47 percent of the total land. *Land and Peasants*, p. 45.
17 Cohen and Weintraub estimated church holdings as 5 percent of the total or 20 percent of the cultivable land. *Ibid.*, p. 43. Dessalegn Rahmato gives an estimate of 10 to 12 percent. See his *Agrarian Reform in Ethiopia* (Trenton, N.J., 1985), p. 19.
18 For Tigrai see Gabre Wolde Ingida-Work, "Ethiopia's Traditional System of Land Tenure and Taxation," trans. Mengesha Gessesse, *Ethiopia Observer*, 4 (1962), 318–19; Mahteme Selassie Wolde Meskel, *Zekre Negger*, 2nd edn (Addis Ababa, 1970), pp. 150–56; Pankhurst, *Economic History*, pp. 514, 516–17; MLRA, "A Detailed Study of Communal Tenure

Systems in Ethiopia," unpublished (1970), pp. 21–22. For Gojjam see Gabre Wolde, "Ethiopia's Traditional System," 321; Hoben, *Land Tenure*, p. 211; Getachew Adamu, "A Historical Survey of Taxation in Gojjam 1901–1969" (BA thesis, HSIU, May 1971), pp. 2–12; Kebede Tessema to Blatta Haile Wolde Kidan, Debre Markos, February 3, 1950 (25 Tir 1942), MIA–G 29/42/2. Mantel-Niecko has relevant information on both provinces scattered throughout most of *The Role of Land Tenure*. Mahteme Selassie, *Zekre Negger*, pp. 144–60; Markakis, *Ethiopia*, pp. 79–80.

19 Mantel-Niecko, *The Role of Land Tenure*, p. 60.
20 Underlying the irregular nature of extraction, D. Crummey has arrived at an estimate of 30 percent of total produce for eighteenth- and nineteenth-century Ethiopia. "State and Society," in D. Crummey and C. C. Stewart (eds.), *Modes of Production in Africa* (Beverly Hills and London, 1981), p. 232.
21 Cited in Gilkes, *The Dying Lion*, p. 61.
22 See the collection of articles in Donham and James, *The Southern Marches*, pp. 51–245; C. W. Mclellan, *State Transformation and National Integration: Gedeo and the Ethiopian Empire, 1895–1935* (East Lansing, 1988).
23 Donham, "Old Abyssinia," pp. 44–45.
24 See, for example, Lubie Birru, "Abyssinian Colonialism as the Genesis of the Crisis in the Horn," *NEAS*, 2, 3 (1980–81) and 3, 1 (1981), 93–99; Teodore Nasoulas, "Ethiopia," *Horn of Africa*, 4, 3 (1981), 3–6.
25 It is true that following the expulsion of the Italians there was scattered resistance in the south against the restoration of the imperial state. Some intellectuals, mainly from Wellega, had also proposed the formation of an Oromo state under British protectorate.
26 Levine, *Greater Ethiopia*, p. 26. Italics in the original.
27 Markakis, *Ethiopia*, p. 32; Marcus, *Menelik II*, p. 193.
28 Acknowledgment is due to the late Baro Tumsa for this quotation.
29 Marx, *The Eighteenth Brumaire*, p. 124; V. I. Lenin, *Collected Works*, Vol. XXIX (Moscow, 1965), p. 421.
30 Mesfin Wolde Mariam, *Rural Vulnerability to Famine in Ethiopia 1958–1977* (New Delhi, 1984), p. 73. For the best analysis of the destruction of the ecosystem and consequent peasant pauperization, see McCann, *From Poverty to Famine*.
31 Dessalegn, *Agrarian Reform*, p. 31.
32 Mesfin, *Rural Vulnerability*, p. 90.
33 An official study disclosed that 40 percent "were made up of single consolidated plots, whereas 36 percent consisted of 30 or more parcels." Dessalegn, *Agrarian Reform*, p. 31.
34 In the *rist* areas the annual gross income of households obtained from the average value of gross production was anywhere between ETH $100 and $250. MLRA, "A Detailed Study," pp. 41–44.
35 For example, in Sidamo, Kaffa, and Wello the distribution of farms measuring less than half a hectare was 94, 92, and 82 percent respectively. Dessalegn, *Agrarian Reform*, p. 29.
36 Mesfin, *An Introductory Geography*, p. 171.
37 Cohen and Weintraub, *Land and Peasants*, p. 51. The authors estimated the southern peasantry as constituting 60 percent of the country's rural population.
38 MLRA, "The Major Features of Prevailing Land Tenure Systems in Ethiopia," unpublished (October 1971), p. 18.
39 CSO, *Report on Land Survey of Tigre Province*, p. 37, and MLRA, "A Detailed Study," p. 24.
40 Mesfin, *Rural Vulnerability*, pp. 91–92; CSO, *Report on Land Survey of Hararge Province*, p. 46.
41 Mesfin, *Rural Vulnerability*, p. 114.
42 *Ibid.*, p. 18.
43 Crummey, "Abyssinian Feudalism," pp. 28–31; Markakis, *Ethiopia*, pp. 298–99.

44 Perham, *The Government*, p. 211.
45 An account of the taxation policies is available in Markakis, *Ethiopia*, pp. 120–23, and Peter Schwab, *Decision-Making in Ethiopia* (London, 1972), pp. 27–86. See also Eshetu Chole, "Towards a History of the Fiscal Policy of the Pre-revolutionary Ethiopian State: 1941–74," *JES*, 17 (November 1984), 88–106.
46 Eshetu, "Towards a History," 93.
47 Taye Gulilat, "The Tax in Lieu of Tithe and the New Agricultural Income Tax," *Dialogue*, 11, 1 (December 1968), 17.
48 Haile Selassie I, *Selected Speeches* (Addis Ababa, 1967), p. 493.
49 Schwab, *Decision-Making*, p. 92.
50 *The Ethiopian Herald*, November 23, 1967.
51 Schwab, *Decision-making*, pp. 91–92. For a fuller account see pp. 89–138.
52 Gilkes estimated that about 75 percent of the rural population earned ETH $300 or less and "50 percent of those probably earned half of this or even less in cash." *The Dying Lion*, p. 125.
53 CSO, *The Public Sector of the Ethiopian Economy* (1974), p. 16; CSO, *Ethiopia: Statistical Abstract* (1972), pp. 8, 31.
54 CSO, *Ethiopia: Statistical Abstract*, pp. 8, 31.

4 Tigrai: provincialism versus centralism

1 Gabre Wolde, "Ethiopia's Traditional System," 326. The imperial claim that payment of tax was a guarantee of the right to hold land is based on traditional grounds.
2 Lt. Colonel G. Peirson, "Account of the Operation," FO 371/35608.
3 *Ibid.*
4 Gabre Egziabher Dare, interviewed, Debub (Wajirat), April 17, 1975.
5 Kifle Dadi to Minister of the Interior, Mekele, May 27, 1943 (19 Ginbot 1935), Ministry of the Interior Archives – Tigrai (henceforth MIA–T) 11/36; Balambaras Tekka Wolde Rufael, interviewed, Mekele, April 15, 1975; Belai Woldiye, interviewed, Addigrat, April 23, 1975.
6 Peirson, "Account," FO 371/35608, and also Brigadier A. E. Cottam, "Interim Report – Tigre Operations," October 18, 1943, FO 371/35608.
7 J. Trimingham, *Islam in Ethiopia* (London, 1952), pp. 192, 194–95; C. Conti Rossini, "Voggerat, Raia Galla e Zobul," *Africa*, 56 (1938), 88–89.
8 J. Millard, "Report on the Azebo and Raya Gallas (1942)," FO 371/35608; Abba Habte Mariam Tedla, interviewed, Mekele, April 5, 1975; Haile Negussie, Abraha Yohannes, and Redaee Abraha, interviewed, Debub, April 17, 1975.
9 Millard, "Report," FO 371/35608.
10 I have benefited from Claude Meillassoux, "The Social Organization of the Peasantry," *JPS*, 1, 1 (1973), 81–90.
11 Zewde, *Yohannes IV of Ethiopia*, p. 4.
12 For some minor exceptions see G. K. N. Trevaskis, *Eritrea* (London and New York, 1960), pp. 14–16.
13 Samir Amin, *Unequal Development* (New York, 1976), p. 15.
14 Haggai Erlich, *Ethiopia and the Challenge of Independence* (Boulder, Colo., 1986), chs. 6–8.
15 Haile Selassie, *My Life*, pp. 246–50; K. Cooke to Ras Haile Selassie Gugsa and to all the people of Tigrai, Mekele, n.d., FO 371/31597; *Addis Zemen*, January 11, 1975 (3 Tir 1967).
16 R. G. Howe to Anthony Eden, Addis Ababa, November 30, 1943, FO 371/35608; also anonymous to R. H. D. Sanford, Addis Ababa, 1943, enclosure FO 371/35608.
17 R. G. Howe to G. Mackereth, Addis Ababa, October 15, 1943, FO 371/35608; see also G. Mackereth, "Memo," September 25, 1943, FO 371/35608.
18 General Officer Commander-in-Chief East Africa (GOC in C) to Commander in Middle East, Nairobi, October 22, 1941, enclosure, FO 371/27522.

19 Bayiu Wolde Giorgis to Leul-Ras Seyum, Addis Ababa, December 7, 1943 (29 Hidar 1935), MIA–T 11/36; Gabre Hiwet Meshesha to Bitwoded Mekonen, November 11, 1943 (3 Hidar 1935), MIA–T 11/36; Aleme Teferru, interviewed, Mekele, April 10, 1975; Fisseha Tekle, interviewed, Wukro, April 20, 1975; Wolde Leul Seyum, October 25, 1974; Kifle Dadi to Minister of the Interior, Mekele, May 27, 1943, MIA–T 11/36.

20 Tessema Tesfai, interviewed, Addigrat, April 23, 1975; Wolde Leul Seyum, October 25, 1974; Fisseha Tekle, April 20, 1975.

21 Sissay Shumiye to Minister of the Interior, Mekele, October 29, 1945 (21 Tikimt 1937), MIA–T 11/36; anonymous to Minister of the Pen, Mekele, October 21, 1945 (13 Tikimt 1937), MIA–T 11/36; Security Department of Ministry of Defense, "Report," Addis Ababa, 1942 (1934), MIA–T 11/36; British Legation to Foreign Office, Addis Ababa, December 4, 1944, FO 371/41466.

22 The group reportedly fabricated a story about a diamond dropped from heaven at the Church of Mary of Tsion in Aksum for the youngest son of Ras Gugsa, Kifle Tsion, as evidence of his divine selection for the kingship. Anonymous, "Memo," December 19, 1945 (11 Tahisas 1937), MIA–T 21/3; Fisseha Tekle, April 20, 1975.

23 Getahun Tessema to Director of Public Security, Addis Ababa, January 16, 1943 (8 Tir 1935), MIA–T 11/36; Kifle Dadi to various bandit leaders, Mekele, December 21, 1943 (13 Tahisas 1935), MIA–T 11/36; Kifle Dadi to Minister of the Interior, Mekele, April 24, 1943 (16 Ginbot 1936), MIA T 11/36.

24 Prominent among them were Haile Mariam Redda, Belai Woldiye, Yikuno Amlak Tesfai, Fassil Teferri, Hadera Tedla, Belai Gugsa, and Assefa Derso. Getahun Tessema to Director of Public Security, January 16, 1943, MIA–T 11/36; Haile Mariam Redda, interviewed, Addis Ababa, October 23, 1974; Belai Woldiye, April 24, 1975.

25 R. G. Howe to A. Eden, Addis Ababa, November 30, 1943, FO 371/35608; Belai Woldiye, April 22, 1975; Kegnazmatch Gessesse Woldiye, interviewed, Addigrat, April 21, 1975. Haile Mariam claimed that he traveled to Addis Ababa not to seek appointment but to gather military intelligence. Not only is this claim contradicted by his uncles, Belai and Gessesse Woldiye, but it also seems highly improbable.

26 Tsegai Gebru, interviewed, Mekele, April 7, 1975; Belai Woldiye, April 22, 1975; Haile Mariam Redda, October 23, 1974.

27 Anonymous to Minister of the Interior, "The People of Mekele District and their Plight," Mekele, June 29, 1943 (21 Sene 1935), MIA–T 11/36; Zewengel Gabre Kidan, interviewed, Addis Ababa, June 6, 1975; Luel-Ras Mengesha Seyum, interviewed in Arlington, Virginia, December 7, 1980. According to Mengesha the misuse of the traditional *afersata* (public gathering) was a source of peasant discontent. It was customary to coerce peasants either to deliver up criminals or to bear a collective penalty.

28 See, for example, Getachew Haile, "The Unity and Territorial Integrity of Ethiopia," *JMAS*, 24, 3 (September 1986), 480, and Erlich, *Ethiopia*, ch. 8. Erlich has assembled a good amount of evidence from the British archives to support his thesis of a "tripartite struggle" in Tigrai. What that evidence suggests is that British military officials may have influenced the unrest in the province; it does not, in any way, indicate that they created it.

29 R. G. Howe to Anthony Eden, Addis Ababa, November 30, 1943, FO 371/35608.

30 Tessema Tesfai, April 23, 1975.

31 Judicial Adviser, Ministry of Justice, to Getahun Tessema, Addis Ababa, May 10, 1943, MIA–T 11/36; Ephrem Tewolde Medhin to Minister of the Interior, Addis Ababa, July 25, 1943 (7 Tir 1935), MIA–T 11/36; Getahun Tessema to Adviser, Ministry of the Interior, Addis Ababa, May 10, 1943, MIA–T 11/36; Ministry of Foreign Affairs to British Legation, Addis Ababa, July 17, 1943, FO 371/35608; Kifle Dadi to Minister of the Interior, Mekele, n.d. but probably written in 1943, MIA–T 11/36; Stephen Longrigg to Minister of the Interior, Asmera, December 13, 1943, MIA–T 11/36.

237

32 Alberto Sbacchi, "Haile Selassie and the Italians 1941–1943," *African Studies Review*, 22, 1 (April 1979), 30–31; 34–35.

33 R. E. Cheesman, "Report," May 25, 1943, FO 371/35606.

34 Lt. General Issayas Gabre Selassie, unpublished manuscript in the possession of his cousin, who preferred to remain anonymous, and consulted in Addis Ababa, January 1974; Secretary of State to Foreign Office, "Memorandum," Addis Ababa, October 15, 1941, FO 371/27522.

35 R. G. Howe to G. Mackereth, Addis Ababa, October 15, 1943, FO 371/35608; Secretary of State for Foreign Affairs, "Memorandum," October 15, 1941, FO 371/27522; HIM Haile Selassie to Emmanuel Abraha, Addis Ababa, August 20, 1941 (14 Nehassie 1933), appendix III in "Policy with Regard to Ethiopia," October 15, 1941, FO 371/27522; HIM Haile Selassie to the Princess Tenagne Work, enclosure, FO 371/27521.

36 Gabre Meskel Odda to Kifle Ergetu, Addigrat, November 16, 1945 (8 Hidar 1937), MIA–T 21/3; Gabre Meskel Odda to Tsehafe-Tizaz Wolde Giorgis, Addigrat, September 20, 1943 (12 Meskerem 1937), MIA–T 11/36; anonymous to Director of Ministry of the Pen, April 9, 1945 (1 Miazia 1937), MIA–T 21/3; Sisay Shumiye to Minister of the Interior, Mekele, October 29, 1943 (21 Tikimt 1937), MIA–T 11/36; Trevaskis, *Eritrea*, pp. 60–63; Peirson, "Account," FO 371/35608.

37 Haile Mariam, October 24, 1974.

38 Erlich, *Ethiopia*, pp. 170–81.

39 Anthony Eden, Memorandum, "Policy with regard to Ethiopia," October 15, 1941, FO 371/27522.

40 Secretary of State for War to Secretary of State for Foreign Office, September 23, 1941, enclosure, FO 371/27521.

41 R. G. Howe to Foreign Office, Addis Ababa, December 6, 1943, FO 371/35608. See also R. G. Howe to Foreign Office, Addis Ababa, October 30, 1943, FO 371/35607.

42 Millard, "Report," FO 371/35608.

43 Tessema Tesfai, April 23, 1975; Kegnazmatch Haile Selassie Belai, interviewed, Adwa, April 26, 1975; Girazmatch Zewoldai Gabre Hiwet, interviewed, Adwa, April 28, 1975; Major Negga Haile Selassie, "Report on the Campaign," n.d., FO 371/35607.

44 Petitions from Raya and Azebo to the Prime Minister, Mekele, August 28, 1968 (20 Nehasie 1960), MIA–T 17596/58; R. E. Cheesman, "Report," May 25, 1943, FO 371/35626.

45 Kifle Dadi to Minister of the Interior, May 27, 1943, MIA–T 11/36; Kifle Dadi to Minister of the Interior, n.d., but no. 229, MIA–T 11/36; Mekonen Endalkachew to Kifle Dadi, Addis Ababa, October 10, 1943 (2 Tikimt 1935), MIA–T 11/36.

46 I am grateful to Fitawrari Belai Woldiye for this information. Other informants thought that though the poem was popular at that time, it may actually have been composed earlier in relation to other events.

47 Balambaras Assefa Asgedom, interviewed, Mekele, April 10, 1975.

48 Kifle Dadi to Minister of the Interior, May 27, 1943, MIA–T 11/36; anonymous to Minister of the Interior, n.d., MIA–T 11/36; Kifle Dadi to Minister of the Interior, Mekele, May 27, 1943, MIA–T 11/36.

49 Issayas, MS; GOC in C East Africa to War Office, Nairobi, September 23, 1943, FO 371/35607; Haile Mariam Redda, October 23, 1974.

50 Cottam, "Interim Report," FO 371/35607; Haile Mariam, October 24, 1974.

51 Issayas claimed (MS.) he had about four hundred men against 30,000 rebels, whereas Haile Mariam put the figure at five thousand troops against 20,000 of his own. Mengesha thinks that Issayas may be closer to the truth. Haile Mariam Redda, October 24, 1974; Mengesha Seyum, December 7, 1980.

52 In Ethiopia proclamations were a major mode of communication. There is little reason to suspect the authenticity of this important and interesting document. Despite some variations with regard to details, all informants agreed on the content of the text. Haile Mariam Redda,

October 23, 1974; Fisseha Tekle, April 20, 1975; Belai Woldiye, April 22, 1975; Girmai Mengesha, April 8, 1975; Tsegai Gebru, interviewed, Mekele, April 7, 1975.

53 Peirson, "Account," FO 371/35608; see also Minister of State to Foreign Office, Cairo, October 1, 1943, FO 371/35607; GOC in C, East Africa, Nairobi, July 15, 1944, FO 371/41478.

54 Cottam, "Interim Report," FO 371/35607; GOC in C East Africa, Nairobi, July 15, 1944, FO 371/41478.

55 From the Foreign Office's translated copies, FO 371/35607.

56 *Ibid.*

57 Minister of State to Foreign Office, London, October 1, 1943, FO 371/35607; Peirson, "Account," FO 371/35608; Haile Mariam, October 24, 1974.

58 Cottam, "Interim Report," FO 371/35607; Peirson, "Account," FO 371/35608; GOC in C, East Africa, to War Office, October 10, 1943, FO 371/35607.

59 Peirson, "Account," FO 371/35608; also A. E. Cottam to Headquarters, East Africa, Addis Ababa, November 11, 1943, FO 371/35608; W. E. M. Logan, "Summary of Air Operations in Tigrai," October, 1943, FO 371/35608; R. G. Howe to Foreign Office, Addis Ababa, October 13, 1943, FO 371/35608.

60 The *gedigedi* is a rare white bird. Here it is used as a metaphor for the plane. Poem as recorded by Issayas Gabre Selassie and translated with the help of Dr. Alem Seged Hailu.

61 Peirson, "Account," FO 371/35608.

62 Cottam, "Interim Report," FO 371/35607.

63 Haile Mariam Redda, October 24, 1974; Habte Mariam Tedla, April 5, 1975; Haile Negussie and Redaee Abraha, April 17, 1975.

64 Pietro Badaglio, *The War in Abyssinia* (New York, 1937), pp. 145–46.

65 Wolde Aregai Gebru to Tsehafe-Tizaz Wolde Giorgis, Mekele, January 16, 1945 (8 Tir 1937), MIA–T 21/3. Haile Mariam was first detained in Gore, Illubabor, and then at Hamer Bako, Gamu Gofa, until his release in 1967. Haile Mariam, October 24, 1974.

66 Haile Mariam's manuscript, in his possession. The MS, consulted in October 1974, is a skeletal outline of the rebellion, perhaps drafted long after the event. It gives some of the possible causes, names of leaders, and government reactions. Although woefully incomplete, it is a useful document.

67 In 1975 he was appointed head of the militia in Tigrai, charged with the difficult task of suppressing what is sometimes called the "Second *Weyane*."

68 Peirson, "Account," FO 371/35608; Haile Negussie, April 17, 1975.

69 Abba Yohannes Gabre Egziabher, *Tigrigna-Amarigna Mezgebe Kalat* (Asmera, 1948–49), p. 638.

70 Mesfin, *An Introductory Geography*, p. 53.

71 Fisseha Tekle, April 21, 1975; Girmai Negash, April 9, 1975; Assefa Asgedom, April 10, 1975; see also Gilkes, *The Dying Lion*, p. 188. Haile Mariam denied that he had advocated neither secession nor restoration of the Tigrean dynasty.

72 This is not the first time that Haile Selassie was accused of a Catholic connection. Ras Gugsa Wolle accused him of it when he rebelled against the emperor in 1929–30. Leonard Mosley, *Haile Selassie* (Englewood Cliffs, N.J., 1964), p. 146.

73 Haile Mariam Redda, October 23, 1974; Tsegai Gebru, April 10, 1975.

74 Haile Mariam Redda, October 23, 1974 and his MS; Tsegai Gebru, April 10, 1975.

75 Girmai Mengesha, April 8, 1975; Assefa Asgedom, April 11, 1975; Zewengel Gabre Kidan, June 6, 1975. For the looting see R. G. Howe to Foreign Office, Addis Ababa, October 15, 1943, FO 371/35607.

76 Badaglio, *The War in Abyssinia*, p. 146; R. E. Cheesman, "Report," May 25, 1943, FO 371/35626.

77 Cottam, "Interim Report," FO 371/35607. According to the same source, British personnel suffered one killed and two wounded.

78 Cottam, "Interim Report," FO 371/35607; Peirson, "Account," FO 371/35608.
79 These included Beyenech Seyum, Lemlem Gabre Selassie, Dejazmatch Marru Aram, Dejazmatch Haile Selassie Gabre Medhin; Shum-Tsiraa Sebhatu Wolde Gabriel, Fitawrari Gabre Medhin Tedla, Dejazmatch Bezabeh Negussie, Kegnazmatch Asberom; Kegnazmatch Alemayehou Wolde Giorgis, Girazmatch Alemayehou, Kegnazmatch Negash Desta, Kegnazmatch Hagos Bula, Tweoldai Gebru, Bashai Assefa Derso, and Bashai Gugsa. "List of Prisoners," MIA–T 11/36; Haile Mariam Redda, October 24, 1974; Sebhatu Wolde Gabriel, April 13, 1975; Gabre Medhin Tedla, April 15, 1975.
80 Perham, *The Government*, p. 357. I have not seen any concrete evidence that directly implicates the man. In the interview of 1980 (see above), Mengesha claimed that though he was accused by some officials whose identity he did not reveal, he had no part in the rebellion.
81 R. G. Howe to G. Mackereth, Addis Ababa, January 8, 1944, FO 371/41477; Peirson, "Account," FO 371/35609.
82 Major Hodgson, Provincial Adviser to Minister of the Interior, Addis Ababa, February 25, 1944, MIA–T 11/36.
83 Yemane Hassen to Minister of the Interior, Maichew, January 6, 1945 (28 Tahisas 1937), MIA–T 11/36; Yemane Hassen to Ras Abebe Aregai, Maichew, January 1, 1945 (23 Tahisas 1937), MIA–T 11/36; see also anonymous to Minister of the Pen, Mekele, March 1944 (Megabit 1937), MIA–T 11/36; Director of Security to Minister of Defense, Addis Ababa, October 3, 1944 (25 Meskerem 1937), MIA–T 11/36; Abiye Abebe to Ras Abebe Aregai, Addis Ababa, April 26, 1944 (18 Miazia 1936), MIA–T 11/36; G. R. Howe to A. Eden, Addis Ababa, January 11, 1944, FO 371/41477.
84 This fee was known as *nai messob* (of the plate) or *mehtsebi id* (for washing the hands).
85 Sebhatu Wolde Gabriel, April 13, 1975; Haile Negussie, April 19, 1975; Girmai Mengesha, April 8, 1975. Haile Mariam in his MS wrongly gives these as precipitants of the revolt.
86 The Raya and Azebo were also deprived of their horses and mules, and were not allowed to possess any weapons, including daggers, for nearly twenty years. Kifle Ergetu to Leul-Dejazmatch Mengesha Seyum, Addis Ababa, June 15, 1963 (7 Sene 1954), MIA–T 1/37; Yemane Hassen to Minister of the Interior, Maichew, October 17, 1946 (9 Tikimt 1938), MIA–T 1/37.
87 Minister of Land Reform and Administration, "Memo," September 5, 1974 (27 Nehasie 1966), MLRA–T M6/L2/65; Dejenu Bedanie and Sahle Dengel, "Report on Menchare," MIA–T 6320/37.
88 MLRA, "A Detailed Study," p. 24.
89 MLRA, *Report on Land Survey of Tigre Province*, p. 28. This compared with 46 percent in Gojjam and 63 percent in Begemedir. MLRA, "Tenurial Constraints on Rural Development in Ethiopia," unpublished paper prepared by Mesfin Kinfu (August 1974), p. 5.
90 Elders of Chercher and Mehoni subdistrict to Dejazmatch Zewde Gabre Selassie, April 7, 1974 (29 Megabit 1966), MLRA–T M6/L2/65.
91 R. Mousnier, *Peasant Uprisings in Seventeenth-Century France, Russia and China*, trans. B. Pearce (New York, 1970), p. 348.
92 Erlich, *Ethiopia*, p. 188.
93 Gilkes, *The Dying Lion*, p. 188.

5 Bale: the nationalities armed

1 This material has been distilled from I. M. Lewis, *A Pastoral Democracy* (London, 1961), ch. 5; Said S. Samatar, *Oral Poetry and Somali Nationalism* (Cambridge, 1982), p. 99; and Lee V. Cassanelli, *The Shaping of Somali Society* (Philadelphia, 1982), pp. 127–29.
2 G. W. B. Huntingford, *The Galla of Ethiopia* (London, 1955), pp. 61, 73, 331; Asmarom Legesse, *Gada* (New York, 1973), pp. 8–10, 38, 47–48.

3 *Gebbar* units, comprising several households and normally cultivating contiguous plots of land, were obliged to give four *dawilla* (120–50 kilos) of cereals, 20 kilos of honey, or four Maria Theresa thalers annually as *gibir*; 10 kilos of *gesho*, a load of wood, and from one-half to one MT thalers on every New Year, Christmas, and Easter to the *neftenya*; and two MT thalers to the district administrator annually. Mahteme Selassie, *Zekre Negger*, pp. 162–63. Belachew Beyan, interviewed in Mena, May 23, 1975.

4 E. A. Powell, *Beyond the Utmost Purple Rim* (London, 1925), pp. 258–59.

5 Belachew Beyan, May 23, 1975; Kebede Wolde Mariam, interviewed in Mena, May 19, 1975.

6 Kebede Haile, interviewed in Mena, May 19, 1975; Sahle Deneke, interviewed in Goba, May 8, 1975; Wolde Selassie Bereka to emperor, Goba, November 21, 1969 (13 Hidar 1961), Ministry of the Interior Archives – Bale (henceforth MIA–B 2401/53/3).

7 From a leaflet written in Amharic and Arabic and that bears the seal of General Wako Gutu, MIA–B 2401/53/3.

8 As the official records were incomplete and not wholly accurate, we do not know the exact amount confiscated under such flimsy claims. What we have are fleeting glimpses. Lique mekwas Tadesse Negash, provincial governor in the 1950s is said to have acquired 500 *gashas* in Delo and Genale alone, in complicity with the royal family. Government records showed, however, that the family's holdings did not exceed 226 *gashas*, of which 134 belonged to the crown prince and the rest to his parents. And, contrary to public belief, the same records showed that Tadesse himself did not own more than 44 *gashas*. Ras Abebe Aregai, Minister of Defense, and one of the casualties of the 1960 coup, claimed 86 *gashas* in Delo; two minor officials held 100 *gashas* each in the same subdistrict. People of Arena to Minister of the Interior, October 13, 1956 (5 Tikimt 1948), MLRA–B MS/N2/65; Abdullahi Delmer to MLRA, Addis Ababa, May 4, 1967 (26 Miazia 1957), MLRA–B M5/N2/65; residents of Sinana subdistrict to Bitwoded Zewde Gabre Hiwet, June 3, 1970 (26 Sene 1962), MIA–B 2401/53/3.

9 John M. Cohen, "Ethiopia after Haile Selassie," *African Affairs*, 72, 289 (October 1973), 379.

10 For example, in 1963 the government expropriated 100 *gashas* in Dinsho, Fasil, which it then leased to a lone Norwegian entrepreneur for sheep production on a commercial scale. The venture failed in the midst of armed conflict, but the extent and purpose of the expropriation signaled the impending threat from capitalist development. People of Sinana to emperor, March 13, 1964 (22 Megabit 1956), MLRA–B M5/N2/65; Ze Emanuel Haile and Shifaw Abagero to Bale Governorate General, Goba, July 13, 1967 (5 Hamle 1959), MLRA–B M5/N2/65.

11 We have instances of this. In Delo, holdings estimated as 13, 45, and 58 *gashas* turned out to be only 9, 7, and 4 after remeasurement. Whereas some landlords should have been liable for 40, 41, and 16 *gashas*, they actually paid tax on only 8, 4, and 7 *gashas* respectively. Gelchu Togie to Minister of the Interior, Meslo, December 12, 1962 (4 Tahisas 1954); Ze Emanuel Haile and Shifaw Abagero to Bale Governorate General, July 13, 1967.

12 Major General Worku Metaferia to MLRA, Goba, July 14, 1967 (6 Hamle 1959), MLRA–B M5/N2/65.

13 For example, little or no tax was paid on as many as 1,721 *gashas* in Genale and 3,545 *gashas* in Wabe; holdings of 95 and 10,341 *gashas* were registered as 6 and 8,329 *gashas* respectively. Bale Governorate General to Ministry of Finance, Goba, July 13, 1967 (6 Hamle 1959), MLRA–B M5/N2/65; anonymous, "memo" to Minister of MLRA, Addis Ababa, July 8, 1972 (30 Sene 1964), MLRA–B M5/N2/65.

14 Compiled from archives of MF/DAR/H.4/22, file nos. 5 and 7. See in particular, Eskender Dehne to Minister of the Interior, Addis Ababa, March 2, 1964 (24 Yekatit 1956), file no. 7, and Bejirond Tamrat Aberra to Bale Governorate General, Goba, September 3, 1964 (24 Nehassie 1956), file no. 5.

15 In El Kere the nomads paid tax not on the land but on their livestock. The difference between the ETH $8,012,226.20 mentioned in the text and the $7,816,751.76 of table 5.1 was perhaps the uncollected sum from this district.
16 Dejenu Bedanie to Assefa Negash, August 20, 1961 (12 Nehassie 1954). In possession of author.
17 Major General Wolde Selassie Bereka to four district governors, March 19, 1969 (11 Ginbot 1961), MIA–B 2401/53/3.
18 In a talk given to a peasant meeting on May 10, 1975 in Goba, at which the author was present. I am grateful to Abdelkadir Gelchu for the translation from Orofima.
19 Gelchu Togie to Minister of the Interior, December 12, 1962.
20 Bekure Gabre Mariam to MLRA, Goba, October 21, 1974 (13 Tikimt 1966), MLRA–B M5/N2/65.
21 John Darnton, "Ogaden Villages begin to Savor Freedom from Ethiopia," *The New York Times*, September 26, 1977.
22 Dejenu Bedanie, "Report on Bale," Addis Ababa, n.d., MIA–B 9847/53/2, special file no. 2.
23 Gilkes, *The Dying Lion*, p. 223.
24 Dejenu, "Report," MIA–B 9847/53/2.
25 *Ibid.*
26 Information Services of the Somali Government, *The Somali Peninsula* (London, 1962), p. ix.
27 Markakis, *National and Class Conflict*, pp. 175–81.
28 Worku Enque Selassie to emperor, September 1965 (Meskerem 1958), MIA–B 2401/53/3.
29 It appears that Kahin Abdi moved, first, to Luuq (Lugh), and then to the border village of Bihol Garasle to become liaison between the rebels and the Somali government – a task he performed until the end of conflict in 1970. Wolde Selassie Bereka to emperor, November 21, 1969 (13 Hidar 1961), MIA–B 2401/53/3; Mohammed Gelchu, interviewed in Goba, May 8, 1975.
30 Worku Enque Selassie to emperor, September 1965.
31 As regards their background see Cassanelli, *The Shaping of Somali Society*, pp. 14–15; E. R. Turton, "Bantu, Galla and Somali Migrations in the Horn of Africa," *JAH*, 16, 4 (1975), 524–29.
32 The two were involved in a land dispute then pending in the district court. Aberra Ketsela, "The Rebellion in Bale 1964–1970," BA thesis, Haile Selassie I University (Addis Ababa, May 1971), pp. 6–7. Bekele Haile, interviewed in Ginir, May 7, 1975.
33 Hussien and Aliye became bandits over matters of taxation, and Ismi turned against the state when, for reasons that are not publicly known, he was barred from practicing law in Ginir. Umar Mohammed, interviewed in Ginir, May 7, 1975; Bekele Haile, May 7, 1975.
34 *Addis Zemen*, March 9, 1964 (1 Megabit 1956). It is interesting that the proclamation made no mention of the unrest in the province.
35 Bekure Tsion Tilahun, handwritten script, Institute of Ethiopian Studies, Addis Ababa, IES 835, No. 39/67; Lt. Colonel Peirson, "Report on the Situation in Borana," Moyale, June 15, 1943, FO 371/35606; Debissa Arero, interviewed in Mena, May 16, 1975.
36 A. E. Butler, "Survey of the Frontier between British East Africa and Abyssinia," September 25, 1903, FO 1/48; Gerald Reece, "Northern Frontier District," FO 371/41477; R. G. Howe to Governor of Kenya, Addis Ababa, January 11, 1944, FO 371/35606; Foreign Office to British Legation, London, July 12, 1943, FO 371/35603.
37 The group included Musa Doya, Adem Jillo, and Ibrahim Korri, three *Burkas* who later played a central role in the rebellion. Kebede Gedibe to Bale Governorate General, March 30, 1965 and June 23, 1965 (22 Megabit and 15 Sene 1957), MIA–B 2401/53/3; see also Aberra, "The Rebellion," p. 9.
38 Kebede Gedibe to Bale Governorate General, June 23, 1965; Aberra, "The Rebellion," p. 9; Kebede Gedibe to Bale Governorate General, March 30, 1965.

39 Worku Enque Selassie to emperor, Addis Ababa, July 5, 1964 (27 Sene 1956), MIA–B 2401/53/3; Worku Enque Selassie to emperor, September 1965, MIA–B 2401/53/3.

40 *Ibid.*

41 Memo of the Defense Committee for Ogaden, December 9, 1966, MIA–B 1/57/2767. See also Lt. General Merid Mengesha to Dejazmatch Kifle Ergetu, April 6, 1966 (28 Megabit 1958), MIA–B 1/57/2767.

42 Colonel Gessesse Retta was appointed commander of the brigade at Neghele and chief administrator of Borana while Brigadier General Kebede Yacob became the commander of the Seventh Brigade assigned to Bale, and which established its base at Goro. Colonel Gessesse Retta to Chief of Staff, Neghele, April 4, 1967 (25 Megabit 1957), MIA–S 1/58.

43 Colonel Gessesse Retta to Chief of Staff, Neghele, April 4, 1967 (25 Megabit 1957), MIA–S 1/58.

44 C. Welch calls this "the politicization of discontent." See his *Anatomy of Rebellion* (New York, 1980), p. 168.

45 Abdelkadir Gelchu (intelligence officer), interviewed in Goba, May 10, 1975; Abdulrahman Dube (former guerrilla), interviewed in Deyiu (Delo), May 21, 1975. See also Dejenu, "Report," MIA–B 9847/53/2; Wolde Selassie Bereka to Minister of the Interior, Goba, December 26, 1968 (18 Tahisas 1960), MIA–B 2401/53/3.

46 Wolde Selassie Bereka to Zewde Gabre Hiwet, Goba, July 5, 1969 (27 Sene 1961), MIA–B 2401/53/3; Wolde Selassie Bereka to Minister of the Interior, Goba, November 21, 1969 (13 Hidar 1961), MIA–B 2401/53/3; Colonel Ketema to Minister of the Interior, Addis Ababa, November 30, 1969 (23 Hidar 1961), MIA–B 2401/53/3; Mohammed Gelchu, May 10, 1975; Getachew Kebede, May 8, 1975.

47 Lt. General Merid Mengesha to emperor, Addis Ababa, January 1964 (Tir 1956), MIA–B 2585/53/3; Lt. General Kebede Gabre to Major General Wolde Selassie Bereka, Addis Ababa, June 16, 1968 (8 Sene 1960), MIA–B 2401/53/3; Wolde Selassie Bereka to Zewde Gabre Hiwet, Goba, February 21, 1970 (13 Yekatit 1962), MIA–B 2401/53/3; Kebede Gabre to Lt. General Iyassu Mengesha, Addis Ababa, August 23, 1969 (15 Nehasie 1961), MIA–B 2401/53/3.

48 Worku to emperor, September 1965.

49 Wolde Selassie Bereka to Minister of the Interior, Goba, December 25, 1968 (18 Tahisas 1960), MIA–B 2401/53/3; Wolde Selassie Bereka to Kifle Ergetu, November 6, 1968, MIA–B 2401/53/3.

50 Mekuria Abiche to Major General Wolde Selassie Bereka, February 25, 1970, MIA–B 2401/53/3; Wolde Selassie Bereka to Zewde Gabre Hiwet, March 10, 1970, MIA–B 2401/53/3.

51 Dejenu, "Report," MIA–B 9847/53/2.

52 Wolde Selassie Bereka to Zewde Gabre Hiwet, February 21, 1970, MIA–B 2401/53/3.

53 Wolde Selassie Bereka to Major General Diressie Dubale, Goba, April 20, 1968 (12 Miazia 1960), MIA–B 2401/53/3; Wolde Selassie Bereka to Kifle Ergetu, Goba, February 5, 1968 (29 Yekatit 1960), MIA–B 2401/53/3; Official Minutes, Gura Damole, March 29, 1969, MIA–B 2401/53/3.

54 Wolde Selassie Bereka to Zewde Gabre Hiwet, March 10, 1970, MIA–B 2401/53/3; Jagaama Kelo to Army Headquarters, Neghele, March 5, 1970 (27 Yekatit 1962), MIA–B 2401/53/3.

55 Jagaama Kelo to Army Headquarters, Neghele, February 28, 1970 (20 Yekatit 1962), MIA–B 2401/53/3; *Addis Zemen*, March 9, 1970 (1 Megabit 1962).

56 Major General Jagaama Kelo to Army Headquarters, Neghele, April 3, 1970 (25 Megabit 1962), MIA–B 2401/53/3.

57 Official Minutes, Gura Damole, March 29, 1969, MIA–B 2401/53/3; Wolde Selassie Bereka to Diressie Dubale, Goba, December 17, 1968 (9 Tahisas 1960), MIA–B 2401/53/3; Jagaama Kelo to Army Headquarters, Neghele, March 16, 1970 (30 Yekatit 1962), MIA–B 2401/53/3; Umar Mohammed, May 7, 1975; Abdelkadir Gelchu, May 9, 1975. Although official

records identified H. Bunni as colonel, some of my informants referred to him as the "other" or "second" general. Their chief lieutenants were Abdullahi Ibrahim, Adem Jillo, Aliye Chirri, Aliye Daddi, Ali Semud, Dubero Wako, Geddu Deber, Hassan Ture, Kedir Wako, Mohammed Belade, Mohammed Bunni, Umar Ader, Umar Kabelo, Umar Mohammed (all colonels), and Girazmatch Wako Lugo.

58 Jagaama Kelo, "Report," Army Headquarters, Neghele, August 19, 1968 (11 Nehasie 1960), MIA–B 2401/53/3; Jagaama Kelo to Army Headquarters, Neghele, March 6, 1970, MIA–B 2401/53/3; Wolde Selassie Bereka to Diressie Dubale, Goba, December 17, 1968, MIA–B 2401/53/3; Wolde Selassie Bereka to Zewde Gabre Hiwet, Goba, March 10, 1970 (2 Megabit 1962), MIA–B 2401/53/3.

59 No concrete information on the relative strengths and distribution of the guerrilla fighters exists. While one source estimated the total force in 1963 at ten thousand, Gilkes thought that it could not have exceeded half that number. The official accounts for the years 1968–70 showed that some 21,510 people surrendered or were captured during that time. Of these, about 8,820 were listed as children and 5,770 as women. We do not know how many of the remaining and those classified as women were actual fighters. See *Tigilachin*, special issue (January 1972) (Tir 1964); Gilkes, *The Dying Lion*, p. 289, n. 13; Major General Wolde Selassie Bereka to Zewde Gabre Hiwet, Goba, March 10, 1970 (2 Megabit 1962), MIA–B 2401/53/3; Major General Jagaama Kelo to Army Headquarters, March 8, 1970 (30 Tir 1962), MIA–B 2401/53/3; Captain Admassu Mekonen to Army Headquarters, Neghele, April 9, 1970 (1 Miazia 1962), MIA–B 2401/53/3; Brigadier General Tesfaye Gabre Mariam to Major General Yilma Shibeshi, April 25, 1969 (17 Megabit 1961), MIA–B 2401/53/3; Jagaama Kelo, "Report," Addis Ababa, August 19, 1968, MIA–B 2401/53/3; Lt. General Kebede Gabre to Lt. General Assefa Ayene, Addis Ababa, January 24, 1970 (16 Tir 1962), MIA B 2401/53/3; Wolde Selassie Bereka to Major General Diressie Dubale, Goba, March 18, 1968 (9 Tahisas 1960), MIA–B 2401/53/3.

60 Two of my informants, Usman Wako and Abdulrahman Dube (both interviewed on May 21, 1975), told me that Wako was "half Oromo and half Somali," his mother being from the latter ethnic group – an ideal combination in such a situation, but one which I was not able to verify. And Debissa Arero and Mohammed Gelchu were helpful in the formulation of this profile.

61 The similarities in the pattern of organization of this revolt and that of the Mau Mau of Kenya are so striking that I have benefited from the insights of Barnett and Njama in the reconstruction and analysis of this part of my account. See Donald L. Barnett and Karari Njama, *Mau Mau from Within* (New York, 1966), especially pp. 169–71, 302–305.

62 Usman Wako, May 21, 1975; Abdulrahman Dube, May 21, 1975; Barnett and Njama, *Mau Mau*, pp. 169, 305.

63 Barnett and Njama, *Mau Mau*, pp. 170, 302.

64 Umar Ader, interviewed with security officers, December 27, 1969, enclosure in Wolde Selassie Bereka to Kifle Ergetu, January 5, 1969, Goba, MIA–B 2401/53/3; Umar Mohammed, May 7, 1975; Abdulrahman Dube, May 21, 1975; Worku Enque Selassie to emperor, September 1965, MIA–B 2401/53/3; Mekuria Abiche to Major General Wolde Selassie Bereka, El Kere, February 25, 1970 (17 Yekatit 1962), MIA–B 2401/53/3; Sileshi Wolde Mariam to Dejazmatch Alula Bekele, Addis Ababa, December 22, 1967 (14 Tahisas 1959), MIA–B 2401/53/3.

65 Major Ayele Tadesse to Bale Governorate General, Ginir, December 13, 1965 (5 Tahisas 1957), MIA–B 2401/53/3; Umar Ader, December 27, 1969, MIA–B 2401/53/3; Mohammed Gelchu, May 9, 1975.

66 Major Getachew Demissie, May 19, 1975; Mohammed Gelchu, May 9, 1975.

67 Gessese Retta to Chief of Staff, Neghele, August 7, 1967, MIA–B 2401/53/3.

68 Kebede Gabre to Diressie Dubale, Addis Ababa, February 28, 1969, MIA–B 2401/53/3.

69 Jagaama Kelo, "Report," Army Headquarters, August 19, 1968, MIA–B 2401/53/3; Wolde

Selassie Bercka to Diressie Dubale, Goba, December 17, 1968, MIA–B 2401/53/3; Jagaama Kelo to Army Headquarters, March 6, 1970, MIA–B 2401/53/3; Wolde Selassie Bereka to Zewde Gabre Hiwet, March 10, 1970, MIA–B 2401/53/3; Major Haile Mariam Kerie to Minister of the Interior, Neghele, February 15, 1970 (7 Yekatit 1962), MIA–B 2401/53/3; Captain Admassu Mekonen to Army Headquarters, April 9, 1970, MIA–B 2401/53/3; Usman Wako, May 21, 1975; Tahir Allo, June 2, 1975; Umar Ader, December 27, 1969, MIA–B 2401/53/3.

70 Mao Tse-Tung, *Selected Works*, Vol. II (Peking, Foreign Languages Press, 1965), p. 94.

71 Gilkes, *The Dying Lion*, pp. 170–71.

72 Information about the early life of the Imam whom the Ethiopians called Ahmad Gragn (the left-handed) is uncertain. Between the years 1531 and 1543 he led an army of Adali and Somali irregulars who, inspired by a *jihad* (holy war), conquered and plundered much of Christian Ethiopia. Today, the Somali state regards him as a national hero. Tadesse Tamrat, *Church and State in Ethiopia 1270–1527* (Oxford, 1972), pp. 297–302; S. Touval, *Somali Nationalism* (Cambridge, Mass., 1963), pp. 49–51.

73 Worku to emperor, September 1965.

74 Muhammad Mini (captain) and Abdo Chirri (major) to Alemayehou Taye, June 5, 1969 (27 Ginbot 1961), MIA–B 2401/53/3; also Kedir Wako (colonel) and Mohammed Gutta (major) to Lt. Abebe Bekele, Fetcha, November 1969 (Hidar 1961), MIA–B 2401/53/3.

75 Gessesse Retta to Chief of Staff, August 7, 1969, MIA–B 2401/53/3; Jagaama Kelo, "Report," August 19, 1968, MIA–B 2401/53/3; Wolde Selassie Bereka to Diressie Dubale, December 17, 1968, MIA–B 2401/53/3; Jagaama Kelo to Army Headquarters, March 6, 1970, MIA–B 2401/53/3; Wolde Selassie Bereka to Zewde Gabre Hiwet, March 10, 1970, MIA–B 2401/53/3; Haile Mariam Kerie to Minister of the Interior, February 15, 1970, MIA–B 2401/53/3; Admassu Mekonen to Army Headquarters, April 9, 1970, MIA–B 2401/53/3; Lt. General Kebede Gabre to Lt. General Assefa Ayene, January 24, 1970, MIA–B 2401/53/3; Tesfaye Gabre Mariam to Yilma Shibeshi, March 25, 1969, MIA–B 2401/53/3.

76 In normal times the average prices of a cow and an ox were ETH $77 and $97 respectively. During the conflict the prices had fallen to about $30. MLRA, "Bale Governorate General" (November 1971), p. 13; Abebe Tessema, interviewed, Mena, May 22, 1975. Even then government earnings were substantial (one auction netted about ETH $130,000); Lt. Colonel Bekele Fire Hiwet to Zewde Gabre Hiwet, Awasa, February 7, 1970 (29 Tir 1962), MIA–B 2401/53/3.

77 Jagaama Kelo, "Report," August 19, 1968, MIA–B 2401/53/3; Wolde Selassie Bereka to Zewde Gabre Hiwet, March 10, 1970, MIA–B 2401/53/3; Jagaama Kelo to Army Headquarters, March 6, 1970, MIA–B 2401/53/3; Admassu Mekonen to Army Headquarters, April 9, 1970, MIA–B 2401/53/3.

78 Cassanelli, *The Shaping of Somali Society*, pp. 252–53.

79 Major Ayele Tadesse to Bale Governorate General, Ginir, December 13, 1965 (5 Tahisas 1957), MIA–B 2401/53/3; Official Minutes, Gura Damole, March 29, 1969, MIA–B 2401/53/3; Kebede Haile, May 18, 1975; Mohammed Gelchu, May 9, 1975.

80 Elemma Terre, May 20, 1975; Kebede Haile, May 19, 1975; and Abdulrahman Dube, May 21, 1975.

81 Among others, Fitawrari Gelchu Togie became subdistrict governor in Delo, and Dejazmatch Fatule Tekene and Kegnazmatch Abdullahi Barud were appointed district and subdistrict governors respectively in El Kere.

82 Official Minutes, El Kere, December 15, 1975 (7 Tahisas 1967), MIA–B 2401/53/3.

83 Solomon Gabre Mariam to Belai Abbay, Addis Ababa, September 22, 1973 (14 Meskerem 1966), MLRA–B M5/N2/65; also Belai Abbay to emperor, Addis Ababa, July 20, 1973 (12 Hamle 1965), MLRA–B M5/N2/65; Belai Abbay to emperor, Addis Abba, July 12, 1973 (4 Hamle 1965), MLRA–B M5/N2/65.

84 MLRA, *Report of Land Tenure Survey of Bale Province*, p. 9.
85 Colonel Belachew Jemaneh to Minister of the Interior, Addis Ababa, January 12, 1968 (4 Tir 1960), MIA–B 2401/53/3.
86 Wolde Selassie Bereka to emperor, Goba, November 21, 1969, MIA–B 2401/53/3; *Addis Zemen*, July 27, 1970 (19 Hamle 1962).
87 Gilkes, *The Dying Lion*, p. 226.

6 Gojjam: a vendée revolt?

1 R. Kapuscinski, *The Emperor* (New York, 1984), p. 95.
2 Zewde, *Yohannes IV of Ethiopia*, p. 2.
3 A brief account of the relationship is provided in Bairu Tafla, "Two of the Last Provincial Kings of Ethiopia," *JES*, 10, 1 (January 1973), 29–43.
4 Marcus, *Menelik II*, p. 105.
5 Mosley, *Haile Selassie*, p. 143.
6 Perham, *The Government*, p. 359.
7 Idea derived from Anderson, *Lineages*, p. 52.
8 Gizachew, "A Historical Survey," pp. 2–12.
9 Nega Ayele, "Centralization versus Regionalism in Ethiopia," (BA thesis, Haile Selassie I University, June 1971), p. 34.
10 *Ibid.*
11 Mosley, *Haile Selassie*, p. 143.
12 Bairu, "Two of the Last," 46.
13 A. E. Southard to Secretary of State, Addis Ababa, December 11, 1928, in Steffanson and Starrett, p. 156.
14 Mosley, *Haile Selassie*, p. 119. Evidently Mosley has a proclivity toward exaggeration. See R. E. Cheesman, *Lake Tana and the Blue Nile* (London, 1968, reprint), p. 33.
15 Petition to emperor, signed by forty people and received on January 10, 1950 (2 Tir 1942), MIA–G 29/42/2.
16 D. W. Lascelle to Herbert Morison, Addis Ababa, March 13, 1951, FO 371/90073.
17 See "The Case of Aberre Yimam," file No. 239/45, Ministry of Justice Archives, Addis Ababa.
18 J. C. D. Lawrence and H. S. Mann, "F.A.O. Land Policy Project (Ethiopia)," *Ethiopian Observer*, 9, 4 (1966), 294.
19 Unidentified Lt. Colonel to Security Department, Addis Ababa, December 7, 1968 (30 Hidar 1961), MIA–G 29/60/3; Hoben, *Land Tenure*, p. 219.
20 Hoben, *Land Tenure*, p. 219.
21 *Ibid.*
22 Kifle Ergetu and Kifle Dadi, "Report" to Tsehafe-Tizaz Aklilu Habte Wold, Addis Ababa, October 2, 1968 (2 Sene 1960), MIA–G 29/60/3.
23 Information was gathered from employees of the Ministry of the Interior, Addis Ababa, in May 1975. See also Markakis, *Ethiopia*, pp. 378–79.
24 Markakis, *Ethiopia*, p. 378.
25 Perham, *The Government*, p. 287.
26 Petitions from Dega Damot, Inarj Inawga, and Nebise, enclosed in Tafesse Tebikie to Kifle Ergetu, June 16, 1968 (8 Sene 1960), MIA–G 29/60/3.
27 Markakis, *Ethiopia*, p. 378.
28 See by-laws of the organization, MIA–G 29/60/3.
29 Captain Ayalew Mekonen and Fekade Tsigie, "Intelligence Report," Addis Ababa, April 20, 1968 (12 Miazia 1960), MIA–G 29/60/3; Tafesse to Kifle, June 16, 1968; Kifle and Kifle to Aklilu, October 2, 1968; People of Nebise to Ministry of the Interior, July 20, 1968 (12 Hamle 1960); Tafesse to Kifle, June 16, 1968; People of Inarj Inawga to Ethiopian Govern-

ment, June 12, 1968 (4 Sene 1960), MIA–G 29/60/3. The Ministry of Community Development and Social Welfare reported that its contributions rose from ETH $0.2 million in 1963–64 to over $1.1 million in 1970–71. Evidence from the Ministries of the Interior and Information showed that the total voluntary contributions for a period of nine months of 1971–72 was $2.3 million. This "figure would be substantially higher if data would be included for contributions in kind and labor." Gojjam's contribution for the ten months between September 1971 and June 1972 was $148,700. Assuming that an average of $150,000 was raised annually for the years 1962–67, it seems reasonable to conclude that the peasants' total contribution might have exceeded a million dollars. IBRD, *Recent Economic Performance and Future Prospects in Ethiopia*, Vol. XI, Confidential Report No. 9–ET, (November 1972), pp. 21–22.

30 See petitions enclosed in Kifle and Kifle to Aklilu, October 2, 1968.
31 Nega, "Centralization," p. 84. The price of a mill varied from ETH $12,000 to $25,000.
32 He was killed in a gun battle during the revolutionary upheaval of 1974.
33 Tafesse to Kifle, June 16, 1968; Kifle and Kifle to Aklilu, October 2, 1968.
34 The two commonly used were *yedagna eger* (judge's foot) and *yesenselch fetch* (chain breaker), and the amount varied from a quarter to as much as five dollars from each household.
35 Ayalew and Fekade, "Report," April 20, 1968; Major Haile Mariam Arrede and Captain Befekadu Demena to Major General Yilma Shibeshi, Addis Ababa, March 1968 (Ginbot 1960), MIA–G 29/60/3.
36 Kifle and Kifle to Aklilu, October 2, 1968. See also Tafesse to Kifle, June 16, 1968, and Ayalew and Fekade, "Report," April 20, 1968.
37 Ayalew and Fekade, "Report," April 20, 1968.
38 Markakis, *Ethiopia*, p. 380.
39 Major General Diressie Dubale to Kifle Ergetu, Addis Ababa, April 23, 1968 (15 Miazia 1960), MIA–G 29/60/3.
40 Security Department, "Report" to Diressie, November 17, 1968.
41 Compiled from enclosures in Tafesse to Kifle, June 16, 1968, and Nega, "Centralization". Amharic poetry does not always lend itself to easy translation.
42 Nega, "Centralization," pp. 38, 75, 81; Tafesse to Kifle, June 8, 1968.
43 Tafesse to Kifle, June 8, 1968; Kegnazmatch Berhanou to Kola ena Dega Damot administration, Jebi Tinhan, July 5, 1968 (28 Sene 1960), MIA–G 29/60/3; enclosure in Yilma Shibeshi to Kifle Ergetu, December 18, 1968.
44 Kapuscinski, *The Emperor*, pp. 96–97.
45 Yilma Shibeshi to Kifle Ergetu, Addis Ababa, May 20, 1968 (12 Ginbot 1960); Kifle Ergetu to Tsehayu Enque Selassie, Addis Ababa, April 17, 1968 (9 Miazia 1960); Lt. General Kebede Gabre to Aklilu Habte Wold, Addis Ababa, April 10, 1968 (2 Miazia 1960), MIA–G 29/60/3.
46 See, for example, Peter Schwab, "Rebellion in Gojjam Province," *CJAS*, 4, 2 (1970), 251, and Nega, "Centralization," p. 90.
47 Tsehayu Enque Selassie, "Report" to Dejazmatch Solomon Abraha, Debre Markos, June 19, 1968 (11 Sene 1960), MIA–G 29/60/3.
48 Governor of Bibugn to Administration of Motta, Bibugn, February 10, 1968 (2 Yekatit 1960) and to Governorate General of Gojjam, February 11, 1968 (3 Yekatit 1960), MIA–G 29/60/3; Police Headquarters to Minister of the Interior, Addis Ababa, October 5, 1968 (27 Meskerem 1961), MIA–G 29/60/3. For an intimate account of the events in Dega Damot see Hoben, *Land Tenure*, pp. 220–26.
49 Colonel Gebrai Egzi to Yilma Shibeshi, Debre Markos, March 18, 1968 (10 Megabit 1960), MIA–G 29/60/3; Yilma to Kifle, May 20, 1968; Tsehayu to Solomon, June 19, 1968.
50 Tsehayu to Solomon, June 19, 1968.
51 Yilma to Kifle, May 20, 1968.

52 Lt. Colonel Kebede Zelleke to Tsehayu Enque Selassie, Mengisto, April 8, 1968 (30 Megabit 1960), MIA–G 29/60/3; enclosure in Tsehayu to Solomon, June 19, 1968.
53 Gebrai Gabre Egzi to Police Headquarters, Debre Markos, April 24, 1968 (16 Miazia 1960), MIA–G 29/60/3.
54 See petition to emperor, Addis Ababa, April 1968 (Miazia 1960), MIA–G 29/60/3.
55 Kifle Ergetu to Tsehayu, April 17, 1968.
56 Proclamation, MIA–G 29/60/3.
57 Members of the commission were Damtew Bereded (Finance), Colonel Ketema Yilma (Police), and Fekadu Tsigie (Security). Kifle Ergetu to Tsehayu Enque Selassie, Addis Ababa, May 30, 1968 (22 Ginbot 1960), MIA–G 29/60/3.
58 Tafesse to Kifle, June 16, 1968.
59 Tafesse to Kifle, June 8, 1968.
60 *Ibid.*
61 Tsehayu to Solomon, June 19, 1968.
62 Kifle Ergetu to Governor of Gojjam, Addis Ababa, June 27, 1968 (19 Sene 1960), MIA–G 29/60/3.
63 The other members were Dejazmatch Dereje Mekonen, Afenegus Haile Leul Chernet, Dejazmatch Bizuwork Gabre, Ato Dilnessahou Retta, and Ato Temesgen Worku.
64 Kifle and Kifle to Aklilu, October 2, 1968.
65 Nega, "Centralization," p. 89.
66 They got away with 32 rifles, 1 pistol, and some 200 bullets. Police Commissioner to Minister of the Interior, Addis Ababa, October 5, 1968 (27 Meskerem 1961); Corporal Berhanou Enbaye to Police Chief of Motta, Hulet Ij Inese, October 19, 1968 (11 Tikimt 1961), MIA–G 29/60/3; Security Department to Diressie, November 17, 1968; Dereje Mekonen to Kifle Ergetu, Debre Markos, November 1968 (Hidar 1960), MIA–G 29/60/3.
67 Proclamation, MIA–G 29/60/3.
68 Dejazmatch Haile Yesus Filate to Dereje Mekonen, Finote Selam, November 7, 1968 (21 Tikimt 1961), MIA–G 29/60/3; Major General Yilma Shibeshi to Kifle Ergetu, Addis Ababa, December 18, 1969 (10 Tahisas 1961), MIA–G 29/60/3; Dereje to Kifle, November 1968.
69 Yilma to Kifle, December 18, 1969.
70 Gizachew, "A Historical Survey," p. 47; Nega, "Centralization," p. 98.
71 Berhanou to Kifle, June 7, 1968.
72 Hoben, *Land Tenure*, p. 226.
73 Tafesse to Kifle, June 16, 1968; Tsehayu to Solomon, June 19, 1968; Yohannes Mehari, interviewed, Addis Ababa, March 20, 1975.
74 Yohannes Mehari, interviewed, Addis Ababa, March 20, 1975; Nega Ayele, interviewed, Addis Ababa, February 15, 1975.
75 Gilkes, *The Dying Lion*, p. 185.
76 Hoben, *Land Tenure*, p. 223.
77 Security Department, "Report" to Diressie, November 17, 1968.
78 Security Department to Diressie, November 17, 1968.
79 Chief of Police to Gojjam Governorate General, Debre Markos, December 7, 1968 (30 Hidar 1961), MIA–G 29/60/3.
80 Lt. Wodajie Wolde Mariam to Mengistu Alemayehou, October 12, 1968, MIA–G 29/60/3; Kebede Gabre to Aklilu, April 10, 1968.
81 Enclosure, Tsehayu to Solomon, June 19, 1968.
82 *Ibid.*
83 Hoben, *Land Tenure*, pp. 66–67.
84 Yohannes Mehari, "Debre Markos Awraja-Gojjam, Local Administration" (BA thesis, Haile Selassie I University, April 1970), pp. 26–27.
85 Nega, "Centralization," p. 89; Tafesse to Kifle, June 8, 1968; Yilma to Kifle, December 18,

1968; Security Department to Diressie, November 17, 1968; Colonel Mengistu Alemayehou to Dereje Mekonen, Debre Markos, October 8, 1968 (30 Meskenem 1960), MIA–G 29/60/3.

86 It is noteworthy that dissidents had reportedly received from their urban supporters ammunition and financial aid amounting to about ETH $80,000. Security Department to Diressie, November 17, 1968; Yilma to Kifle, December 18, 1968.

87 Enclosed in Tsehayu to Solomon, June 19, 1968.

88 *Ibid.*

89 Wodajie to Alemayehou, October 12, 1968; Lt. Mamo to Police Chief, Finote Selam, July 2, 1968 (24 Hamle 1960), MIA–G 29/60/3; Tsehayu to Solomon, June 19, 1968.

90 Hess, *Ethiopia*, p. 195.

91 Chief of Police to Gojjam Governorate General, December 7, 1968; Security Department to Diressie, November 17, 1968.

92 Kebede to Aklilu, April 10, 1968.

93 Markakis, *Ethiopia*, pp. 382–83.

94 Colonel Ketema Yilma to Minister of the Interior, October 23, 1968; Police Chief to Gojjam Governorate General, December 8, 1968; Ambaw Teferri to Dereje Mekonen, Borana, Wello, September 21, 1968 (13 Meskerem 1960), MIA–G 29/60/3; Security Department to Diressie, November 17, 1968.

95 Mengistu to Dereje, October 8, 1968.

96 Gilkes, *The Dying Lion*, p. 178.

97 Nega, "Centralization," p. 63.

98 Schwab, *Decision-Making*, pp. 158, 164; Hoben, *Land Tenure*, pp. 9–10; Markakis, *Ethiopia*, pp. 385–87.

7 Conclusion

1 Zagorin, *Rebels and Rulers*, Vol. I, p. 227.

2 Tilly, "Reflections on the History," p. 44.

3 Markakis and Nega, *Class and Revolution*, pp. 27, 39.

4 Wolde Selassie Bereka to emperor, Goba, December 21, 1969 (13 Hidar 1961), MIA–B 2401/53/3.

5 Enclosure in Kifle and Kifle to Aklilu, MIA–G 29/60/3.

6 Harris, "The Revolutionary Role," 19.

7 Zagorin, *Rebels and Rulers*, Vol. I, p. 225. See also Mousnier, *Peasant Uprisings*, pp. 343–44, and Moore, *Social Origins*, p. 457.

8 E. J. Hobsbawm, "Peasants and Politics," *JPS*, 1, 1 (1973), 12.

9 *Ibid.*, 13.

10 Gilkes, *The Dying Lion*, p. 226; Halliday and Molyneaux, *The Ethiopian Revolution*, p. 76.

11 Wolf, *Peasant Wars*, p. 293.

12 Skocpol, *States and Social Revolutions*, pp. 113, 140.

13 Zagorin, *Rebels and Rulers*, Vol. I, p. 224.

14 Barnett and Njama, *Mau Mau*, ch. 1, and Welch, *Anatomy of Rebellion*, pp. 185–94; 218–29.

Epilogue

1 Antonio Gramsci, *Selections from the Prison Notebooks* (New York, 1980), p. 276.

2 Halliday and Molyneaux, *The Ethiopian Revolution*, p. 74.

3 *Ibid.*, p. 158.

4 Markakis's *National and Class Conflict* gives the most comprehensive treatment of these issues.

5 TPLF, *Ye hizb Weyane harnet Tigrai Communist Ye asir amet guzo gimgema*, Hamle 1979 (July 1985), pp. 95–97.

6 There were three competing groups led by Yohannes Tekle Haymanot, Seba'agadis Dori, and Dejen Tessema. Information provided by Aregawi Berhe, former military commander and Central Committee member of the TPLF, in Washington, D.C., August 29, 1989.

7 For more on the TPLF, see my "Preliminary History of Resistance in Tigrai, Ethiopia," *Africa*, 39, 2 (Guigno 1984), pp. 201–26; Markakis, *National and Class Conflict*, pp. 252–58.

8 Aregawi Berhe, August 30, 1989.

9 Aregawi, Gidey, Asfeha, Misgena, and Negussie, all members of the Central Committee, were either forced out or voluntarily left the movement.

10 Markakis, *National and Class Conflict*, p. 225.

11 John Darnton, "Somali Front Leader Bars Ceasefire with Ethiopia," *The New York Times*, September 25, 1977.

12 Markakis, *National and Class Conflict*, p. 181. See also chapter 5, n. 64 above.

13 OLF, *Oromia Speaks*, 4, 1 and 2 (December 1983), 32.

14 *Africa Confidential*, 27, 16 (July 30, 1986), 6.

15 Detailed descriptions of the three organizations are found in Markakis, *National and Class Conflict*, pp. 222–34; 258–64.

16 Basil Davidson, *The People's Cause* (London, 1981), p. 115.

17 I. M. Lewis, "The Western Somali Liberation Front (WSLF) and the Legacy of Sheikh Hussien of Bale," in Joseph Tubiana (ed.), *Modern Ethiopia: From the Accession of Menilek II to the Present*, Proceedings of the Fifth International Conference on Ethiopian Studies, Nice, December 19–22, 1977 (Rotterdam, 1980), p. 410.

18 Clapham, *Transformation and Continuity*, p. 59.

19 Marx, *The Eighteenth Brumaire*, p. 15.

20 Bereket Habte Selassie, *Conflict and Intervention in the Horn of Africa* (New York and London, 1980), pp. 88–89. The phrase "dissident nationalist" was coined by Markakis in his *National and Class Conflict*, p. xvii.

21 Markakis, *National and Class Conflict*, p. xiv.

22 See, for example, Getachew, "The Unity and Territorial Integrity," 484.

23 Wolf, *Peasant Wars*, p. xv.

24 Anonymous, interviewed in New York, May 26, 1987.

25 Markakis, *National and Class Conflict*, p. 296, n. 18.

26 Clapham, *Transformation and Continuity*, p. 165.

27 TPLF representative, interviewed in Washington, D.C., October 12, 1988.

28 Markakis, *National and Class Conflict*, pp. 257–58.

29 Gebru, "Preliminary History," 219.

30 Aregawi Berhe, August 29, 1989.

31 Any gains made by 1986 were not apparently enough to curtail rebel success. Clapham, *Transformation and Continuity*, p. 158.

32 *Ibid.*, p. 168.

33 These were Fitawrari Simieneh Desta (who later joined EDU), Fitawrari Awdew Abesha, Lt. Sileshi Beyene, and Lt. Bewketu Kassa. Except for Awdew, the rebels were killed. This information was obtained from Alem Seged Yohannes, a former major in the imperial police force, in Washington, D.C., August 30, 1989.

34 The troops that committed the alleged massacre were commandeered by Major Endale Tessema, a member of the *Derg*. Information from Alem Seged Yohannes.

35 Dessalegn Rahmato, "Settlement and Resettlement in Mettekel, Western Ethiopia," *Africa*, 43, 1 (Marzo 1988), 32; EPRP, *Abyot* (February–March 1985), 5–8.

36 TPLF, *Ye-hizb Weyane*, pp. 24–25.

37 TPLF, *Tigray* (February 1982), 8–9.

38 TPLF, *Ye-hizb Weyane*, p. 26.

39 James C. Scott, "Revolution in the Revolution," 97.

40 A controversial political concept developed by Amilcar Cabral in his *Revolution in Guinea* (New York, 1969), p. 110.
41 Teferra Waluwa, member of the EPDM's Central Committee, interviewed in Washington, D.C., December 20, 1989.
42 Gramsci, *Selections*, p. 349.

Bibliography

Archives

Ethiopia

Ministy of the Interior

Bale 1/57/2767; 5645/3; 2401/53/3; 9847/53/2
Gojjam 29/42/2; 29/60/3; 8273/3/2
Sidamo 1/58; 1/51/2269
Tigrai 11/36; 11/37; 21/3; 1097/43; 6320/37; 17596/58

Ministry of Land Reform and Administration (MLRA)

Bale M5/N2/65
Tigrai M6/L2/65

Ministry of Finance, Department of Agricultural Revenue (MF/DAR)

Bale H/4/22, Nos. 5, 7
Tigrai 40/7

Ministry of Justice

"The Case of Aberre Yimam" (Amharic), file no. 239/45

Great Britain

Public Record Office, Foreign Office (FO)

FO	1/48				
FO	371/27521	FO	371/35607	FO	371/41468
FO	371/27522	FO	371/35608	FO	371/41477
FO	371/31597	FO	371/35626	FO	371/41478
FO	371/31602	FO	371/35627	FO	371/41479
FO	371/35603	FO	371/35628	FO	371/41480
FO	371/35604	FO	371/41450	FO	371/80231
FO	371/35605	FO	371/41466	FO	371/90073
FO	371/35606	FO	371/41467		

Official publications

Ethiopia

Ministry of Land Reform and Administration, *Report of Land Tenure Survey of Bale Province*,
December 1969; *Hararghe Province*, July 1971
    A Policy Oriented Study of Land Settlement, Vol. II, prepared by V. E. M. Burke and
    F. Thonley, December 1969
Central Statistical Office (CSO), *The Public Sector of the Ethiopian Economy*, 1974
    Ethiopia: Statistical Abstract, 1972
    Report on Land Survey of Gojjam Province, July 1970; *Hararghe Province*, July 1980; *Tigre
    Province*, July 1970

Somalia

Information Services of the Somali Government, *The Somali Peninsula: A New Light on
Imperial Motives*, London: Staples Printers Ltd., 1962

United States

Steffanson, Borg G. and Ronald K. Starrett (eds.), *Documents on Ethiopian Politics, Vol. II, the
Consolidation of Power of Haile Selassie 1920–1929*, Salisbury, N.C.: Documentary Publications, 1977

Other

International Bank for Reconstruction and Development (IBRD), *Recent Economic Performance and Future Prospects in Ethiopia*, Vol. XI, Confidential Report No. 9–ET, November
1972
    Agricultural Sector Survey: Ethiopia, 3 vols., July 1972
    Economic Growth and Prospects in Ethiopia, September 1970
World Bank, *Ethiopia: Recent Economic Developments and Future Prospects*, December 1983

Manuscripts, papers

Bekure Tsion Tilahun, n.d., Institute of Ethiopian Studies, IES 835–No. 39/67
Haile Mariam Redda, n.d., in his possession.
Issayas Gabre Selassie, n.d., in his uncle's possession.
MLRA, "Tenurial Constraints to Rural Development in Ethiopia," prepared by Mesfin Kinfu,
August 1974
    "Bale Governorate General: A Short Geographical Account," November 1971
    "The Major Features of the Prevailing Land Tenure System in Ethiopia," October 1971
    "A Detailed Study of the Communal Tenure System in Ethiopia," 1970
    "Report on Tigre Province: System of Land Holding," prepared by Taame Beyene and
    Zagaye Asfaw, 1970

Theses

Aberra Ketsela, "The Rebellion in Bale 1964–1970," BA thesis, Haile Selassie I University
(HSIU), Addis Ababa, May 1971
Bruce, John W., "Land Reform Planning and Indigenous Communal Tenures: A Case Study of

253

Bibliography

the Tenure Chiguraf–gwoses in Tigray, Ethiopia," unpublished SJD Law dissertation, University of Wisconsin, Madison, May 1976

Fantahun Birhane, "Gojjam 1800–1855," BA thesis, HSIU, 1973

Gebru Tareke, "Rural Protest in Ethiopia, 1941–70: A Study of Three Rebellions," Ph.D. dissertation, Syracuse University, 1977

Gizachew Adamu, "A Historial Survey of Taxation in Gojjam, 1901–1969," BA thesis, HSIU, May 1971

Mehari Yohannes, "Debre Marcos Awraja-Gojjam, Local Administration: The Role of Traditional Elements," BA thesis, HSIU, April 1970

Mohammed Hassen, "The Oromo of Ethiopia, 1500–1850: With Special Emphasis on the Gibe Region," Ph.D. thesis, University of London, 1983

Nega Ayele, "Centralization versus Regionalism in Ethiopia: The Case of Gojjam 1932–1969," BA thesis, HSIU, June 1971

Yohannis Birhanu, "The Patriots of Gojjam 1936–41: A Study of Resistance Movement," BA thesis, HSIU, 1972

Newspapers, periodicals, pamphlets

Addis Zemen, 8 Tir 1962 (January 16, 1970); 1 Megabit 1962 (March 9, 1970); 19 Hamle 1962 (January 27, 1970); 3 Tir 1967 (January 11, 1975)

Africa Confidential, 21, 24 (November 26, 1980); 22, 11 (May 20, 1981); 27, 16 (July 30, 1986); 29, 13 (July 1, 1988); 29, 1 (April 29, 1988)

Negarit Gazetta, March 30, 1942

The Ethiopian Herald, November 23, 1967; March 19, 1975

The New York Times, September 25 and 26, 1977

The Washington Post, August 5, 1976

Struggle, 5, 2 (November 17, 1969; 111, 1 (September–October 1975) (University Students' Union of Addis Ababa)

Tigilachin, special issue, Tir 1964 (July 1972) (Ethiopian Students' Union in Europe)

Oromia Speaks, 4, 1 and 2 (December 1983) (Oromo Liberation Front)

Hurggie Dima, 2, 1(1977) (Yokkuma Oromo Organization in North America)

Tigray, February 1982 (TPLF Foreign Mission Bureau)

Books and articles

Abir, Mordechai, *Ethiopia: The Era of the Princes*, London: Longman, 1968

Addis Hiwet, *Ethiopia: From Autocracy to Revolution*, Review of African Political Economy, Occasional Publication No. 1, London: Merlin Press, 1975

Afework Gabre Yesus, *Dagmawi ate Menelik*, Rome, 1901

Almagor, Uri, "Institutionalizing a Fringe Periphery: Dassanetch–Amhara Relations," in D. Donham and Wendy James (eds.), *The Southern Marches of Imperial Ethiopia*, Cambridge: Cambridge University Press, 1986

Amin, Samir, *Unequal Development: An Essay on the Social Formations of Peripheral Capitalism*, New York: Monthly Review Press, 1976

Anderson, Perry, *Lineages of the Absolutist State*, London: Verso Press, 1976

Asmarom Legesse, *Gada: Three Approaches to the Study of African Society*, New York: The Free Press, 1973

Badaglio, Pietro, *The War in Abyssinia*, New York, 1937

Bahru Zewde, "An Overview and Assessment of Gambella Trade (1904–1935)," *IJAHS*, 20, 1 (1987)

"Economic Origins of the Absolutist State of Ethiopia (1916–1935)," *JES*, 17 (November 1984)

254

Bairu Tafla, "Two of the Last Provincial Kings of Ethiopia," *JES*, 10, 1 (January 1973)

Barnett, Donald L. and Karari Njama, *Mau Mau From Within: An Analysis of Kenya's Peasant Revolt*, New York: Monthly Review Press, 1966

Bartnicki, Andrzei and Joanna Mantel-Niecko, "The Role and Significance of the Religious Conflicts and People's Movements in the Political Life of Ethiopia in the Seventeenth and Eighteenth Centuries," *Rassengna di Studi Etiopici*, 24 (1969–70)

Bauer, Dan Franz, *Household and Society in Ethiopia: An Economic and Social Analysis of Tigray Social Principles and Household Organization*, Ethiopian Series Monograph No. 6, African Studies Center, Michigan State University, East Lansing, Michigan, 1977

Bereket Habte Selassie, *Conflict and Intervention in the Horn of Africa*, New York and London: Monthly Review Press, 1980

Bloch, Marc, *Feudal Society*, 2 vols., London: Routledge & Kegan Paul, 1971

Blok, Anton, "The Peasant and Brigand: Social Banditry Reconsidered," *CSSH*, 15 (September 1972)

Bondestam, Lars, "People and Capitalism in the Northeastern Lowlands of Ethiopia," *JMAS*, 12, 3 (1974)

Cabral, Amilcar, *Revolution in Guinea*, New York: Monthly Review Press, 1969

Callaghy, Thomas M., "External Actors and the Relative Autonomy of the Political Aristocracy in Zaire," in Nelson Kasfir (ed.), *State and Class in Africa*, London: Frank Cass, 1984

Cassanelli, Lee V., *The Shaping of Somali Society: Reconstructing the History of a Pastoral People 1600–1900*, Philadelphia: The University of Pennsylvania Press, 1982

Caulk, Richard A., "Bad Men of the Borders: Shum and Shefta in Northern Ethiopia in the Nineteenth Century," *IJAHS*, 17, 2 (1984)

"Armies as Predators: Soldiers and Peasants in Ethiopia, c. 1850–1935," *IJAHS*, 11, 3 (1978)

Cheesman, R. E., *Lake Tana and the Blue Nile: An Abyssinian Quest*, London: Frank Cass, 1968 (reprint)

Chege, Michael, "The Revolution Betrayed: Ethiopia, 1974–9," *JMAS*, 17, 3 (1979)

Chesneaux, Jean, *Pasts and Futures, or What is History For?*, London: Thames & Hudson, 1978
Peasant Revolts in China, 1840–1949, trans. C. A. Curwen, New York: Norton, 1973

Clapham, Christopher, *Transformation and Continuity in Revolutionary Ethiopia*, Cambridge: Cambridge University Press, 1988
Haile Selassie's Government, London: Longmans, Green, 1969

Cohen, John M., "Ethiopia after Haile Selassie: The Government Land Factor," *African Affairs*, 72, 289 (October 1973)

Cohen, John M. and Dov Weintraub, *Land and Peasants in Imperial Ethiopia: The Social Background to a Revolution*, Assen, The Netherlands: Van Gorcum, 1975

Conti Rosini, Carlo, "Voggerast, Raia Galla e Zobul," *Africa*, 56 (1938)

Crummey, Donald, "Banditry and Resistance: Noble and Peasant in Nineteenth-Century Ethiopia," in D. Crummey (ed.), *Banditry, Rebellion and Social Protest in Africa*, London: James Currey/Heinemann, 1986
"State and Society: 19th-Century Ethiopia," in Donald Crummey and C. C. Steward (eds.), *Modes of Production in Africa: The Precolonial Era*, Beverly Hills and London: Sage, 1981
"Abyssinian Feudalism," *Past and Present*, 89 (November 1980)
"Society and Ethnicity in the Politics of Ethiopia during the Zamana Masafent," *IJAHS*, 8, 2 (1975)
"Tewodros as Reformer and Modernizer," *JAH*, 10, 3 (1969)

Darkwah, R. H. Kofi, *Shewa, Menilek and the Ethiopian Empire 1813–1889*, London: Heinemann, 1975

Davidson, Basil, *Let Freedom Come: Africa in Modern History*, Boston: Little, Brown, 1978
The People's Cause: A History of Guerrillas in Africa, London: 1981

Davidson, Basil, Lionel Cliffe and Bereket Habte Selassie (eds.), *Behind the War in Eritrea*, Nottingham: Spokesman, 1980

255

Bibliography

Deal, Douglas, "Peasant Revolts and Resistance in the Modern World: A Comparative View," *JCA*, 5, 4 (1975)

Dessalegn Rahmato, "Settlement and Resettlement in Mettekel, Western Ethiopia," *Africa*, 43, 1 (Marzo 1988)

   Agrarian Reform in Ethiopia, Trenton, N.J.: The Red Sea Press, 1985

   "Conditions of the Ethiopian Peasantry," *Challenge*, 10, 2 (July 1970)

Dobb, Maurice, *Studies in the Development of Capitalism*, New York: International Publishers, 1970

Donham, Donald, "Old Abyssinia and the New Ethiopian Empire: Themes in Social History," in D. Donham and Wendy James (eds.), *The Southern Marches of Imperial Ethiopia*, 1986

Ellis, Gene, "The Feudal Paradigm as a Hinderance to Understanding Ethiopia," *JMAS*, 14, 2 (June 1976)

Erlich, Haggai, *Ethiopia and the Challenge of Independence*, Boulder, Colo.: Lynne Riener, 1986

Eshetu Chole, "Towards a History of the Fiscal Policy of the Pre-revolutionary Ethiopian State: 1941–74," *JES*, 17 (November 1984)

Fernyhough, Timothy, "Social Mobility and Dissident Elites in Northern Ethiopia: The Role of Banditry, 1900–69," in Crummey (ed.), *Banditry* (1986)

Gabre Hiwet Baykedagn, "Ate Menelik ena Itiopia," in *Berhan Yihun*, Asmera (1912)

Gabre Wolde Ingida-Work, "Ethiopia's Traditional System of Land Tenure and Taxation," trans. Mengesha Gessesse, *Ethiopia Observer*, 4 (1962)

Gamst, Frederick, "Peasants and Elites Without Urbanism: the Civilization of Ethiopia," *CSSH*, 12, 4 (1970)

Gebru Tareke, "Continuity and Discontinuity in Peasant Mobilization: The Case of Bale and Tigray," in Marina Ottaway (ed.), *The Political Economy of Ethiopia*, New York: Praeger Publishers, 1990

   "Preliminary History of Resistance in Tigrai, Ethiopia," *Africa*, 39, 2 (1984)

   "Peasant Resistance in Ethiopia: The Case of *Weyane*," *JAH*, 25 (1984)

Gedamu Abraha, "Wax and Gold," *Ethiopia Observer*, 11, 3 (1968)

Getachew Haile, "The Unity and Territorial Integrity of Ethiopia," *JMAS*, 24, 3 (September 1986)

Gilkes, Patrick, *The Dying Lion: Feudalism and Modernization in Ethiopia*, London: Julian Friedmann, 1975

Girma Beshah and Merid Wolde Aregay, *The Question of the Union of Churches In Luso-Ethiopian Relations*, Lisbon, 1964

Gramsci, Antonio, *Selections from the Prison Notebooks*, New York: International Publishers, 1980

Haile Selassie I, *My Life and Ethiopia's Progress 1892–1937*, translated and annotated by Edward Ullendorff, Oxford: Oxford University Press, 1976

   Selected Speeches, Addis Ababa: Artistic Printers, 1967

Halliday, Fred and Maxine Molyneaux, *The Ethiopian Revolution*, London: Verso, 1981

Harris, Nigel, "The Revolutionary Role of Peasants (1)," *International Socialism*, 41 (December 1969–January 1970)

Henze, Paul, *Rebels and Separatists in Ethiopia: Regional Resistance to a Marxist Regime*, Santa Monica, Calif.: Rand, 1985

Hess, Robert L., *Ethiopia: The Modernization of Autocracy*, Ithaca and London: Cornell University Press, 1970

Hilton, Rodney (ed.), *The Transition from Feudalism to Capitalism*, London: Verso, 1976

Hoben, Allan, *Land Tenure among the Amhara of Ethiopia: The Dynamics of Cognatic Descent*, Chicago and London: University of Chicago Press, 1973

Hobsbawm, Eric J., "Peasants and Politics," *JPS*, 1, 1 (1973)

   Bandits, London: Penguin, 1972; 2nd edn, 1981

Huntingford, G. W. B., *The Galla of Ethiopia: The Kingdoms of Kafa and Janjero*, London: International African Institute, Oxford University Press, 1955

Jordan, Gabre-Medhin, *Peasants and Nationalism in Eritrea: A Critique of Ethiopian Studies*, Trenton, N.J.: The Red Sea Press, 1989

Kapuscinski, Ryszard, *The Emperor: Downfall of an Autocrat*, New York: Vintage Books, 1984

Kasfir, Nelson, "Relating Class to State in Africa," in N. Kasfir (ed.), *State and Class in Africa*, 1984

Kebede Tessema, *Yetarik Mastawesha*, Addis Ababa: Artistic Printers, 1970 (1962)

Klein, A. Martin (ed.), *Peasants in Africa: Historical and Contemporary Perspectives*, Beverly Hills: Sage, 1980

Kobischchanov, Yuri M., *Axum*, trans. Lorraine T. Kopitanoff, University Park, Pa. and London: The Pennsylvania State Press, 1979

Lan, David, *Guns and Rain: Guerrillas and Spirit Mediums in Zimbabwe*, London and Los Angeles: James Currey and University of California Press, 1985

Landsberger, Henry (ed.), *Rural Protest: Peasant Movements and Social Change*, London: Macmillan, 1974

Lange, Werner, *Domination and Resistance: Narrative Songs of the Kafa Highlands*, Ethiopian Series Monograph No. 8, African Studies Center, Michigan State University, East Lansing, Michigan, 1979

Lawrence, J. C. D. and H. S. Mann, "F.A.O. Land Policy Project (Ethiopia)," *Ethiopia Observer*, 9, 4 (1966)

Lefort, Rene, *Ethiopia: An Heretical Revolution?*, trans. A. M. Berrett, London: Zed Press, 1983

Lenin, V. I., *Collected Works*, Vol. XXIX, Moscow: Progress Publishers, 1965

Levine, Donald N., *Greater Ethiopia: The Evolution of a Multiethnic Society*, Chicago and London: University of Chicago Press, 1974

Wax and Gold: Tradition and Innovation in Ethiopian Culture, Chicago and London: University of Chicago Press, 1965

Lewis, Herbert S., "Spirit Possession in Ethiopia: An Essay in Interpretation," in Rubenson (ed.), *Proceedings* (1984)

Lewis, I. M. (ed.), *Nationalism and Self-Determination in the Horn of Africa*, London: Ithaca Press, 1983

"The Western Somali Liberation Front (WSLF) and the Legacy of Sheikh Hussien of Bale," in Joseph Tubiana (ed.), *Modern Ethiopia: From the Accession of Menilek II to the Present*, Proceedings of the Fifth International Conference on Ethiopian Studies, Nice, December 19–22, 1977, Rotterdam: A. A. Balkama, 1980

A Pastoral Democracy: A Study of Pastoralism and Politics Among the Northern Somali of the Horn of Africa, London: International African Institute, 1961

Lipsky, George A., *Ethiopia: Its People, Its Society, Its Culture*, New Haven: Hraf Press, 1962

Littmann, Enno (ed. and trans.), *Publications of the Princeton Expedition to Abyssinia*, Vol. II, *Tales, Customs, Names and Dirges of the Tigre Tribes: English Translation*, Leyden, 1910

Lonsdale, John, "States and Social Processes in Africa: A Historiographical Survey," *African Studies Review*, 24, 2/3 (June/September 1981)

Lubie Birru, "Abyssinian Colonialism as the Genesis of the Crisis in the Horn: Oromo Resistance 1855–1913," *NEAS*, 2, 3 (1980–81) and 3, 1 (1981)

McCann, James, *From Poverty to Famine in Northeast Ethiopia: A Rural History 1900–1935*, Philadelphia: University of Pennsylvania Press, 1987

Mclellan, Charles W., *State Transformation and National Integration: Gedeo and the Ethiopian Empire, 1895–1935*, Ethiopian Series Monograph No. 19, African Studies Centre, Michigan State University, East Lansing, Michigan, 1988

Mahteme Selassie Wolde Meskel, *Zekre Negger*, 2nd edn, Addis Ababa: Berhanena Selam Printing Press, 1970 (1962)

Bibliography

"The Land Systems of Ethiopia," *Ethiopia Observer*, 1, 9 (August 1957)

Yabatoch Kerse, Addis Ababa: Nestanet Printing Press, 1945 EC

Mantel-Niecko, Joanna, *The Role of Land Tenure in the System of Ethiopian Imperial Government in Modern Times*, trans. Krzystog Adam Bobinski, Warsaw: Wydawnictwa Uniwersytetu Warszawskiego, 1980

Mao Tse-Tung, *Selected Works*, 4 vols., Peking: Foreign Languages Press, 1965

Marcus, Harold G., *Ethiopia, Great Britain, and the United States, 1941–1974: The Politics of Empire*, Berkeley/Los Angeles/London: University of California Press, 1983

The Life and Times of Menelik II: Ethiopia 1844–1913, Oxford: Clarendon Press, 1975

Markakis, John, *National and Class Conflict in the Horn of Africa*, Cambridge and London: Cambridge University Press, 1987

Ethiopia: Anatomy of a Traditional Polity, Oxford: Clarendon Press, 1974

Markakis, John and Nega Ayele, *Class and Revolution in Ethiopia*, Nottingham: Spokesman, 1978

Marx, Karl, *The Eighteenth Brumaire of Louis Bonaparte*, New York: International Publishers, 1975

Marx, Karl and Frederick Engels, *The German Ideology*, New York: International Publishers, 1970

Meillassoux, Claude, "The Social Organization of the Peasantry: The Economic Basis of Kinship," *JPS*, 1, 1 (1973)

Merid W. Aregay, "Millenarian Traditions and Peasant Movements in Ethiopia 1500–1855," in Sven Rubenson (ed.), *Proceedings of the Seventh International Conference of Ethiopian Studies*, University of Lund, April 26–29, 1982, Institute of Ethiopian Studies, Scandinavian Institute of African Studies, and African Studies Center, Michigan State University, Berlings, Arlov, Sweden, 1984

Mesfin Wolde Mariam, *Rural Vulnerability to Famine in Ethiopia 1958–1977*, New Delhi: Vikas, 1984

An Introductory Geography of Ethiopia, Addis Ababa: Berhanena Selam HSI Printing Press, 1972

"The Rural–Urban Split in Ethiopia," *Dialogue*, 11, 1 (1968)

Moges Uqbe Giorgis, *Nay Etiopiawian Tintawi Misale biTigrinya*, Asmera: Kokobe Tsebah Printing Press, 1958 EC

Moore Jr., Barrington, *Social Origins of Dictatorship and Democracy: Land and Peasant in the Making of the Modern World*, Boston: Beacon Press, 1969

Mosley, Leonard, *Haile Selassie: The Conquering Lion*, Englewood Cliffs, N.J.: Prentice-Hall, 1964

Mousnier, Roland, *Peasant Uprisings in Seventeenth-Century France, Russia and China*, trans. Brian Pearce, New York: Harper & Row, 1970

Nasoulas, Teodore, "Ethiopia: The Anatomy of an Indigenous African Colonial Empire," *Horn of Africa*, 4, 3 (1981)

Nicolas, Gildas, "Protest in Ethiopia," *Ufahamu*, 2, 3 (1972)

"Peasant Rebellions in the Socio-political Context of Today's Ethiopia," *PAJ*, 7, 3 (1974)

Ottaway, Marina and David, *Ethiopia: Empire in Revolution*, New York: Africana Publishing Co., 1978

Paige, Jeffrey M., *Agrarian Revolution: Social Movements and Export Agriculture in the Underdeveloped World*, New York: The Free Press, 1975

Pankhurst, Richard, "'Fear God, Honour the King': The Use of Biblical Allusion in Ethiopian Historical Literature, Part II," *NEAS*, 2, 1 (1987)

Economic History of Ethiopia 1800–1935, Addis Ababa: Haile Selassie I University, 1968

State and Land in Ethiopian History, Monograph in Ethiopian Land Tenure No. 3, The Institute of Ethiopian Studies, Addis Ababa: Oxford University Press, 1966

258

"Some Factors Depressing the Standard of Living of Peasants in Traditional Ethiopia," *JES* 4, 2 (July 1966)

"The Ethiopian Army in Former Times," *Ethiopia Observer*, 7, 2 (1963)

Pausewang, Siegfried, "Peasant Society and Development in Ethiopia," *Sociologica Ruralis*, 13, 2 (1973)

Perham, Margery, *The Government of Ethiopia*, Evanston, Ill.: Northwestern University Press, 1969

Pool, David, *Eritrea: Africa's Longest War*, Anti-Slavery Society, Report No. 3, rev. edn., London: Calverts Press, 1982.

Powell, E. Alexander, *Beyond the Utmost Purple Rim*, London: John Long, 1925

Rubenson, Sven (ed.), *Proceedings of the Seventh International Conference of Ethiopian Studies*, Institute of Ethiopian Studies, Addis Ababa, Scandinavian Institute of African Studies, Uppsala, African Studies Center, Michigan State University, East Lansing: Berlings, Arlov, Sweden, 1984

The Survival of Ethiopian Independence, London: Heinemann Educational Books, 1978

"Adwa 1896: The Resounding Protest," in R. I. Rotberg and Ali A. Mazrui (eds.), *Protest and Power in Black Africa*, London: Oxford University Press, 1970

Wichale XVII: The Attempt to Establish a Protectorate over Ethiopia, Haile Selassie I University Historical Studies No. 1, Addis Ababa: Oxford University Press, 1964

King of Kings, Tewodros of Ethiopia, Addis Ababa, 1966

Rudé, George, *Ideology and Popular Protest*, New York: Pantheon Books, 1980

Samatar, Said S., *Oral Poetry and Somali Nationalism: The Case of Sayyid Mohammad Abdille Hassan*, Cambridge: Cambridge University Press, 1982

Saul, John S. and Roger Woods, "African Peasantries," in Shanin (ed.), *Peasants and Peasant Societies*, London: 1971

Sbacchi, Alberto, *Ethiopia under Mussolini: Fascism and the Colonial Experience*, London: Zed Press Ltd., 1985

"Haile Selassie and the Italians 1941–1943," *African Studies Review*, 22, 1 (April 1979)

Schwab, Peter, *Decision-Making in Ethiopia: A Study of the Political Process*, London: C. Hurst, 1972

"Rebellion in Gojjam Province," *CJAS*, 4, 2 (1970)

Scott, James C., *Weapons of the Weak*, New Haven and London: Yale University Press, 1985

"Revolution in the Revolution: Peasants and Commissars," *Theory and Society*, 7, 1 (1979)

"Protest and Profanation: Agrarian Revolt and the Little Tradition, Part I," *Theory and Society*, 4, 1 (spring 1977)

The Moral Economy of the Peasant: Rebellion and Subsistence in Southeast Asia, New Haven and London: Yale University Press, 1976

Sergew Hable Sellassie, *Ancient and Medieval Ethiopian History to 1270*, Addis Ababa: United Printers, 1972

Shack, William A., *The Gurage: A People of the Ensete Culture*, London: Oxford University Press, 1966

Shanin, Teodor, "Peasantry as a Political Factor," in T. Shanin (ed.), *Peasants and Peasant Societies*, London: Penguin, 1971

Sherman, R., *Eritrea: The Unfinished Revolution*, New York: Praeger, 1980

Simoons, F. J., "Some Questions on the Economic Pre-history of Ethiopia," in J. D. Fage and R. Oliver (eds.), *Papers in African History*, London: Cambridge University Press, 1970

Skocpol, Theda, *States and Social Revolutions: A Comparative Analysis of France, Russia and China*, Cambridge and London: Cambridge University Press, 1979

Spencer, John H., *Ethiopia at Bay: A Personal Account of the Haile Sellassie Years*, Algonac, Mich.: Reference Publications, 1984

Stahl, Michael, *Ethiopia: Political Contradictions in Agricultural Development*, Stockholm: Liber Treyk, 1974

Bibliography

Steer, George L., *Caesar in Abyssinia*, Boston: Little, Brown, 1937

Steinhart, Edward, *Conflict and Collaboration: The Kingdoms of Western Uganda, 1890–1907*, Princeton: Princeton University Press, 1977

Taddesse Tamrat, *Church and State in Ethiopia 1270–1527*, Oxford: Clarendon Press, 1972

Taye Gulilat, "The Tax in Lieu of Tithe and the New Agricultural Income Tax: A Preliminary Evaluation," *Dialogue*, 11, 1 (December 1968)

Taye Reta, "Gojam Governorate General," *Ethiopian Geographical Journal*, 1, 1 (June 1963)

Tekle Tsadik Mekuria, *Ye Itiopia Tarik, ke Aste Tewodros eska Kedamawi Haile Selassie*, Addis Ababa: St. George Printing Press, sixth reprint, 1968 (1960)

Therborn, Goran, *The Ideology of Power and the Power of Ideology*, London: Verso Editions and NLB, 1980

Tilly, Charles, "Western State-Making and Theories of Political Transformation," and "Reflections on the History of European State-Making," in C. Tilly (ed.), *The Formation of National States in Western Europe*, Princeton, N.J.: Princeton University Press, 1975

Touval, Saadia, *Somali Nationalism: International Politics and the Drive for Unity in the Horn of Africa*, Cambridge, Mass.: Harvard University Press, 1963

TPLF, *Ye-hizb Weyane harnet Tigrai Communist Ye asir amet guzo gimgema*, Hamle 1979 (July 1985)

Trevaskis, G. K. N., *Eritrea: A Colony in Transition 1941–52*, London and New York: Oxford University Press, 1960

Trimingham, J. S. Spencer, *Islam in Ethiopia*, London: Oxford University Press, 1952

Turton, E. R., "Bantu, Galla and Somali Migrations in the Horn of Africa: A Reassessment of the Juba/Tana Area," *JAH*, 16, 4 (1975)

Ullendorff, Edward, *The Ethiopians: An Introduction to Country and People*, 3rd edn, London and Oxford: Oxford University Press, 1973

Wallerstein, Immanuel, *The Modern World System*, New York and London: Academic Press, 1976

Welch Jr., Claude E., *Anatomy of Rebellion*, Albany, New York: State University Press, 1980

Wipper, Audrey, *Rural Rebels: A Study of Luo Protest Movements in Kenya*, Nairobi: Oxford University Press, 1977

Wolf, Eric R., *Peasant Wars of the Twentieth Century*, New York and London: Harper and Row, Publishers, 1969

Peasants, Englewood Cliffs, N.J.: Prentice-Hall, 1966

Yohannes Gabre Egziabher, *Tigriniya-Amarigna Mezgebe Kalat*, Asmera: Antigraphic Printing Press, 1948–49 EC

Zagorin, Perez, *Rebels and Rulers, 1500–1660*, 2 vols., Cambridge: Cambridge University Press, 1982

Zewde Gabre Sellassie, *Yohannes IV of Ethiopia: A Political Biography*, Oxford: Clarendon Press, 1975

Index

Index

Aliye Daddi, 141, 242 n. 33, 244 n. 57
Allawaha, river, 99
Allomata [Allamata] district, 120
Amba Alage, *see* Alage
Amhara people, 33, 93, 113, 189, 206, 207, 222; rivalry with Oromo–Somali, 125, 131, 136–37, 157, 159, 212–13; Shewan Amhara domination, 50, 71–72, 98, 103, 116, 193, 197, 220; *see also* Amharic language and culture
Amhara regions, 33, 157, 160
Amharic language and culture, 28, 36, 48, 81–82, 161, 197; *see also* "Abyssinianization"
Amin, Samir, 95–96
Anda Abuna, battle of (1943), 107
Anderson, Perry, 49
Anglo-Ethiopian Agreement (1942), 103
Angola, 2
Anuak people, 33
Arabic language, 48
Arabs, 74, 213
Araya Degela, Dejazmatch, 99, 113, 120
Araya Selassie, 96
aristocracy, landed, 11, 12, 18, 73–74, 81, 96–99; relations with state, 57, 79, 85, 195; *see also* landlords
armaments, 101–102, 118, 146, 153, 191, 204, 220
Armenians, 74
army/armed forces: imperial, 39, 42, 43, 45, 46, 198; law disbanding private armies, 81; postrevolutionary, 204, 225; role in Bale rebellion, 140, 145, 146–47, 148; role in Gojjam revolt, 180, 182–83, 190; role in Tigrean uprising, 106, 108–12 *passim*; United States aid, 52; *see also* military organization, rebel
Arsi people, 33, 128, 151, 154
Arsi region, 76, 168, 210, 218, 219, 222, 230 29
artisans, 65
Arusi, *see* Arsi
Asberom, Kegnazmatch, 240 n. 79
Asseb–Dessie road, 105
Asfa-Wosen, Prince, 92–93, 106
Asmera, 97, 99, 102, 105, 120, 122; United States military base, 52
Asseb, 34
Asseb region, 33, 91
Assefa Derso, 237 n. 24, 240 n. 79
Assimba, 208
Ausa, 69, 70
Awasa, 222
Awash river, 36, 40, 47, 69, 134, 210
Awdew Abesha, Fitawrari, 250 n. 33
Aweytu people, 128

Awobal, 179
Ayalew Desta, 183, 184
Aychem, battle of (1930), 45, 48
Azebo district, 99, 106, 107, 108, 119, 120
Azebo people, 89, 91, 93, 118; role in Tigrean uprising, 94–96, 102, 106, 112, 113, 115, 122; social system, 93, 115, 117; treatment of, after uprising, 120–21, 123, 240 n. 86
Azwari river, 178

Bahir Dar, 178 (table), 179, 189, 201
Bale province, 127, 230 n. 29; Abyssinian domination, 129–30, 158; ethnic and class hostility, 125, 130, 136, 142–43, 154, 158, 159; native gentry, 125, 134, 136–38, 142, 147, 150, 151, 157; popular revolts (*see also* Bale rebellion), 18, 48, 130–31; population density, 34, 76, 126; postrevolutionary conflict, 203, 207, 210–11, 212–13; religious discrimination, 125, 136, 155, 158; social formation, 128–29; Somali communities, 33, 125, 126, 128, 130, 137, 142–43, 212–13; topography, 126–28, 146
Bale rebellion (1963–70), 21, 85, 125–59, 198, 199–200, 201, 212; bureaucratic corruption as factor, 52, 125, 133–34, 137–38, 142, 145–46, 158; course of, 140–49; government action on intercommunal strife as contributory cause, 142–43; guerrilla tactics, 153, 200; ideological ambiguity, 151, 153–55; Islam as ideology of mobilization, 126, 154–55, 200; issue of ethnicity, 125, 126, 130, 131, 136–37, 154, 157, 158; land alienation as major cause of discontent, 125, 129, 131–32, 134, 157, 158, 241 n. 8; leadership and organization, 126, 149–55; postrevolt treatment of rebels and peasants, 156–8; religious factors, 136, 137, 154–55, 158; resentment at government restrictions on trade and pastoral nomadism, 125, 134–36; role of militia, 135, 146–48 *passim*; role of peasants, 152, 156; role of Somalia, 126, 131, 135–41 *passim*, 144–45, 148–50, 152–54 *passim*, 158–59, 200, 212; taxation as issue, 125, 131–35 *passim*, 142; *see also* bandits; Haile Selassie I; Oromo people; Orthodox Church
Bamlaku Ayele, 185, 187, 188
bandits/banditry, 4, 16–18, 20, 82; in Gojjam, 167, 172, 174, 187; peasant attitudes toward, 16–17; role in Bale rebellion, 138, 140–41, 143, 149–50; role in Tigrean uprising, 89, 91, 99–101, 105, 106, 113–14, 122; social origins, 17, 18, 38, 100

262

Index

Index

266

Index

Mecha people, 33; Mecha and Tulema cultural association, 221
mechie, 165
Meda Welabu, 156
Mehoni region, 99, 107, 108, 120–21, 122
Mekele, 98, 101; captured by rebels (1943), 108–109, 117, 118; retaken by government forces, 111, 113
Melka Gersi, 148
Melka Jimma, 148
Melka river, 147
Mena, 144, 147, 156
Menchere region, 107, 108
Menelik II, Emperor, 38, 39–42, 44, 70, 94, 163, 232 n. 25
Mengesha of Tigrai, Ras, 96
Mengesha Seyum, Dejazmatch, Leul Ras, 107, 119, 208, 209, 240 n. 80
mengist ("unsettled zones"), 68, 69
Mengisto, 180
Menz, 167
mercantilism, 164, 166
Metekel, 163, 177, 178 (table), 189, 219
Metemma, battle of (1889), 41
Metemma valley, 69
migration, 4, 38; labor, 77, 216; *see also* nomadism
military, *see* army
Military Convention of 1942, 102
military coup, attempted (1960), 82
military organization and effectiveness, rebel, 200, 224; in Bale, 126, 140, 144–45, 147–53 *passim*; in Gojjam, 178–80, 183–87 *passim*, 190–92, 200; in Tigrai, 106–13 *passim*, 114, 117–18; *see also* armaments; guerrilla warfare
militias, 12–13, 14, 198; *see also* Bale rebellion; Gojjam revolt; Tigrean uprising
millenarianism, 3, 13, 118, 155
minerals, 32
ministerial system, 42
Ministry of Defense, 52
Ministry of the Interior, 51, 53
Ministry of Land Reform, 85
Mitchell, Sir Philip, 103
Mitsiwa, *see* Massawa
"modernization," politics of, 38, 194–95
Mogadishu, 138, 141, 142, 143, 149, 154
Mohammed Abdi Nur Takani, Sheikh, 141
Mohammed Abdille Hassan, Sayyid, 130, 154
Mohammed Ali Rube, Colonel, 150, 210
Mohammed Belade, 244 n. 57
Mohammed Bunni, 244 n. 57
Mohammed Gedda, 130
Molyneaux, Maxine, 11, 205
monetarization of the public economy, 42, 47–48, 164

mosques, 63
Motta, 171–72, 177–84 *passim*, 188, 190, 219
Mousnier, Roland, 121
Moyale, 210, 211
Musa Doya, 242 n. 37

National Bank of Ethiopia, 48
nationalism, 38, 48, 104, 151, 210; of postrevolutionary movements, 207, 208, 210, 212–13, 214; tension between regionalism/localism and, 29, 36, 221
Nech Lebash (paramilitary force), 52–53
neftenya (overlord's representative), 129
Negash Desta, Kegnazmatch, 240 n. 79
Neghele, 140, 141, 144, 145
Nekemte, 70
Nigeria, 2
Nilo-Saharan linguistic groups, 33, 219
Nilotes, 33
nobility, 14, 17, 56, 78; fief holdings and subsidiary rights, 65, 66, 74, 80, 81, 83; relations with crown, 18–19, 42–4, 46, 48, 49–50, 74, 81, 123, 196; relations with peasants, 13–14, 19, 37, 58, 74, 114, 169, 198; relationship to aristocracy, 73–74; *see also* Tigrean uprising
nomadism, pastoral, 93, 129–30, 134–35, 141, 142–43, 242 n. 15
nonconfrontational tactics, peasants', 4–5, 8, 14, 16, 20, 67
North Korea, 210
northern provinces of Ethiopia, 12, 34, 47, 197, 221, 230 n. 29, 233 n. 51; effect of state centralization, 18; interdependence and shared traditions of nobility and peasants, 13–14, 19, 37, 74, 198; labor migration, 77, 216; nobility, 49–50, 66, 74, 80, 81, 83, 196; poverty, 76–77; social relations, 64–67, 73, 80; *see also* Begemedir; Eritrea; Gojjam; Haile Selassie I; land tenure; Tigrai
Nur Gurwein, 130

oath-taking, rebel, 116–17, 186
Oberso, 144
Oddo, 142
officials, *see* administration
Ogaden, 33, 34, 126, 130, 141, 143, 210; Ogaden Campaign (1964), 172; Ogaden War (1977–78), 211; Somali designs on, 139–40
Omo, 40, 142
Organization of African Unity (OAU), 139, 148
Oromifa language, 33, 48, 222
Oromo Liberation Front (OLF), 29–31, 211–12, 213, 221–22, 224, 225

Index